Tao-sheng's Commentary on the Lotus Sūtra

SUNY Series in Buddhist Studies
Kenneth K. Inada, Editor

Tao-sheng's Commentary on the Lotus Sūtra

A Study and Translation

Young-ho Kim

State University of New York Press

Published by
State University of New York Press, Albany

Printed in the United States of America

For information, address State University of New York
Press, State University Plaza, Albany, N.Y., 12246

Library of Congress Cataloging-in-Publication Data

Kim, Young-ho, 1941–
Tao-sheng's commentary on the Lotus Sūtra : a study and translation / Young-ho Kim.
p. cm.—(SUNY series in Buddhist studies)
Originally presented as the author's thesis.
Bibliography: p.
Includes index.
ISBN 0-7914-0227-4.—ISBN 0-7914-0228-2 (pbk.)
1. Chu tao-sheng, d. 434. Fa hua ching shu. 2. Tripiṭaka. Sūtrapiṭaka. Saddharmapuṇḍarīkasūtra—Commentaries. I. Chu-tao -sheng, d. 434. Fa hua ching shu. English & Chinese. 1990. II. Title. III. Series.
BQ2055.C553K55 1990
294.3'85—dc20 89-4629
CIP

10 9 8 7 6 5 4 3 2 1

Contents

Preface

This work grew out of my initial (and abiding) quest for the origin and whole spectrum of the Ch'an (Zen) doctrine of enlightenment, which is noted for the controversy involving two apparently irreconcilable and diametrically opposed approaches, traditionally distinguished as northern and southern or gradual and sudden. The distinction between North and South seems symbolic of the state of the world today, with its various forms of confrontation created by the differences of ideology, religion, and so on, which reflects humankind's schizophrenic, divided mind, viewing things through a black-and-white prism. Acutely aware, rather empirically, of the extra dimension of human suffering, I wondered; Are two parties or arguments really apart from each other without any junction whatsoever between them, like the South and North Poles? Isn't now the time to focus more on similarities than on differences, common identities rather than distinct identities, genera rather than species—on the assumption that all humanely motivated ideas, unless ill-motivated for self-serving purposes, must have some common ground to share? Perhaps, we need a comprehensive perspective innate in the religious dimension, which, having been long forgotten, should be recouped, yet, of course, not at the cost of truth. With such a train of thought, I was inclined, in search of a classical paradigm, to review the Ch'an tradition, which has long dominated the Buddhist practice in East Asia to this day, assuming that the two approaches may represent no more than the methodological focus on one aspect or another of the whole process of enlightenment. Yet, the two arguments have been exaggerated in reductionist hands as if they were two alternatives that could never harmonize or fuse. Two conceptions seem to typify the processes of knowledge involving all the human spiritual endeavors seeking truth and reality. If two aspects are taken to represent, say, rationalism and intuitionism in the epistemological terms, Buddhism, from its inception, has never been free of either means of knowledge, as has the whole Indian tradition. Some trace of evidence for such a line of thinking seemed to have been reemerged in some eminent Ch'an masters in Chinese and Korean traditions, in their syncretist or synthetist approaches.

Against this background, with perhaps arguable hypotheses and evidence, one might find it necessary to pursue the matter to its point of origin as an issue in Chinese Buddhism. Hence, the subject figure of the present study as the initial promulgator of the doctrine of enlightenment. This particular conception, however, cannot be isolated from the rest of his thought, the ramifications of which seem to be unusually varied and integrally linked with each other. Thus, a more comprehensive study is called for.

The problem of enlightenment as such may not be addressed fully here, not being the sole subject, but I have attempted to establish a plateau from which to view and reexamine afresh the problem and other matters. Ideally, a proper context has been reconstructed here to ward off further misguided interpretations taken out of the context. The kind of context furnished here is philological and philosophical, not social or anything else, for I believe that, in earlier days, more individual initiatives were and could be taken for religious salvation than today. The era and material concerned here also involve a setting of multireligious cultural tradition. How Buddhism of Indian provenance underwent the process of acculturation while maintaining the fundamental identity toward Chinese Buddhism in the context concerned may show a classic pattern to those interested in comparative religion and concerned with the world today, in turmoil mainly caused by what can be reduced to religious conflicts. We thus have come around again to my initial quest and intent, the search for common substructure or a rule for coexistence and harmony.

The translation of the fifth century text, more than one and half millenniums apart from us now, was not so easy a task, requiring the time that otherwise would be devoted to a more extensive, balanced study, especially of the "prehistory," but this goal remains an ideal to achieve in the future; and I believe this text-centered thesis as it is now has fulfilled more than its objectives generally expected of such a work.

In the course of writing this time-consuming, double-edged work comprising many subject matters, originally presented as a doctoral thesis at McMaster University, many people have been helpful in one way or another. Yün-hua Jan, McMaster University, long has been a constant source of information, guidance, and inspiration. I have benefited enormously from his erudition in Chinese thought and language. He and Leon Hurvitz, University of British Columbia, put themselves at my disposal for many difficult passages of the text; the latter gladly sharing one summer with me in Vancouver. Yet, I am solely responsible for any misinterpretations or shortcomings. Graeme MacQueen, McMaster University, whose concern for the cause of peace I also share, provided many useful comments, making me ponder the relevancy of the work to our shared ideal. Koichi Shinohara helped restrain me to the present perimeter of research. For all of those scholars, I remain sincerely grateful. For the actual process leading to this publication, my sincere thanks are due to Sung Bae Park, SUNY at Stony Brook, for having encouraged and supported me toward publication, and Kenneth Inada, SUNY at Buffalo, editor of the present series, for having found my work worthy to be in the series. I am thankful to Kang-nam Oh, University of Regina, who introduced me to the good institution of McMaster as we were caused to share the brahmacarin stage of life together at two places. I am also very grateful to another friend of mine, Sang-shih Lee, now at Oxford for his second doctoral degree, who has given me unfailing support, moral and otherwise, I cannot overstress the help and support rendered by my wife, Eun-kyung, in numerous ways for the completion of the work, including repeated typing while rearing two children, Haeda and Aramie. I also should like to express my gratitude to her parents and brother for helping materially in the cost of preparation for publication. My student, Young-ja Lee, kindly offered her help for typing a part of the final version of the MS.

Young-ho Kim

Prolegomena

History recognizes Chu Tao-sheng (ca. 360–434) as a seminal Buddhist scholar with prophetic acumen. His original, creative mind is revealed in a number of doctrines[1] that when enunciated seemed unorthodox and revolutionary. Unfortunately, all expository writings relating to those doctrines are lost; therefore, we have only an indirect knowledge of the exact substance and background of Tao-sheng's arguments, let alone any way of reconstructing his entire system of thought.

Under such circumstances, it is necessary to make the most of what is left and to try to see the whole through the fragments. The staple of the material is Tao-sheng's commentary on the *Saddharmapuṇḍarīka Sūtra* or *Lotus Scripture*: the subject of the present monograph. This commentary, in fact, is Tao-sheng's only work preserved in full. Its size is sufficient for drawing out something tangible without losing sight of the context. The work was composed toward the end of Tao-sheng's life (in 432), a product of his mature scholarship, presumably incorporating the doctrines pronounced earlier.

Any data based on fragmentary statements gleaned from second-hand sources, or even the direct information from the commentaries themselves obtained without consulting its context, may be incomplete and open to arbitrary understanding and appropriation.[2] This can be all the more true when the statements are collected and grouped in accordance with certain methods of classification or translated into another language. Ideally, the original may be served best when rendered in a modern language with the least intervention and mediation by the translator's philosophy or beliefs. The translation of the isolated statements of Tao-sheng's writing into English fails to do full justice to his mind, as does the way the material is sometimes lumped together as, for example, by Walter Liebenthal (possibly on account of misguided presuppositions, despite his great service of opening our eyes to Tao-sheng).[3] A translator can easily fall victim to reading his own ideas and knowledge into the text instead of letting the text speak for itself.

The aims of this study are twofold: (1) to prepare a faithful, undistorted translation of the commentary in its entirety, in order to provide a basis and vantage point for further study and understanding of Tao-sheng; and (2) to attempt to illuminate Tao-sheng's system of religious knowledge by examining the commentary in conjunction with other doctrines and writings, and thus to evaluate Tao-sheng's contribution to implanting (or transplanting) the alien religious system in Chinese soil. Of course, the two objectives are not to be seen as separate tasks; they are closely bound up with one another.

Apart from its value as a means to our goals, the commentary has its own significance.[4] The *Lotus Sūtra* was to become possibly the single most important scripture for the full-fledged Chinese Buddhist schools, especially for the T'ien-t'ai school. Also, as the first commentary on the *Lotus* written in Chinese, Tao-sheng's work, including the ever-important schema of the classification of teaching (*p'an-chiao*),[5] set the tone for subsequent commentators to follow, modify, or diverge from.

In pursuit of our aims, we are naturally faced with some difficulties and problems. As a rule, a commentary by nature tends to confine the range of the commentator's activity within a certain boundary; that is, the general direction and motifs of the *sūtra* concerned. A commentator may select and concentrate on certain words and expressions without paying much attention to their context in order to support his own philosophical presuppositions, but it generally can be assumed that the commentator will stay within the scope of the foundational scripture. A commentator confronts an almost insurmountable barrier when dealing with a religious scripture, for any criticism regarding the document of the founder's testimonial (*śabda*) might be seen as sacrilegious. One should be cautious, therefore, when considering Tao-sheng's "unorthodox" and "revolutionary" reputation. Furthermore, certainly more than one tradition is involved in the commentary, with many specifically Chinese philosophical terms and presuppositions found in the text, creating exegetical and hermeneutical complexities. Nevertheless, a *sūtra* the size of the *Lotus*, which puts a variety of concepts and phrases at the commentator's disposal, may still provide a versatile thinker such as Tao-sheng some room to maneuver. The *Lotus* revolves around the motif of three vehicles dialectically turning into One Vehicle, a form of the diversity-in-unity principle, which seems to accommodate what some of Tao-sheng's contemporaries regarded as unorthodox and idiosyncratic patterns in his thought. After all, he elected to compose or compile a commentary on the *sūtra* before anyone else.

To what extent has Tao-sheng left the imprint of his own thinking and language on the commentary? A clue to that question may be found in the commentary's preamble, in which Tao-sheng speaks as if he had acted merely as the editor or compiler of the text, using input from various sources. If that is the case, the text would amount to no more than the upshot of collective thinking or a compendium of some sort. It might also suggest the view that an individual person is the product of an era and to that degree, in the final analysis, his work is not so much a product of personal labor as the fruit of a collective process.[6] Regarding the problem of language, the commentary is replete with Taoist and other Chinese concepts and terminology. However, the borrowing of language is not a trait unique to Tao-sheng; it is common among the writings of his contemporary Buddhists. Even if his acknowledgment of his "editorship" cannot be dismissed as a self-effacing gesture, Tao-sheng probably could never have eschewed the form of language in current use as a tool for both communication with others and accommodation and expression of the elements of his own thought. There is no evidence that his language in other documents, including the remains of two other commentaries, was markedly different from the language of this work. Then, the problem boils down to this: Where does Tao-sheng's identity as an independent person and thinker lie? Where is his originality?

In the case of Tao-sheng and his contemporaries, part of the thinker's identity has to do with whether he is to be regarded as a Buddhist, a Taoist, some kind of hybrid, or something else altogether. Put differently, what system is Tao-sheng's primary frame of reference?[7] Does the label *Buddho-Taoist*,[8] by which many of Tao-sheng's contemporaries were known, apply without qualification to Tao-sheng? If so, what exactly does the label mean? Two lines of thinking seem to be involved here: Buddhism and neo-Taoism. However, the latter is really a syncretism of Taoism and Confucianism, as interpreted by such systematizers as Wang Pi and Kuo Hsiang. Therefore, no simplistic, single-term answer can be adequate. Tao-sheng, like anyone in that period, was exposed to the major components of the Chinese tradition, and his individual imprint may be found in the way he assimilated the foreign concepts with the existing patterns of thought.

At a glance, the titles of Tao-sheng's expositions could sound bizarre and shocking, and certainly thought provoking, to his contemporary Buddhists. From this we can surmise either that Tao-sheng was far ahead of his time in grasping the essence of the Buddhist doctrines or that he deviated from the traditional Indian Buddhist presentation and thinking. If the first is true, he remained a Buddhist in every sense of the word; if the second is true, he may turn out to be a Taosit in disguise or a Buddho-Taoist at best. But rather than seeing him from a single perspective, we might prefer to view him from the perspective of comparative religion, as a kind of harmonizer or syncretist of the two traditions. Tao-sheng seemed to insist upon seeing beyond external structures and symbols.[9] His boigraphy in the *Kao-seng chuan* tells how through illumination he came to realize the limit of exigency and symbols and proceeded to write the two propositions—"The good deed entails no retribution" and "By way of sudden enlightenment one achieves Buddhahood"—both of which seem implicit in the commentary. Hence, we might conjecture that Tao-sheng intended either to transcend the external forms of the religious systems involved or to see the common properties behind their various expressions. Or, he may have merely borrowed the language of one system to explain another.

The key to these hypotheses seems to lie in the language of the text, which has to do with the neo-Taoist philosophy, the most recently developed system then in vogue. Right from the beginning of the text, the reader can hardly pass any statement of philosophical significance without encountering one or more terms of non-Buddhist origin, terms that certainly are not found in the text of the *Lotus* translated by Kumārajīva nor in other *sūtras* rendered in Chinese thus far. Perhaps, Tao-sheng had no choice but to resort to the contemporary philosophical language to express his ideas and to address the general public. Such style of expression and diction also may reflect exactly the way Tao-sheng's own process of thinking took place. This problem of the language will be properly examined as the central theme of Part II.

Our analysis will be carried out in several ways. The critical analysis will be highlighted by two major analytical approaches: first, a general examination of the philosophically significant concepts and expressions of Chinese origin; second, a comprehensive survey of the use of the term *li*.

In the first approach, some fifteen terms and concepts, which clearly stand out as recurrent rather than casual, will be identified and examined for their roles in Tao-sheng's vocabulary. Some are closely associated with the "Sage" and will be discussed in connection with him. Their original meanings and implications as found in the Chinese texts will be correlated with the implications suggested by Tao-sheng in the commentary and the related parts of the *sūtra*. This will help clarify whether the borrowed terms retained their original meanings or underwent some transformation to take on new connotations, as with the word *wu-wei* or nondoing, a Taoist concept that had already been transformed into the symbol for the Buddhist term for "the unconditioned" (*asaṃskṛta*). Whether such terms function merely as new symbols for certain Buddhist concepts without any remnant of conceptual content remains to be seen. There is also the possibility—and it is our hypothetical position—that Tao-sheng could not escape being a syncretist on the matter. In that case, there is the question of precisely in what fashion Tao-sheng blended the two traditions, and whether the original content of the terms was lost.

Reliance on an existing form of expression or terminology for interpreting and introducing a new tradition would not be unnatural, and it would merely add another dimension of difficulty to the complexities in our search for Tao-sheng's identity. Yet, there may be room for an individual's mark in the very process of borrowing, in the choice of vocabulary, in the way both the existing and new forms are reconciled; that is, the mode of transfusion or assimilation. Depending on who uses the old symbol, there can be differences in its expanse of denotation and connotation; a thinker's distinctly personal imprint may well lie in the manner and extent of his borrowing of existent symbols or concepts. One glaring example in this sense is the concept *li*, rendered variously by the sinologists as "principle," "reason," "norm," "order," or "noumenon." One cannot afford to overlook the omnipresence of the term in the text, more recurrent throughout than any other abstract noun, including *tao*, an already established term. *Li* was to become probably the most significant and pregnant philosophical concept in Chinese philosophy, especially in neo-Confucianism and in Hua-yen Buddhism.[10] Tao-sheng picked up the term *li* while it was still in its nebulous stage of evolution and made it a functional term, which can be considered an immeasurable contribution. Indeed, a separate study could be devoted to Tao-sheng's appropriation of this significant term.

Here, I take *li* as a medium through which to understand Tao-sheng's apprehension of the Buddhist doctrine as represented in the *Saddharmapuṇḍarīka*, and possibly the inner structure of Tao-sheng's own mind. All expressions or statements of the *sūtra* worthy of comment seem to be filtered down and reduced to *li*. What underlies such statements is represented symbolically in miniature, as it were, encoded and stored in *li*. *Li* can thus be regarded as a key to Tao-sheng's understanding of the *sūtra*. But its importance does not lie just in its role as a convenient tool for interpreting the *sūtra* and as the principle underlying its statements; in its own right, *li* stands for an ontological entity or the ultimate reality. *Li* can be both particular and universal. What has remained a problem arising from the coexistence of several systems in the interpretation of one Buddhist commentator therefore may find an explanation or even a solution in the structure of *li*.

There is a concept that merits a scrupulous review in connection with *li*: the process of enlightenment. Tao-sheng is noted for the theory of sudden enlightenment. The text nonetheless teems with expressions that apparently contradict Tao-sheng's alleged position. Tao-sheng's original theory is believed to be the one that *li* is analytically unpartitionable. Now we are confronted with what seems to be the antithesis of the theory, although *li* remains the key term. How can we account for the discrepancy?

In addition to the two-way analysis of the text, part II, a study of

Tao-sheng's commentary on the *Saddharmapuṇḍarīka Sūtra* proper will be further reinforced by other facts and data related to the *CSPS*. Starting with how Tao-sheng became familiar with the *Lotus* (Chapter 6), they will include the structure and style of the text (Chapter 7), basic ideas to be correlated with the tenets of the *sūtra* (Chapter 8), any other traces or new development of his thought identifiable in the text (Chapter 9), and finally, a brief review regarding the significance of the *CSPS* for the study of Tao-sheng and subsequent Buddhist schools (Chapter 10).

To help illuminate the text and Tao-sheng, it is also necessary to identify where Tao-sheng stood historically and note his works, influence, and doctrines. Thus, as a prolegomenon to the study of the *CSPS*, general surveys of Tao-sheng's background and relevant facts will precede the textual study.

Against this background information, Tao-sheng's position in history and his line of thinking may be delineated more clearly. Included in the first part will be a sketch of Tao-sheng's doctrines, under three major theme groups, based on all the available sources, direct or indirect, with the *CSPS* being the last source drawn on when necessary. The sketch will provide a comprehensive overview of Tao-sheng's thought and serve as the base for tracing (in chapter 5) Tao-sheng's influence on the thoughts of subsequent Buddhist thinkers, and for identifying (in Part II) the traces of those doctrines in the text itself.

Finally, the translation of the text is offered as the chronicle and result of the foregoing investigation and analysis. Every effort will be made to render the fifth-century writing as literally as possible.[11] Apparently the safest way to keep the writer's intended meaning intact would call for every letter, word, and idiom of the text to be taken in the sense that would have been understood in the days of its composition, particularly in the literary or religious circle to which our author belonged, rather than in the sense that would have been meant in other times or currently.

As is the case with the term *tao* when it occurs alone (and nontechnically), the pregnant term *li* will be left untranslated throughout for the obvious reason that it has too many connotations to define or fix in a word or two. Apart from consistency, my intent is to acknowledge the fact that *li* usually stands as a substantive in Tao-sheng's vocabulary.

The best way to illuminate the expressions in the text and find their most appropriate meanings is to trace and identify them in the classical sources, which turns out to be related mostly to neo-Taoism. Thus, we will determine if the meanings drawn from classical contexts are applicable to the commentary or are adjusted in compliance with the Buddhist sense of the equivalent terms or the general intent of the appropriate passage or phrase in the *sūtra*.[12]

We should be cautious in reading the text, because it abounds with corrupted letters, undecipherable letters that were omitted, and especially copying errors, both homophonous and homographic. We also must be wary of the text's punctuation. Every chapter of the translation will be preceded by a brief synopsis of the corresponding section of the *sūtra*, to familiarize the reader with the general setting and context in which a certain word or phrase is being interpreted. Still, despite all our efforts, there may be many baffling phrases. Tao-sheng's cryptic writing—a millenium and a half apart from us—is certain to leave many points unresolved and hypothetical solutions moot.[13] Nevertheless, translation should and will be attempted. We may simply hope, as Tao-sheng himself humbly stated, that the reader "may not abandon [the search for] the *Tao* due to [my] human insignificance (or folly)" (*CSPS* 396d); here, "the *Tao*" is the path traversed by Tao-sheng.

Notes

1. The evaluation of Tao-sheng's greatness and importance may be based on two grounds: historical records and theoretical analysis. For the first there are two biographies, in *Kao-seng chuan*, 7, Taishō (T), 50.366b–367a; and in *Ch'u san-tsang chi-chi*, 15, T55.110c–111b. There is also a eulogy by (Hui-lin) found in *Kuang hung-ming chi*, T52.256c–266b. In other records, Tao-sheng is listed among the best four, eight, or ten disciples of Kumārajīva. In his encyclopaedic work *Han Wei liang-Chin Nan-pei-ch'ao Fo-chiao shih* (Shanghai, 1938), encompassing several centuries from the beginning of the history of Buddhism in China up to the sixth century, modern historian T'ang Yung-t'ung devotes more space to Tao-sheng than to anyone else, comparing his place in Chinese Buddhism to that of Wang Pi in neo-Taoism (see Taiwan reprint, 1974, vol. II, 155). For the theoretical grounds Hu Shih, ("Development of Zen Buddhism in China," *Chinese Social and Political Science Review*, 15, no. 4 [1932]: 483f.) calls Tao-sheng "a revolutionary thinker," considering him the founder of "Chinese Zenism" or "School of Sudden Awakening or Enlightenment." T'ang (p. 179) similarly refers to Tao-sheng as the "founding father" of the theory of sudden enlightenment of the Ch'an school.

2. Richard H. Robinson, *Early Mādhyamika in India and China* (Madison, Wisc., 1967), p. 18, quotes S. Schayer, *Ausgewählte Kapitel aus der Prasannapadā* (Krakow, 1931), p. xxviii: "The danger lies in the arbitrary isolation of individual thoughts, which are only understandable in systematic connection, as elements of structural unities." Because we deal with basically the same period of Chinese Buddhism and the "Buddho-Taoists," I will follow closely the arguments of Robinson's book, particularly Chapter 2, "Questions and Method,"

and will refer to it when appropriate for comparing my arguments, though we are far apart in terms of subject matter, scope, and intermediate, if not ultimate, goals.

3. See Walter Liebenthal, "The World Conception of Chu Tao-sheng," *Monumenta Nipponica*, 12 (1956). Of Liebenthal's work, Robinson remarks: "At that time I supposed that it would be necessary merely to summarize existing works on early Indian Mādhyamika and to do a modest amount of further research on the Buddho-Taoists on whom Liebenthal had already published his studies. But it soon became clear that the presuppositions, problems, and methods of previous writers were such that I could not extract from them what my purpose required" (p. 3). And again: "My expectation that the Buddho-Taoists could be dealt with easily and briefly was disappointed as soon as I began to examine Liebenthal's work carefully and to probe the texts. I found that I disagreed with most of Liebenthal's philosophico-religious interpretations, as well as with his methods of translation" (p. 4). It is not clear whether Liebenthal's writings on Tao-sheng are included here, or whether Tao-sheng can be counted among the Buddho-Taoists for that matter, because Tao-sheng never became part of the subject matter in Robinson's study; anyway, the same is no less true of the case of Tao-sheng in my view.

4. A study with focus on Tao-sheng's understanding of the *Saddharma-puṇḍarīka* and some relevant information surrounding it can be found in Ōchō Enichi's monographic article, "Jikudōshō sen Hokekyōso no kenkyū," *Ōtani daigaku kenkyū nempō* 5 (1952): 167–276, the best comprehensive study on the subject so far. See also his more recent, condensed article, "Jikudōshō no hoke shisō," in Sakamoto Yukio, ed., *Hokekyō no Chūgokuteki tenkai* (Kyoto, 1972), pp. 145–173.

5. In 760, Tao-i of the T'ang period writes in his colophon to the collection of the commentaries on the *Vimalakīrti-nirdeśa Sūtra*, Taishō, No. 2777, p. 440a: "In the case of the *Lotus*, people took [Tao-] sheng's commentary as the basis [of its interpretation]."

6. Cf. Robinson, *Early Mādhyamika*, p. 10: "Selection and rejection, operating in individual and collective choices, are major factors in modifying traditions. This affects both native and imported elements . . . we could not wholly reduce the lives and thoughts of these men to typological generalities. We must allow for the qualitative uniqueness, and value the intrinsic worth of the outstanding men whose biographies happen to have been recorded."

7. Cf. Robinson, ibid., p. 5: "In what respects was the Buddhism of Kumārajīva's disciples Indian, and in what respects was it Chinese?"

8. The term *Buddho-Taoism* has a wide range of applications, from the early stage of conflict and interaction between the two components to the process of cultural amalgamation and synthesis of the two systems; Tao-sheng probably belonged to the last stage of the development. E. Zürcher, when using the term in *The Buddhist Conquest of China* (Leiden, 1972), p. 288ff., refers to the

relatively earlier stage, whereas Robinson seems to allude to the later stage when he says: "There is not yet an adequate lexicon of the Buddho-Taoist vocabulary, which possesses a rich stock of formations that are unique to it" (p. 16).

9. Cf. Robinson, *Early Mādhyamika*, p. 12: "I suspend judgment on the thesis that the structure of right thought and the structure of reality are identical"; and p. 15: "It cannot be assumed that the structure of language corresponds to the structure of thought, or that all thoughts can be represented by symbols, or that language is the only kind of symbol-system."

10. *Li* as a central concept associated with various canons and writings throughout the Chinese tradition is dealt with in Wing-tsit Chan, "The Evolution of the Neo-Confucian Concept *Li* as Principle," *Tsing Hua Journal of Chinese Studies* n.s., 4, no. 2 (February, 1964): 123–148, reprinted in *Neo-Confucianism, Etc., Essays by Wing-tsit Chan*, (Hanover, N. H., 1968), pp. 45–87. See also, T'ang Chün-i, "Lun Chung-kuo che-hsüeh szu-hsiang shih chung li-chih liu-i" ("Six Meanings of *li*"), *Hsin-ya hsüeh-pao (New Asian Journal)* 1, no. 1 (1955): 45–98. In *An Outline and an Annotated Bibliography of Chinese Philosophy* (New Haven, 1969), p. 111, Chan calls *li* "the cardinal Chinese philosophical concept".

11. Cf. Liebenthal, *The Book of Chao* (Peking, 1948), p. viii: "My translation is fairly literal, but sometimes it seemed to be impossible to render the meaning without changing the phrasing. In one or two cases the translation is so free that almost amounts to a mere outline of the content."

12. Cf. Robinson, *Early Mādhyamika*, p. 15f.: "If these two conditions are fulfilled, then the technical meaning of the term is understood, and whatever the term may or may not mean in Chinese texts from an earlier period is an extraneous question. However, the other meanings of a term may mislead the reader and prevent him from identifying its technical sense in the restricted context." This observation, however, need not apply to the present case, partly because the two languages involved are not identical.

13. Cf. Robinson, ibid., p. 14f.: "The thoughts of men who lived fifteen centuries ago are imperceptible and only partially inferable. The only evidence for them is strings of written symbols representing a dead language for which only a limited corpus of texts now exists. This means that the writer's mood, his irony and humor, the triteness or novelty of his expressions, cannot be known with certainty, because the sample is defective. Not only are the lineaments of his literary mask discernable imperfectly, but the mental events that accompanied the composition of the text are even more inscrutable."

PART I

Introduction

Chapter 1

TAO-SHENG'S PREHISTORY: THE STATE OF BUDDHIST STUDIES IN CHINA

Tao-sheng's life (ca. 360–434) lies mainly within the period of Eastern Chin (317–419), extending a little further to that of the Sung Dynasty (House of Liu) (420–477). The Chin era witnessed the development of "gentry Buddhism," a product of interchanges between monks and intellectuals who fled from the north after its conquest and helped found a new dynasty in the south. *Gentry Buddhism* thus refers to the class of people involved and their tendency to focus on philosophical rather than religious issues. Tao-sheng was first initiated into this form of Chinese Buddhism.

The introduction of Buddhism to China had taken place about three centuries earlier, generally believed to have occurred around the time of the Christian era. In spite of this great length of time, Buddhism had not really taken root in Chinese soil. Only since the middle of the second century, with the influx of missionaries from the Indian subcontinent and its perimeter (including An Shih-kao, from Parthia, the first missionary ever recorded), could tangible signs of development be found. The influx of missionaries led to the introduction and translation of *āgamas*, *sūtras*, and expositions, activities that had increased greatly by the time of Tao-sheng, due mainly to the missionary zeal of Kumārajīva, with whom the former studied for some time. These thinkers were to encounter and challenge the presuppositions of the existing traditions and face a number of new hermeneutical and exegetical problems.

Buddhism's confrontations with other religious traditions brought about diverse forms of interaction, from outright rebuttal to mutual identification on a number of levels. Increasingly discernible were attempts to accommodate Buddhism within the framework of existing systems. In the course of assimilating Buddhism into the Chinese tradition, there was a need for both comparative linguistics and a perspective geared to envisioning more than one religion—in other words, for an early, primitive form of comparative religion. This syncretism is demonstrated in the Chinese religious and philosophical literature of the time, ranging from a fabricated "*sūtra*" to highly polemical writings to a falsified Taoist scripture[1] based on the theme that Lao-tzu became the Buddha. Tao-sheng's period had a precedent for this syncretic approach in the hybrid of neo-Taoism, a fusion of Confucianism and Taoism in which, however, Confucianism was deemed primary. Similarly, the absorption of Buddhism into Chinese culture was to involve not only Taoism but Confucianism as well.

A typical course for a would-be Buddhist was to study Confucianism first, switching later to Taoism, and finally settling in Buddhism. This pattern is a process of spiritual evolution typically found in the careers of Chinese Buddhists throughout all eras.[2] Tao-sheng was no exception; he, too, passed through the secular stages of training (though they were relatively brief in his case)[3] to arrive at Buddhism. The extent to which these secular disciplines influenced his later thought is a question we will look at later.

As religious practices became more diversified with the introduction of Buddhism, it became an accepted idea that the way (Tao), which is one by nature, can be arrived at via different paths. This view became a fundamental proposition for Tao-sheng's contemporaries, repeated in their writings as it had been formulated earlier in the *I Ching*: "[In the world] there are many different roads but the destination is the same."[4]

The dominant system during Tao-sheng's day was neo-Taoism, or Hsüan-hsüeh (Dark Learning), and Buddhists at the time could not separate themselves from this philosophical system in either terminology or concepts. They in fact were versed in both canons, distinguished as the "inner" and "outer." The "outer" canon of secular texts consisted of three "profound (dark) works": the *Lao-tzu*, the *Chuang-tzu*, and the *I Ching*. These three are the non-Buddhist works on which Tao-sheng draws most heavily in the CSPS for language and conceptual reference.[5]

This syncretic tendency was evident in the practices of the advanced Buddhist circle at Lu-shan led by Hui-yüan, to which Tao-sheng may have belonged. (We know that he stayed in Lu-shan from 397 to 405 and briefly thereafter.) Hui-yüan himself could not remain outside of the trend. Although he was a disciple of Tao-an, who put an end to the practice of *ko-i*, an expedient method of matching Buddhist and Taoist concepts,[6] Hui-yüan did use the *ko-i* method on some occasions.

Likewise, one of his lay disciples, Tsung Ping (375–443 or 447) in his work "On the Elucidation of Buddhism" (*Ming-fo lun*) maintains that Confucius, Lao-tzu, and the Tathāgata all lie in the same path to salvation.[7] Nonetheless, they remained strong adherents of the Buddhist religion in practice and its staunch defenders in debates.

A similar tendency towards syncretism can be seen in the poetry of Hsieh Ling-yün (385–433), the versatile lay Buddhist scholar-poet. For example, in his compilation "Discussion of the Fundamental Sources" (*Pien-tsung lun*, hereafter referred to as the *PTL*), the discussants talk of the theory of sudden enlightenment as advocated by Tao-sheng from the standpoint of Confucianism, arriving at the view that the Confucian and Buddhist paths are identical. We also find such statements as "Confucianism and Taoism are identical (in their goals)"[8] and that they are "compatible."[8] It is worth noting that when a part of the *PTL* was presented to Tao-sheng for comment (see *PTL* postscript), he did not register any major objection to its general line of thought.

The reconciliation of Buddhism with Taoism and Confucianism was often formulated in terms of "origin" and "end" (*pen-mo*). In this approach it was held that the Taoist scriptures, the *I Ching*, and the Buddhist *Dharma* all are concerned with the search for the original source of existence. They suggest that salvation lies in returning to this "origin."[10] The "end" has to do with "traces" (*chi*) and "expediency" (*ch'üan*), means of arriving at the origin. The conceptual relation of *pen-mo* again can be translated into the better-known classical form of *t'i* (substance) and *yung* (function), which originated in the neo-Taoist Wang Pi's commentary on the *Lao-tzu* (Chapter 38).[11] This formulation, glimpsed in such an early period, helps explain the frame of thought expressed by Tao-sheng and others, especially the syncretic T'ien-t'ai Buddhists, who focused on the *Lotus Scripture* and saw its motif of three vehicles dialectically evolving into the One Vehicle.

In what general forms was Buddhism transmitted to Tao-sheng? One approach to this question is to survey the scriptures and doctrines that were first brought by the missionaries. The first scripture to be rendered into Chinese is *An-pan shou-i ching* (*Sūtra* on Mindfulness through Breathing Exercises), translated by An Shih-kao (second century). This text of Hīnayāna meditation helped give the Chinese a more favorable impression of what they initially considered to be an unpalatable religion from foreign parts. It helped minimize the effects of resistance in Han society, deeply penetrated by Taoism, because in the eyes of the Chinese the text apparently dealt with the same matters of hygiene, longevity, and immortality that characterized Taoist practices.[12]

Another set of texts, the series of *Prajñāpāramitā Sūtras*, arrived almost at the same time with, or soon after, the *dhyāna* scripture. A smaller version of the texts (in ten rolls), called *Tao-hsing Prajñāpār-amitā Sūtra*, was translated in 181 by Lokakshema (Chih Lu-chia-ch'en), an Indo-Scythian monk, who later also translated the *Pan-chou san-mei ching* (*Pratyutpanna-samādhi Sūtra*) and twenty-one other works. Thus, the Buddhist doctrine of emptiness (*k'ung*, *śūnyatā*) really started Buddhism's interaction with the indigenous Taoist tradition; and it was to become a dominant subject of Chinese Buddhist philosophy, discussed up to the time of Kumārajīva (fourth century). However, in this early stage of interaction, the concept of emptiness was crudely taken to be equivalent to that of Taoism's *wu*, void or nonbeing. The study of the *Prajñāpāramitā Sūtras*, was later reinforced by an 8000-line translation of the same *sūtra* by Chih-ch'ien about a half century after Lokakshema. The large "wisdom" *sūtra*, in 25,000 lines, was translated by Dharmaraksha (Fa-hu) in 286 and by Mokśala (Wu-cha-lo) in 291.

In the fourth century, these *sūtras* became a focal point of Chinese Buddhist activity; however, an understanding of the doctrine embodied in the *sūtras* had not yet emerged from the neo-Taoist pattern of thought. The comprehension based on these translations was epitomized in Tao-an (312–385) and his contemporaries, only to be supplanted by Kumārajīva and his group, with new and more authentic translations of the same texts. Dharmaraksha covered in his voluminous translations what had been left out by Lokakshema, including the *Saddharmapuṇḍarīka* (in 286), which was translated anew in 406 by Kumārajīva, whose version was to become the basis of Tao-sheng's commentary. The *Nirvāṇa Sūtra*, which made Tao-sheng famous in connection with the universal Buddha-nature and which resulted in his temporary excommunication from the church, was also translated by Fa-hsien in collaboration with Buddhabhadra in 418, and again in a complete version by Dharmakshema in 421.

Another scripture of significance to Tao-sheng and the Kumārajīva circle, *Vimalakīrti-nirdeśa Sūtra*, on which both wrote commentaries, received several renderings, including those by Chih-ch'ien in the third century and Kumārajīva in 406. Thus, before and during Tao-sheng's period, so many of the major *āgamas* and *sūtras* were made available in translation that Tao-sheng was prompted to attempt in the *CSPS* to devise a schema to accommodate the varied teachings of the Buddha long before the T'ien-t'ai and the Hua-yen Buddhists concocted their systems of classifying the Buddha's teaching (*p'an-chiao*).

Many Buddhist concepts ran contrary to ingrained modes of Chinese thought and had to overcome considerable resistance before finally gaining acceptance. Two of the philosophical issues current in the time of Tao-sheng were "retribution" (*pao-ying*) and "extinction [or survival] of spirit (*shen*)." The two problems are related. The Chinese were baffled by what they saw as a contradiction between the two Buddhist postulates of the existence of *karma*, the agent or force causing reincarnation, and the nonexistence of spirit, as an offshoot of the doctrine of *anātman* or no-self. They saw an obvious contradiction in the fact that the subject who receives reward or punishment for the *karma* committed is then said not to exist. Tao-sheng actively participated in the debates on these questions by committing himself to dealing with at least one of them in writing.

The theory of no-self was a difficult idea for the Chinese to grasp. As late as the fourth century, *anātman* was identified in the *Feng-fa yao* (Essentials of *Dharma*)[13] by Hsi Ch'ao with the absence of physical body or constant abode and was seen as an entity moving and changing without ceasing. The style and terminology of expressions used resemble those of the *I Ching*. Nurtured in such a frame of thinking, the Chinese Buddhists, later including Tao-sheng, came to embrace readily the notion of the true self,[14] seemingly contradicting the concept of *anātman*. The related issue of rewards for good deeds gave rise to numerous writings by Tao-sheng's contemporaries, including two essays[15] by Hui-yüan and one by Tao-sheng himself, who used the bold title: "Good Deeds Entail No Recompense."

The study of the *Prajñā* texts by Chinese Buddhists, influenced as they were by neo-Taoist thought and expression, gave rise to diverse interpretations of ontological reality. The result was the emergence of schools in a loose and nebulous pattern, grouped under the appellation of "six houses and seven schools."[16] Their names reveal a blending of Buddhist and Taoist terms such as *emptiness*, *nonbeing* (*wu*), *illusion*, *form* (*rūpa*), *mind*, and *causation*. Classified under these schools are the thinkers Tao-an, Chih Tao-lin, and Chu Fa-t'ai, who, as immediate predecessors of Tao-sheng, were directly or indirectly influential in his early education. During this generation, the exegetical device of *ko-i* or concept-matching, drawing what seemed to be categorically parallel concepts from the Taoist scriptures, was used to help make abstract Buddhist concepts, especially those associated with the *prajñā* doctrine, more intelligible to both Buddhist neophytes and non-Buddhists. This technique was employed even by Tao-an and Hui-yüan in the early stages of their careers. It was soon to be abolished, however, as the Buddhist glossary in Chinese developed further. Yet, even though the explicit method of matching concepts was abandoned, there always was a need for exploiting familiar native Taoist terms and concepts to attract prospective converts.[17] Whether Tao-sheng furthered this ongoing practice or veered from it to find his own way we will explore presently.

In addition to the philosophico-religious aspect, socio-political conditions should be taken into account when we examine Tao-sheng's background. How philosophico-religious concepts of foreign origin were introduced and understood was not entirely unrelated to external factors. One line of demarcation drawn in China at this time was between the North and the South. The rise and fall of small, short-lived states brought social and political instability, especially to the northern region. The partition of China proper into North and South actually started with the establishment of the Eastern Tsin in 317, after the Tsin court seceded from the northern territory. This state of disunion continued, resulting in the era of Nan-pei-ch'ao (Southern and Northern Dynasties), which lasted until 589, when China was unified by the Sui dynasty. This geopolitical division brought about distinctive cultural patterns in the North and South, and Buddhism as a cultural phenomenon was naturally filtered through these. The period we are concerned with here is mainly the fourth century, extending a little into the fifth, during which time Tao-sheng's thought was nurtured.

Tao-sheng was originally of southern background. Born in P'eng-ch'eng (the modern Hsü-chou in Kiangsu), one of the major Buddhist centers in Han times, he moved a little farther south to Chien-k'ang, the southern capital, to start his Buddhist studies. He stayed there longer than any other place in his life, initially from 371 to 397, studying in part under the tutelage of Chu Fa-t'ai (who died in 387) and again from 409 to 428. Fa-t'ai may have instilled in Tao-sheng some elements characteristic of the northern tradition, but Tao-sheng, like other converts to the new religion, must have been swayed in his religious orientation by the two dominant philosophical and intellectual trends of the era: *Ming-chiao* (Doctrine of Names) and *Hsüan-hsüeh* (Dark Learning). The former, a synthesis of the Confucian tradition with Legalist precepts, provided principles for social praxis by defining the roles individuals play in society. The latter, a form of revived Taoism founded on the writings of Wang Pi, addressed the metaphysical question of reality in terms of being (*yu*) and nonbeing (*wu*). Both lines of thought finally were combined in Kuo Hsiang's commentary on the *Chuang-tzu*.

The Buddhist centers that arose in the capital and surrounding eastern region were closely connected ideologically and politically to the imperial court. At the same time, other centers came into existence in the Central and Southeast areas. About those centers outside the capital, E. Zürcher writes:

> Ideologically they were more independent and creative, and at the same time more open to influences from the North. . . . The clerical leaders at these centres (Tao-an at Hsiang-yang, Hui-yüan at the Lu-shan) and many of their disciples came from the North. Their

> doctrinal views represent an amalgamation of Northern Buddhism with its stress on devotional practices, trance and thaumaturgy and based upon the translated scriptures of the archaic period of which it is a direct continuation, and the more intellectualized Southern gentry Buddhism with its peculiar mixture of Dark Learning and Mahāyāna notions and its ontological speculations based upon the *Prajñāpāramitā* and the *Vimakīrti-nirdeśa*.[18]

Northern Buddhism was a strong influence on Tao-sheng's first mentor, Chu Fa-t'ai, who, along with Tao-an, had been under the tutelage of Fo-t'u-teng, a monk from central Asia. Northern Buddhism experienced a period of profound growth when Tao-an was made to move to Ch'ang-an in 379, and later, when Kumārajīva was taken captive in the North and brought there in 401:

> a new chapter in the history of Northern Buddhism begins, characterized by a renewed influx of missionaries, scriptures and ideas from Central Asia and India, huge translation projects, state patronage and supervision, and the emergence of a body of scriptural and scholastic literature (both Hīnayāna and Mahāyāna) together with a new method of exegesis and a new translation technique. In the first decades of the fifth century some elements of Northern Buddhism become gradually known in the South, especially at the Lu-shan where Hui-yüan entertained close relations with Kumārajīva's school at Ch'angan. Around 416 political conditions in the North brought about the disintegration and dispersal of the Buddhist community at Ch'angan. For the third time since the end of the Han a mass emigration of monks to the South took place, and the propagation of the new ideas and theories resulted in a complete reorientation of Southern Buddhism and, eventually, in the rise of Chinese schools.[19]

Tao-sheng stood right in the middle of these events, moving between northern and southern Buddhist centers, including Lu-shan and Ch'ang-an, as well as Chien-k'ang. He was not rigidly bound by existing divisions, however; he eventually outgrew them, becoming probably more creative and original than any other contemporary Chinese Buddhist and emerging as a dynamic thinker with a host of fresh ideas.

Notes

1. I am referring to the *Lao-tzu hua-hu ching* (*Sūtra on Lao-tzu's Conversion of the Barbarians*) written, or rather forged, by Wang Fu at the turn of the

4th century A.D. For studies on this work, see Kamata Shigeo, *Chūgoku Bukkyōshi* (Tokyo, 1968), p. 44, note 3.

2. Of Tao-sheng's contemporaries, Hui-yüan (334–416) and Seng-chao (374–414) are most typical. For Hui-yüan's case, see Arthur F. Wright, *Buddhism in Chinese History* (Stanford, Calif., 1959), p. 46; Paul Demiéville, "La pénétration du Bouddhisme dans la tradition philosophique chinoise," *Cahiers d'histoire mondiale*, 3 (1956): 23–24.

3. His brightness in conventional subjects prior to his conversion to Buddhism is suggested in his biography in the *Kao-seng chuan*, T50.366b20f., and his eulogy by Hui-lin in T52.266a1f.

4. *T'ien-hsia t'ung-kuei erh shu t'u* in "Appended Remarks" (*Hsi-ts'u chuan*), Part 2, Ch. 5; Wing-tsit Chan, comp. and trans., *A Source Book in Chinese Philosophy* (Princeton, N. J., 1963), p. 268.

5. See Hu Shih, "The Development of Zen Buddhism in China", *The Chinese Social and Political Science Review*, 15, no. 4 (1932): 484: "Tao-sheng was only the natural product of an age which . . . was one of Taoist revival."

6. See T'ang Yung-t'ung, "On 'Ko-yi,' the Earliest Method by Which Indian Buddhism and Chinese Thought Were Synthesized," in W. R. Inge et al., eds., *Radhakrishnan, Comparative Studies in Philosophy* (London, 1951), pp. 276–286.

7. See T52.9–16. For a discussion of the document from a different perspective, see Kenneth Ch'en, "Anti-Buddhist Propaganda during the Nan-Ch'ao," *Harvard Journal of Asiatic Studies*, 15 (1952): 176f.

8. See T52.225a.

9. T52.225b2f.

10. See, for example, *Pien-tsung lun*, T52.226c7.

11. *Lao tzu i*, vol. 3, b/5:3; Ariane Rump with Wing-tsit Chan, trans., *Commentary on the Lao Tzu by Wang Pi* (Honolulu, 1979), p. 112.

12. For the Taoist aspect, see Holmes Welch, *Taoism: The Parting of the Way* (Boston, 1966), p. 89.

13. In the *Hung-ming chi*, vol. 13 (T52.86a–89a) translated in E. Zürcher, *The Buddhist Conquest of China* (Leiden, 1959), vol. 1. pp. 164–175.

14. Actually the concept and the word itself were carried to them by the *Nirvāṇa Sūtra*, a predominant subject of extensive study of the day, which, as Tao-sheng and other Chinese Buddhists rightly found out, puts forward the eternal reality and the true self, or eternal self; see Tao-sheng's commentary to the *Nirvāṇa Sūtra* in T37.452a, 452b, 453b, 453c, 463a, 532c, and 550b. Also what appears to be Tao-sheng's statement of doctrine is found in the *Ming-seng chuan*

ch'ao (Excerpts of the Biography of Famous Monks) by Pao-ch'ang, in *Hsü tsang ching*, vol. 134, p. 8d10.

15. *Ming pao-ying lun* (On the Explanation of Karmic Retribution), in *Hung-ming chi*, vol. 5, T52.33f.; and *San-pao lun* (On Three Kinds of Karmic Retribution), ibid., T52.35. For discussions and translation in part especially of the first article, see Fung Yu-lan, trans. Derk Bodde, *A History of Chinese Philosophy*, vol. 2, pp. 272ff.; Liebenthal, "Shih Hui-yüan's Buddhism as Set Forth in His Writings," *Journal of the American Oriental Society*, 70 (1950): 243–259.

16. See Kenneth Ch'en, "Neo-Taoism and the Prajna School during the Wei and Chin Dynasties," in *Chinese Culture* 1, no. 2 (1957): 35ff.; Fung, *History of Chinese Philosophy*, vol. 2, pp. 243ff.; Zürcher, *Buddhist Conquest*, p. 148.

17. An episode involving Hui-yüan's practice of the analogical method is recorded in his biography in the *Kao-seng chuan*, (hereafter *KSC*), vol. 6, p. 348a. But Zürcher, *op. cit.*, p. 184, holds that Tao-an later had abolished the method.

18. Zürcher, *Buddhist Conquest*, p. 114.

19. Loc. cit. For the characteristic development of Buddhism in north and south in the subsequent period, see Hurvitz, *Chih-i* (538–597), Mélanges chinois et bouddhiques (Bruxxells, 1962), vol. 12, pp. 74ff.

Chapter 2

TAO-SHENG'S BIOGRAPHY

Biographical Sources

As in the case of most of the contemporary and earlier masters of Chinese Buddhism, the primary source of our knowledge of Tao-sheng's education, life, and works is the *Kao-seng chuan* (*Biographies of Eminent Monks*, hereafter referred to as the *KSC*), compiled in 519 by Hui-chiao (who died in 554). Tao-sheng tops the list of thirty-two masters in *ch'üan* 7 (T50.366b–367a). Another major source is the *Ch'u san-tsang chi-chi* (Collection of Records Pertaining to the Tripiṭaka), compiled in about 518 by Seng-yu (445–518), specifically *ch'üan* 15 (T55.110c–111b). The two records on Tao-sheng are basically identical in content, except for one episode: the account of Tao-sheng's influence immediately after his death is found only in the *KSC*. It is possible that one text derives from the other but it is more likely that both derive from a third fundamental *Urtext*.

The only extant contemporary writing with any biographical value is the eulogy for Tao-sheng by Hui-lin, found in the *Kuang hung-ming chi* (*Further Collection of Essays on Buddhism*), compiled by Tao-hsüan (596–667) (T52.265c–266b). The basic biographical information contained in its first paragraph concurs with the two sources just cited, although the second half is sentimental in style and subjective in content.

A potentially informative document of which, unfortunately, we have only sketchy excerpts is the *Ming-seng chuan* (*Biographies of Eminent Monks*) written by Pao-ch'ang in the period of the Liang dynasty (502–557). In these excerpts (HTC, vol. 134, p. 15a–b) we find six items concerning or seemingly attributed to Tao-sheng, the first of which is titled "The Story of Chu Tao-sheng at the Western Monastery on Lu-shan." The rest deal with topics advocated by Tao-sheng, probably at the community. Since the first article refers to Tao-sheng's first sojourn at Lu-shan, the document seems to provide not a full-fledged biography, but accounts of single incidents and arguments. Nonetheless, it gives very informative details of the period.

Tao-sheng is mentioned in a couple of other sources whose themes are related to him in one way or another. One is the *Fa-hua chuan-chi* (*Biographies and Records Related to the Lotus*) (T51, nr. 2068), compiled by Seng-hsiang of the T'ang dynasty (618–907). A brief biography of Tao-sheng in *chüan* 2 (T51.56a) is based mostly on the *KSC*, with the additional information coming from "later commentaries" about Tao-sheng's lectures on the *Lotus* held in an "auspicious atmosphere" and the fact that he wrote the commentary. Another record is the *Lu-shan chi* (*Chronicle of Lu-shan*), (T51, nr. 2095), compiled by Ch'en Shun-yü during the Sung period (960–1127). Although it is primarily a repetition of the *KSC*, the biography (T51.1040c–1041a) nevertheless provides some new information in its last passage: The first ruler of the Posterior T'ang, who reigned from 923 to 926, issued a decree to dedicate a hall in memory of Tao-sheng, conferring a posthumous title "the Great Master of Universal Deliverance (or Salvation)" (P'u-chi ta-shih). This illustrates the esteem in which the work of Tao-sheng was held even as late as the tenth century. Kumārajīva's biography in the *KSC* (T50.323b) is another minor source of some importance.

Tao-sheng's Early Years in Chien-k'ang under Chu Fa-t'ai

Tao-sheng was born around 360[1] in P'eng-ch'eng, located in the central eastern part of the mainland (in modern Kiangsu), lying approximately midway between the two great rivers, Hwang Ho and Yangtze. Having been one of two major Buddhist centers during the Han Dynasty in the first and second centuries A.D., the place must have furnished a favorable environment for a potential Buddhist. Although it was no longer important as a Buddhist center, a few eminent Buddhist figures in fact had been born there or associated with the center.[2] Tao-sheng's father, a local magistrate, allowed the boy, barely eleven years old, to study with Chu Fa-t'ai (319–387) in Chien-k'ang, a little south of Tao-sheng's home. Tao-sheng stayed there as an outstanding disciple of Fa-t'ai for a number of years during the formative phase of his Buddhist education, and he probably remained beyond his master's death. Fa-t'ai's influence on Tao-sheng therefore may have been greater than one can gather from the extant record (which is hardly detailed).

Fa-t'ai had been a disciple of Fo-t'u-teng (died 349), probably a Kuchean missionary. A thaumaturge, "a great propagandist," and "the practical propagator of the faith in its most elementary form by the most simple and adequate means which appealed to most of an illiterate population,"[3] Fo was anything but a translator or exegete.[4] Unlike Tao-an (312–385), a fellow student under Fo, Chu Fa-t'ai did not establish himself as a scholarly monk in a serious sense. That line of practice and the mantle of the community presided over by him devolved to Tao-sheng, who adopted the master's clerical surname "Chu" ("Indian"). This may account for the relatively late blooming of Tao-sheng's critical mind. Nonetheless, Tao-sheng seems to have stood on his own, emerging as a brilliant lecturer and debater. He was probably familiar with some basic Buddhist texts, including the *Prajñāpāramitā Sūtras*, because Fa-t'ai had lectured at one point on the *Pañcaviṁśatisāhasrikā Prajñāpāramitā Sūtra* (*Fang-kuang ching*).[5]

The First Sojourn at Lu-shan with Hui-yüan

Tao-sheng became an itinerant mendicant in middle age, probably upon the death of his master in 387. In 397, he settled down in Lu-shan, which was in the process of becoming a celebrated Buddhist center in the South. Two important figures Tao-sheng met then were Hui-yüan (334–417), the founder of the community in around 380, and Sanghadeva, a Kashmir missionary and a specialist in *Abhidharma* hailing from the Sarvāstivāda school of Hīnayāna Buddhism. Despite the big difference in age between Tao-sheng and Hui-yüan, there is no evidence that their relationship ever became intimate or developed into that of mentor-student.[6] They may have shared the chores of community life and even the same compound, but they probably were separated by different living quarters (*vihāras*). They may have discussed some problems debated at that time, not only in the community but outside it, including the question of *karma* and reward (*pao-ying*). Yet, it seems preposterous to assume that the two shared views or basic approaches to any of these questions simply because they stayed in the same community. For example, both wrote articles on the question of retribution, but because only Hui-yüan's writing is extant, some scholars speculate that one can deduce Tao-sheng's position from it.[7] Hui-yüan and Tao-sheng are alike in that they struggled, on the one hand, to comprehend the Buddhist frame of thinking as distinct from the Chinese perspectives in which they had been trained, and, on the other hand, to find the way to assimilate these two ways of thinking.[8] But the two are widely apart in training, subject matter, methodology, style, the scriptures they dealt with, and the substance of their understanding. In general, Hui-yüan remained more conservative, sometimes doggedly faithful to the literal meaning of the texts, including monastic rules (*vinaya*),[9] whereas Tao-sheng was more liberal, with a wider perspective, often boldly rejecting the literal sense of a text while attempting to capture its spirit.

Though his interest was not limited to one school or area, Hui-yüan can be put in the category of the Mādhyamika in light of his training under Tao-an (312–385) and his writings, including correspondence with Kumārajīva. Tao-sheng, however, did not specialize in one doctrine or another, and the texts on which he wrote commentaries, including one of the *Prajñāpāramitā Sūtras*, are diverse in doctrinal origin. Metaphysically and practically, as Itano Chōhachi points out, Hui-yüan is more or less a dualist who, for one thing, distinguishes between the two orders, secular and sacred, whereas Tao-sheng's thinking appears to have a somewhat monistic tinge.[10] Tao-sheng's monistic perspective is seen in his stress on the identification of *nirvāṇa* and *saṃsāra*,[11] which is a point also made by the *Mādhyamika*,[12] as well as in his emphasis on the dialectical identification of three vehicles and One Vehicle, the theme of the *Lotus Sūtra*. In short, Tao-sheng was in a position subordinate to Hui-yüan in the communal hierarchy, but Tao-sheng's vision and grasp of Buddhism even then may have been too far advanced beyond Hui-yüan's to be influenced by it. However, Tao-sheng shared with Hui-yüan the teaching of Gautama Saṅghadeva on the Sarvāstivāda and its version of the *Abhidharma* literature of Hīnayāna. In a sense, Tao-sheng took the path to Mahāyāna philosophy following in the steps of Kumārajīva, and in fact he is credited for having fused the Sarvāstivādin doctrine and Mahāyāna speculations as enunciated by Kumārajīva.[13]

Study under Kumārajīva in Ch'ang-an

In 405 or 406, after staying at Lu-shan for about seven years, Tao-sheng made a long-cherished and eagerly awaited move to Ch'ang-an to study with Kumārajīva, who had been there since 401, attracting about 3000 aspiring pupils to Mahāyāna doctrines. However, Tao-sheng's sojourn in Ch'ang-an was relatively brief, only about two years, for some unidentified reason. This brief period, however, was sufficient to demonstrate Tao-sheng's ability and warrant him a position on contemporary "honours lists," ranging from one of the four "(great) philosophers"[14] to one of the fifteen great disciples, more often than not being listed first.

Despite his fame, the specific role Tao-sheng played and how much he contributed, particularly to Kumārajīva's major task, translation, are not certain. Although Tao-sheng is reported by Seng-chao to have been on hand when Kumārajīva translated the *Lotus*, Tao-sheng does not figure prominently in any record as a close assistant to Kumārajīva in his translation activities. Rather, Seng-jui (352–436) was Kumārajīva's scribe and, perhaps, his chief disciple,[15] and Seng-chao (374–414) accompanied Kumārajīva from his pre-Ch'ang-an days until his death (414) and directly assisted Kumārajīva in many ways, including writing the prefaces and colophons to many *sūtras* under translation.[16] Tao-sheng's relatively brief stay may not have allowed him to leave a visible mark on the translations.

When Tao-sheng arrived in Ch'ang-an, the captial of the Eastern Chin (317–420), the massive 100-volume work of the *Great Wisdom Treatise* (*Mahāprajñāpāramitā-śāstra, Ta Chih-tu lun*) was almost (or just) completed. In the course of the brief period between 405 and 408, however, an assortment of important texts was translated. These included *Vimalakīrti-nirdeśa*, *Lotus*, and *Aṣṭasāhasrikā-prajñāpāramitā* (*Hsiao-p'in*) *Sūtras*. It may not be just coincidental that in the ensuing years Tao-sheng wrote commentaries on these three, the last of which is not extant today in any form; he may have commented on them not only because they represented important doctrines but also because of Kumārajīva's influence. In fact, in the preface to his commentary on the *Lotus* (CSPS, 396d), Tao-sheng says something to this effect. In the case of the *Vimalakīrti-nirdeśa*, Seng-chao's commentary on the text, written between 406 and 410, prompted Tao-sheng to write his own.

In 408 Tao-sheng returned to Lu-shan, bringing with him Seng-chao's essay "*Prajñā* has no knowing" (*pan-jo wu-chih lun*), which was read widely and favorably in the community. Tao-sheng's role as a messenger of the literature shows his unique ability to bridge the nascent northern and southern Buddhist traditions represented by Ch'ang-an and Lu-shan respectively.[17]

The Second Sojourn at Chien-k'ang

Soon afterwards, in 409, Tao-sheng moved to Chien-k'ang for the second time. He remained in the area more than twenty years, taking up residence in the monastery called Ch'ing-yüan ssu (later Lung-kuang ssu) from 419 on. Tao-sheng thus began to tread the path of an independent thinker.[18] In addition to winning respect from the court and the general populace as well as the intelligentsia, he was able to meditate on the status of Chinese Buddhism and indentify some significant points to be clarified or rectified. This period, which also marks the point of his maturity as a thinker, was his most productive in terms of writings, most of which are presumed to have been drafted during this period,[19] with one obvious exception: the present commentary under study, composed in 432 in Lu-shan. A controversial theory Tao-sheng advocated at this time concerned the question of whether the *icchantikas*, regarded traditionally as outcasts from the path of enlightenment, were also Buddha-natured. Tao-sheng decided they were while reading an incomplete version of the *Mahāparinirvāṇa Sūtra*, a complete version of which was still to come. The absolute universality of the Buddha-nature was the logical conclusion he reached by inference from the first part of the *sūtra*, even though it contained an explicit statement excepting the *icchantikas*.[20] This bold new interpretation, amounting to a challenge of an accepted channel of the Buddha's doctrines, brought about his expulsion from the Buddhist community sometime between 428 and 429.

The Third Sojourn at Lu-shan and Death

Lamenting that people had not been able to transcend the symbols of the translated *sūtras* to grasp the true meaning behind the words and predicting that he would be proven right and eventually exonerated, Tao-sheng retreated to Lu-shan in 430, via Hu-ch'iu-shan in 429. It was not long, after the complete text of the *Nirvāṇa Sūtra*, translated by Dharmakshema, had made its way there, that Tao-sheng turned out to be correct.[21] He was vindicated and praised for his penetrating insight. Instead of returning to Chien-k'ang, however, he remained at Lu-shan until his death in 434.[22] In 432, Tao-sheng composed a commentary on the *Lotus Sūtra* on the basis of information and lecture notes he had collected throughout many years. Hence, from the chronological point of view, this work—the subject of our analysis and translation—may represent the culmination of Tao-sheng's scholarship.

Evaluation of Tao-sheng's Life

Throughout his Buddhist career, Tao-sheng lived and worked primarily at three locations: Chien-k'ang for some thirty-six years altogether, split between two periods; Lu-shan for about thirteen years over three periods; and Ch'ang-an for three years. These three locales were evolving three different interpretive traditions, and Tao-sheng's exposure to many sources nutured him as a Buddhist thinker, a rare fortune that distinguished him from other contemporary Buddhists. At Ch'ang-an, under Kumārajīva, he studied the Mādhyamika doctrine in conjunction with the *Prajñāpāramitā* and other related texts, as well as the *Lotus* under translation. At Lu-shan he learned the *Abhidharma* doctrine with Sanghadeva, among others. Yet Tao-sheng had already spent his formative years in Chien-k'ang, the first seventeen years under Chu Fa-t'ai, until the latter died in 387. Thus, what Tao-sheng learned at Lu-shan and Ch'ang-an reinforced and consolidated the basic knowledge he had acquired at Chien-k'ang.

Tao-sheng's maturation at Chien-k'ang remains largely in the dark; nevertheless, a few things about Chu Fa-t'ai and the community can be mentioned in this connection. Fa-t'ai, as mentioned earlier, gave lectures on a *Prajñāpāramitā Sūtra*. Of the six "houses" and seven "schools" that arose in this period in connection with the interpretation of the concept of emptiness, Fa-t'ai belonged to the school of Original Nonbeing, or a variant, which argues for the centrality of the concept of nonbeing (*wu*) in Buddhist ontology.

Fa-t'ai's community was not entirely isolated from other centers in terms of ideological exchange; he shared his interpretation of the Mādhyamika with his senior colleague under Fo-t'u-teng, Tao-an, who stayed in Ch'ang-an until his death in 385. (Fa-t'ai had been sent to Chien-k'ang when the community under Teng was dispersed.[23]) Fa-t'ai exchanged correspondence with Tao-an on the question of the three vehicles,[24] the theme of the *Lotus*, and probably on other issues, too. According to Chi-tsang's commentary on the *Lotus*,[25] Tao-an and Fa-t'ai lectured on the old version of the *Lotus*, a translation by Dharmaraksha from the third century. Here, it becomes evident that Tao-sheng's interest in the *Lotus* may have antedated his contact with the new translation by Kumārajīva, and so his commentary naturally reflects the two lines of tradition in which he was involved, as he himself suggests in the beginning of his work.

The doctrine of vehicles was not the sole subject dealt with in the communities of Fa-t'ai and Tao-an; they also were involved with the questions of stages (*bhūmi*) and enlightenment,[26] subjects that are to an extent interrelated. These three concepts all appear very prominently in Tao-sheng's *CSPS*. Tao-sheng reportedly also wrote a pamphlet entitled "Explaining the Meaning [of the Proposition] that in the Initial [Moment of] Thought upon Entering the Eighth Stage, [a Bodhisattva] Intends to Achieve *Nirvāṇa*." This line of thought naturally could lead to the conclusion that Tao-sheng in fact did reach in his later work: that enlightenment is instantaneous. His work under Fa-t'ai thus paved the way for the development of this theory.

Tao-sheng stood at an ideological intersection, a good position from which to synthesize the varying traditions. He may owe the basic structures of some of his major doctrines to his early masters,[27] yet otherwise, he seems to have emerged from his early days on as an independent thinker. His biography in the *KSC* reports his fame as a talented lecturer at the age of only fifteen. Later, Tao-sheng journeyed to other Buddhist centers, but his encounters with other masters and their teachings appear not to have had any major impact on him as far as the basic structures of his thought are concerned, and he developed no close master-disciple relationship.

Notes

1. Kamata Shigeo, *Chūgoku Bukkyōshi*, p. 76, gives the date 355–434 with no explanation for the new date of birth.

2. For example, Liu I-min (Ch'eng-chih) (354–410), a prominent contemporary layman at Lu-shan.

3. Zürcher, *Buddhist Conquest*, p. 183.

4. See Arthur F. Wright, "Fo-t'u-teng: A Biography," *Harvard Journal of Asiatic Studies*, 11 (1948): 324: "He had come to China with the intention of starting a religious center in the imperial capital, and, had he reached there at a less disturbed time, he would no doubt have become a great translator and exegete."

5. *KSC*, vol. 5, 354b.

6. The master-disciple relationship is assumed by Robinson, *Early Mādhyamika in India and China* (Madison, Wisc., 1967), p. 99; Kamata, *Chūgoku Bukkyōshi*, p. 74; Ch'en, *Buddism in China*, whereas T'ang Yung-t'ung, *Ham-Wei liang-Chin Nan-pei-ch'ao Fo-chiao shih* (Shanghai, 1938), vol. 2, p. 142, defines their relationship to be that of peers.

7. See Fung, *History of Chinese Philosophy*, vol. 2 pp. 272ff.; Ch'en, Buddhism in China, pp. 118f.; Fung, *A Short History of Chinese Philosophy* (New York, 1948), p. 249.

8. For an assessment of Hui-yüan in reference to his understanding of the Mādhyamika doctrine, see Robinson, *Early Mādhyamika*, pp. 104, 114.

9. See the biography of Hui-yüan in the *KSC*, T50.361b, translated in Zürcher, *Buddhist Conquest*, vol. 1, p. 253.

10. See Itano Chōhachi, "Dōshō no tongosetsu seiritsu no jijō," *Tōhō gakuhō*, 7 (1936): 125–186, particularly 164ff. and 175ff. See the text, 396d3f.

11. See CVS, 392a17.

12. See the *Mādhyamikakārikās* by Nāgārjuna, 25:19, translated in Frederic J. Streng, *Emptiness: A Study in Religious Meaning* (Nashville, 1967), p. 217.

13. See his biography in the *KSC* T55.110c29. It may not be easy to prove or disprove the point in the text concerned, for the third element, the Taoist view, makes the question more complex. Nonetheless see *CSPS* 397a5, for ex-

ample, for the possible trace of such connection. Liebenthal, "A Biography of Chu Tao-sheng," *Monumenta Nipponica*, 11, no. 3 (1955): 68, holds that close contact with the *Abhidharma*, though it may have enriched his knowledge, left Tao-sheng's thinking processes virtually untouched.

14. The other three are Tao-jung, Seng-chao, and Hui-kuan; see *KSC*, vol. 7, 368b.

15. See T50.332b23.

16. It does not necessarily mean his knowledge of Sanskrit was poor or insufficient to make him an assistant. As a matter of fact, Tao-sheng is listed as a cotranslator, along with Buddhajīva, of the text of Mahīsāsaka vinaya translated in 423 in Chien-k'ang; see his biography in *CSTCC*, vol. 15, T55.111b1ff.

17. See Ōchō, "Jikudōshō sen Hokekyōso no kenkyū," *Ōtani Daigaku kenkyū nempō*, 5 (1952), p. 173.

18. See Robinson, *Early Mādhyamika*, p. 169; Demièville, "La pénétration du bouddhisme dans la tradition philosophique chinoise," *Cahiers d'historie mondiale*, 3, no. 1 (1965): 32–35.

19. Itano Chōhachi, "Dōshō no tongosetzu", p. 168, believes that the theory of sudden enlightenment was expounded in the period between 409 and 414.

20. See the *Mahāparinirvāṇa Sūtra*, vol. 4, translated by Fa-hsien, T12. 881b.

21. See the *Mahāparinirvāṇa Sūtra*, vol. 5, translated by Dharmakshema, T12.633b.

22. Robinson, *Early Mādhyamika*, p. 169, wrongly puts the date of death at 432, probably following Liebenthal, "A Biography," p. 89.

23. See *KSC*, vol. 5, 354b.

24. See Ōchō, "Jikudōshō no hokke shisō," p. 204.

25. *Fa-hua hsüan-lun*, T34.363b.

26. See Ōchō, "Jikudōshō no hokke shisō," pp. 202ff.

27. See ibid., p. 205; Paul Demiéville, "La pénétration," p. 32.

Chapter 3

TAO-SHENG'S WORKS

Tao-sheng's works consist of commentaries (*shu*), treatises (*lun*), expositions (*i*), a translation, letters, and other forms of writing. The main source of the works in the following list is the *Ch'u-san'tsang chi-chi* (*Collection of Records of Tripiṭaka*, hereafter referred to as the *CSTCC*), vol. 15 (T55), compiled by Seng-yu in 518, unless otherwise indicated. With the exception of some of the commentaries, Tao-sheng's works are all lost, making it virtually impossible to put them in chronological order. Apart from the *Lotus Sūtra* (432), no work can be dated; only rough dates in terms of *terminus a quo* and *terminus ad quem* can be assigned for some.

Commentaries

Commentary on the Vimalakīrti-nirdeśa Sūtra

The translation of the *sūtra* by Kumārajīva, on which Tao-sheng's commentary is based, was completed in 406, while Tao-sheng stayed in Ch'ang-an with Kumārajīva. Tao-sheng must have participated in or familiarized himself with the process of translation. He was motivated to write his commentary by Seng-chao's commentary, which was sent to Lu-shan in 410, when he was in Chien-k'ang after a brief sojourn at Lu-shan from 408 to 409. Tao-sheng's commentary thus can be dated shortly after 410. The "exegetical commentary" (*i-shu*) is preserved in the excerpted form in the collection entitled *Chu Wei-mo-chieh ching* (T38, nr. 1775) compiled by Seng-chao (374–414), along with the commentaries by Seng-chao and Kumārajīva. The date of the commentary therefore can be placed between 410 and 414. It also is found in basically the same form in the *Ching-ming ching chi-chieh Kuan-chung shu* (T85, nr. 2777), compiled by Tao-i in 674 (or 760).

Commentary on the Mahāparinirvāṇa Sūtra

There were two versions of the *sūtra*, one (six volumes) translated by Fa-hsien, another called the "northern version" (forty volumes), by Dharmakshema. The first one, *Ta-p'an ni-heng ching* (T12, nr. 376), appeared in 418; the second one, *Ta-p'an nieh-p'an ching* (T12, nr. 374), reached Tao-sheng in 430. A revised edition (thirty-six volumes) of the latter, called the "southern version," was compiled by Hui-kuan, Hui-yen, and Hsieh Ling-yün, probably after Tao-sheng's death.

The commentary listed in the *CSTCC* is called *Ni-heng ching i-shu* (*Exegetical Commentary on the Nirvāṇa Sūtra*). Hence, Tao-sheng is believed to have written a commentary on Fa-hsien's version. Yet, we find Tao-sheng's comments, probably selectively, in the collection of commentaries to the *sūtra* called *Ta-p'an nieh-p'an ching chih-chieh* (71 volumes) (T37, nr. 1763), which was compiled by Seng-liang and Pao-liang (444–509) by the decree of Emperor Wu of the Liang dynasty. The commentaries of ten masters representing the tradition of the Nirvāṇa School are collated in the collection, Tao-sheng's being placed on top. Because the collection is based on the longer version of the *sūtra*—that is, *Nieh-pan ching*—it can be presumed that Tao-sheng wrote another commentary.[1] The first commentary could have been written between 418 and 430, whereas the second was written after 430, but probably before 432, when the commentary on the *Lotus* was written.

Commentary on the Smaller Version [of the Prajñāpāramitā Sūtra] (Hsiao-p'in ching i-shu)

The *sūtra* (*Aṣṭasāhasrikā*) (T8, nr. 227) was newly translated by Kumārajīva in 408 when Tao-sheng stayed in Ch'ang-an,[2] while there already had been an old translation (called *Tao-hsing ching*) by Lokakshema in 179 A.D. Tao-sheng thus must have been instigated by Kumārajīva's interpretation of the doctrine embodied in the *sūtra*. The commentary, unfortunately not extant, would have revealed another dimension of Tao-sheng's thought-sphere, which is party shown in the fact that he did not neglect to include the basic, earliest Prajñāpāramitā text in his catalogue of the scriptures to comment on.

Commentary on the Lotus (Saddharmapuṇḍarīka) Sūtra (Miao-fa lien-hua ching shu)

The only writing remaining intact, this commentary (the subject of our present study) was completed in 432. Based on also a new translation by Kumārajīva in 406 (old one by Dharmaraksha in 286), when Tao-sheng was around in Kumārajīva's circle, the commentary certainly took an extended process of production—and so much thought-process.

Treatises (lun)

"On the Two Truths" (*Erh-ti lun*).
"Buddha-Nature Is That Which One Will Realize in the Future" (*Fo-hsing tang-yu lun*).
"Dharma-kāya Is Formless (*arūpa*)" (*Fa-shen wu-se lun*).
"[The Buddha's] Response Is Expressed in [various] Conditions" (*Ying yu-yüan lun*).[3]
"The Buddha Has [in Reality] No 'Pure Land' [in the Realm of Dharma-kāya]" (*Fo wu ching-t'u lun*).[4]

Expositions (i)

"[Ethically] Good Deeds Do Not Lead One to Receive [Religious] Retribution."[5]
"By Sudden Enlightenment One Achieves Buddhahood."[6]
"Explaining the Exposition that [a Bodhisattva] with the first Thought upon His Entering the Eighth Stage (*bhūmi*) Is Likely to Achieve *Nirvāṇa*."
"Discussing the Meaning of Buddha-Nature."
"On the 'Thirty-six Questions' in the *Nirvāṇa*." Reference is to the same number of questions raised by Kāśyapa Nalagramaka to the Buddha in the *Nirvāṇa Sūtra* (T37.379; cf. 619bf.).
"Expositions of the Fourteen Topics."[7] This writing is listed in some historical sources, and some of the topics along with the title are mentioned in several places, including a subcommentary to the *Hua-yen Sūtra*, the *Hua-yen ching sui-shu yen-i ch'ao* (T36, nr. 1736) by Ch'eng-kuan (760–820), the fourth patriarch of the Hua-yen School, and a subcommentary to the *Nirvāṇa Sūtra, Nieh-p'an hsüan-i fa-yüan chi-yao* (T38, nr. 1766, p. 19a17) by Chih-yüan during the Sung period (976–1022). We can gather from the last two sources that the topics include "the doctrine of the eternally abiding [*nirvāṇa* or *li*]" (T36.291a); "the doctrine of the reality" (T36. 400a); "the doctrine that good deeds do not entail rewards" (T36.318c); and the tenth topic, "the doctrine that sentient beings possess Buddha-nature" (T38.19a17). Thus, this writing seems to contain most of Tao-sheng's ideas, ontological or Buddhological, that he put

forward and formulated up to the point of the *icchantika* question (see T38.19a17).

Translation

Tao-sheng is listed as a cotranslator of a work of *vinaya* ("discipline") called *Five-division law of the Mahīśāsakā* [*School*] (T22, nr. 1421) along with the principal translator, Buddhajīva. The work was translated in 423 or 424, when they were together at the Lung-kuang ssu in Chien-k'ang. It is not certain how much and in what way Tao-sheng participated as a cotranslator in the process, but it was very rare for a Chinese to share the position with a native speaker of Sanskrit. Even Seng-chao and Seng-jui, the able assistants to Kumārajīva, could not entertain that honor in any of the translations in which they participated. This suggests that Tao-sheng probably was equipped with a working knowledge of the Buddhist Sanskrit language and that his scholarly and practical interest extended to and encompassed *vinaya* or the monastic rules.

Letters

Letter to Wang Hung

A brief letter answering Wang's inquiry about the doctrine of instantaneous enlightenment is found at the end of the *Pien-tsung lun* (T52. 228a8ff.), compiled by Hsieh Ling-yün (385–433), which deals exclusively with Tao-sheng's doctrine. In the letter, Tao-sheng generally agrees with Hsieh's interpretation of the doctrine, adding, however, that true knowledge consists in what one has experientially illuminated in oneself. The letter confirms the value of this document as the only legitimate source for Tao-sheng's doctrine in the absence of his writings proper.

Letters to Fan Po-lun, Fu Chi, and Other Monks

A series of four letters were exchanged between Fan Po-lun (Fan-t'ai) and Tao-sheng, Fu Chi (d. 426), or other related monks. Listed in Fa-lun's catalogue (CSTCC 12, in T55.83 a–f.), it is not certain how many letters Tao-sheng himself wrote in this correspondence. The date is before 426.

Other Writings

The *Ming-seng chuan* (*Biographies of Eminent Monks*, hereafter referred to as the *MSC*) by Pao-ch'ang (during the period of the Liang dynasty, 502–557) lists five items.[8] They may represent the topics of Tao-sheng's lectures or writings, just quotes from them, or Tao-sheng's statements. Three of them are

> "The proposition that 'those who are endowed with the two factors of life (namely, *yin* and *yang*) are (or have in) themselves [potentially] the right causes of *nirvāṇa* [and their reincarnation in the three realms (*triloka*) is simply the result of delusion]. The *icchantikas* being [also] the class of beings partaking of reincarnation, how is it possible that they are solely excepted from possessing Buddha-nature?' "[9]
>
> "The proposition that 'the knowledge of the two vehicles is to view emptiness (*śūnyatā*) as universal characteristics while the knowledge of the bodhisattvas is to view emptiness as specific characteristics'."
>
> "The proposition that 'by doing good and suppressing evil one is said to have attained the [good] *karma* of [being reborn as] man or god (deva), yet in reality this is not a case of the good deed entailing reward'."
>
> "The proposition that 'animals enjoy riches and pleasure while there are those who, born among humans as the result of [good] retribution, are afflicted with poverty and suffering'."
>
> "The proposition that 'an *icchantika* is not equipped with the root of faith, yet, though they are cut off from the good root, they still possess Buddha-nature'."

Notes

1. See T'ang, *Fo-chiao shih*, p. 149.

2. Liebenthal, "A Biography," p. 71, is misinformed on two counts, with regard to the Sanskrit title "*Daśasāhasrikā*" and the year 407. For the first see Zürcher, *Buddhist Conquest*, p. 65, and Robinson, *Early Mādhyamika*, p. 117; and for the second see Seng-jui's preface to the translation, T55.55a4.

3. Liebenthal, "A Biography," p. 94, lists the title as "The Response of the Buddha Is Conditioned".

4. Also quoted in Chi-tsang, *Fa-hua hsüan-lun*, T34.442a9ff., in which the writing called "The Treatise on the Dharma-kāya Having No 'Pure Land'" is identified with "The Treatise on the 'Seven Treasures'." For the identification of "pure land" and "seven treasures," see *CVS*, 334b–c28; *CSPS*, 410b15ff.

5. Liebenthal, "A Biography," p. 94, translates the title: "True Piety

Requires No (Mundane) Rewards." It thus is contentious whether "good" has ethical or religious implications and, likewise, to what dimension retribution refers. One can consider the next topic in close association with the present one, and one of the "propositions" to be listed is on a similar subject. Anyway, it is evident that Tao-sheng talks of the two different planes, moral and religious.

6. The close connection of the present theme with the last one is apparent in the sources of information; namely, Tao-sheng's biographies. *KSC*, 366, lists the present writing right after the last topic without any hiatus or any word interpolated, even the word (*i*). *CSTCC*, T55.111a5 adds the word *chi* ("and") between the two. See Fuse Kōgaku, *Nehanshū no kenkyū* (Tokyo, 1973), pp. 22, 192.

7. T'ang, *op. cit.*, 150, doubts the authenticity of this work. See Kamata, *Chūgoku Kegon shisōshi no kenkyū* (Tokyo, 1978), p. 418.

8. Liebenthal, "A Biography," p. 94.

9. The full statement of the article now translated is found in the *I-ch'eng fo-hsing hui-jih ch'ao* (*Transcript of the One Vehicle Buddha-Nature Wisdom*) by the Japanese monk Ensō (d. 883), in T70.173c. See Fung, *History of Chinese Philosophy*, vol. 2, p. 271. Cf. translation by Liebenthal, "A Biography," p. 94.

Chapter 4

TAO-SHENG'S DOCTRINES

Here we will try to sketch an overall view of Tao-sheng's doctrines based on all the available sources excluding the *CSPS*, as much as possible. This will serve two purposes: first, it will provide a basis by which his influence can be measured; second, we can then compare this picture of Tao-sheng's thought with what has been found in the commentary (see Part II). The titles of the expository writings ascribed to Tao-sheng but now lost reveal him as a seminal thinker with a vast range of scholarly insight. Many of his writings were interrelated variations on a number of major distinct themes, interconnected to form a unified system of thought. For this reason, we will closely examine two of the more conspicuous topics and aggregate the rest. We can list Tao-sheng's two main subjects and miscellaneous theories as follows:

1. The doctrine of sudden enlightenment.
2. The doctrine of Buddha-nature, related to the *Nirvāṇa Sūtra* (and the *icchantika* issue).
3. Miscellaneous theories, which include "a good deed entails no retribution"; "the Buddha has [in reality] no Pure Land"; "the *Dharma-kāya* is formless"; and "on the double truth."

This listing shows Tao-sheng's main concerns: the nature of the Buddha, how Buddhahood is achieved, and the theoretical underpinnings of this process.

Sudden Enlightenment

Because Tao-sheng's exposition of the subject, "On Sudden Enlightenment [as the Means] to Achieve Buddhahood," is lost along with all of his other thematic writings, relevant information on the doctrine can be gleaned only from other sources. The doctrine is cited or touched upon briefly here and there in various sources, contemporary to him and later, which attests to the range of its impact on other thinkers.

The most important of these sources is the *PTL*, compiled by Hsieh Ling-yün, which contains some seventeen sets of questions and answers regarding Tao-sheng's proposition, involving six questioners and one respondent. The anthology begins with Hsieh's brief preface and ends with Tao-sheng's brief comment. But Hsieh's interpretation may not be identical with Tao-sheng's in phraseology and logical method. In fact, though Tao-sheng, in his letter to Wang Hung (one of the questioners) praises the way Hsieh answers, he points out the need for clarifying the fact that illumination, unlike ordinary perception, must be realized in one's personal experience.

As firsthand sources, of course, one immediately thinks of the three commentaries by Tao-sheng himself. In the *CNS* and the *CVS* one can find some statements or expressions suggesting his approach, but very few. The two *sūtras* concerned do not provide proper opportunities for the commentator to play with the topic. In the *CSPS* we find numerous statements on the process of enlightenment, yet most of these speak for what appears to be the antithesis of Tao-sheng's original thesis, that is, for a gradual path to enlightenment. This fact requires a close analysis, which will be attempted later.

Although Tao-sheng's theory of sudden enlightenment is touched on in some documents, there is no reference to the background of the theory nor to a particular scripture involved, if any. One can merely conjecture as to the factors that may have led to the development of the doctrine. First, the doctrine could be viewed as a natural upshot of the development of Buddhist thought in China following its introduction about three centuries earlier. The doctrine of sudden enlightenment encapsulates the Chinese understanding in practical terms of what Mahāyāna Buddhism stands for, in contradistinction to Hīnayāna, which stresses gradual self-realization. A series of scriptures on meditation from the Hīnayāna tradition had already been translated, and the translation and study of the *Prajñāpāramitā Sūtras* came soon afterward, marking the introduction of the Mahāyāna tradition, furthered by Kumārajīva through accurate renderings of the Sanskrit texts and interpretations of the related doctrines. Hailing from and continuing this line of development, Tao-sheng may have arrived at his theory of sudden enlightenment by way of the doctrine of the *Prajñāpāramitā Sūtras*, realizing that the discriminating intelligence (*prajñā*) exercised through emptiness (*śūnyatā*) could imply a theory of intuitive knowledge through instantaneous illumination.[1]

Another factor related to Mahāyāna that probably prompted Tao-sheng to propound the doctrine, as Ōchō observed,[2] was the concept of stages (*bhūmi*). The concept of *bhūmi* obviously implies a graduated process of achieving Buddhahood, but Chinese Buddhists in the fourth century saw an element of instantaneity in it as well. In fact, it was in connection with the concept of *bhūmi* that the question of enlightenment was discussed. Chih Tun (314–366) is the first on record to have touched on the matter. According to a biography of Chih, he "scrutinized the ten stages and then he realized that instantaneous enlightenment occurs in the seventh stage."[3] Thus, Chih took the seventh stage as the crucial juncture of gradual path and sudden breakthrough, when the virtue of intellectual receptivity, called "acquiescence in the truth that all phenomena are unoriginated [and illusory]" (*anutpattika-dharma-kṣāntiḥ*)," sets in.[4] This line of argument can be seen in eminent Buddhist thinkers including Tao-an (312–385), Hui-yüan, and Seng-chao.[5] The theory they advocated was referred to as *minor subitism* (sudden-enlightenment)—a clear indication that it is a term invented after Tao-sheng appeared on the scene with his "major subitism."

Of the masters of minor subitism, Seng-chao was the closest contemporary to Tao-sheng. However, unlike other contemporaries like Hui-kuan, who wrote "On Gradual Enlightenment" to counter Tao-sheng, it is not certain whether Seng-chao actually was engaged in the debate, which may have been going on toward his last years (374–414), (if we date Tao-sheng's theory between 409 and 414, in agreement with Itano Chōhachi).[6] The last part (IV) of Seng-chao's essays (*Chao-lun*), especially sections 8–13, is devoted to the question of enlightenment in terms of gradualism, but these sections in fact are spurious.[7] Hui-ta (551–589) in his commentary on the *Chao-lun* sums up Seng Chao's actual position on the matter as follows: "Up to the point of the sixth stage, [the two realms of] existence (*yu*) and nonexistence (*wu*) are not synthesized. Therefore one is not yet enlightened to *li*. If one is beyond the seventh, [the two realms of] existence and nonexistence are experienced simultaneously. Only then can we speak of it as enlightenment to *li*."[8]

It is not certain how much of Seng-chao's actual language is reflected in this statement, but the analytical style and terminology are typical of Seng-chao, who here seems to be in basic agreement with Tao-sheng. Tao-sheng does not reject the doctrine of the stages but merely pushes the critical juncture to after the eighth[9] or the tenth stage. He refutes the "minor subitists" by describing anything short of the ultimate stage as unreal, saying: "From birth-and-death (*saṃsāra*) to the diamond perception all belong to dream. In the perception after the diamond one opens up to great enlightenment."[10] Here the *diamond* refers to the tenth stage or later. In Tao-sheng's commentary on the *Lotus*, we find the ten stages mentioned, but only in the sense that they are limited as a representation of the process of enlightenment (409c).

Instead of identifying Tao-sheng's doctrine with the Mahāyāna tradition from India, one may be tempted to ascribe it to a Chinese pattern of thinking, a pragmatic simplification of the time-consuming, complex learning process formulated in Indian Buddhism.[11] Support for this view is found in the *PTL*. In the anthology of queries about Tao-sheng's theory, Hsieh Ling-yün characterizes Tao-sheng's "new theory" as blending two cultures: the element of instantaneity drawn from Confucian teaching and the idea of Buddhahood from the Indian tradition.[12]

Behind this cultural trend may have been Tao-sheng's own mystical experience. A description in his biography in the *Kao-seng chuan* may be cited: "After having deeply meditated for a long time, Sheng's understanding penetrated to what lies beyond words, whereupon he exclaimed: 'The purpose of symbols is to gain a complete understanding of ideas, but once the ideas have been gained, the symbols may be forgotten.'"[13] Although a gradual process is suggested here, an instantaneous penetration or breakthrough at a certain point of the process also may be implied.

It is possible to get a picture of Tao-sheng's theory of sudden enlightenment from scattered comments and quotes. The *PTL* carries an account of what Tao-sheng is said to have proposed: "The illumination (or mirror) of the extinction (*nirvāṇa*) (or the quiet domain) is so subtle and mysterious that it does not allow any grade or class. To learn it accumulatively will be endless. How can it stop by itself?"[14]

The *illumination of the extinction* later is redefined as the ultimate substratum (*tsung-chi*). This is the object of enlightenment, and it implies a kind of ultimate reality or noumenal domain, which in turn suggests that an equally distinct and transcendent epistemological approach is necessary. Here Tao-sheng is challenging a linear, accumulative learning process. In his view, this type of cultivation serves only a limited purpose, stopping short of the ultimate experience. Liu Ch'iu, a later follower and faithful interpreter of Tao-sheng, quotes the latter as saying:

> By means of [thirty-seven] factors of practice leading to enlightenment (*bodhipākṣya-dharmāḥ*), one may be able to go near *nirvaṇa*, but one may not be called an arhat yet. By means of the six perfections (*pāramitās*), one may be able to reach Buddhahood, but one is not to be referred to as a bodhisattva yet. In the case of the analogy of cutting a tree [you gradualists take up in defense of

> your argument], [it can be said that] one can cut away the tree gradually foot by foot, inch by inch, because the tree still exists. Yet in the case of realizing the nonorigination (of *dharmas*), since birth (or origination) has to be exhausted, illumination must be sudden.[15]

"The stages and gradations," in the words of Heinrich Dumoulin, may "refer to the way and not to the liberating insight itself."[16] The analogy of woodcutting was used initially by the gradualists, but Tao-sheng may be attempting to make his own point that the woodcutter is bound to reach an instant when no more is left to cut.

More similes are employed in the arguments on both sides, taken up first by one party, then exploited by the opposite party for its own cause. In the *PTL* we find the simile of North and South: the North representing the place of the ignorant; the South, the residence of the Sage. The gradualists characterize travel from North to South as a gradual progress, whereas the subitists focus on arrival in the South and the sudden encounter with the Sage.[17] Hui-kuan, the chief adversary of Tao-sheng's theory, drew the analogy of mountain climbing, in which a climber advances step by step toward the peak in view from afar.[18] The proponents of subitism cite this analogy to suggest how, on arriving at the peak, the climber finds the vista opened up wide. As can be seen in this mutual appropriation of imagery, although the focuses were different, the two positions were not necessarily incompatible, particularly from the syncretic standpoint that was to emerge after Tao-sheng.[19]

Does Tao-sheng provide adequate metaphysical and epistemological grounds for sudden enlightenment? The key to this question lies in the concept of *li*: a term of extreme significance in the Chinese philosophical tradition, and one that is ubiquitous in Tao-sheng's writings. *Li* has a wide spectrum of implications embracing both the particular and the universal, yet it may be safe to relate *li* to the essential substance underlying all things, including the Buddha's teachings. However, Tao-sheng seems to take particulars as representations of the universal, and therefore, in his view, there is no serious conflict between the two levels. It may be possible to see *li* as a metaphysical term for the ultimate reality. *Li* is identified with what is immutable (ch'ang): *nirvāṇa, Dharmatā*, and *Dharma-kāya*. By losing it one enters into the bondage of birth-and-death (*saṃsāra*); and by attaining it one reaches *nirvāṇa*. Whatever it is, *li* represents that by which one is to be enlightened; that is, it is the content of enlightenment.

Then, why sudden enlightenment? Because *li* is indivisible and nonanalytic, and the ontological nature of *li* dictates its epistomological mode. Tao-sheng makes this point in his *CNS*: "The true *li* (or Truth) is self-so (*tzu-jan*): enlightenment also is [the process of] mysteriously identifying oneself with [Truth]. What is true being not gradational (nondifferentiated), then can enlightenment allow any [stages of] changing?"[20] The interrelation of ontology and epistemology seen here receives a clearer exposition by Tao-sheng in the following quotation: "What is the meaning of *sudden*? It means that *li* is indivisible; while the word *enlightenment* means illuminating the ultimate [that *li* is]. Hence, nondual enlightenment matches with indivisible *li*. [The distinction between] *li* and knowledge being done away with, we call it *sudden enlightenment*."[21] Thus, the indivisible nature of *li* requires an equally indivisible means to grasp it.

As a corollary, one also can consider the expression *one*. *Li* is often described as "one," especially in the *CSPS*. *One* is found along with such words as *ultimate* (or "final") (*chi*), *mysterious* (*miao*), *everlasting* (*ch'ang*), as well as *vehicle* (*yāna*), referring to *One Vehicle* as the point of synthesis in the dialectial process involving the three vehicles. Hsieh's argument in the *PTL* begins with the premise that "*li* is united with the One ultimate (or one and final)."[22] As a logical consequence in his view, "one enlightenment" therefore is in order: "with one enlightenment all the fetters of existence are dispensed with simultaneously."[23]

Tao-sheng does not specifically reject the established doctrine of stages (*bhūmi*), which apparently typifies gradual enlightenment, but he locates the ultimate *li* beyond the confines of the ten stages.[24] The ten stages and four grades of sagehood are merely the means that the Buddha devised to bring *li* within reach of all sentient beings.[25]

Faith (*hsin*) is relegated by Tao-sheng as something short of enlightenment. "Understanding through faith" (*hsin-chieh*) in his view is not genuine enlightenment: when enlightenment sets in, faith gives way.[26] In the *PTL* we find this view reiterated by Hsieh Ling-yün; "Understanding is not to be gradually reached, whereas faith arises [gradually] from instruction. What do I mean by this? The fact that faith arises from instruction [shows that] there is such a thing as the work of daily advancement. But since [final] understanding is not gradual, there can be no such thing as partial entry into illumination."[27] In this way, Buddhahood does not allow gradual access, but rather an all-or-nothing, once-and-for-all situation.

The Buddha-Nature and Related Ideas

Unlike Tao-sheng's concept of sudden enlightenment, his interpretation of the concept of Buddha-nature has a clear connection with a particular scripture—the *Nirvāṇa Sūtra*. His study of the *Nirvāṇa Sūtra* occupied a relatively long span of time, from 426 to 432, at least. His interpretation of Buddha-nature also involved him in such related issues as the icchantika, the concept of conditions (*yüan*), and the notion of stimulus-response (*kan-ying*).

Let us first look at the historical facts surrounding Tao-sheng's interpretation of the *Nirvāṇa Sūtra*. A question arose in Tao-sheng's mind when he read an early version of the *sūtra* translated by Fa-hsien in 418. There he came across a phrase in Volume 4 stating that all living beings possess the Buddha-nature, with the exception of a lowly class of men called *icchantika*.[28] Tao-sheng believed this statement to be inconsistent with the Buddha's message as embodied in the whole of the *Nirvāṇa Sūtra*. The principle of the universally applicable Buddha-nature was the logical conclusion Tao-sheng arrived at after penetrating the gist of the scripture. One of the propositions Tao-sheng is said to have promulgated reads: "Beings who are subject to the interaction of the two elements (*yin* and *yang*) are all primary causes of *nirvāṇa*. One's birth in the three realms invariably refers to nothing but the effect of delusion. The icchantikas belong to the life-sustaining species; then how can only they be deprived of the Buddha-nature?"[29] Similarly he proposes again: "The icchantikas do not possess the root of faith. [Yet], though they are cut off from [the root of] the good, they still possess the Buddha-nature."[30]

This daring challenge of scripture provoked the established church, and as a result Tao-sheng was excommunicated in 428 or 429, but was exonerated later when another, larger version of the *Nirvāṇa Sūtra* (40 vols.), translated by Dharmakshema, reached the capital. The new translation, in Chapter 23, contained a statement verifying Tao-sheng's conclusion that the icchantikas, too, are Buddha-natured.[31]

This event demonstrated Tao-sheng's systematic comprehension of the Buddhist teachings, his view of Buddha-nature thus representing one part emanating from the whole of his thought. Likewise, his theory of enlightenment and his doctrine of Buddha-nature also are integrally connected.[32] What makes sudden enlightenment possible for sentient beings? The cause that accounts for it is the Buddha-nature. Tao-sheng identifies sudden enlightenment with self-realization or internalized knowledge. This link is found in the *CSPS*, where Tao-sheng writes: "The sentient being's endowment with [the potential for] great enlightenment leads all to succeed in becoming a Buddha" (408d3). And again: "Sentient beings all possess the endowed [capacity] for great enlightenment; there is no one that is not a potential bodhisattva" (409c3). Developing the point further, Tao-sheng writes: "All sentient beings, without exception, are Buddhas, and all are also [already in the state of] *nirvāṇa*" (408b16).

The innate nature originally constituted in all sentient beings is thus posited as the "primary cause (*yin/hetu*)" of Buddhahood. For the mass of suffering, unenlightened beings this original nature is covered up with "veils of dirt" (400b10), "bondages" (408b17), or "defilements" (400b11). For this reason, ignorant beings are alienated from their originally pure state of being; enlightenment is the regaining of that original state. In this sense the title of Tao-sheng's treatise on the subject, "The Buddha-nature is something which a being is bound to possess [again when enlightened]" (*Fo-hsing tang-yu lun*)[33] must be interpreted. Furthermore, Tao-sheng in the *CNS* makes the point (also implicit in the *CSPS*) that the Buddha-nature does not exist uninterruptedly through all three time-periods: past, present, and future:[34] "Because living beings are originally endowed with 'the Buddha's knowledge and insight,' yet these are not manifested on account of dirt and obstacles, when Buddha [helps] open and get rid of the veils of dirt, they are now able to obtain them" (400b9). (Here the "endowment of the Buddha's knowledge and insight" is identical with Buddha-nature, adapted to the terminology of the *sūtra*.)

The concept of Buddha-nature might seem to imply a concept of self—a self that is to have this Buddha-nature.[35] Yet, the concept of self (*ātman*) was rejected by Buddhism in favor of the idea of selflessness (*anātman*),[36] a problem that comes to the fore in the *Nirvāṇa Sūtra*, as seen in its use of the phrase *true self* (*chen-o*). In his interpretation, Tao-sheng merely follows the *sūtra*, solving the apparent conflict by identifying *no self* with *true self*, together representing two sides of a single reality,[37] the former implying a means to express the latter. Tao-sheng thus sometimes speaks of the "self of the Buddha-nature" in agreement with the *Nirvāṇa* and the *Vimalakīrti sutras*.[38] He also uses the term *Buddha-nature* synonymously with such terms as *Dharma, the true, origin* (*pen*),[39] *Tao, self-soness* (*tzu-jan*), *li*,[40] *the immutable*,[41] *the middle path*,[42] and *nirvāṇa*.[43] In the *CNS* Tao-sheng states: "Those who have realized the *Dharma* are darkly merged with the self-soness. All the Buddhas are invariably in such a state. The *Dharma* by which [such a process] is effected is the Buddha-nature."[44]

Although Buddha-nature is the cause of enlightenment—more specifically, its primary or "right" cause (*cheng-yin/hetu*)—alone it is not sufficient to bring about enlightenment. Because it is dormant, there must be something else to harness its latent power—what Tao-sheng calls the *supporting conditions* (*yüan/pratyaya*).[45] Buddha-nature and the supporting conditions are bound together in the enlightenment process. Tao-sheng writes in the *CNS*: "Cause and conditions can not be separated from each other. Because there are cause and conditions, learning can lead to attainment of Buddhahood. How can no self and self be separated?"[46] What is suggested here is that cause and conditions are related to two separate levels of truth represented by no self and self, respectively, the two inseparable both ontologically and epistemologically.

What then constitutes the conditions? Tao-sheng appears to have tackled the question in an essay of which only the title is known; and it apparently has some bearing on the interaction betwen beings and the Buddha, for the title is "On the Proposition that [the Buddha's] Response (or Reflex) Is Expressed through Conditions." This refers to the role of the Buddha as the mediator and prime mover of the enlightenment process. The thrust of Tao-sheng's argument may be glimpsed in the following quotation, apparently taken from the writing in question: "The *Dharma*-master [Tao-sheng] says: [The Buddha] illuminates the conditions and response; the response should lie in knowledge. What does it mean that his response should lie in knowledge? It means that he consciously (or voluntarily) responds."[47]

This approach contrasts with the "unconscious response" of the Sage advocated by Tao-an, Seng-chao, and Fa-yao, where no "condition" is involved. *Response* (*ying*) refers to the Sage's role in the process of a being's enlightenment.[48] Sequentially, response or reflex is preceeded by *kan*, stimulus that comes from the being to be enlightened. *Kan-ying*, or *Ying-kan*, as they often occur together in a compound form, is an indivisible sequence, almost a simultaneous process. The terms are obviously borrowed from the *Chuang-tzu* and the *I Ching*. In the *Chuang-tzu* we find the following description of the Sage: "Roused (*kan*) by something outside himself, only then does he respond (*ying*); pressed, only then does he move; finding he has no choice, only then does he rise up."[49] A similar idea is expressed in the *I Ching, Hsi-t'zu chuan*: "But if it (the Change) is stimulated it penetrates the *raison d'être* of the world."[50] The same formula is found in the *CSPS*.[51] Yet, as will be substantiated later (in Part II), there is a fundamental difference between the Taoist and the Buddhist Sage: one is self-oriented or introverted, whereas the other is altruistically oriented or extroverted.

How does the stimulated Sage's response come about? His response must be channelled through concrete actions, which in turn require supporting conditions. Hui-ta quotes Tao-sheng speaking of the Sage's response: "The *Dharma*-master [Tao-] sheng said: "Stimulus-(reflex) has conditions [through which it is expressed]; sometimes by way of being born in suffering situations to share sorrowful commiseration, sometimes through love and desire to share the bondage of delusion, or sometimes by way of the *dharma* of the good. Therefore [the Buddha] consciously responds."[52] What is implicit here is the notion of expedient means (*upāya-kauśalya*), but the *Dharma* of the Sage is not restricted to a particular approach applied at particular point in time. As

Tao-sheng writes, "The *Dharma*-nature illuminates the round (or perfect), and *li* the real remains eternal. When it comes to stimulus-reflex, how can it be inactive even for a while?"[53]

The *kan-ying* stage is preceded by the being's active approach to the Sage. This is essential because illumination, as Tao-sheng points out to Wang Hung in a brief letter found attached to the *PTL*, denotes empirical knowledge internalized in oneself.[54] Although *kan* signifies what is received by the Sage through stimulus from outside, the initiative taken on the part of the being is called *k'ou* (to "tap, strike, fasten"). Recurrent particularly in the *CSPS*,[55] the term symbolizes an intense plea to the Sage for guidance toward the goal of enlightenment, signaling at the same time the being's readiness to undergo the enlightenment process.[56]

Our description of the enlightenment process would not be complete without the addition of one more term, *chi*, the agent that makes the being's contact with the Sage possible. As Tao-sheng puts it in the *CSPS*, "If [a being] has internally no subtle triggering-mechanism (*chi*) of *Tao*, the Sage then will not respond" (412b). It becomes evident here that *chi* as an inner property is related to the Buddha-nature. In fact, they are interchangeable in many contexts: they may be seen as different aspects of one and the same faculty, but *chi* is more dynamic and external, whereas the Buddha-nature represents the latent substructure that awaits reactivation at the time of enlightenment. Originating in the *I Ching* and other Taoist texts and further evolved by the neo-Taoists, the concept *chi* was excavated by Tao-sheng to reinforce and complement the otherwise nebulous concept of the Buddha-nature.

The hybrid nature of Tao-sheng's interpretation becomes clear when we put together the pieces of his view of the process of enlightenment: when "the being with the subtle triggering-mechanism for enlightenment (*wu-chi*) actively invites (*k'ou*) the Sage [to come to his aid]", the latter "stoops down (or condescends) to respond."[57] Practically all these terms came from Chinese philosophical texts; nonetheless, couched in this originally non-Buddhist terminology is Buddhist content, with the effect that the concept of Buddha-nature has received a new structural framework.

Miscellaneous

Besides the two major themes just examined, in Tao-sheng's expository writings titled with the words *i* (exegesis) or *lun* (discussion) one can distinguish four other distinct subjects: good deeds entailing no retribution; two truths; the Dharma-kāya formless; and no Pure Land in the domain of the Buddha. At a glance, one finds that only one of these themes is postulated in the positive, leading one to believe that Tao-sheng set out to correct misconceptions he thought prevalent in contemporary Buddhist circles. This recalls the way the Indian Mādhyamika Buddhists attempted by means of the doctrine of emptiness (*śūnyatā*) to uncover flaws in the concepts and doctrines propounded by other Buddhist sects as well as by orthodox Hindu schools. In this respect, one can put the one positive title, "two truths", into the same category.

As a matter of fact, Tao-sheng was exposed to the *Prajñāpāramitā* texts and the Mādhyamika doctrine through different channels from the early stage of his Buddhist career. The doctrine found its way into his writing, especially in the conception of the real.[58] It should be noted that what is subject to rejection by Tao-sheng may not be the real as such but certain ill-conceived notions about it. Tao-sheng appears to be more explicit on this point than the Mādhyamika.

The Good Deed Entails No Retribution

The biographies of Tao-sheng lists this title ahead of all others, suggesting that it is Tao-sheng's earliest major writing. The question of retribution for deeds committed—cause and effect—intrigued the pragmatic Chinese mind. It was a subject much talked about in Tao-sheng's time, along with the question of spirit (*shen*) as the immutable entity or subject to receive this retribution.

As for the substance of Tao-sheng's theory, a key may be found in the terms *good* and *retribution*; both of which he radically redefined in this context. Tao-sheng is quoted as writing: "By overcoming evil through good, one is entitled to obtain the *karma* of man or god (deva). [Yet] in reality this is not what is truly good but is just [karmic] retribution."[59] In a different proposition Tao-sheng talks of retribution: "[Even] animals enjoy richness and pleasure [whereas] the retribution of men includes poverty and suffering."[60] As long as one remains in the cycle of reincarnation one has done nothing "good" in the true sense of the word. As he says, "retribution belongs to the phase of change and transcience; birth-and-death belongs to the domain of a great dream."[61] The cycle of retribution in *saṃsāra* does not lift one to the ultimate reality of *nirvāṇa*. In the *CVS* Tao-sheng illustrates this point: "When one practices meditation (*dhyāna*) in the hope of receiving retribution, one then has attachment to the practice. Since one has attachment to the practice, one's retribution must be a delusion. One who is deluded in retribution is tied to birth [-and-death]."[62] He then contrasts this with positive, undeluded karmic retribution: "When [a bodhisattva], in hopes of saving other lives, is born [into the sahā world], he is being born as an expedient means. Because he is not motivated for his own sake, his retribution is without delusion."[63]

We must now determine what is meant by the word *good*. The *good*, as Tao-sheng understood it, must be defined in terms of *li*, posited as the object of ultimate knowledge. In the *CNS* Tao-sheng writes: "The attainment of *li* is "good." To deviate from *li* means "not good." He goes on to say: "What is *good* and what is *not good*? Deviating from *li* is *not good*. Returning to it, one achieves *good*. . . . In deviation from *li*, one gets tied [in bondage]. By achieving it one is [in the state of] *nirvāṇa*, released (*mokṣa*), and cut off [from bondage]."[64] Merely disliking suffering and seeking pleasure is not the good.[65] What is valued by Tao-sheng is not based on biological, aesthetic, or ethical values.

Goodness can be measured only on a religious scale.[66] All other values are subservient to the religious value. Tao-sheng declares in the *CVS*: "Seeking pleasure is the endless *dharma*; it is 'the conditioned (*saṃskṛta*) [*dharma*]'. 'The unconditioned (*asaṃskṛta*)' is the *dharma* embodying *li*. Therefore, [in the latter *dharma*] there is no actual [worldly] merit and benefit."[67] As long as a deed stands to contribute to the path to enlightenment it is "good." Chi-tsang, the San-lun master, in his commentary to the *Lotus* cites Tao-sheng's original treatise: "Previously Chu Tao-sheng wrote a treatise titled 'The Good Deed Entails No Retribution.' In it he states: 'One tiny act of goodness also helps all to become Buddhas, but not to receive the retribution of birth-and-death.'"[68] The significance of "one tiny act of goodness" is clearly indicated in the *CSPS*.[69] Accumulation of these bits of goodness in an individual being leads to the accomplishment of Buddhahood. All good deeds, therefore, must be directed toward the final goal of enlightenment. When the good is presented by the Buddha as something less than religious knowledge, this should be considered as an expedient device designed to induce unenlightened beings on to the bodhisattva path.

There Is No Pure Land in [the Realm of] the Buddha

The notion of the Pure Land is found in most of the *sūtras* known to Tao-sheng, including the *sūtras* on which he wrote commentaries, the *Prajñāpāramitā* (small version), the *Vimalakīrti-nirdeśa*, and the *Lotus*. The notion of the Pure Land interested Chinese Buddhists as a tangible picture of a world transcending the present one. Hui-yüan is said to have led a group at Tung-lin ssu to make a vow before statue of Amitābha, wishing to be reborn in the Pure Land in the Western Paradise. This was in 402, when Tao-sheng was staying on the mountain, leading to speculation that he might have joined the group.[70] In any case, this activity could have motivated him to delve into the theme, especially as rebirth in the Western Paradise might be interpreted as recompense for good deeds. Popular interest led Tao-sheng to define the notion of the Pure Land in an exposition (*Fo wu ching-t'u lun*) that is now lost. He also could not afford to overlook this important issue in the commentaries.

The *Vimalakīrti-nirdeśa* in its first narrative (Chapter 1) deals with the question of the Pure Land in regard to "the Bodhisattva deeds that lead to the realization of the Pure Land."[71] Tao-sheng begins his comment with the words: "The deeds that lead to the Pure Land means that these deeds bring about the Pure Land, but it is not something to be produced. Producing the land lies with living beings."[72] In contrast, Tao-sheng then turns to the Sage in the *CSPS*: "Phenomena and images appear only due to the existence of fetters. Since the Sage is the one who has comprehended *li*, he has had his fetters all destroyed. The fetters being destroyed, then, how can there be any land?" (406a). Hence, one can arrive at his thesis that "the Buddha has no Pure Land [in his domain]." The idea of *land* thus applies only to beings. Tao-sheng further substantiates this point in the *CVS*: "Land refers to the territory of beings. When there is no impurity in it, we call it pure. There is no impurity, hence, it is nonexistent. There is the territory, hence, it is existent. Existence is caused by deliverance (*mokṣa*). If deliverance is accomplished, delusion will be completely gone."[73]

The idea of Pure Land in reality is unsubstantial. It is merely a convenient designation. Tao-sheng reasons in the *CSPS*: "The untainted purity thus means none other than no land. [The Buddha] resorts to land to speak of nonexistence. Hence he speaks of the Pure Land" (410b). Yet, Tao-sheng does not stop at simple negation of the locus: "Even though it is said that there is no land [in reality], there is nonetheless no place that is not any land. There is neither bodily form nor name, yet bodily form and name are existent all the more" (406a). Here, Tao-sheng seems to apply with some modification the Mādhyamika style of logical argument, stopping at the two stages of negation and not continuing to the complete negation of the four-pronged negation or tetralemma (*catuṣkoṭi*). The result is a monistic picture.

In regard to the Pure Land, Tao-sheng is closer to the Mādhyamika doctrine than his contemporaries, including Seng-chao, who was reputed to be the foremost Mādhyamika scholar after Kumārajīva. Seng-chao and Kumārajīva do not challenge the basic idea of the Pure Land as such, except for the concept of the two vehicles.[74] Seng-chao also is less exhaustive than Tao-sheng in applying the Mādhyamika logic to the concept of the Pure Land.[75]

Chi-tsang, the systematizer of Chinese Mādhyamika, the San-lun school, however, cites Tao-sheng's writing and comment as follows:

> The Master Sheng wrote "On the Seven Treasures." This is [the same as] the writing "The *Dharma-kāya* Has No Domain of the

> Pure Land." Now I would like to comment on it. [Tao-sheng argues as follows:] If it is said that the *Dharma-kāya* does not rely on the impurity of earth and sand [for its representation], then it does not consist in the purity of treasures and jades, either. Hence, [Tao-sheng] speaks of no land. . . . [I would say:] If we accept that the *Dharma-kāya* dwells in form (*rūpa*) [for representation] but its reality is in the middle path, we can also arrive at [the premise] that there is no such land. [Yet] that is not the case [with Tao-sheng]. If we scrutinize the idea meant by Tao-sheng, it is merely the case that there is no land of treasures and jades. [But I say:] You cannot say that there is no land of treasures and jades. [But I say:] You cannot say that there is no land of the middle path. If that is the case, Master Sheng attains the land of the Dharma-kāya, and then loses the land of traces.[76]

Chi-tsang's approach certainly reflects one of the Mādhymika conceptions of the middle path: that *nirvāṇa*, represented by *Dharma-kāya* here, and *saṃsāra*, represented by *traces*, remain undifferentiated. But Chi-tsang failed to heed the overall orientation of Tao-sheng's thought. Tao-sheng's approach tends of focus on the reality itself but not its traces or representations. This imparts the impression of a monistic position, the influence of the neo-Taoists, whose language Tao-sheng borrows heavily. Yet Tao-sheng is not a simplistic monist. He says in the *CSPS*: "Even though I say that there is no land; yet there is nothing that is not [a part of] the land" (406a). He also does not fail to recognize *saṃsāra* as the actual locus of enlightenment. In the *CVS*, Tao-sheng states: "Enlightenment in the Greater Vehicle does not consist in departure from birth-and-death (*saṃsāra*) the near, to seek it in the far."[77]

Tao-sheng's monistic frame thus accomodates all Buddhist frames, including the middle path. In the *CNS*, Tao-sheng says: "What is said here, that birth-and-death is the middle path, illustrates that there is what is original."[78] He goes on to say:

> The twelve causes-and-conditions (*pratītya-samutpāda*) are the middle path. This illustrates that living beings are originally possessive of [the Buddha-nature]. If [this nature] is taken to be permanent (*śāsvata*), then it will not agree with the fact that there is suffering (*duḥkha*). If it is taken as something annihilated (*uccheda*), then there will be no *li* for attaining Buddhahood. In this way those who see the middle path will see the Buddha-nature.[79]

The domain of the Buddha is to be found in saṃsāric existence. As Tao-sheng puts it in the *CSPS*, "the nonexistence of the Buddha is because beings are impure and evil; since the Buddha is not present due to [beings'] impurity, when they are pure he will certainly be present" (410b).[80] In short, the Buddha is not to be found removed in the fictitious Pure Land, which as is made clear in the *CSPS* (410c), merely is an extemporaneous teaching device employed by the Buddha.

The Dharma-kāya Is Formless

Listed in the biography alongside his writing on the Pure Land, Tao-sheng's article "The *Dharma-kāya* Is Formless" may not much differ from the former in essential substance. The Buddha meant by Tao-sheng in the former essay is taken largely in the sense of the *Dharma-kāya*, the real, permanent, omnipresent entity transcendent to the saṃsāric state of existence, "the ultimate reality that underlies all particular phenomena."[81]

One of the most provocative Mahāyāna conceptions, the *Dharma-kāya* gave rise to many interpretations among Chinese Buddhists, especially Buddho-Taoists familiar with notions of Heaven (*t'ien*) and the Sage. This prompted Tao-sheng to rebut some prevailing misconceptions. In the *CVS*[82] we can get a glimpse of Tao-sheng's position on the *Dharma-kāya* as it is juxtaposed with Seng-chao's—an example of diverse contemporary views. Tao-sheng comments on the phrase from the *sūtra*, "the Buddha body is called *Dharma-kāya*."[83] In the beginning he locates the *Dharma-kāya* in the stratum under the Buddha body and the "sixteen feet" (or Transformation) body (*Nirmāṇa-kāya*). Then he defines *dharma*—that "there is nothing that is not *dharma*"[84]—which may be based on either a monistic perspective or Sarvāstivādin realism. Next he identifies *body* (*kāya*) with the substance (*t'i*) embodying that meaning. Thereupon he advances to say:

> *Dharma-kāya* is true and real while the sixteen feet (transformation) body is extemporaneous, in response [to the need of beings]. . . . He who is enlightened to the *Dharma* of such nature will have his covers and delusion eliminated and blind illusion also removed. He will mysteriously transcend the three realms (*triloka*). *Li* darkly merges with the sphere of the formless. There being no form, there is no form that he is not capable of taking. Three realms having been cut off, there is no realm he is not capable of having. One who is [capable of becoming] any form is ready to respond to any stimulus. The Buddha is in the state of the unconditioned (*asaṃskṛta*). . . . Thus the sixteen feet and eight feet all

are Buddhas visualized by beings in the water of their thoughts. The Buddha remains always formless. How can there be two [different things, form and formless]?[85]

Here emerges a picture of Tao-sheng's theory. The *Dharma-kāya* is certainly without form. But this should not be interpreted as a simple negation; it is an expression that implies an absolute affirmation. Tao-sheng's negation here applies only to any particular form that can be conceived by an unenlightened being. This framework of double negation invariably partakes of the Mádhyamika doctrine of emptiness. And yet Tao-sheng seems to propose something more than the rejection of the popular conception of the Buddha's form. The preceding quote ends with a monistic overtone.

When one compares Tao-sheng's viewpoint on the matter with Seng-chao's expressed in the latter's commentary on the same passage of the *Vimalakīrti*,[86] one may identify some fundamental differences in their approaches. They agree on the monistic conception of the *Dharma-kāya* as the common basis of the two levels of reality, both of which they formulate *via negativa*, certainly reflecting the Mādhyamika doctrine. But they diverge on how the levels are related to each other with respect to the *Dharma-kāya*. In Seng-chao the connection between formless and not formless is copulative, with the conjunctive *and* between them, whereas in Tao-sheng the relation is causal, with the resulting structure that "because it is not *ens*, it is not non-*ens*." Seng-chao's pattern of description is simple and linear whereas Tao-sheng's is correlative through a cause–effect relationship. Thus Tao-sheng's definition produces a more integral, tightly knit relation between the two levels of *Dharma-kāya*.[87]

Tao-sheng's approach is summed up in the last paragraph of the quotation just analyzed: "The Buddha is ever formless; how can there be two, [*Dharma-kāya* and Transformation body]?" But again this "one" assumes many forms: "Although the physical bodies of the Buddhas are different, they are one." Likewise, "One Buddha has no form that he can not possess. Hence, [it is said that] they are all the same."[88] Tao-sheng connects the physical body with the Buddha's response to the need of beings. As he puts it: "The physical body is in existence as his external response. It comes from 'unobstructed knowledge.' Yet 'unobstructed knowledge' has no physical body."[89]

Again, as he says in the *CSPS*, "The Buddha in the form body comes into existence invariably in response to [the need of beings]; he has no fixed real form" (409d). Its substance being incorporeal, the *Dharma-kāya* is identifiable only by correspondingly abstract knowledge. It is not an object (*viṣaya*) in the ordinary sense, but something that requires a "dark," mystical perception. Object and knowledge in this case are so closely correlated that it is hardly possible to distinguish them. *Li*, the ultimate principle of reality, often represents what is to be perceived or known. Tao-sheng declares: "The Buddha is the substance (*t'i*) of knowing *li* and transcends and surpasses the territories [of the three realms]."[90]

Tao-sheng attempts to tackle squarely the grounds underlying the premise of formlessness in a logical analysis elsewhere in the *CVS*:

> The Buddha, incarnated as a human being, is nothing more than the composite of the five aggregates (*skandhas*). If it is [assumed to be] existent, then it follows that the form (or physical body) is identical with the Buddha. If the form is not identical with the Buddha, then it follows that there is the Buddha outside the form. The Buddha being outside the form can further be considered in three categories: the Buddha existent in the form, the form existent in the Buddha, and the form belonging to the Buddha. In case the form is identical with the Buddha, it does not follow that [the Buddha] is not dependent upon the four [other aggregates to reincarnate]. In case the Buddha exists outside form, it does not follow that [the Buddha] is dependent upon form. In case the Buddha is found in the midst of the form, the Buddha would be impermanent. In case the form is found in the midst of the Buddha, then the Buddha would have divisions. In case the form belongs to the Buddha, the form would not be subject to change, [which would be against its nature].[91]

Hence, the Buddha, in the sense of the *Dharma-kāya*, has no connection with the form, which technically accounts for one of the five aggregates that make up the human anatomy.

Tao-sheng's argument on the *Dharma-kāya* is consistent with the monistic absolutism dominant throughout his writings. Itano Chōhachi aptly characterizes Tao-sheng's line of thought as "the monistic perspective of the absolute nonbeing (*wu*)."[92] *Nonbeing*, like the Buddhist term *emptiness* (*k'ung/śūnyatā*), symbolizes not only negation of the self-existence (*svabhāva*) of things or concepts, but also of the original or ultimate substratum. For the former sense, we can mention as an example in Tao-sheng's vocabulary the word *wu-hsiang*, "the markless" or "without external mark"; for the latter, the antonym of *wu-hsiang, shih-hsiang*, "the real" or "the real mark." The origin of both senses may be traced to Chu Fa-t'ai, who was the theorizer of the doctrine of original nonbeing (*fen-wu i*), listed first in the so-called "six houses and seven schools," in connection with the interpretation of the *Prajñāpāramitā* doctrine.[93] This position is believed to have been shared by Tao-an, Fa-t'ai's colleague.[94] Their understanding of *wu* in connection with the Buddhist concept of "emptiness" can be compared with that of Seng-chao, representative of the new breed of *Prajñāpāramitā* interpreters stemming from Kumārajīva, who were more faithful to the Mādhyamika texts. *Wu* as conceived by Seng-chao is used largely in the sense of the antipode of *yu* or existence, whereas *wu* was taken by earlier interpreters as something fundamental, transcending phenomena and the antithesis of being and nonbeing.[95] These two interpretations both influenced Tao-sheng, as he was exposed to both during his early training. The view of *wu* Tao-sheng received from Chu Fa-t'ai was reinforced through two channels: from the Chinese side, by the neo-Taoist Wang Pi's metaphysics, strongly tinged with monistic undertones, and from the Buddhist side, by the *Nirvāṇa Sūtra*, which encompasses the idea of the true self and the Womb of the Thus Come One (*Tathāgata-garbha*). Tao-sheng has been portrayed by historians as the one who succeeded in harmonizing "the genuine 'emptiness' and the mysterious 'existence'" (*Chen-k'ung miao-yu*): *emptiness* refers to the doctrine associated with the *Prajñāpāramitā Sūtras* and *mysterious existence* to the *Lotus* and *Nirvāṇa Sūtra*.[96] The ultimately real as a facade of *wu* finds expression in some of the terms Tao-sheng frequently uses, such as *li, emptiness, Dharma* (*fa*), *Dharma-nature*, the *foundational* (*pen*), *One*, the *ultimate* (*chi*), *Tao*, and the signless (*wu-hsiang/animitta*).

On the Two Truths

The concepts of the two truths, worldly or conventional (*saṃvṛti-satya*) and supreme or ultimate (*paramārtha-satya*), also were common subjects much talked about in connection with diverse Mahāyāna *sūtras*.[97] Tao-sheng's view on the question may be found in the *CNS*, the only substantial source available. He did not fail to notice the part of the *Nirvāṇa Sūtra* touching on this fundamental doctrine of Buddhism; the position of the *sūtra* expressed in Chapter 6 coincides in essence with Tao-sheng's own. In the *sūtra*, the Buddha recognizes only one truth, the supreme, as the real, in which the conventional truth, as an expedient means, is ultimately subsumed. Tao-sheng, in agreement with the *sūtra*, declares: "The worldly truth is identified with [the truth of] the supreme meaning. There is only the supreme meaning. There is no worldly truth."[98] Tao-sheng then elaborates: "Those who are deluded all take what they are deluded about as real. We call it the worldly truth. Although we refer to it as the worldly truth, it does not follow that there is a real [truth] that is different from it. Hence it is the [truth of] ultimate meaning. The ultimate truth never changes the worldly truth."[99] Why, then postulate two types of truth when they are ultimately one? Tao-sheng introduces the notion of expedient device: "*Li*, as mentioned, is only one, without a second. [The Buddha] speaks of it as two [truths] only as an expedient means and to follow convention."[100]

The recognition of conventional truth (*su*) presupposes the existence of a higher truth (*Tao*). This distinction represents a social and philosophico-religious perception of the Sage that Tao-sheng felt it necessary to rectify. In the very beginning of the *CSPS*, Tao-sheng deplores this viewpoint, the effect of which is that those who approach the profound, mysterious words of the Sage are few, whereas those who superficially fondle them are many. He ends with the lament: "Is it not a case of the sacred (*Tao*) and the profane (*su*) in opposition?" (396d). The phrase "*Tao* in opposition to *su*" in fact was in vogue in the period and can be found in many contemporary writings,[101] indicating how the two words usually were juxtaposed. Tao-sheng's ideal, however, was to unify the two from a religious standpoint.

For a view in contrast with Tao-sheng's, we can cite Hui-yüan. He vehemently defended the differentiation of the two value-systems, religious and secular, the former being superior to the latter.[102] This point of view is expressed in "A Priest Does Not Bow down before a King."[103] In contrast, according to Itano Chōhachi, Tao-sheng rejects such dualism, as also is demonstrated in his doctrine of "sudden enlightenment."[104]

How are enlightenment and "truth" interrelated? The truth that can be realized only through enlightenment is primary, real, and absolute, whereas the worldly truth for the unenlightened or deluded is secondary, temporary, and relative. Tao-sheng writes:

> Because there is the delusion that there are "many" [realities], it is called the worldly truth; because there is comprehension that there are not "many" [realities], it is called the [truth of] supreme meaning. Things near and far [in the relative realm] are the worldly truth; attaining to the real is [the truth] of the supreme meaning. Because one comprehends and sees [the reality], we call it [the truth of] the supreme meaning. What one is deluded about is the worldly truth.[105]

That the two truths are related to enlightenment appears in the following: "Hence, the one whose letters and words are in accord with *li* is the Buddha. When [one's letters and words] are discordant [with *li*], one is an ordinary man. All that is related to the Buddha is true and real. All that is related to an ordinary man is the conventional truth."[106]

Li symbolizes the object of enlightenment, constituting "truth" and what is real. *Truth* requires empirical verification and investigation of the real. As Tao-sheng puts it, "*Li* should be verified and realized. This is thus called 'truth.' 'Truth' denotes investigating what is real. Hence it is called real."[107] This again is illustrated in a quotation of Tao-sheng by Chün-cheng (of T'ang):

> The *Dharma*-Master Chu Tao-sheng says: Things are necessarily caused and conditioned, without self-nature (*svabhāva*). Hence they are not existent. They arise in accordance with cause and conditions. Hence they are not nonexistent. Being not existent and not nonexistent both show the *Dharma* to be real. Being real, it is referred to as "true" (or supreme). No error, hence it is called "truth." Contradicting what is "true," it is called "conventional." Not "true," hence it is not "truth." Therefore what is unreal and what is real are relative to each other, and the designations of "true (supreme)" and "conventional" [truths] are produced.[108]

Here, Tao-sheng seems to suggest that the conventional as such does not constitute "truth," but the latter is qualified by the former to compose conventional truth as one term; whereas in the case of the real (or supreme) truth, the two words match naturally with each other in their true senses.

The supremacy of the absolute domain over the relative, nonetheless, does not abrogate the value of worldly truth for the enlightened. That is so, not only because *li* as the symbol of the final reality unites the two domains, but also because it represents an expedient means for helping unenlightened beings. As Sangharakshita aptly puts it, "only by means of the conventional truth could the absolute truth be realized; the one was the stepping-stone to the other."[109] As cited previously, Tao-sheng clarifies: "Mahāyānistic enlightenment consists originally in not discarding what is near, the realm of birth-and-death (*saṃsāra*), to seek it in the far." That *nirvāṇa* is not to be sought apart from *saṃsāra* is a Mahāyāna principle: the Mādhyamika Buddhists arrive at identification of the two by way of the principle of "emptiness." In light of this and the fact that Tao-sheng does not depart from the *Nirvāṇa Sūtra* in this, it may be concluded that, as far as the notion of two truths is concerned, Tao-sheng remains a Mahāyānist, though the metaphysical structure behind the argument is shared, and probably reinforced, by neo-Taoist philosophy.

Notes

1. As will be discussed in the next section, the interconnection of the doctrine of emptiness and sudden enlightenment also is identifiable in the Ch'an tradition. The respect for the *Prajñāpāramitā Sūtras*, especially the *Diamond Sūtra*, and its doctrine is demonstrated clearly in the *Sixth Patriarch Platform Scripture*, the subitist's text, which is in one version (Tun-huang) also titled "Southern School Sudden Doctrine, Supreme Mahāyāna Great Prajñāpāramitā Scripture. . . ." See Philip Yampolsky, *The Platform Sutra of the Sixth Patriarch* (New York, 1967), p. 125.

2. Ōchō, "Jikudōshō no tongosetsu," *Zen kenkyūsho kiyō*, 3: 108.

3. Cited in T'ang, *Fo-chiao shih*, vol. 2, p. 170, quoting from *Shih-shuo wen-hsüeh p'ien-chü*.

4. See Liu Ch'iu, Preface to the *Wu-liang i ching*, T9. 384a (cf. the *I ching*, 388b); Hui-ta, *Chao-lun shu*, in HTC vol. 150, p. 425d. For the definition of the term, see *BHSD*, p. 27.

5. See Hui-ta, ibid.

6. Itano Chōhachi, "Dōshō no tongosetsu seiritsu no jijō," *Tōhō gakuhō* 7 (1936): 168.

7. See T'ang, *Fo-chiao shih*, II, p. 184; Liebenthal, *Chao Lun*, p. 152. Robinson left out the part in his translation in *Early Mādhyamika*, pp. 212-232. Cf. Ōchō's article in Tsukamoto Zenryū, ed., *Jōron kenkyū* (Kyoto, 1955), pp. 197ff.

8. Hui-ta, *Chao-lun shu*.

9. See CSPS 406a11. Cf. Hui-ta, ibid., p. 426b4.

10. Quoted in Chi-tsang, *Erh-ti i*, T45.111b (cf. 121c).

11. For instance, see Hu Shih, "The Development of Zen Buddhism in China," p. 483.

12. See T52.225a.

13. T50.366c, translated in Fung, *History of Chinese Philosophy*, vol. 2, p. 270.

14. T52.225a. Cf. tranlation in Fung, ibid., p. 275: "the state of mirror-like voidness (of Nirvāṇa) is abstruse and mysterious and does not admit of any stages (for its attainment). But the accumulating of learning is an endless process, for how can it stop of itself?"

15. T9.384a. Cf. *Chao-lun*, chapter 9, in T45.160a.

16. Dumoulin, *History of Zen Buddhism*, p. 64.

17. See T525c. Cf. Hui-ta, *Chao-lun shu*, p. 426b. A translation is found in Liebenthal, *The Book of Chao*, p. 189.

18. See Hui-ta, ibid., p. 426c; Liebenthal, "The World Conception", I, p. 80, and II, p. 89.

19. For further discussion, see Part II, Chapter 7.

20. T37.2377b. Cf. translation by Liebenthal in "The World Conception," 77: "The Inner Order (or things) is [*sic*] that of Nature and Recognition is a transcendal act of union (with that Order). Inner (Order) is without distinctive features; how then can Recognition change (with its object)?"

21. Hui-ta, *Chao-lun shu*, p. 425c.

22. T52.225a2.

23. T52.225b28.

24. Cf. *CSPS*, 409c8, 410c15.

25. See Hui-ta, *Chao-lun shu*, p. 425c15.

26. See ibid., p. 425c13. For a fresh discussion on faith and enlightenment, see Sung Bae Park, *Buddhist Faith and Sudden Enlightenment* (Albany, 1983), especially pp. 1–18, 55–58.

27. T52.225b25, translation from Fung, *History of Chinese Philosophy*, vol. 2, p. 278. For a comprehensive sketch of Tao-sheng's argument, see Whalen Lai, "Tao-sheng's Theory of Sudden Enlightenment Re-examined," Peter Gregory, ed., *Sudden and Gradual* (Honolulu, 1987), pp. 169–200.

28. For the definition of the word in the contexts of the *Nirvāṇa* and other sources, see Mochizuki Ryōko, "Itsusendai towa nanika," *IBK*, 17, no. 1 (1968): 112–118.

29. Originally in the *Ming-seng chuan* (vol. 10) by Pao-ch'ang, now lost, condensed in a work by the Japanese monk, Soshō, in T70.173c; see Hurvitz, *Chih-i* p. 102. Also found in a shortened form in *HTC*, vol. 134, p. 15a Cf. a translation in Fung, *History of Chinese Philosophy*, vol. 2, p. 271: "All those who receive the two principles have the right cause that may lead to *Nirvāṇa* and (continued) endurance of life within the Threefold World is (simply) the result of delusion. Since the icchantikas fall within the class of beings who partake of life, why should they be the only ones to lack the Buddha nature?" Cf. also Liebenthal, "A Biography," p. 94.

30. *HTC*, vol. 134, p. 15b.

31. See T12.393b.

32. See Itano, "Dōshō no busshōron," pp. 4ff.

33. For the definition of the word *tang* and a discussion of the problem, see T'ang, *Fo-chiao shih*, II, p. 160ff.; Kenneth Ch'en, *Buddhism in China*, p. 128f.

34. Chün-cheng (of T'ang), *Ta-ch'eng ssu-lun hsüan-i*, in *HTC*, vol. 74, p. 46b.

35. See *CSPS*, 403c18, 404a2.

36. See Nakamura Hajime, ed., *Jiga to mūga* (Kyoto, 1974), especially pp. 119ff.

37. See *CNS*, 452a, 453b.

38. See *CVS*, 354b.

39. See *CNS*, 532b, 531c (cf. 277b; *CSPS*, 407c).

40. See *CNS*, 543b, 547c.

41. Cf. *CNS*, 277b.

42. See *CNS*, 546c.

43. See *CNS*, 547c; *SCPS*, 408b. Also see Fang, Li-t'ien, *Wei Chin Nan-pei-ch'ao Fo-chiao lun-t'sung* (Peking, 1982), pp. 171f.

44. *CNS*, 549a.

45. See *CSPS*, 399d.

46. *CNS*, 461a.

47. Chün-cheng, *Ta-ch'eng*, p. 40a.

48. See *CNS*, 394b.

49. In Chapter 15, translated by B. Watson, *The Complete Works of Chuang Tzu* (New York, 1968), p. 168.

50. Part 1, Chapter 10; Legge, trans., *I Ching*, p. 270: "When acted on, it penetrates forthwith to all phenomena and events under the sky."

51. See *CSPS*, 412b.

52. *HTC*, vol. 150, p. 421a.

53. *CNS*, 420a

54. See *PTL*, 228a; CVS, 343a.

55. *CSPS*, 402b, 403a, 404b. 412b.

56. See Morie Shunkō, "Jikudōshō no kannō shisō," *IBK*, 21. no. 2 (1972): 140–141; Liu, Kuei-chieh, "Chu Tao-sheng ssu-hsiang chih li-lun chi-ch'u," *Hua-kang Fo-hsüeh Hsüeh-pao*, no. 5 (December 1981): 364f.

57. See *CSPS*, 412b2, 403d1.

58. See Kobayashi Masami, "Jikudōshō no jissō gi ni tsuite," *IBK*, 28, no. 2, (1979): 764; Liu, Kuei-chieh, "Chu Tao-sheng ssu-hsiang chih li-lun t'e-se chi ch'i chia-chih i-i," *Hua-kang Fo-hsüeh Hsüeh-pao*, no. 6 (July 1980): 390f.

59. Listed in Pao-ch'ang, *Ming-seng chuan ch'ao*, in *HTC*, vol. 134, p. 15b. See Liebenthal, "A Biography," p. 94: "By doing the good and suppressing the evil one attains what is called the Karma of men and gods; in the aspect of truth getting reward for doing the good is not (the issue)."

60. Ibid. (MSC). Liebenthal, ibid., translates the title: "Animals may be happy; among men there are poor people. (Is that a suitable) reward (for good deeds)?"

61. In Chi-tsang, *Erh-ti i*, T45, 111b.

62. *CVS*, 378b.

63. Ibid.

64. *CNS*, 532c; cf. 531c.

65. See *CNS*, 396b.

66. See P. C. Bagchi's article in S. Radhakrishnan, ed., *History of Philosophy Eastern and Western*, p. 577: "When Tao-sheng speaks of 'goodness requiring no reward', he speaks not from the relative point of view but from the absolute."

67. *CVS*, 357c.

68. T34.505a. Cf. translation by Liebenthal, "World Conception," I, p. 84: "Every pious act, insignificant as it may be, leads to Buddhahood; it does not receive a mundane reward."

69. See *CSPS*, 397a, 400d.

70. One hundred and twenty-three participants in the vow mentioned in the biography of Hui-yüan, *CSTCC*, vol. 15, in T55.109c. Kamata, *Chūgoku Bukkyō shi*, p. 75, counts Tao-sheng, one of the eighteen celebrated pundits in the community at the Tung-lin monastery, among them.

71. Charles Luk, trans., *The Vimalakīrti Nirdeśa Sūtra* (Berkeley, Calif.: 1972), p. 8.

72. *CVS*, 344b.

73. *CVS*, 344c.

74. Following closely what is set out in the *Vimalakīrti*, Seng-chao maintains that purity of Buddhaland is inseparaby bound up with the purity of the beings (*CVS*, 335b15). The Pure Land of the Tathāgata is essentially unrestricted (334b) and remains always pure (337b); the sin and impurity of beings keep them from seeing it (337b24). The land being unrestricted, there is no other land that belongs to the ordinary beings (334b27). Here, Seng-chao exhibits some trait of the Mādhyamikas holding no difference between *nirvāṇa* and *saṃsāra* in a sense.

75. See Furuta Kazuhiro, "Jikudōshō no Butsu-mu-jōdo-setsu," *IBK*, 19, no. 2 (1970): 318.

76. In *Fa-hua hsüan-lun*, T34.422a9. Liebenthal translates: "If he wants to define the Middle Path saying that the *dharmakāya* moves his body into Reality, and therefore is not found in paradise, then he is wrong. For he has expressed (only one side of the picture) saying that the Land is free (even) from the Precious Things and calling that the Middle Path. He has in this way described the Land of the *dharmakāya* (non-World) but omitted that of the Traces (World)—(which is the other side of the picture) ("World Conception," II, p. 86).

77. *CVS*, 392a.

78. *CNS*, 546b.

79. CNS, 546c.

80. See also Chi-tsang's commentary on the *Lotus*, in T34,441c.

81. D. T. Suzuki, *Outlines of Mahāyāna Buddhism*, p. 46.

82. *CVS*, 343a.

83. Charles Luk, *Vimalakīrti*, p. 18.

84. Cf. *CSPS*, 397a6.

85. Cf. rendering of the paragraph by Liebenthal, "World Conception," II, pp. 85–86.

86. Seng-chao's comment on the same passage reads: "In the *sūtra* it is said: 'the *Dharma-kāya* is the body void and empty.' [*Dharma-kāya*] is not something born, yet there is nothing that it is not born into. It is without form, yet there is nothing that it does not take form of. It transcends what the three realms represent. It is separated from the realm of the conscious. . . . Being subtle and mysterious, it cannot become the existent (*yu*); ready to respond to myriad forms, it cannot become the nonexistent (*wu*). Extending fully out to the eight directions, it cannot become small, minutely entering [any space] with-

out leaving any room uncovered. Hence, it is capable of coming out of birth and getting into death, it remains penetrative and comprehensive in its inexhaustible transformation. . . . How can one afford to discard what is nearby, that is, the sixteen feet [body], and seek the *Dharma-kāya* in the distance!" (*CVS*, 343a). As in the case of Tao-sheng, *Dharma-kāya* is defined here in binary terms with two contrasting elements: negation of an element and again the negation of its antithesis. The elements employed are identical or similar. Both Tao-sheng and Seng-chao share the proposition that the *Dharma-kāya* is transcendental to the manifestation of the three realms and unconditioned. Tao-sheng predicates the Buddha as the unconditioned. Seng-chao later also characterizes the *Dharma-kāya* as the unconditioned (412a). Seng-chao uses the expression "fully extending to the eight directions." We find in the *CSPS* (402c, 404b) the same expressions applied to *li* that is identified with the embodiment of the *Dharma-kāya*. The implied approach for a practitioner, according to Seng-chao, is to seek the real by way of the visible representation in the Transformation body. Later Tao-sheng, as quoted earlier, makes a statement in a similar vein: "The enlightenment of the Greater Vehicle consists, in its original sense, not in discarding what is in the near, namely, birth-and-death, and seeking it again in the distance" (392b, cf. 392c, 406b).

87. See Furuta Kazuhiro, "Jikudōshō no hosshin mushoku setsu," *IBK*, 17, no. 2 (1967): 128-129.

88. *CVS*, 405a.

89. Ibid.

90. *CVS*, 360a.

91. *CVS*, 410b.

92. Itano, "Dōshō no tongosetsu seiritsu no jijō," pp. 184–185.

93. For description of and discussion of them, see *KSC*, in T50.354; Fung, *History of Chinese Philosophy*, vol. 2, pp. 243ff.; Kenneth Ch'en, "Neo-Taoism and the Prajñā School during the Wei and Chin Dynasties," *Chinese Culture*, 1, no. 2 (1957): 35ff.; Liebenthal, *Chao Lun* (Hong Kong, 1968), pp. 133ff.

94. See Fung, ibid., p. 247f.; Ōchō, "Jikudōshō sen," p. 201f, 35f.; Mikiri Jikai, "Jikudōshō no shisō," *Ōtani gakuhō*, 46, no. 1 (1065): 31ff.; T'ang, *Fo-chiao shih*, I, p. 169.

95. See Kobayashi, "Jikodōshō no jissō," p. 759.

96. See T'ang, *Fo-chiao shih*, II, p. 179; Ōchō, "Jikudōshō sen," p. 173.

97. Found also in Hīnayāna; see Sangharakshita, *A Survey of Buddhism* (Bangalore, 1976), p. 282.

98. *CNS*, 487b.

99. *CNS*, 487a.

100. *CNS*, 487b.

101. See Part III (Translation), Preface, note 5. Cf. Hui-ta, *Chao-lun shu*, p. 443a10.

102. See Itano, "tongosetsu seiritsu", especially p. 171ff.

103. Preserved in *HMC*, vol. 5, T52.29c–32b; translated in Leon Hurvitz, "'Render unto Caesar' in early Chinese Buddhism," *Liebenthal Festschrift* (Santiniketan, 1957), pp. 80–114.

104. Itano, "tongosetsu seiritsu," pp. 164ff.

105. *CNS*, 488a.

106. *CNS*, 464a.

107. *CNS*, 489b.

108. Chün-cheng, *op. cit.*, p. 23c Cf. for a little interpretation, see Mikiri Jikai, "Jikudōshō no hannyā shisō," *Bukkyōgaku seminā*, vol. 4, pp. 56f.

109. Sangharakshita, *Survey of Buddhism*, p. 283.

Chapter 5

TAO-SHENG'S INFLUENCE AND THE IMPACT OF HIS DOCTRINES

The spectrum of Tao-sheng's scholarly interest in the themes and *sūtras* was so vast that his thinking cannot be classified easily. Tao-sheng's orientation remained largely philosophical, yet it involved the question of salvation, although it was not religious in the sense of a system with clearly defined programs, practices, and organization. At the time, it was too early for any contemporary Chinese Buddhist to consciously chart his way with an eye to the formation of a school. Tao-sheng was at least one century ahead of any such movement, for not until the sixth century did any "school" in the true sense begin to appear on the Chinese scene.[1] Understandably some sectarians tended to trace their lines to the past as far back as possible,[2] but connections are historically tenuous except those of Indian origin, such as the Chinese Mādhyamika or the San-lun school, in which Kumārajīva and Seng-chao figured prominently. Yet, as the tendecy to adhere to specialized doctrines and text swept the land, Chinese Buddhists were expected to belong to a certain school or line of tradition. Tao-sheng's influence can be measured along the lineages of five schools. We will now identify the influence of doctrines Tao-sheng advocated in the thoughts of other monks.

The Doctrine of Sudden Enlightenment

The Contemporary and Following Period

Tao-sheng was certainly a controversial theoretician and debater. The impact of his style of thinking must have been felt in the contemporary scene; however, we find no record of any eminent figure who argued and wrote in favor of Tao-sheng's theory exactly as it was. Tao-sheng alone was listed as the champion of "major subitism," whereas many eminent masters—including his contemporaries Seng-chao and Kumārajīva, and earlier figures like Chih Tun (314–366) and Tao-an (312–385)—advocated "minor subitism." (The distinction between *great* and *small* was based on which stage (*bhūmi*), that is, the tenth or the seventh was considered the critical point of enlightenment.)[3] This suggests that Tao-sheng's position on the matter was unique and that the theory represented a fresh, revolutionary perception of the existing tradition. Yet, at least one contemporary work supported the sudden enlightenment view, the *Pien-tsung lun* compiled by Hsieh Ling-yün; but the arguments and the terminology used there are not identical with those of Tao-sheng.

Reportedly at least two polemical writings argued against Tao-sheng's view, attesting to a strong opposition in the established church and thus also to the impact Tao-sheng's theory registered. One is "In Arguing for Gradual Enlightenment" (*Chien-wu lun*) by Hui-kuan (d. 446), Tao-sheng's chief opponent, who accompanied Tao-sheng to Kumārajīva in 405 and was to become, along with Tao-sheng, one of the four "wisest" disciples. The other work is "In Arguing that Illumination Is Gradual" (*Ming-chien lun*) by T'an Wu-ch'eng (ca. 383–446),[4] also a disciple of Kumārajīva, and one of thirty-three or thirty-five "greats." These works are lost now, but the gist of Hui-kuan's argument is known to have laid focus on the individual difference in the capacity for enlightenment, using the analogy of climbing a mountain peak.[5]

The line of argument in favor of the gradualist view is partially documented in some other writings, including part of Seng-chao's essays, namely Part IV ("*Nirvāṇa* Has No Name"), Chapters 8 to 13.[6] Scholars are divided on the question of whether this part of Seng-chao's work is authentic.[7] If we follow Itano and place the date of Tao-sheng's argument somewhere between 409 and 414, it is possible that Seng-chao, probably alive until 414, was drawn into the dispute, as were Hui-kuan and T'an. The document nevertheless testifies to the extent of the controversy sparked by Tao-sheng.

Along with the concept of Buddha-nature, the doctrine of instantaneous illumination clearly remained a topic of intense, ongoing discussion after Tao-sheng. Yet his view suffered some setbacks, partly because Hui-kuan (d. 446), spokesman of the gradualist camp, outlived Tao-sheng by some twelve years and effectively attacked the subitist position. But the theory continued to find its proponents at least for the balance of the century. Some of Tao-sheng's own disciples and junior contemporaries defended and expounded his position. They include

Pao-lin (d. ca. 453), his disciple Fa-yao (d. ca. 480), and a certain Hui-sheng, all at the Lung-kuang ssu, where Tao-sheng sojourned from 419 to 428 or 429.[8] And there were other proponents of the doctrine besides those in the direct line of transmission from Tao-sheng. King Wen of the (Liu) Sung dynasty took a keen interest in the theory and was impressed by Fa-yüan (409–489) and Tao-yu (ca. 405–475) as they spelled out Tao-sheng's doctrine. The king's successor, the Emperor Hsiao-wu, also had high regard for Tao-yu and his disciple Fa-tzu (Tao-tzu), considering them the "orthodox line" of Tao-sheng's school.

In the midst of continuing interest among clergy and nobility[9] in Tao-sheng's doctrine of sudden enlightenment, Tao-sheng's thought was reembodied in the lay scholar Liu-ch'iu (436–495). Although chronologically far removed from Tao-sheng, Liu-ch'iu's works were remarkably similar in subject matter and methodology to Tao-sheng's. He "expounded the meaning of [the premises] that good does not entail reward and that one achieves Buddhahood through sudden enlightenment, wrote commentaries to the *Saddharmapuṇḍarīka* and others, and lectured on the *Nirvāṇa*, the large and small (*Prajñāpāramitā*) *Sūtras*, and so on,"[10] all of which are now lost. He discussed the issue of enlightenment from the subitist perspective in his preface to the *Wu-liang i ching* ("The *Sūtra* of Immeasurable Meaning").[11] The *Sūtra* itself is a peculiar product, believed to be a counterfeit made during the Liu Sung period (420–479), influenced by both the *Lotus Sūtra* and Tao-sheng's theory of enlightenment. (The reason for its connection with the latter is that its theme is the fast attainment of Buddhahood).[12] Here we see yet another mark of Tao-sheng's impact throughout the fifth century. Tao-sheng's influence may be detected not only in individual thinkers but also in several schools, to which we now turn.

Tao-sheng's Doctrine and the Ch'an School

Attempts have been made by some modern historians to place Tao-sheng in the lineage of the Ch'an School. Hu Shih, for instance, takes him as "the founder" of the school.[13] However, it may be safe to consider Tao-sheng a theoretical forerunner of the Ch'an.[14] The one possible link is the doctrine of sudden enlightenment; but if we take into consideration the fact that sudden enlightenment did not come into Ch'an history until the latter half of the seventh century, then there is an almost unbridgeable hiatus between Tao-sheng and the sudden enlightenment faction of Hui-neng (638–713) or his disciple Shen-hui (668–760).[15] This gap includes the period between Tao-sheng and the alleged beginning of the school, around 520 at the earliest, when the legendary founder Bodhidharma (470–534) is said to have arrived in China during the reign of Wu-ti (reigned 502–550) of the Liang Dynasty.

Aside from the question of any historical connection, one may argue, in agreement with Ui Hakuju, that there is a fundamental, qualitative difference in approach between Tao-sheng and the Ch'an: the former is theoretical whereas the latter is practical.[16] Tao-sheng's approach may be termed *noetic* or *cognitive*, whereas the Ch'an's is intuitive. Nevertheless, what Tao-sheng means by intellectual knowledge in its religious sense may not differ essentially from intuitive wisdom (*prajñā*) after all. Similarly, suddenness as intended by Tao-sheng may not differ in substance from suprasensory perception as implied by the Ch'an. And the Ch'an practice also can be seen as an "intellectualistic approach."[17] The general approach adopted by Shen-hui, mastermind behind the successful campaign to establish "the school of Sudden Awakening or Enlightenment" (Tun-tsung) in the seventh century, finds expression in the dictum: "The one word *knowledge* (or cognition) is the gateway to all mysteries."

One can perceive this noetic orientation not only in Shen-hui but also in Bodhidharma, who spoke of "entering [the absolute realm] by means of *li*" (*li-ju*), as opposed to "entering by means of practice" (*hsing-ju*).[19] This approach, based on the absolute dimension over and above the ethical one, is discernable also in the words exchanged between Bodhidharma and Emperor Wu of the Liang Dynasty. To the latter's question if there was any merit in his good deeds to further the cause of Buddhism, the Bodhidharma said flatly: "none!"[20] This is exactly identical with Tao-sheng's proposition that "a good deed does not entail retribution," implying an insurmountable gap between the two realms of relative and absolute, conventional and religious.[21]

The two systems share many expressions describing the awakening per se, including two typical words that are used throughout the history of Ch'an: "sudden" (*tun*) and "[penetrating] all of a sudden [open and clear]" (*huo-jan*),[22] with qualifying attributes such as "great"[23] and "immediate" (*pien*).[24] The *locus classicus* of these words for the Ch'an is the *Platform Scripture of the Sixth Patriarch*, the basic "*sūtra*" of the Sudden Enlightenment Sect, which shows similarities to Tao-sheng in phraseology and ideology, as typified in the passage: "Ignorant people cannot understand completely. Although [the Buddha's] speeches are made in myriad ways, they are all congruous with *li* (principle) and end up becoming one ('return to One')" (section 36 of the Tun-huang version).

More significantly, the idea of Buddha-nature, with its variants, *nature* (*hsing*), *self-nature* (*tzu-hsing*), and *original nature* (*pen-hsing*), resounds throughout the scripture (section 3 et passim). Indeed, if all variations are put together, the term *nature* (*hsing*) represents the single most recurrent concept in the text. It appears in the first meaningful statement by Hui-neng, the sixth patriarch, who characteristically rejects the idea of gradual cultivation advocated by Shen-hsiu (section 6): "*Bodhi* (enlightenment) originally has no tree . . . Buddha-nature is always pure and clean; where is there room for dust?" (section 8). Buddha-nature even constitutes the object or the content of sudden illumination. The pure nature exists in the midst of delusions (section 36). Its aspects are identical with or similar to those described by Tao-sheng.

In an enlarged version of the *Platform Scripture* edited by Tsung-pao in 1291 (T48.345–365), even the *Nirvāṇa Sūtra* is discussed with reference to the Buddha-nature and the *icchantika* (349c31ff.). It adopts the same position first developed by Tao-sheng. The notion also characteristically is incorporated in the Ch'an dictum "to [experientially] see the [Buddha-] nature and become a Buddha (*chien-hsing ch'eng-fo*)." Intuition of one's Buddha-nature and sudden enlightenment may be related as cause and effect or as the expression of a process in which each entails the other.[25] In fact, this interrelationship is suggested in the title of Tao-sheng's writing: 'Buddha-Nature Is Something that Will Be Manifested in the Future [when one becomes a Buddha] (*Fo-hsing tang-yu lun*)."

It is worth noting that one of the longer sections (section 42 of the Tun-huang version) in the Ch'an text is devoted to the *Lotus*, including references to the (one) Buddha-Vehicle, three vehicles that serve as the expedient means for the deluded, and the four stages or "gates" (T9.7a) used to explain the Buddha's purpose for coming into the world; namely, the "opening," "demonstrating," "realizing" (*wu*), and "entering into" his wisdom and insight. These concepts are then combined with the notion of "to practice with the mind."

The connection of this doctrine to the *Lotus* also can be seen in Tao-sheng's commentary on the *sūtra*. Some scholars have recognized the *CSPS* as a source of Tao-sheng's theory of sudden enlightenment.[26] Ōchō, for instance, identifies the *Lotus* and the *Dasábhūmika Sūtra* as the stimuli behind Tao-sheng's argument.[27] The concept of One Vehicle as the ultimate principle, presented in the *Lotus*, and the doctrine of stages in the other *sūtra*, both appear recurrently in the *CSPS*. The theme of the fourfold purpose of the Buddha's appearance in the sahā world also is discussed in the *CSPS* in terms of stages. This discussion ends with the statement that "what a practitioner takes as one enlightenment consists, [in analysis], of these four meanings" (400b).[28]

In general, however, the *Platform Scripture* is a repository of various doctrines and gives references to their sources. The *sūtras* mentioned in the smaller version (Tun-huang edition) include (besides those already mentioned) the *Diamond Sūtra* (Vajracchedikā), which belongs to the *Prajñāpāramitā* literature; the *Laṇkāvatāra Sūtra*, which is rooted in the Yogācāra doctrine of consciousness only; and the

Vimalakīrti-nirdeśa, a *Bodhisattva-vinaya Sūtra*. Of these the *Diamond* is cited more than the others; to a lesser degree, the *Vimalakīrti*, which can be regarded as a Mādhyamika-related text, also is frequently quoted. As a matter of fact, the scripture calls itself a *Mahāprajñāpāramitā* scripture, an attempt to trace the theoretical basis of meditational practice to the doctrine of emptiness (*śūnyatā*). In this context, one can still relate the Ch'an tradition to Tao-sheng, because he belonged to the circle of Kumārajīva, who translated and lectured on the *Prajñāpāramitā* scriptures more than on any other line of texts.

Nonetheless the *Platform Scripture* ideologically is far too complex to be associated with one particular line of tradition. For instance, the emphasis on mind or thought (*hsin*), taken not only in the negative sense, as in "no thought," but also in a positive sense, can be related to the Vijñānavāda or Yogācāra doctrine.[29] With the two major doctrines of Mahāyāna (and others) represented, the scripture synthesizes many sources. Under the idea of sudden enlightenment, for example, lies a recognition of the two alternatives of sudden and gradual as due to differences in individual faculties (section 39). The *Platform Scripture* thus stands in the line of tradition started by Tao-sheng that gradually developed syncretic tendencies.[30]

The relation of Tao-sheng and the Ch'an is defined in a similar way by Ōchō. In an article dealing with Tao-sheng's doctrine as the source of the Ch'an ideology, he traces the continuity of the tradition with regard to three points of contact.[31] First, he argues that Tao-sheng's stress on "forgetting the symbols to get hold of the ideas," a well-known notion of the period that originated in Taoist and neo-Taoist texts, set an early model for the Ch'an, whose motto was "separate transmission outside of the (written) teachings and no setting-up of words and letters." Second, Ōchō claims that Tao-sheng set forth for the first time the question of sudden as opposed to gradual enlightenment. Third, Ōchō proposes that the concept of *chi* as the enlightenment-triggering mechanism inherent in man was first introduced into the Buddhist vocabulary by Tao-sheng, finding a significant place in the Ch'an glossary.

This interpretation presupposes the rejection of Ui Hakuju's contention that the Ch'an and Tao-sheng were of different orientation (the former practical and the latter theoretical) and consequently incompatible. Ui depends on two premises: (1) that there is no connection whatsoever between theory and practice; and (2) that Tao-sheng was a theoretician with no religious practice, whereas the Ch'an practitioner had no theory. But these assumptions are not valid. Theory and practice are closely interrelated: the Buddha warned against indulging in metaphysical speculation and insisted that truths should be verified empirically in practice. There is no reason to believe that Tao-sheng departed from this tradition. The Ch'an practitioners belonged to this tradition as well. Reduction to one aspect or another thus does not do full justice either to the Ch'an or to Tao-sheng. There is no evidence that Tao-sheng was not also a mystic. As a matter of fact, as Ōchō points out, he looked beyond symbols and words to the ineffable mystical reality.

Although it cannot be said that Ch'an practice was derived directly from the doctrines of Tao-sheng, it is likely that Tao-sheng had a seminal influence on Ch'an ideology and practice. Tao-sheng's thought was revived in the seventh century in Hui-neng and his disciple Shen-hui, and its influence was felt far beyond the date of the *Platform Scripture*. Tao-sheng is cited as much as Seng-chao in many Ch'an works produced during and after the T'ang era (618–907).[32]

Tao-sheng's Doctrine and the Hua-yen School

The influence of Tao-sheng's doctrine on the Hua-yen philosophy can be examined in three ways: through the classification of teachings, the concept of *li*, and the idea of instantaneous enlightenment.

It has been pointed out that Tao-sheng was the first to attempt to schematize the Buddha's diverse, if not conflicting, teachings, as found in so many distinct scriptures. The most representative of the Chinese Buddhist schools, the T'ien-t'ai and the Hua-yen, developed their own systems for classifying the Buddha's teachings. The Hua-yen system can be regarded as a variant of the T'ien-t'ai, the latter historically preceeding the Hua-yen. The T'ien-t'ai, in turn, was modeled after Hui-kuan's *p'an-chiao*. Hui-kuan's division of the teachings into two, "sudden" and "gradual," originated in Tao-sheng's doctrine, by all accounts. One can say, therefore, that the whole of the *p'an-chiao* system owes its origin to Tao-sheng. In Hui-kuan's and the T'ien-t'ai's models, the "sudden" method of teaching refers to the *Hua-yen Sūtra* about which it was said that the Buddha first put forward the *Hua-yen Sūra* but, because it turned out to be too difficult, he moved to a gradual process of teaching, enunciating other *sūtras*. The fact of individual differences in aptitude was recognized by Hui-kuan, and Tao-sheng repeatedly makes the same point in the *CSPS*, in agreement with the *Lotus*, suggesting differences between "sharp" and "dull" faculties. The interconnection is evident in the *Platform Sūtra*, where the teaching is repeatedly referred to as the "Sudden Doctrine (or Teaching)" (sections 29, 35, 53, et passim). Nevertheless, in the Hua-yen's *p'an-chiao*, the "sudden" teaching refers to the *Vimalakīrti* and the Ch'an doctrine, whereas the *Hua-yen Sūtra* represents the fifth and final "round" (or perfect) doctrine; that is, the position taken by the *Lotus* in the T'ien-t'ai system. The *Hua-yen* represents "One Vehicle" (*Ekayāna*), whereas the "three vehicles" refers to Hīnayāna, the gradual, and the sudden. The relationship of the One and the three is defined in a twofold way, as both "identical" and "distinct": identical in the sense that the One is inclusive of the three; and distinct in the sense that the One is permanent whereas the three are temporary.[33] Although the three vehicles refer to different groups, this pattern is similar to Tao-sheng's interpretation of the theme of the *Lotus* in the *CSPS*, as well as to the T'ien-t'ai's, which probably inherited Tao-sheng's interpretation.

As to the second point of contact, the concept of *li*, as conceived by the Hua-yen, particularly as the key term defining the Dharma-realm (*dhātu*), *li* reaches the culmination of its long history as the major philosophical term in Chinese Buddhism. Tao-sheng contributed more to this trend than any other thinker. In Tao-sheng's glossary, *li* is instilled with a wide range of exegetical and metaphysical implications, including a connotation compatible with the "totalistic"[34] cosmology that charactezizes the Hua-yen philosophy. The ontological *li*, when translated epistemologically, also may imply the concept of sudden enlightenment.

These points can be seen in Ch'eng-kuan's (738–839) thought. The fourth patriarch of the Hua-yen school, Ch'eng-kuan purified and consolidated the tradition, also giving it a new dimension. In his writings one can find the unmistakable trace of Tao-sheng's influence. In Kamata Shigeo's analysis,[35] Ch'eng-kuan departed from his predecessors by putting more stress on the *Dharma-dhātu* of the noumenon–phenomena (*li-shih*) interpenetration, the third of the fourfold universal realities, as opposed to that of phenomena–phenomena (*shih-shih*) interpenetration, the fourth. *Li* in this context bears some similarities to *li* as established by Tao-sheng. *Li*, for example, is posited as indivisible.[36] Ch'eng-kuan recognizes the importance of realizing "one" *li*, as he follows Tao-sheng's soteriology, actually quoting Tao-sheng's words.[37] Tao-sheng's relativistic view on the relationship of the two truths, real (*paramārtha*) and conventional (*saṃvṛti*), lends support to Ch'eng-kuan's interpretation of the question; they share a belief in the undifferentiated aspect of the absolute realm.[38] This shared ontological understanding of *li* naturally leads to an identical position on enlightenment. Ch'eng-kuan quotes Tao-sheng's statement in that regard, adding his own approving remarks.[39] Ch'eng-kuan also cites Tao-sheng's other works, including the commentaries on the *Nirvāṇa, Vimalakīrti*, and *Lotus*, to substantiate his own views.

Conversely, one may ask whether there was any influence of the *Hua-yen Sūtra* on Tao-sheng's thought, particularly since the *Hua-yen (Avataṃsaka) Sūtra* (60 *chüan*) was translated by Buddhabhadra (359–429), during the period 418–421, in none other than Chien-k'ang, where Tao-sheng then resided.[40] It is possible that he was exposed to the text, but there is no indication that the *sūtra* exercised any influence upon him. It is conceivable, for instance, that Tao-sheng may have encountered the idea of individual differences in intelligence and faculty in the *sūtra*; but this was not new to him, for he had already encountered it in the *Lotus* during his youth. Nor is there room for the *Hua-yen Sūtra* in Tao-sheng's division of the Buddha's teaching career, as there is in other *p'an-chiao* models, including that of his contemporary, Hui-kuan.[41]

The Doctrine of Buddha-Nature

The study and exegesis of the *Nirvāṇa Sūtra* continued during the fourth century and into the beginning of the fifth, largely due to Tao-sheng's study of the text and the controversy over the related theory of Buddha-nature he initiated. This textual study did not evolve into a full-fledged system or "school" in the full sense of the term, and it was to be overshadowed by the development of other schools in the sixth century. Yet, such a continued interest in a specific text and its doctrine, without any missionary or Indian founder involved in the lineage, was almost unprecedented in China. In this respect, Tao-sheng stood very much in the forefront of the formation of the schools that would emerge in the centuries to come.

Tao-sheng was placed at the top of the list of exegetes of the *sūtra* and expounders of the theory of the Buddha-nature as well; he was first not just chronologically but also as the initiator of the tradition. In 509, upon the order of the Emperor Wu (reigned 502–550) of the Liang dynasty (502–557), Pao-liang (444–509) or Seng-liang or both collected various commentaries on the *sūtra* and compiled ten works, ranging from Tao-sheng's commentary to Pao-liang's own commentary, into an anthology of seventy-one volumes.[42] This line of study in the South waned afterwards, giving way to and being absorbed into other sectarian movements. Yet the tradition continued in the North from the sixth century to the seventh, enlisting many eminent monks ranging from T'an-yen (516–588) to Fa-ch'ang (567–645).

Tao-sheng's theory of Buddha-nature also gave rise to diverse interpretations: at first three "houses," later to be further divided into ten or eleven interpretations.[43] Tao-sheng's position constitutes the first listed in both classifications. The scriptural source given is the *Nirvāṇa Sūtra* (chapter 12): "'Self' means none other than Tathāgata-garbha (Womb of the Thus Come One). All sentient beings possess Buddha-nature and that is what 'Self' precisely means."[44]

The basic issue for the three "houses" was whether sentient beings possess the Buddha-nature originally, at present, or in the future. The essence or substance (*t'i*) of Buddha-nature in other practical terms was also discussed. Tao-sheng defined it as "what sentient beings are going to have (or realize as the fruit of cultivation and enlightenment)." His argument is believed to have been formulated in an essay bearing the title "Buddha-Nature Is [the Property] One Will Acquire [in the Future]." There were three more relevant essays: "Defining the Meaning of Buddha-Nature," "Explaining the Proposition That a Bodhisattva Is Likely to Attain *Nirvāṇa* at the First Moment of Thought upon Arrival at the Eighth Stage (*bhūmi*)," and "Thirty-Six Questions in the *Nirvāṇa [Sūtra]* (or on *nirvāṇa*)."

Dharmakshema, master of the second "house" or interpretation and translator of the large version of the *Nirvāṇa Sūtra* (in forty rolls, T.12, near 374), identifies the substance of Buddha-nature with what beings originally have, the Middle Path (*Madhyamā-pratipad*) and Suchness (*Bhūtatathatā*). The third view, held by Ta-yao (ca. 400–475), is a middle position between the first two. Buddha-nature as the "right cause" (*cheng-yin*) consists of the *li* for attaining Buddhahood already in a being's possession. In the case of the ten viewpoints, the descriptive terms identified with Buddha-nature include the *li* of the Buddha, true spirit, pleasure principle, sentient beings, storehouse (*ālaya*) consciousness, or pure consciousness (*amala-vijñāna*). The last two were associated with the masters of the Ti-lun (Dashabhūmi) School (sixth century); the predecessor of the Hua-yen (Avataṃsaka) School (seventh century); and She-lun (Mahāyāna-saṃparigraha) (sixth century), the predecessor of the Fa-hsiang (Vijñāptimātratā) School (seventh century). All these facts indicate that Tao-sheng's shadow extended beyond both his own century and the Nirvāṇa School. As a matter of fact, the Nirvāṇa School is considered a forerunner of the T'ien-t'ai School, as it became absorbed into the latter. Likewise, the universality of the Buddha-nature came to be incorporated into Hua-yen Buddhism[45] and also permeated the Ch'an literature; the concept is central to the *Platform Sūtra*.

Tao-sheng and Other Schools

Tao-sheng and the T'ien-t'ai School

Tao-sheng's connection with the T'ien-t'ai School can be viewed in terms of, among others, the two scriptures, the *Nirvāṇa Sūtra* and the *Lotus Sūtra*. It may be suggested that the importance placed on them by Tao-sheng prior to any other masters was faithfully relayed to the T'ien-t'ai tradition. The two scriptures are lumped together in the T'ien-t'ai schema of classification of teachings (*p'an-chiao*): in the category of the Five Periods the *Nirvāṇa* and the *Lotus* belong to the final period.[46]

There is a subtle distinction between the two, of course,: for the T'ien-t'ai School, the *Louts* represents the ultimate ("round") doctrine of the Buddha's teaching career; whereas the *Nirvāṇa*, taught simultaneously, represents a résumé of all other teachings expounded before, thereby taking a somewhat penultimate position, supplementary and subsidiary to the *Lotus*.

In addition to his exegesis of the scriptures, Tao-sheng contributed to the development of the T'ien-t'ai School in two other ways. First, he is credited with the invention of one of the two earliest prototypes[47] of the *p'an-chiao* system itself. In the *CSPS* (396d), Tao-sheng puts forward a scheme of four *Dharma wheels*, representing the Buddha's teaching career: the good-and-pure, the expedient, the true, and the residueless. Although Tao-sheng does not explicitly match any of the *sūtras* with these stages, the last two seem to suggest the *Lotus* and the *Nirvāṇa*, in that order.[48] Being the case, this is in contrast with the *p'an-chiao* system of the T'ien-t'ai, in which, as said before, the two *sūtras* are both classified as of the final period, with the *Lotus* accorded the more significant role. Yet, the T'ien-t'ai schema, along with a similar schema in the Hua-yen school, represents an upshot of the development started by Tao-sheng.

The second way Tao-sheng contributed to the development of T'ien-t'ai has to do with its Eight Doctrines, consisting of one set of four "transforming methods" and a set of four doctrines. The first two, gradual and sudden teachings, probably had their origin in Tao-sheng's theory of enlightenment,[49] as did the later tendency to view the problem of sudden versus gradual syncretically, whereby the two were accommodated without contradiction.[50] The germ of this perspective can be seen even in Tao-sheng and his gradualist opponent and contemporary, Hui-kuan. Gradualism can be found throughout Tao-sheng's commentary—his division of the Buddha's teachings itself implies nothing less than a gradual learning process. Similarly, behind Hui-kuan's theory is a clear tolerance toward Tao-sheng's theory.[51] Hui-kuan in fact came up with a *p'an-chiao* scheme a little closer to the T'ien-t'ai and Hua-yen models than Tao-sheng's. The two main branches of Hui-kuan's scheme are "gradual teaching" and "sudden teaching." *Sudden* refers to the *Hua-yen Sūtra* whereas *gradual* encompasses other *sūtras* and doctrines, including the *Nirvāṇa* and *Lotus*.[52]

There are still other points of connection. For example, Tao-sheng speaks of "to converge and return" (*hui-kuei*, 396d17) with implicit reference to the theme of the *Lotus Sūtra* that the three vehicles as provisional devices give way to the One Vehicle as the true goal. Tao-sheng interprets this as a dialectical process, with an overtone of "returning," a notion harking back to the Taoist idea of "returning to the origin" (*fan-pen*).[53] In T'ien-t'ai, it is paraphrased as "the three being converged to return to the One" (or "unity of three in One") (*hui-san kuei-i*).[54] The description of the "three" as "provisional" (*ch'üan*) and the "One" as real (*shih*), encapsulated in the T'ien-t'ai phrase, "to lay the exigency [of three] open and manifest the real" (*k'ai-ch'üan hsien-shih*) was originally coined by Tao-sheng.[55] Tao-sheng is cited frequently by Chih-i (538–597), the actual systematizer of the school, throughout his various commentaries on the *Lotus*.[56]

Tao-sheng and the San-lun School

Tao-sheng's connection with the San-lun ("Three Treatise") School, the Chinese Mādhyamika, can be treated historiographically as well as from the standpoint of internal evidence. In one old tradition,[57] Tao-sheng is listed as the second patriarch of the sect, after Kumārajīva as the founder, leading to Seng-lang (d. ca. 615) and Chi-tsang (549–623), the two principal contributors to the establishment of the school proper, called *New Three Treatise Sect*. This record has been questioned, especially by some Chinese and Japanese scholars. Some have come up with other names, like Seng-chao and Seng-sung, in place of Tao-sheng.[58] However, the honor given to Tao-sheng, chosen over fifteen to thirty-five prominent disciples of Kumārajīva to represent the tradition as torchbearer, merely suggests how highly respected Tao-sheng was even in the San-lun tradition.

There is no evidence that Tao-sheng actively promoted the texts constituting the "three treatises"—the *Mādhyamika Śāstra, Dvādaśa-nikāya Śāstra*, and *Śata Śāstra*— and his relatively brief stay at Ch'ang-an probably did not allow him to participate in the translation of these and other related texts, except one. Nonetheless, Tao-sheng managed to write a commentary on one of the *Prajñāpāramitā Sūtras*, the original source of the Mādhyamika doctrine. Earlier he probably participated in the lecture on the *Tao-hsing Prajñāpāramitā* given by Chu Fa-t'ai. Thus there is no question that he was exposed to and familiar with the doctrine. More significantly, he wrote a work, "Discussion of the Two Truths" (*Erh-ti lun*), apparently dealing with this concept, closely associated with the Mādhyamika, as we know by the fact that Chi-tsang discusses the same topic in his exposition of Tao-sheng's work, "The Meaning of the Two Truths" (*Erh-ti i*) (three volumes, T45, nr. 1854). Tao-sheng's writing is lost, as is the commentary; however, his conception can be glimpsed partly in his commentary on the *Nirvāṇa Sūtra*, the fragments of which are preserved in the collection (T37, nr. 1763).[59] Although Tao-sheng's words may be too fragmentary to present any coherent picture, no point seems to be particularly at variance with Chi-tsang's views, though Chi-tsang presents a far more complex framework, involving three levels of double truth; rather, at some points similarities are shown in their basic conceptions. At one point Tao-sheng says: "*Li* does not consist in two realities, yet there are two designations. Although their marks (*hsiang*) exist, it does not follow that [*li*] presupposes two [realities]. As their marks do not exist, two thus become false."[60] And Chi-tsang states: "However, it is not merely illusion that is to be discarded, for 'reality' too does not [actually] exist. The reason is that reality exists only because originally there is illusion (*i.e.*, only as the antithesis of illusion)."[61] Tao-sheng also identifies illusion (*huo*) with the worldly truth (*saṃvṛti-satya*).[62] Here, he refers to the monistic nature of true reality (*li*), whereas Chi-tsang refers to the Mādhyamika conceptions of "Emptiness" (*Śūnyatā*) and Middle Path. But both attempt to arrive at the negation of bifurcated realities, hinting at the ultimate reality transcending the relativistic perspective. In the text, Chi-tsang quotes many sources including the *Nirvāṇa Sūtra*,[63] also the source of Tao-sheng's view of the concept. In various places, Chi-tsang frequently refers to Tao-sheng's statements[64] as often as any contemporary of Tao-sheng, including Seng-Chao, who was perhaps a Śūnyavādin.

Notes

1. One can talk of the "six houses and seven schools" in the fourth century that came into being, as found later, due to the divergent views on the *prajñā* doctrine, often interpreted in terms of Taoist concepts. Yet, it could be a convenient grouping by the later historians including T'an-chi in the fifth century. Those "schools" lasted too briefly, mostly for a single generation, to be regarded as the sects, as found later. See Chapter 1, note 16.

2. For example Hui-yüan (344–416) sometimes has been regarded as the founder of the Ching-t'u (Pure Land) School because he, as early as in 402, organized a group called the White Lotus Society to worship Amitābha, aspiring to be born in the Pure Land in the Western Paradise. But T'an-luan (476–542) is accepted as the real founder. See Ch'en, *Buddhism in China*, p. 105f.; Takakusu, *The Essentials of Buddhist Philosophy*, p. 168 and p. 15. Incidentally, Tao-sheng is listed arguably as one of the "eighteen eminent savants"; see T'ang, *Fo-chiao shih*, II, p. 142.

3. See Ch'i (of Sui), *San-lun yu-i i*, T45.121c; Hui-ta, *Chao-lun shu*, *HTC*, 150.425cf. and 428d; Chi-tsang, *Erh-ti i*, T45.111b; Liu Ch'iu, preface to the *Wu-liang i ching*, T9.384a. But in the CSPS Tao-sheng talks of the eighth stage, not the tenth, as the demarcation; see the Translation, Chapter 5, p. 245 (5.4.11).

4. Kamata, *Chūgoku Bukkyō shi kenkyū*, p. 404, talks mistakenly of the two works as if they were available.

5. Hui-kuan's view appears in Hui-ta, *Chao-lun shu*, p. 426b–c. Also his theory seems to be reflected in the *Ming-seng chuan ch'ao*, excerpts from the p. 8c. See T'ang, *Fo-chiao shih*, II, p. 184.

6. T45.159ff. Hui-kuan's argument may be found in Chapters 8–10 particularly. See T'ang, ibid., p. 184.

7. See T'ang ibid., p. 184; Itō Takatoshi, "Jōrono meguru shomondai," *Komazawa Daigaku Bukkyō gakubu kenkyū kiyō* 40 (March 1982): 206ff.

8. See Tao-sheng's biography in the *KSC*, T50.367a.

9. The theory, believed to be declared in the period from 409 to 414 according to Itano, *op. cit.*, p. 168, still excited the gentry Buddhists in 422–423 when the *Pien-tsung lun* was compiled. See T'ang, *Fo-chiao shih*, II, p. 153.

10. See the letter to Liu Ch'iu by Hsiao Tzu-liang in *KHMC* 19, T52.233a.

11. T9.383b.

12. See Kamata, *Chūgoku Bukkyō shi*, p. 143; T9.384b, 385c, 386a, b, c et passim for the concept of speedy enlightenment.

13. Hu Shih, "Development of Zen Buddhism in China," *Chinese Social and Political Science Review* 15, no. 4 (January 1932): 483; and "Ho-tse ta-shih shen-hui chuan" *Hu Shih wen-ts'un* 4: 261f. Liebenthal disagrees with Hu, who views Tao-sheng as "the actual founder of Ch'an (Zen)" ("A Biography," p. 90) or "the virtual founder of Ch'an Buddhism" ("World Conception," I, 103).

14. T'ang, *Fo-chiao shih*, II, p. 179 (see also p. 156) regards him as "the founder" (or the first patriarch) in reference with doctrines; Fung, *History of Chinese Philosophy*, vol. 2, p. 388, says: "Ideologically speaking, the origin of the Ch'an school goes back to Tao-sheng (ca. 360–434)." In the last chapter we discussed his two famous theses that "a good deed entails no retribution" and that "Buddhahood is achieved through instantaneous enlightenment". These provide the theoretical basis for Ch'an philosophy.

15. See Philip B. Yampolsky, The *Platform Sutra of the Sixth Patriarch* (New York, 1967), pp. 23ff.; Hu Shih's articles on Shen-hui, including a biography of Shen-hui in *Hu Shih wen-ts'un*, IV, 245–288, especially 288.

16. Ui Hakuju, *Zenshū shi kenkyū*, vol. 1, pp. 20f.

17. Hu Shih, "Ch'an (Zen) Buddhism in China, Its History and Method," *Philosophy East and West*, 3, no. 1 (April 1953): 15.

18. The expression is employed by Tsung-mi (779–841), as he interprets or quotes Shen-hui, in the *Ch'an-yüan chu-ch'üan chi tu-hsü* (General Introduction to the Collection of Expositions on the Sources of the Ch'an), T48.403a1f.,

cited and discussed in Hu Shih, "Ho-tse ta-shih shen-hui chuan," *Hu Shih wen-ts'un*, IV, p. 261, and *Shen-hui ho-shang i-chi*, p. 35.

19. See Hu Shih, "P'u-t'i-ta-mo k'ao," *Hu Shih wen-ts'un*, III, 296ff., and *Hu Shih chiang-yen chi*, I, p. 161. Though it is not exactly the same, we can speak of "entering *li*," which Tao sheng uses in the commentary (409a); cf. his biography (T50.366c). Kamata, *Chūgoku Kegon shisōshi no kenkyū*, p. 405, identified it with "a kind of sudden enlightenment (*satori*)".

20. Found in the *Platform Sūtra*, section 34, Yampolsky, *Sixth Patriarch*, p. 155.

21. See Hu Shih, "Ho-tse ta-shih shen-hui chuan," p. 262f.

22. The expression is originally found in the *Vimalakīrti-nirdeśa Sūtra*, T.14.541a. For Tao-sheng, see T45.111b; *CVS*, 354b. For the Ch'an, see the *Platform Sūtra*, sections 19 and 30: "suddenly" (Yampolsky, pp. 141 and 151).

23. See Tao-sheng's commentary, 398b9, 408d4, 409c3, et passim, the *Platform Sūtra*, sections 37 and 42.

24. See *CSPS*, 401a14; the *Platform Sūtra*, section 40 et passim.

25. Cf. Fuse, *Nehanshū no kenkyū*, p. 193; *Hu Shih chiang-yen chi*, I, 118f.

26. See Ōchō, "Jikudōshō no tongosetsu," p. 107; Kamata, *Chūgoku Kegon shishō shi no kenkyū*, p. 406.

27. Ōchō, ibid., p. 108.

28. Liebenthal, "World Conception," I, p. 88, commits a logical error by rendering the passage (400b17) with "that these four steps are taken by the believer in one single act of illumination."

29. T'ang, *Fo-chiao shih*, II, p. 179 (also see p. 156), traces the idea of mind associated with enlightenment as found in the Ch'an ideology to Tao-sheng.

30. See Ōchō, "Jikudōshō no tongosetsu," p. 109.

31. Ibid., p. 99ff.

32. See Kamata, *Chūgoku Kegon shisō shi no kenkyū*, p. 413.

33. See Takakusu, *Essentials of Buddhist Philosophy*, pp. 116f.

34. Ibid., p. 113.

35. *Chūgoku Kegon shisōshi no kenkyū*, p. 416f.

36. See T36. 219s.

37. See T36.220a.

38. See T35.575b.

39. See T36.187a.

40. Tao-sheng is believed to have studied at least the *Ten-stage Sūtra (Daśa-bhūmi Sūtra)*, Vasubandhu's commentary to which was to become a base text for the Ti-lun (Daśa-bhūmi) School, the predecessor of Hua-yen; see Ōchō. *Hokke shisō*, p. 229.

41. Tao-sheng's colleague at Lu-shan and Ch'ang-an as well as his adversary in the doctrine of enlightenment, Hui-kuan, acknowledges the position of the *Hua-yen Sūtra* in his *p'an-chiao*; see Tsukamoto, *Collected Works*, III, 93.

42. Found in T37, near 1763. Ch'en, *Buddhism in China*, p. 128, mistakes the (seventy-one) volumes as commentaries.

43. See T'ang, *Fo-chiao shih*, II, pp. 189ff.; Itano, "Dōshō no busshōron."

44. T12.648b.

45. Takakusu, *Essentials of Buddhist Philosophy*, p. 117.

46. See Hurvitz, *Chih-i*, p. 237ff.

47. The other one is the schema formularized by Seng-jui in the postface to the *Saddharmapuṇḍarīka*, in *CSTCC*, T55.57b–c, in which the *Prajñāpāramitā* and the *Lotus* are in mutual relationship; see Ōchō, "Jikudōshō sen," p. 232.

48. See Hurvitz, *Chih-i*, p. 218; Tsukamoto Zenryū, *Collected Works*, III, 96.

49. See Hurvitz, ibid., p. 197.

50. See Fuse, *Nehanshū no kenkyū*, p. 38f.

51. See ibid., p. 42.

52. For Hui-kuan's *p'an chiao*, see Hurvitz, *Chih-i*, p. 219, the chart being based on Itō Giken, "Tendai izen no kyohan no tsuite," in *Ryūkoku Daigaku ronsō*, no. 284 (February 1929): 26–77.

53. Tao-sheng uses the term in his commentary on the *Vimalakīrti*, T37.531c.

54. See, for example, Chih-i, *Miao-fa lien-hua ching wen-chü*, T34.127a–b; Ti-kuan, *T'ien-t'ai ssu-chiao i*, T46.775b. Also Chi-tsang, the systematizer of the San-lun School, to be discussed later, frequently employs the phrase in his commentaries to the *Lotus*; see, for example, T34.363a–b.

55. For Tao-sheng, see the text 397a; for the T'ient-t'ai, see Chih-i, ibid.,

and Ti-kuan, ibid. Cf. Ōchō, "Jikudōshō no tongosetsu," pp. 234 and 236, for the use of the phrases applicable to Tao-sheng.

56. For example, see Chih-i, ibid., T34.127a. The point is also made by Sakamoto Yukio, in the same edition, *Hokekyō no Chūgokuteki tenkai*, Introduction, p. 2. For more connections, general and particular, identifiable between Tao-sheng and T'ient-t'ai, see Fuse Kōgaku, "Hokke koryū no kenkyū," *Shūkyō kenkyū* 6, no. 6 (1929): 25–54, especially 33ff.

57. See Prebish, ed., *Buddhism: A Modern Perspective* p. 190; Takakusu, *Essentials of Buddhist Philosophy*, p. 99; Kamata, *Chūgoku Bukkyō shi*, p. 185.

58. Hatani Ryōtai, "*Sanron Kaidai*," pp. 3–6, cited by Robinson, *Early Mādhyamika*, p. 162f.

59. See T37.487af.

60. T38.487a1f.

61. Translated in Fung, *History of Chinese Philosophy*, vol. 2, p. 297.

62. See T38.488a.

63. See, for example, T37.79a,b.

64. For example, in *Erh-ti i*, T45.111b, Chi-tsang quotes Tao-sheng: "It is also identical with the meaning of the great sudden enlightenment. This is what Chu Tao-sheng talked about. he said: 'Retribution [for good or evil *karma*] belongs to the sphere of change and decay. Birth-and-death belongs to the realm of great dream. From birth-and-death to the diamond-consciousness, all are dreams. After the diamond-consciousness one achieves instantaneous wide-open great enlightenment.'"

PART II

A Critical Study of Tao-sheng's Commentary on the *Lotus Sūtra*

Chapter 6

TAO-SHENG AND THE *SADDHARMAPUṆḌARĪKA*

The only credible information about how Tao-sheng came to take an interest in the *Lotus* is his own statement found in the preface to the commentary itself (396b). He writes that earlier, "when young," he happened to attend a series of lectures on the *Lotus*, which were "rich in literary content and meaning" and "deep in reflection in the explanatory medium (*shih*) and underlying principle (*li*)." The notes he jotted down then, he goes on to say, became the basis of the present commentary compiled toward the end of his life in 432. The lecturer is not specified. Possibly, it could have been either Chu Fa-t'ai (320–387) or Kumārajīva (344–413). The expression "when I was young" makes Chu sound like the more plausible author, because Tao-sheng was presumably with Chu between ages eleven (ca. 371) and twenty-seven (ca. 387), whereas he studied under Kumārajīva in his late forties, between 405 and 408.

However, no other evidence supports the theory of the earlier master.[1] Furthermore, the commentary is based on the text of Kumārajīva, not on any other translation, though it is not categorically impossible that he initially attended the lecture based on another version and later used the new translation. The oldest of the three extant translations is the one by Dharmarakshita (translated in 286). Tao-sheng may have studied it at some point in the thirty years following his conversion to Buddhism. Yet, the study of the *Prajñāpāramitā Sūtras* (expecially in the circle of Chu Fa-t'ai as in the circle of the latter's colleague Tao-an) dominated and overshadowed the study of other scriptures.

As a matter of fact, Tao-sheng was in Ch'ang-an when Kumārajīva translated the *Lotus*. The translation was not limited to rendering the Sanskrit text into the Chinese language but involved the master's interpretation of the text, eliciting lively discussions among students concerning the most appropriate translations of the original Sanskrit terms. It may be pointed out here that in his colophon to the *Lotus*, Seng-chao recognized Tao-sheng's presence in the translation, also stating that "the letters and meanings (as suggested by Kumārajīva) were both penetrative," resembling Tao-sheng's description cited earlier.[2] In any event, a long gap of at least twenty-seven years lies between Tao-sheng's introduction to the *Lotus* and the compilation of his commentary. During this period Tao-sheng was occupied with many subjects and *sūtras*, covering practically all of his theories and writings. The commentary thus marks the culmination of his scholarship.

The commentary was completed in 432 while Tao-sheng was at Lu-shan after being excommunicated in 430 because of the icchantika issue. Tao-sheng apparently took up the *Lotus* as a medium to voice his thoughts and feelings about the Buddhist study and practice of his time. This is expressed in the first passage of the commentary, as he laments: "those who seriously tackle and grasp [the subtle words] are few while those who superficially touch and sneer at them are many" (396d). In fact the doctrine of universal Buddhahood is manifestly embodied in the text (400b9f., 408b16f., et passim).

Doctrinally, the *Lotus* is close to the *Nirvāṇa*. In the view of contemporary and later Chinese Buddhists, they represent two final stages of the Buddha's teaching career, as evidenced in the archetypal schema by Tao-sheng as found in the commentary (396d13f.). In this schema, the fourth ultimate stage refers to the *Nirvāṇa Sūtra*, whereas the *Lotus* is in the third, penultimate. Tao-sheng is credited with having worked out a synthesis of "the true (*chen*) emptiness (*k'ung/śūnyatā*) and the mysterious (*miao*) existence (*yu*)" in this schema. *K'ung* and *yu* sum up the whole spectrum of the Buddha's teaching. *Yu* represents the "eternally abiding wondrous intent" suggested in the *Nirvāṇa*. The *Lotus* elucidates the ultimate unity of the diverse "vehicles." The *Lotus* thus occupies an essential, if not ultimate as with the *Nirvāṇa*, place in the stratification of the teaching—a view transmitted to (and later consolidated by) East Asian Buddhists, especially the T'ien-t'ai.

One thing to be examined and clarified about the commentary is the composite nature of the content, considering Tao'sheng's own statement in the Preface (396d) to the effect that he edited and compiled the commentary from lecture notes and other commentaries. Where is Tao-sheng's own thought reflected? The commentary, according to Fuse Kōgaku, reflects an early line of tradition concerning exegesis of the

Lotus associated with Kumārajīva and his circle.[3] Yet that does not deny the impact of Tao-sheng's own thought on the text; numerous statements and expressions undoubtedly are Tao-sheng's own. Although it thus is clear that the content consists of Tao-sheng's own thoughts plus the elements of two or more other sources, it is hard to sort out and identify the concepts and interpretations drawn from other sources. We can merely guess that the information from other sources might include exegetical definitions of some words and structural analyses of some passages and chapters. Arguably, those parts of the text for which Tao-sheng does not directly give credit to others (with the words "a certain exegesis," and so on) (400b) represent his own original interpretation. If this is so, the commentary stands as an authentic treasury of Tao'sheng's original thought. And it has an added significance in that, being broadly based on a variety of sources, it also can be seen as an outgrowth of the tradition concerning the *Lotus Sūtra* up to the culmination of Tao-sheng's career. This being the case, it is a product of collective thinking merging with Tao-sheng's own speculation. However, he may not be much different from other contemporary Chinese Buddhist thinkers in this respect.

Lastly, one may raise the question of authenticity: Does the work stand as the genuine writing of Tao-sheng in every sense? If so, how can one verify it? As a matter of fact, much of the literature of that period has been viewed with suspicion by some modern scholars. A part of the corpus of Seng-chao's writing and the *Wu-liang i ching* (Scripture of Immeasurable Meaning)[4] are cases in point. Coincidentally, these two questionable sources also deal with the problem of enlightenment: the former documenting the theory of gradualism and the latter reflecting Tao-sheng's own subitism. They indicate the impact that Tao'sheng's theory made on the contemporary and ensuing ages.

In the case of the *CSPS*, however, there is no reason to doubt Tao-sheng's authorship. His name is written down at the head of each of the two volumes. The commentary also is mentioned in Tao-sheng's biography, the *CSTCC* by Seng-yu, a usually infallible compilation completed ca. 518.[5] It is also listed in two other sources: *Fa-hua ch'uan chi*[6] and *Tung-yü ch'uan-teng lu*.[7] In this regard we can also cite the preface to a later edition of the collected commentaries to the *Vimalakīrtinirdeśa*, stating that Tao-sheng's commentary became the standard base for the commentaries to come.[8] Further, we can cite the colophon to the *Lotus* written by Seng-chao, describing how the translation was conducted with Kumārajīva in the center, and with the participation of Tao-sheng, top on the list, and other eminent students. In fact, in the *CSPS*, Tao-sheng traces the original meanings in Sanskrit of the proper nouns appearing in the first chapter in almost the same way Kumārajīva does in the commentary on the Vimalakīrti.[9] Furthermore, Tao-sheng's words in the commentary are quoted verbatim in various commentaries to the Lotus by some eminent masters, including Chih-i[10] of the T'ien-t'ai school and Chi-tsang[11] of the San-lun. Tao-sheng's style and phraseology in the commentary show no noticeable discrepancy with those identified in the other two commentaries, *CVS* and *CNS*; sometimes almost identical expressions are found. Perhaps more significant, many of his ideas are readily identifiable in the commentary: the text abounds with variations on the theme of the Buddha-nature; other discernable themes include the Pure Land, the *Dharma-kāya*, and goodness. On the other hand, one subject, that of enlightenment in terms of a temporal process, apparently contradicts the picture of the doctrine represented by the original title itself. However, the text may merely show that the nature of the process is more complex than one would surmise from the title, because the other facet of the concept, gradual realization, also is emphatically presented in the commentary.

Notes

1. Liebenthal, "A Biography," p. 92. Other scholars including Ōchō and Hurvitz mention Kumārajīva for that matter. See Part III, Translation, Preface, note 6.

2. T51.54b.

3. Fuse, "Hokke koryū no kenkyū," especially p. 32ff.

4. Found in T9.384–389. See Wogihara Unrai, "Muryōgikyō, to wa nani-ka," *Nippon Bukkyō Gakkai nempō*, no. 7; Ōchō Enichi, "Muryōgikyō ni tsuite," *IBK*, 3 (1954), pp. 456–462.

5. T55.111b.

6. T51.56a.

7. T55.1164c.

8. T85.440a.

9. T28.328–331; compare *CSPS*, 397b–398a.

10. See, for example, T34.127a, matching with *CSPS*, 409d.

11. See, for example, T34.277a, matching with *CSPS*, 409d.

Chapter 7

LITERARY ASPECTS

Structure

The commentary in the extant edition is divided into two rolls (*chüan*): one from Preface to Chapter 4, another from Chapters 5 to 27. The first roll, although it has fewer chapters, is still slightly longer than the second; this suggests that the first few chapters are more important. It is difficult to tell whether the original text was divided in this manner. In the text (396d) Tao-sheng mentions "one roll."[1] In any event, the first four chapters are the longest and most elaborate. The text may be divided into three distinct parts: the preface; an explanation of the meaning of the title of the *sūtra*; and an exegesis of the twenty-seven chapters, the main body of the text.[2]

Preface

The first paragraph, an introductory remark or preface, tells briefly of the state of Buddhist study in the period and Tao'sheng's motivation to write the commentary, followed by the background of writing or compilation. The second paragraph describes the implication of the four elements that make up the title of the *sūtra*: *miao* (*sad*), *fa* (*dharma*), *lien-hua* (*puṇḍarīka*), and *ching* (*sūtra*). In the course of explaining the title, Tao-sheng schematizes the entire teaching span of the Buddha under the four "*dharma* wheels," nearly the earliest type of *p'an-chiao*. Also defined is "*Mahā-yāna*," the hierarchical source (*tsung*) of the *sūtra*. The explanations of these terms converge on the theme that the three vehicles are set to turn into the One Vehicle.

In the first paragraph of the Introductory Chapter (397a), Tao-sheng breaks down the entire *sūtra* into three sections according to content. The first section, consisting of the first thirteen chapters, deals with the theme that the cause of the three is identical with the cause of the One. The second section, chapters 14 through 21, expounds this theme in terms of effect. The third section, encompassing the remaining chapters, is keyed to the theme that the men of the three vehicles turn out to be none other than the men of the One Vehicle. This thematic division into three was unique at the time. Tao-an already had introduced a method of dividing a scripture into three parts—introduction, the Buddha's main discoure, and talk of propagation[3]—and this system became a standard for later commentators. However, although Tao-an's segmentation is concerned with external structure, Tao-sheng's is concerned with internal structure. Here the leitmotif stands out clearly: the eventual identification of the three and the one in a sort of dialectical process.

Interpretation of Chapters 1–27

Each chapter begins with a description of the content and general intent of the chapter of the *sūtra*, explaining why a given chapter has the title it does. Tao-sheng was a pioneer in the method known as *k'o-wen* (compartmentalized composition), which "consisted of summing up each chapter of a scriptural text in a few clear, well-chosen words and showing its relation to the whole work."[4]

Then follows an analysis of the content. In longer chapters, like the first four of the commentary, an entire *sūtra* chapter is anatomized into a number of distinct paragraphs. Metric parts (*gāthās*) also are included in the breakdown, taken as a recapitulation of what was said in prose. But Tao-sheng fails to take a critical look at the text of the scripture as it is as a composite product consisting of two layers of tradition, represented by prose and metric parts.[5]

Among these divisions, some terms and passages are singled out for comment. Each paragraph begins with a synopsis. The sections that follow are probably to help unravel the general intent of the paragraph, also substantiating or reinforcing the import of the chapter or the main ideas of the commentary. In the actual exegesis of particular phrases, Tao-sheng is less interested in the definition of the word, phrase, or passage than in its implications for the wider context. This is true not only of the longer chapters but also the shorter ones. The passages chosen are knit closely together with Tao-sheng's own words. Thus, it is easy to misinterpret any given statement taken out of context, as Liebenthal often does in his translations and interpretations of Tao-sheng's statements.[6]

This pattern generally applies to individual chapters, except those chapters (9, 12, 21, 26, and 27) which are made up of a single paragraph. Chapter 1, the introduction, has a slightly different structure; it is elaborate in etymological definitions of personal names of the congregation surrounding the Buddha and some of the participants' cosmological positions. This suggests that the commentary also was intended as a primer for neophytes. In general, however, Tao-sheng's approach is exegetical rather than purely literary;[7] in essence it is an "exegetical commentary" (*i-shu*), as it was called in some records. Not just in that connection but in broader range, Tao-sheng's commentary set the pattern for later commentators to follow.

Style and Exegetical Method

Tao-sheng's literary style, as found in the commentary, does not appear to be unique or idiosyncratic. It well may have been a style current among his contemporaries, expecially Buddhists, who in the course of translating Buddhist literature developed somewhat peculiar styles. In translating *sūtras* they had to adjust to the more complex Sanskrit style and syntax. The text of the *Lotus*, translated by Kumārajīva, for instance, shows a complex sentence structure, particularily in prose parts, which alternate with four or five character verses. Technical terms and proper nouns transliterated from Sanskrit into Chinese make sentences even more complex. Compared with their translations, expository essays and polemical writings by Buddhists are refined, but they remain reflective of the Indian stylistic influence.

Because a commentary must stay close to the scripture it analyzes, the *CSPS* exhibits a complex style. Tao-sheng nonetheless endeavors to simplify and economize language as much as possible by using native Chinese terms and symbols. As he tries to deliver to the reader the central ideas in a given paragraph of the *sūtra*, Tao-sheng often succeeds in producing terse, articulate philosophical statements, though some of them, heavily laden with Taoist terms, remain elusive to us. Although no fixed form of literary style was prevalent in the period, Tao-sheng employs various rhetorical forms, including parallelism and antithesis. His prose is punctuated frequently by four-character clauses, repeated as the essential elements of syntax, creating an internal rhythmic structure. Very often he uses rhetorical questions, interjections, and exclamatory phrases for emphasis.

Tao-sheng's method of exegesis is unique: the focus is on the unified idea rather than on the literal meaning of the individual words or expressions. This method is discernable everywhere in the commentary. Sometimes Tao-sheng dissects a word into its constituent phonemes, irrespective of the equivalent original Sanskrit word. By glossing words in this way, Tao-sheng illustrates his main theme directly or indirectly. One of his favorite expressions is "borrowed (or metaphorical) statement" (*chia-ts'u*) or its variants. He uses these expressions in reference to parts of the Buddha's speeches or stories.

Tao-sheng makes no reference to any other Buddhist *sūtra*; nor is any specific phrase or passage actually quoted from any source, except in one paragraph of Chapter 2 (400b), in which "according to a certain exegesis" is said four times successively. It seems vey unusual for a mature scholar like Tao-sheng, having been exposed to various scriptures and other Buddhist literature, to stay away from the scriptural and literary sources. By contrast, his contemporary, Seng-chao, in his essays, widely cites the sources. However, Tao-sheng's text is strewn with Chinese philosophical idioms and dictums, seeming to suggest that he concentrates on the doctrine of the *sūtra* per se, speaking in, and making full use of, the current language.

Vocabulary: The Language of the Text with Special Reference to Neo-Taoism

At a glance, a student of Chinese tradition familiar with the classical literature will not fail to notice that the commentary is full of words and phrases that are not Buddhist. It is hard to find a single passage without such a term, especially when the passage is a significant statement from Tao-sheng himself. Because language and thought are inseparably related, this poses a serious intellectual challenge to understanding Tao-sheng's thought.

It may be argued that a Buddhist glossary had yet to be established, and that Tao-sheng had no alternative but to resort to this style of writing. However, this view is immediately weakened by recalling that Kumārajīva managed to render the same *sūtra* without drawing heavily from the Chinese philosophical lexicon. The *sūtra* translation of Kumārajīva does contain a few native Chinese philosophical terms, borrowed particularly from Taoist literature,[8] but they do not create any exegetical problem because, as a consequence, they were deprived of the philosophical implications intended in the original sources.

One plausible explanation for Tao-sheng's use of Taoist terms may be pedagogy: Tao-sheng was obliged to speak the language of his day out of missionary zeal. Expediency is a pronounced theme of the *sūtra* and also a notion commonly found in the native Chinese tradition.[9] One notable precedent for this practice is the system of *ko-i* (concept matching), a crude, superficial form of exegesis invented immediately preceding Tao-sheng but believed not to have been in practice at the time of Tao-sheng.

The questions then are the following: Does language in Tao-sheng's case serve only as a missionary tool or does it mirror the actual content of his thought? In what frame of reference did Tao-sheng's thinking take palce? Was Tao-sheng, in this commentary, primarily a Buddhist, a Taoist, a Buddho-Taoist hybrid, or something else?

The source of Tao-sheng's borrowing was not restricted to a single system, but if one is to be singled out, neo-Taoism is the candidate, for most of the terms with semantic and philosophical significance are traceable to the canons and related works of neo-Taoism.[10] Neo-Taoism represented the dominant philosophico-religious system of the day. Doctrinally, it is an amalgam of the two major traditions, Confucianism and Taoism. Tao-sheng, in the days before his conversion to Buddhism, was widely read in neo-Taoist works.[11]

In the following sections, we will examine a select number of concepts, thirteen in all, identifiable in the two sources. These terms have been selected for analysis on the basis of their prominent positions in Tao-sheng's terminology; put together, they constitute the backbone of his interpretation. Mostly they occur in the scripture only in some technical, fixed applications. The connotations of these terms will be drawn from the classical sources and then juxtaposed with the meanings apparently intended by Tao-sheng. Thus, we will be able to determine whether these Buddhist ideas become imbued with Chinese philosophical presuppossitions.

Li

Li is the most conspicuous abstract noun in the commentary, occurring 139 times in the text.[12] A key term in Tao-sheng's thought, *li* demands intensive analysis, a task for our next section. Here we will examine the term as a part of Tao-sheng's borrowed vocabulary.

In its extensive usage, unprecedented for a Buddhist text,[13] the term involves many elements of meaning that reflect neo-Taoist conceptions. *Li* had become a pivotal term for the neo-Taoists in interpreting what the *Lao-tzu*, the *Chuang-tzu*, the *Analects*, and the *I Ching* had loosely proposed. Tao-sheng is in the neo-Taoist tradition, first of all in the way the term is used as an object or goal: something "to be searched exhaustively" (*chin*);[14] "to be consummated" (*ch'iung*),[15] the ultimate point "to reach" (*chi*);[16] or "to encounter".[17] He also, however, adds a Buddhist color by describing the goal as something "to be enlightened to" (*wu*),[18] and "to be seen (directly) or experienced" (*chien*).[19]

Li is employed in the text either independently or with a qualifier. When it is qualified, the word is preceded by such indicative adjectives as *this* or *that*, or an adjectival phrase with *chih* (. . . of), a word that makes a possessive case, though sometimes *chih* does not appear but is implicit. What is suggested here are the dual facets of the concept: the universal and the particular. This harks back to the distinct features emphasized by Wang Pi and Kuo Hsiang: Wang's focus is on the *li* that transcends phenomenal representation; Kuo puts stress on the *li* immanent in phenomena.[20] As a corollary, in connection with *li*, Wang views the world from the perspective of the absolute domain of *wu* or nonbeing, whereas Kuo deals mainly with the relative realm of *yu* or being. In Kuo's cosmic map, every being has its own *li*.[21] When a being stands in compliance with its own *li*, it is following nature at the same time: *li* is that which is self-so or self-caused.[22] This relativism, however, does not preclude a higher plane; there is also the unifying principle of the heavenly *li*[23] or the ultimate *li*.[24] Wang, in contrast, stresses the all-conserving *li* of Heaven or Nature that "unites and commands all particular concepts and events."[25] Although Kuo talks of the plurality of things and their *li*, taking *T'ien* or Heaven as "name for the sum total of all things,"[26] Wang underscores the universal unity of things and the singular principle underlying them; for Wang, the universe is one single whole.[27]

These two contrasting pictures of *li* have both found places in Tao-sheng's metaphysical model. The particular, however, appears to be overshadowed by the universal, with the possible implication that *li* as an all-conserving entity has more weight than *li* as an individual principle underlying a particular fact, thing, or statement. However, although the word more often appears unqualified than qualified, an unqualified usage does not necessarily refer to *li* in its universal sense. Even when occurring by itself, *li* often turns out to be closely related to a particular case in the same passage or paragraph. It is likewise questionable whether the term, although particularized in its form, always remains particular in implication. For examples we can cite "the ultimate,"[28] "the Buddha's (*li*)," "the Tathāgata's (*li*)," "the mysterious (*li* of Mahāyāna)," and, probably to a lesser degree, "(*li*) of emptiness (*k'ung/śūnyatā*)."

There are some words that were considered conducive to rendering the very abstruse *li* more accessible to "ignorant" beings. Among such words is *shih* or "profane fact." There is some trace of this concept in Kuo Hsiang's philosophy as well as in Tao-sheng's. However, the close relationship between *li* and *shih*, later advanced by the Hua-yen to the extent of interpenetration of the two domains, had not yet developed.[29] *Shih* in Tao-sheng's system, as in Wang Pi's, is subservient to *li* as a teaching aid, stopping short of the sense of "phenomenon," as opposed to *li* as "noumenon." *Li* becomes manifest through *shih*, if not actually in *shih*. As long as *shih* is taken as the material manifesting *li*,

Tao-sheng remains loyal to the *sūtra*: *shih* accounts for the parables and similes concocted by the Buddha in order to present his original purport or *li* more comprehensibly to ignorant sentient beings.

How extensively Tao-sheng exploits metaphysical terms from other systems is epitomized in this passage: "*Li* transcends the realm of calculation . . . it fills up and covers the ultimate of nonbeing (*wu-chi*)."[30] The style and diction of this quote are anything but Buddhist: the key words are unmistakably identifiable in texts associated with neo-Taoism.[31] And yet it is clear in context that the epistemological implication is Buddhist. "Transcending" (*ch'ao*) seems to refer to a dialectical process in which two realms, being (*yu*) and nonbeing (*wu*), are synthesized, and "the ultimate of nonbeing" may represent such a synthesized state. Hence, as Tao-sheng points out elsewhere, there is nothing that *li* does not penetrate, which is identical in substance with the statement that the *Dharma-kāya* is omnipresent.[32]

Still inherent in the notion of the transcendence of *li* (a point of emphasis for Wang Pi) is its immanence, which finds expression in *tzu-jan* or "self-soness" (also Kuo Hsiang's term for the ultimate). Tao-sheng follows the neo-Taoists in identifying *li*, as used by the Buddha in the *sūtra*, with *tzu-jan*.[33] The word *tzu-jan* occurs frequently in Tao-sheng's commentary, functioning variously as a noun, adjective, or verb.[34] When used as a substantive term, it seems to have affinity with the Taoist usage. *Tzu-jan* refers not only to the mode in which cause and effect interact, but also to the very thing that regulates their interaction.[35] The locus of transformation (*hua*) lies in *tzu-jan*,[36] identifiable with the Buddha-nature.[37] By returning to the state of *tzu-jan* one becomes transformed, which is tantamount to saying that by departing from "delusion" one becomes enlightened to *li*.[38] This notion of "regress" (*fan*) in reaching out to "the ultimate point of origin (*pen*)" can be traced back to Taoism. But here again, Tao-sheng, by combining *fan* and *pen* with the terms "delusion" (*huo, moha*) and "enlightenment" (*wu, bodhi*), interpolated them into what he probably intended as an irrevocably Buddhistic statement.[39]

Fen (Endowed Potential in Human Nature)

Thus Tao-sheng is assumed to follow the Taoists on the basic concept of nature as a self-existing state. Unlike the Taoists, however, he is concerned more with human nature in particular than with nature as a universal principle. More specifically, Tao-sheng deals with the natural element in (human) beings pertaining to their capacity for becoming Buddhas. Though the term *Buddha-nature*, which has its scriptural source in the *Nirvāṇa Sūtra*, does not occur in Tao-sheng's text, the idea is there in such expressions as "all sentient beings are to become enlightened,"[40] because they are "potential bodhisattvas,"[41] and by extension, Buddhas.

This notion finds a Chinese equivalent in the word *fen* ("allotment"). The Taoists contend that all beings should strive to live in accord with their assigned allotments, naturally varied from one individual to another.[42] One's happiness lies not only in realizing this inborn share of capacities but also in translating it into an appropriate position in the social context, which is what Confucianists call the unity of "name and actuality" (*ming-shih*[43]). But instead of delving into its social and ethical implications subsumed by his religious vision, Tao-sheng has borrowed the term to refer to the ontological structure of beings and the subsequent emerging epistemic method for realizing reality as a whole. More specifically, all beings are endowed with the common capacity for "great enlightenment" (*ta-wu/mahābodhi*),[44] or "the Buddha's knowledge and insight";[45] human beings, by their very nature, possess "the subtle triggering-mechanism (*chi*) for enlightenment."[46]

The neo-Taoist premise that natural allotment varies from one person to another remains intact in Tao-sheng's distinction of "sharp" and "dull" capacities.[47] The traditional concept of allotment thus finds a Buddhist application in the notion of potential capacity for enlightenment. The epistemological implications of the concept also show an essential similarity with the neo-Taoist approach. In dealing with *li* or enlightenment, Tao-sheng speaks as if there were an archetypal image of being, which can be retrieved by humans through dispensing with the bondages and crusts superimposed on the original, true self in the course of individual and collective history.[48] Salvation consists not so much in an increment of positive elements as in a decrement of negative ones, not in progression but in retrogression. For description of this approach Tao-sheng follows the Taoist line of thinking. He writes: "*Li* cannot be attained to instantaneously. One should grind the coarse in order to reach the fine; decrease it and further decrease until one arrives at the point of no decrease."[49]

In language, style, and message this is remarkably similar to a passage in the *Tao-te ching* (Chapter 48): "The pursuit of learning is to increase day after day. The pursuit of *Tao* is to decrease day after day. It is to decrease and further decrease until one reaches the point of taking no action."[50] Yet the message couched in these borrowed words is not incompatible with the *sūtra*, as it also advocates a gradualist view of enlightenment. This is but another example of internal affinities enshrouded in different expressions.

The Role of Language

Taoism treats language as a tool somewhat deficient in unfolding ultimate reality to the full extent, as epitomized by the adage in the *Lao-tzu*: "Those who know do not speak; those who speak do not know" (Chapter 56) Also the *Hsi-tz'u ch'uan* ("Commentary on the Appended Judgements" of the I *Ching*), which is a text of Wang Pi's commentary, quotes Confucius as stating: "Writing does not do full justice to words, which in turn do not do full justice to ideas" (11–12). The ineptness of words can be seen in the ineffable nature of *li*. Kuo Hsiang echoes this point: "The ultimate *li* is not something to be spoken of. . . *li* is not that which can be verbalized."[51]

Tao-sheng is in agreement with the Taoists on the limits of language. Various adjectival modifiers descriptive of *li*, such as *deep, profound, wide, mysterious, far-off,* and *dark*, all clearly identifiable in the Taoist literature,[52] express the unspeakable nature of *li*. At best the role of language is to circumscribe *li* through approximation. He pointedly declares: "*Li* is transcendent of words."[53]

Implicit in the limitation of words, on the other hand, is their intermediary value. Language belongs to the category of exigency (*ch'üan*) or expediency (*fang-pien, upāya*). Tao-sheng declares: "*Li* by nature is unspeakable, and yet we speak of it by resort to words in their temporary and false role, which we call expedient means."[54] Words as a medium or "ferry" are indispensable, especially to those who have not "witnessed" *li* in the course of their self-realization.[55] In this respect, language can be best described as a catalyst in the realization of *li*.[56] In Buddhist terms, it can be counted among the supporting causes (*pratyaya*), whereas the primary cause (*hetu*) making realization possible lies in the original capacity innate in human nature.[57]

The utility and limit of language is delineated in the classic simile of fishnets and traps: tools are to be dispensed with once the desired goal is achieved. Tao-sheng appropriates this simile, originally from the *Chuang-tzu* (Chapter 26), in his own way: "Since he has realized *li*, what is the use of words? They are like fishes and hares: once they have been caught, what utility do the nets and traps have?"[58] The simile also receives a lengthy elaboration in Wang Pi's *Chou-i lüeh-li* (Exemplifications of the *Book of Changes*), in which he writes: "Now, the words are fishnets for images, and images are traps for meaning. . . . Thus only by forgetting the images can one grasp the meaning, and only by forgetting the words can one grasp the images."[59] As an extension of this premise, Tao-sheng likewise holds that the pure object is too recondite for both words and relative human knowledge.[60]

Nevertheless, language, especially in connection with the Sage, is sometimes credited with more than a catalytic role. Here, Tao-sheng also finds common ground with the neo-Taoists. The words of the Sage, who has had an experiential encounter with *li*, are an authentic testimonial, a right source of mystical knowledge.[61] Language here does not remain merely descriptive but becomes prescriptive.[62] Therefore, in the adulation of the *sūtra*, repeatedly urged by the *sūtra* itself, there may not be anything unacceptable to Tao-sheng,[63] whose approach in the commentary otherwise reflects a rationalist frame of mind.

The inscrutableness of *li* as the symbol of the core reality is evident in the profuse expressions about the unfathomable nature of *li* (and its closest synonym, *Tao*).[64] Wang Pi portrays *Tao* as "bottomless," "deepest," "most remote," and makes much of the difficulty of realizing it.[65] In line with this standpoint, Wang "opposes the symbolism of numbers" represented in the *Book of Changes* and focuses instead on "the (cosmic) situation and (individual) position."[66] Likewise, using the word *number* (*shu*),[67] Tao-sheng stresses the gulf between *li* and the world of numbers: "The profound *li* is in so dark an abyss that it transcends what the numerical realm represents."[68] Included here is the proposition that "the ultimate image has no form,"[69] *form* symbolizing the domain of calculative and discursive thinking, as the *Chuang-tzu* asserts that "What is ultimately fine (or essence) has no form . . . the formless is of such dimension that it is beyond the reach of numbers."[70]

In his stress on the limits of language, Tao-sheng clearly puts himself in the indigenous Chinese setting.[71] Nonetheless, the point is also implicit in Mahāyāna philosophy, expecially in the *Prajñāpāramitā Sūtras*.[72] Tao-sheng was familiar with both the indigenous and Buddhist views on language, and because of the common ground between them, the mixture of terminologies would not have sounded unnatural to him. The expression *k'ung-li*, "*li* of Emptiness (Śūnyatā),"[73] is a case in point. It is open to varying interpretations, but it seems here that, because in syntax the two nouns are in apposition, the word *li* reinforces the preceding word's general import as the principle underlying phenomena. Hence, through blending the indigenous Chinese philosophical term *li* and the imported Buddhist term *k'ung*, a shared concept is articulated in a new way.

The Sage and Related Terms

In Tao-sheng's text the words *the Sagely Man* (*Sheng-jen*) and its abbreviation *Sage* (*Sheng*) are used more frequently than *the Buddha*, constituting a departure from the *sūtra*. Are they merely interchangeable synonyms? *Sage* embraces broader connotations than Buddha, even if the latter is combined with the concept of the *Dharma-kāya*. The term naturally has an added significance, for it is a concept that originates and figures conspicuously in the established Chinese philosophical and religious systems.

The Sage: "the Inner" and "the Outer"

The Sage personifies the prototype of man in both traditions, Confucian and Taoist, yet with different orientations: the one, a type of socially oriented leader, the other, an introversive recluse. In the neo-Taoist tradition, the two pictures merge in a syncretic form, with Confucius emerging as the foremost archetype of sagehood. Sagehood thus actually accounts for only half of the Chinese ideal of man, succinctly expressed in the idiom, "*Tao* of sageliness within and kingliness without."[74] *Sage-king* does not necessarily have socio-political implications but may refer to a spiritual ideal; the expression then simply suggests a perfect model of man in his two parts.[75]

This two-part division is a recurrent pattern in the text. Of the two, internality overshadows externality in importance, as illustrated in the repeated motif: "As virtues fill within, fame spreads without."[76] This undoubtedly is a variation of the Taoist theme, typified in Kuo Hsiang's words: "As virtues fill within, (other) beings respond to (one's) outside," or "then spirit fills up the outside."[77] The centrality of the internal also is implicit in the words of Tao-sheng: "As the *Tao* is great, it combines kingliness."[78]

Tao-sheng proceeds to translate this Taoist frame into Buddhist terms. The outer part of the *Tao* is equated with external activities compassionately carried out for the sake of other beings.[78] "The equal emphasis on external and internal life"[80] laid out by Kuo Hsiang applies also to the process of enlightenment. Tao-sheng writes: "Since internally they have cherished the wondrous comprehension and externally they have further practiced the six perfections (*pāramitās*), and their thought and reflection (*shih*) are both in so advanced a state, right awakening (*samyaksaṃbodhi*) is the matter of any moment, in the morning or evening."[81] In Tao-sheng's thought lies a monistic tendency, also identifiable in neo-Taoism, in which diverse elements are fused together in a single concept.[82] Thus *t'i* (substance) represents the unity of *hsiang* (lakṣaṇa) or external mark and *hsing* or nature.[83] The Sage thus is one who is "equipped with the *Tao* or expertise for penetrating" and unifying the two layers of being, interior and exterior.[84]

The Sage as envisioned by Tao-sheng participates actively in the enlightenment of other sentient beings, as both initiator and guide. His work is summed up in the word *hua*, which means not just "to teach," but "to instigate metamorophosis" or "conversion."[85] The Sage's program for teaching other sentient beings is geared to varying existential conditions and circumstances, including intelligence, temperament, ethos, and receptivity. This view brings Tao-Sheng closer to the *sūtra* than to native Chinese views of the Sage.

Although there are parallel notions in these two views—the Buddhist "skill-in-means" (*upāya-kauśalya*) and native Chinese "exigency" (*ch'üan*)—they are different in orientation. In actual application, the Chinese Sage, especially the Taoist Sage, primarily is concerned with himself rather than with others, teaching them, if ever, by example rather than direct instruction. But the Buddhist teacher acts as a spiritual mentor, leading sentient beings directly to salvation.

Form borrowing also can be discerned in Tao-sheng's interpretation of the concept of concentration (*ting, samādhi*). The Sage of the *Chuang-tzu* and Kuo Hsiang is the one who freely roams between the two realms of being (*yu*) and nonbeing (*wu*), between movement (*tung*) and quiescence (*ching*), without obstruction, without any deliberation of his own (*wu-hsin*) in a state of nonaction (*wu-wei*).[86] The Taoist Sage is tilted toward quiescence, in contradistinction to the king. In comparison, the Sage in Tao-sheng's portrayal is not subject to movement and quiescence, particularly in the state of concentration or *samādhi*, in which, unlike in the Taoist reveries termed *tso-wang* (sitting in forgetfulness),[87] *li* is never to be forgotten of lost.[88] Among what ought to be forgotten instead are the external mark (*lakṣaṇa*) and existential bondage (*lei*), which hinder one's path to *li*.[89] *Lei* is another term adopted by Tao-sheng from Taoism.[90] Identifiable with defilement (*kleśa*),[91] *lei* also meaning "ties" refers to something that helps feed and cause attachment—a new feature added to its otherwise similar meaning in Taoism.

Chi and Its Beyond

Tao-sheng's Sage, not subject to either of the two modes of existence, remains always in the state of *wu-wei* or nonaction,[92] in much the same way as the *Dharma-kāya*,[93] the incarnation of *li*, is omnipresent.[94] In the Chinese classics something eternal and ubiquitous, an ontological ground of being, is generally postulated. Terms like *t'ien* (heaven), *Tao*, and *li* clearly suggest the idea, and it becomes more explicit in Kuo hsiang. He identifies the true nature of the Sage with "that by which traces are caused" (*so-i-chi*).[95] The Sage thus is revealed through his "function,"[96] beneath all external traces (*chi*). In this schema *so-i-chi* is the substructure, with the Sage working between the two levels of *li* and *chi*. The word *so-i-chi* does not occur in Tao-sheng's commentary, but its intent is implicit in other abstract terms, such as *shih* (the real or actuality) in the apposition of name and reality" (*ming-shih*),[97] a much discussed subject in the native tradition. But *chi*, identical with *ming*, occurs more often than *ming* (in twenty places). It is juxtaposed with "*li*" (398a), "the real" (399b, 403d), and "Dharma" (400a), and it is connected with "words" (399c, 408a), "feeling" (402b), "exigency" (401a, 407b, 412d), and "affairs" (411d *et passim*). It is also coupled with "transformation" (406d), and "(past) conduct" (407b).

Typically, *chi* has to do with "the external" (398a et passim). Although it is found juxtaposed with the true, *Dharma*, or *li*, it is not bogus but is still in touch with the ultimately real,[98] although it can be said to be short of reaching the real.[99] *Chi* implicitly suggests some locus from which it emanates and to which it is to "return" (396d), alluding to "the ultimate source" (411d); the terms involved are invariably traceable to Taoist texts.

Behind Tao-sheng's indebtedness to the Taoists for the general framework of the concept, however, there emerges a fundamental discrepancy. Tao-sheng's "trace," represented by "three vehicles," has a temporary but necessary value for the process of salvation, whereas the Taoist "trace" is something that has to be rejected from the beginning. The Taoist ideal is expressed in the *Tao-te ching*, chapter 27: "The skillful traveler leaves no traces of his wheels or footsteps."[100] On this, Wang Pi comments: "If one acts according to *tzu-jan* without creating or starting things, things will reach their goal and leave no track or trace."[101]

It is true that what Tao-sheng borrowed from the neo-Taoists extends beyond the form of the term to its conceptual framework. It is delineated, for example, in the juxtapositioning of the word *chi* with *li*, as is shown in Kuo Hsiang's enunciation: "Once *li* is arrived at, *chi* is extinguished."[102] However, as to how the notion applies to interaction between the Sage and beings, the fundamental philosophical difference between Buddhism and neo-Taoism unfolds again. This difference can be seen in neo-Taoism's contention that the Sage does not exhibit a "trace." Kuo writes:

> The Sage causes beings to act for themselves. Therefore, he is without trace. Hence, what we call "Sage" refers to the one whose self (or substance) has no trace. Thus, when the beings obtain [what they believe to be the Sage's] trace and the trace obtained is given a forced name of "Sage," the "Sage" then refers [in reality] to the designation for [the one whose essence is] traceless.[103]

Implicit in these different perceptions of "trace" are two different ways in which the Sage deals with beings didactically and soteriologically. Although the Taoist Sage exhibits a distanced attitude toward other beings, assuming a posture of strict aloofness from them, the Buddhist

Sage, by means of "trace," closely follows the emotional conditions of beings on his way to saving them.[104]

This divergence is clearly identifiable in the implications of *ch'üan* or exigency, a concept interpreted differently by the two sides. Like *chi* or trace, *ch'üan* is something from which the real is distinguished: "*chi* stops short of reaching the real;" "*ch'üan* shows the unreal."[105] Yet, it also is an essential part of the learning process, with a transitory value and validity, just as the three vehicles are the harbinger of the One Vehicle.[106] In fact, *ch'üan* is the favored synonym of the otherwise more standard technical term *fang-pien* (*upāya*).[107] Tao-sheng keeps within the bounds of the Taoist tradition when he states that "the exigent approaches (of the Sage) are unrestricted in pattern."[108] However, similarities stop there. The Taoist emphasis is on the Sage's ability to adapt himself to the changing circumstances he encounters, whereas the Buddhist emphasis is on the Sage's effort to comply with the different existential conditions of the recipients of his teaching traditions. Thus, although they take their common term *hua* to refer to both process and goal, teaching cum transformation, the Taoists and Tao-sheng are widely apart on how this can be achieved.

Kan (Perception), *ying* (Response), and *chi* (Subtle Triggering Mechanism)

Tao-sheng's points of contact with and departure from the Taoist and neo-Taoist line of thought, especially in regard to didactic methodology, become manifest more distinctly in a set of terms descriptive of the way the Sage and beings interact with each other in the teaching–learning process. The concepts involved all are firmly rooted in the Chinese philosophical tradition, although one of them, *chi*, partly coincides with the Buddhist concept of "faculty," long a dormant concept that Tao-sheng rehabilitated.

The enlightenment process is initiated by the activation of *chi*, the subtle triggering mechanism, as it "actively appeals to (*k'ou*) the Sage."[109] The *locus classicus* of the term is in the *I Ching*,[110] but more relevantly in the *Chuang-tzu*,[111] and subsequently in Kuo Hsiang's commentary.[112] *Chi* is closely connected to *ken*, "root" or "faculty." It does not specifically occur in Tao-sheng's commentary, but in other Buddhist contexts the two combine to make a compound,[113] and the link is implicit in Tao-sheng's analysis. Only *ken* is found in the *sūtra*.[114] Although *ken* also is used by Tao-sheng,[115] *chi* is used in many contexts. It becomes evident that Tao-sheng fully exploits the term, already impregnated with the Taoist and neo-Taoist perspectives, in order to apply Buddhist doctrines. The connection of *ken* and *chi* was already forged by Kuo Hsiang. On the passage of the *Chuang-tzu*, "Where lusts and desires are deep, the springs of the Heavenly (*T'ien-chi*) are shallow,"[116] Kuo Hsiang states: "Only after the deep root reaches the ultimate, can one revert once (and for all) to the desireless state."[117]

Chi's relation with human nature also is clear in Kuo Hsiang's words: "as they employ their own nature (*hsing*) the Heavenly *chi* darkly issues forth."[118] "Heavenly" (*t'ien*) here may not be entirely foreign to Tao-sheng in its practical implication, because for Kuo Hsiang "'Heaven' represents the general designation for the ten thousand (or myriad) things."[119] Viewed in this light, with its connecion to inherent nature (*hsing*) the "spirtual (*shen*) *chi*"[120] of Tao-sheng is not far removed from the "Heavenly *chi*" of the neo-Taoists.[121]

The terms *chi* and *ken* are interrelated in that they denote the inside and outside of one and the same spiritual entity: *chi* refers more to the kinetic superstratum of faculty and being, and *ken* more to the inner substratum. This *chi* enables beings to establish a point of contact with the Sage.[122] But this contact can be only established as an extension of a being's own internal capacity.[123] The concept in its original Taoist form is based on the premise that human nature contains a positive element conducive to man's advance to the *Tao* or *li*, parallel with Tao-sheng's view that all beings are Buddha-natured. But Tao-sheng exhibits more affinity with the *Lotus* than with neo-Taoism by underlining differences of *chi*, as well as of *ken*, among individuals.[124] Although the Taoists admit variable individual allotment, they do not dwell on it.

Subsequent to the activation of *chi*, the Sage, stimulated or moved (*kan*) by beings who indicate they are ripe for his teaching,[125] responds (*ying*) to them with his teaching program. The Sage's response is an automatic reflex to stimuli reaching him from these beings, because the Sage is capable of intuitive realization (beyond discursive reasoning).[126] Hence, the two events, being moved and then responding, form a chain of reaction, as illustrated by the compound *kan-ying*.

Here again, however, analysis of the schema in concrete terms indicates that beyond this shared framework there is a fundamental difference between the two philosophical systems. In the case of the Chinese Sage, stimuli come from the environment, but not, as in the case of Tao-sheng's Sage, from other beings in the course of his interaction with them. Furthermore, the Chinese Sage's response is self-directed, a self-adaptation to his changing environment, not for the sake of others in a direct way. This self-oriented Chinese Sage, grammatically, has no object for his actions,[127] in contradistinction to Tao-sheng's use of the word, in which the subject and the object are almost always stated explicitly or implicitly.[128]

The feeling (stimulus)–response (*kan-ying*) pattern employed by Tao-sheng concerns the interaction between the Sage and sentient beings, with the capacity for achieving Buddhahood at its center. The traditional Chinese pattern, however, is based on *yin* and *yang*.[129] There is an original chasm between the Sage and ordinary beings; they are situated in different realms. The gap is bridged by the Sage as he assumes a "deigning"[130] posture to "respond" (*ying*) to other beings. However, in the context of the Chinese tradition, this posture applies to when a superior man (*chün-tzu*) or an emperor, not necessarily a Sage, "stoops down" in order to "search for principle in the world."[131] Thus the concept does not apply to the situation of Tao-sheng's Sage.

The Sage's next move is the teaching itself,[132] which can ferry his pupils up to the seventh stage (*bhūmi*) of the bodhisattva path.[133] The image of the Sage as teacher, largely missing in Taoism, comes from the *sūtra*.[134] Otherwise, the phraseology in which the teacher–learner relationship is delineated is drawn largely from classical texts associated with neo-Taoism. This can be seen in Tao-sheng's use of the expression "the exhaustive realization of *li*".[135] The Sage is equipped with "the methodology (*tao*) of thorough penetration (or propagation)."[136] This resembles the mode represented in the *Book of Changes*, in which Change (*i*), when it moves to act, "thoroughly penetrates the raison d'être of the world."[137]

The Sage as Savior: *chi-wu* (to Ferry Beings)

As the term *hua* suggests, the function of the Sage extends beyond teacher to savior. The work "to ferry" (*chi*) is contained in the *sūtra* in the expression *chi-tu*: to ferry (living beings) across (the sea of reincarnation to the shore of *nirvāṇa*).[138] The notion also is found in Taoist works in similar forms, including the expression *chi-wu* to ferry beings across (to salvation), frequently employed by Tao-sheng throughout the text. Implicitly proposed in the phrase *chi-wu* as used by Tao-sheng is the agent of salvation, the Sage. In Taoism, on the other hand, the agent, at best, is the amorphous abstract *Tao* or Change. So whenever the soteriological aspect is mentioned by Tao-sheng, the Sage gives way to the Tathāgata or the Buddha.[139] Saving other beings was an essential mission for the Buddha, constituting his raison d'être in the world. In contrast, the idea of salvation in the *Chuang-tzu* appears to take up a secondary position; saving is relegated to the category of "the knowledge of petty man": "The understanding of the little man never gets beyond gifts and wrappings . . . He wastes his spirit on the shallow and trivial, and yet wants to be the saviour of both world and the Way, to blend both form and emptiness in the Great Unity. Such a man will blunder and go astray in time and space; his body entangled, he will never come to know the Great Beginning."[140]

In so far as it is held that transformation is self-induced or spontaneous (*tzu-hua*), there is no substantial difference between the two systems regarding the goal of universal salvation. However, there is a clear-cut difference in methodology. Recalling the premise in the *Tao-te ching*, that "Tao never does; yet through it all things are done. If the barons and kings would but possess themselves of it, the ten thousand creatures would at once be transformed,"[141] Wang Pi goes on to say: "Do not inhibit the nature (*hsing*) of beings, then beings will help (save) themselves."[142] In brief, as Kuo Hsiang puts it, "If there is deliberate action (*yu-wei*), there is no way of helping (themselves for working out their own salvation)."[143]

The Buddhists and the neo-Taoists thus start from a common basis, but they diverge when it comes to methodology. They then merge in the same goal at the end, universal salvation. Both ways of thought set as their goal bringing the Sage and beings together through the latter's self-enhancing acts, with some aid from the former, but this point is emphasized more in Buddhism. After his own enlightenment, the Buddha set the goal of bringing beings to the same realization, that is, to save (others) as the next step.[144] To be considered along this line is the Taoist idea of "seeing things equal" or "making all things equal" (*chi-wu*).[145] Although referring to the state of consciousness "in which any distinction between It and Other is seen to be illusory and all language dissolves in the immediate experience of an undifferentiated world,"[146] the notion connotes the fundamental equality of all beings.[147] Likewise, Tao-sheng also recognizes the "universality or sameness" (*p'ing-teng*) when he glosses the term *Mahāyāna*.[148] In this framework, even "one trickle of goodness" is conducive to achieving the "topmost knowledge."[149] The underlying implication is that all beings are equally able to realize the truth.

A striking similarity to indigenous Chinese thought is demonstrated in the way Tao-sheng makes the point of universal salvation. While discussing the efficacy of calling upon the name of the bodhisattva Avalokiteśvara (Kuan-yin) as one of the numerous methods the Sage designed for the sake of beings, Tao-sheng says that the Sage is intent on saving all by evervarying approaches without missing any one.[150] Likewise, it is said in the *I Ching, Hsi-tz'u chuan* (Commentary on the Appended Judgements): "[The knowledge of spirit] molds and encompasses all transformation of Heaven and Earth without mistake, and it employs diverse approaches to bring things into completion without missing any."[151]

Nevertheless, there is an indelible mark of Mahāyāna in Tao-sheng's perception of salvation. He does not fail to note that the Tathāgata or the Buddha acts on the salvation of all beings, motivated by "great compassion" (*mahākaruṇā*).[152] Although feelings or affection can be exchanged between the Taoist Sage and beings,[153] and the consequential effect might be identical, the route taken must be different. This becomes clear in the words of Lao Tzu: "And, therefore, the sage is always skillful and wholehearted in the salvation of men, so that there is no deserted man, he is always skillful and wholehearted in the rescue of things, so that there is no abandoned thing."[154] And yet it does not seem to match the Buddha-sage's compassion in its direct interaction and immediate impact. The adjective *great*, which always appears as a qualifier when Tao-sheng uses the word *compassion*, perhaps is intended to accentuate what he may have considered a distinctive concept.

The Emotional Factor (*ch'ing*)

One conspicuous element that is closely involved in the interaction between the Sage and beings is *ch'ing* (feeling, mood). An essential faculty in the biological and mental makeup of the human psyche and mind, it plays a significant part in the human drive toward illumination. One of the recurrent terms in the text, it has no exact Sanskrit equivalent. Its closest equivalent in the *sūtra* may be *adhimuktatā*, "disposition," which can be the basis for nurturing faith and understanding. Although both terms describe the condition that prompted the Buddha to employ various approaches in teaching beings, *adhimukti*, "strong inclination, attachment, earnest, zealous application,"[155] is limited to an emotion that could become "faith and understanding" (*hsin-chieh*), whereas *ch'ing* has a wider range of application, covering neutral and negative, as well as favorable aspects, referring more often to the somewhat rudimentary, volatile part of human emotion that is to be neutralized and brought under control. It does not stop just at sensory feeling in its limited sense.[156] Naturally, it readily can be assumed that Tao-sheng had recourse to the native Chinese sources for this conception. But first let us see how the term is placed in the text semantically and syntactically.

A prominent medium through which *ch'ing* is rendered is the term *li*. *Ch'ing* is antithetically juxtaposed with *li* in many places, defining the locus of *li* outside *ch'ing*'s domain:[157] *li* is darkened by *ch'ing*;[158] and *ch'ing* succumbs to *li*.[159] In brief, *ch'ing* has to be overcome in order for *li* to prevail.[160] In other words, *ch'ing* differs from what constitutes the original state or nature.[161]

Now, turning to Buddhist terminology, Tao-sheng puts *ch'ing* in the same category with illusion (*moha*),[162] illusive thought,[163] mind of impaired vision,[164] and the five desires.[165] However, *ch'ing* also signifies the inner tendency[166] that can become meritorious and conducive to a being's search for *Dharma* and the One. *Ch'ing* is something to be grappled with by the Sage to steer beings to the realization of the One. In this respect, it retains something of the term *disposition* (*adhimukti*).[167] One finds the Buddhist element more strongly imprinted in the application of the concept, which extends beyond individual or private emotion to a collective public mood (*shih-ch'ing*)[168] prevailing in the congregation surrounding the Buddha. Tao-sheng thereby elevated the Chinese concept from its originally individualistic content to a dimension of "social emotion"[169] in harmony with the Mahāyānic notion of compassion. There is no indication that other contemporary and earlier Chinese Buddhists treated the concept in such a way.

There is no doubt that Tao-sheng is indebted to the indigenous sources for the basic idea of *ch'ing*. In fact, *ch'ing* has been a subject of discussion throughout the Chinese tradition, from Mencius to the neo-Confucianists. In Tao-sheng's period it already had intrigued the major figures of neo-Taoism, including Ho Yen (d. 249) and Wang Pi, who represented contrasting views. The gist of their difference was whether the Sage, like ordinary beings, possesses emotions, usually broken down into five: joy, anger, sorrow, delight, and hatred. Behind their differing views, Ho Yen and Wang Pi are in agreement that the Sage is not "ensnared" (*lei*) by emotions in his response to beings or objects (*wu*), but their reasons differ: according to Ho Yen, the emotions are totally absent; for Wang Pi, though the emotions are present, the Sage has the ability to remain nonchalant and disinterested in the entangled affairs of the world.[170]

In any case, the neo-Taoists saw *ch'ing* as much a part of the corpus of human nature as *hsing*, the two representing two different levels of nature, a posteriori and a priori, respectively. According to Wang Pi, these two entities (whose relationship also is much debated in Chinese philosophy)[171] ideally are to be brought into harmony with human action so that an equilibrium of mind may be attained.[172] In actual usage, however, the neo-Taoists texts also fed into the word *ch'ing* some of the connotations found in Tao-sheng's conception, which point to those elements of *ch'ing* that are counterproductive to enlightenment. Thus, *ch'ing* is synonymously coupled with the word *wei*, or false.[173] In the context of Kuo Hsiang's philosophy, *ch'ing* is assumed to be something existentially real by which beings may explore and finally realize the ultimate reality of *li*.[174]

Tao-sheng is not directly concerned with the question of whether the Sage is under the influence of feelings, because he assumes that the Buddhist Sage, by virtue of being enlightened, has brought the senses (*indriyas*), the source of feelings, under complete control. On a few occasions, however, *ch'ing* still applies to Tao-sheng's Sage, but it signifies only good intention or will, activated and exercised for the sake of others.[175] The same is true of the word *yü* (to desire),[176] the very term otherwise equivalent to *tṛṣṇā* (*tanhā*), the arch cause of suffering (*k'u/duḥkha*) and thus of transmigration. In contrast, the Taoist Sage has no such will or desire, neither for his own sake nor for others.[177] Even when Wang Pi argues that the Sage is subject to feelings, this refers to situations concerning external objects (*wu*) surrounding him. In Tao'sheng's vocabulary, the same word primarily refers to human beings. Tao-sheng is more concerned with human situatins. Therein lies the fundamental difference between the teaching methods of the two sides: the one employs a passive, static exemplification; the other, a direct, dynamic approach. They share much in their conceptions of the feelings, but Tao-sheng moves to a religious dimension: "delight" (*lo*), for instance, has been transformed in his thought into the holy blissfulness associated with meditation and is presented as something antithetical and thus antidotal to suffering.[178] For Tao-sheng's Sage, *ch'ing* is transformed into the pathos felt for and directed toward suffering beings.

Lei (Ensnarement, Bondage)

Due to their alienation from *li*, unreleased beings are conditioned to remain in the entangled state of existence, often called *lei*. The word is found together with "external mark" (*hsiang/lakṣaṇa*), both being things to be forgotten after the "wondrous fruit" of enlightenment is obtained.[179] The worldly forms (*shih*) and images (phenomena) are listed as effects brought about by *lei*.[180] It appears to have something in common with impurity or depravity (*kleśa*)[181] and attachment, constituting a stumbling block to one's passage to *li*. Naturally, for the Sage who has apprehended *li*, *lei* is gone forever.[182] It is something that used to occur less often in beings of antiquity, whose "naturally endowed original stuff" was pure and untainted.[183]

Tracking the classical source of the term, one comes across a similar, though somewhat nebulous, usage in the neo-Taoist literature. Wang Pi writes: "The emotion of the Sage responds to things, but is not ensnared by them."[184] The *li*-versus-*lei* pattern already took place in Kuo Hsiang: "to advance to the ultimate *li*, thus to dispel *lei*";[185] the process is identical with that found in Tao-sheng's commentary. The objects that give rise to attachment or bondage include "form and name,"[186] which account for what is real. It is described as a process that the deliberate mind (*yu-hsin*) effects on the self-so state (*tzu-jan*).[187]

Thus what seems to have begun as a verb in Taoism and neo-Taoism through Wang Pi, used loosely to describe the deluded condition of beings entangled in phenomenal factors, came via Kuo Hsiang to be fixed by Tao-sheng's time as an abstract noun, referring to a kind of existential bondage, which the Tathāgata can help untie. This clearly is demonstrated in the *Pien-tsung lun* by Hsieh Ling-yün, which contains a series of inquiries about Tao-sheng's theory of sudden enlightenment. There, the term is used as a noun, as in the phrases "annihilation of *lei*" and "supression of *lei*,"[188] the former identified with sudden enlightenment. In Buddhist terminology, *lei* seems to play the same role as the twin "hindrances" or "veils" (*chang*/*āvaraṇas*), intellectual (*jñeya-*) and moral (*kleśa-*).[189] In its practical implication *lei* seems to be equivalent to "delusion" (*huo*/*moha*), a cause of nescience (*avidyā*). And we find these terms in the *Chuang-tzu* in a similar context: "Such a man will get confused and deluded in the entanglement of forms of the universe, and will never come to know the Grand Beginning."[190] Tao-sheng found in *lei* a link with the indigenous Chinese tradition and saw no contradiction between his use and the original.

One Ultimate

One of the major themes resonant throughout the commentary is the process of the three vehicles evolving into One. This theme, which can be regarded as the leitmotif of the *sūtra*, especially appeals to Tao-sheng, as he returns to it time and again. The proposition can be considered from two perspectives. In a narrow, textual context, the numbers refer to three kinds of discipleship; namely, *śrāvaka*, *pratyekabuddha*, and *arhant* (or *bodhisattva*). In broader terms, *three* symbolized multiple approaches to one single reality or truth, necessitated by the inevitable divergence in the perceptive powers of the multitudinous beings (*chung-sheng*).[191] In this respect, the three vehicles can be seen as merely symbolical.

In the text, all vehicles, each of which is claimed to be a right channel to the Buddha's path, are assigned proper places in the Buddha's didactic program. This was done to prompt Chinese Buddhists to come up with frameworks for classifying the Buddha's diverse teachings (*p'an-chiao*). Its original form is put forward by Tao-sheng, breaking down the Great Sage's career chronologically into four *Dharma* wheels (*-cakra*): of the good and pure, of the skill in means (*fang-pien*/*upāya*), of the true and real, and of the no remainder (*wu-yü*/*anupadhiśeṣa*).[192] Implicit in *Dharma* wheels is the process of three turning one—a dialectical *one* in the sense that three are synthesized into One. *One* stands for a unity,[193] which explains in part why the One and the process itself are described identically as "mysterious" (*miao*).[194] Apart from the schema as a whole, "two" or "three" vehicles can be termed *false* or *unreal*.[195] Tao-sheng generally follows the line of argument advanced in the *sūtra*, and yet there is an added shade of emphasis laid more on the positive aspect of the interim stages than on the negative one. The position of the *sūtra* is succinctly illustrated in the passage: "Therefore the Buddhas, with their expedient power, make distinctions in the One Buddha Vehicle and speak of three.[196] Tao-sheng interprets the passage thus: "Although he spoke of three, he always talked of the One."[197]

In its broader sense, in many respects this is parallel to the concept of the *One* as defined in Taoist thought. The *Tao-te ching* (Chapter 42) puts *One* at the penultimate point, right after *Tao*, portraying it as the fountainhead of all forms of existence. As Wang Pi puts it, "One is the beginning of numbers and the ultimate of things."[198] It is the point of return as well as departure.[199] It is that which the Sage has embraced.[200] Similar patterns of description are readily recognizable in Tao-sheng's writing. Some of these may be seen contextually as connected with particular vehicles, but in many cases they assume the form of a metaphysical statement with universal applicability. Typically, "*Li* is nondual and *Tao* of the Tathāgata is one."[201] Here one can assume that there is a clear connection between the *One* and *one*; the *One* is not merely symbolical, but it still implies oneness. This already has become evident in Wang Pi. On the passage in the *Tao-te ching*, Chapter 42: "*Tao* produced the One. The One produced the two. The two produced the three. And the three produced the ten thousand things," Wang Pi comments: "The ten thousand things have ten thousand different forms, but in the final analysis, they are one. . . . If there is One, there are two, and consequently three is produced."[202]

Tao-sheng returns to the theme that all diversified approaches are destined to return to or merge into One Ultimate or one unity.[203] In Tao-sheng's system (as in neo-Taoism), therefore, *One* denotes not only the final goal to be achieved,[204] or the original source to return to,[205] but also the unity of all varied and seemingly conflicting elements.[206] *One* conveys the monistic picture of reality, which is borne out by the extensive use of the term by Wang Pi, also a monist. Likewise, the ultimate goal to be pursued by beings is union with the one.[207] Tao-sheng, like the Taoists, talks of returning to the One ultimate (397a) or the origin. For Tao-sheng, salvation, after all, consists in regaining the original state of being. In the sense of unity, *One* is similar to his use of *Great*;[208] Tao-sheng in fact uses them interchangeably. Similarly, Lao Tzu designates the "master" source to which a myriad of things belong, namely, *Tao*, which also gave birth to One, as the *Great*.[209]

Middle Way (Chung-tao)

One expression for the One Vehicle is "the *Tao* of the middle and right" (*chung-cheng-chih-tao*).[210] Is its source Buddhist or Chinese? It can be traced to either source. The same can be said of *chung-tao* or *cheng-tao*,[211] which can be taken either as abbreviated forms of this phrase or as separate phrases. In the Buddhist context, the term *chung-*

cheng can be broken down into two characters, the first standing for the middle path (*chung-tao/madhyamā-pratipad*) and the second for the eightfold right (Skt. "noble") path (*cheng-tao/āryamārga*), consisting of as many right (*samyak*) ways. Then is *chung-tao* in Tao-sheng's vocabulary used in the first sense?

The expression and the idea involved are traceable in Chinese scriptures. The idea of middle, in the sense of (golden) mean, occupies a salient place in Chinese thought. It is engraved in the classical texts, particularly in the *Doctrine of Mean* (*Chung-yung*). On moral and psychological planes, the golden mean points to a moderate position, avoiding extreme behavioral patterns,[212] or it points to an indeterminate unstirred state of feelings,[213] which largely is compatible with what the Buddha meant by the middle path, the theme of his first sermon, in which he taught the avoidance of two extremes of asceticism and hedonism. On the philosophical plane, *chung* signifies what is central, in the sense of exactly hitting the point right.[214] The two implications may not necessarily be distinguished, for moderation, by extension, means what is proper and right, which in turn must be in accord with what is ultimately true in the absolute order.

A text imbued with the notion and its related terms more explicitly than any other is the *I Ching*. It is replete with the terms *chung*, *chung-cheng*, *chung-tao* and other variants. The right-in-the-middle state is symbolized by the most balanced arrangement of the lines of the hexagrams, either "middle" or "right." Hence, the prime target of the *I Ching* practice consists in obtaining the mean or the middle way. Wang Pi translates this occult expression into functional and philosophical terms: "*Chung* means not overdoing (or no mistake); *cheng* means not depravedness."[215] By being situated in the right-in-the-center position, one achieves a state of harmony (*chung-ho*) between the opposing elements (*yin* and *yang*), such as inside and outside, firm and yielding, fine and coarse, and movement and quiescence, most of which are found in Tao-sheng's vocabulary. The state of equilibrium (*ho*), according to the *Doctrine of the Mean*, refers to the condition in which the feelings, once aroused, are balanced in due proportion, whereas *chung* means the state before the feelings are welled up.[216] The welling up of feelings should be contained in equilibrium with changing situations: this is called *the timely mean*.[217]

When Tao-sheng speaks of "advancing toward the middle way,"[218] the style of the expression and the mode of the action involved are similar to those found in the *Doctrine*. Yet the subject of the action is not exactly the same. In the Confucian text, it is a Sage that always is "in harmony with the Way" (*chung-tao*),[219] whereas Tao-sheng refers to *li* in his commentary as that which is in harmony with the Way, suggesting that this is so through the varied means applied by the compassionate Buddha.

A variant or emphatic expression of "middle" or "middle way" is found in the cryptic expression *huang-chung* ("yellow and middle").[220] *Huang* is identified with the earth in the *I Ching*[221] and with the middle[222] by Wang Pi. In Tao-sheng, as in its sources, the word refers to some kind of centrality or ultimate limit in the physical or metaphysical sense, alluding to "golden mean." Tao-sheng apparently has drawn on the *I Ching*, for the passage containing this phrase—"*Li* has extended to (or penetrated) the yellow and middle (or center of the earth)"—resembles in style and terminology the passage from the book, "The superior man is in the yellow and middle and has penetrated *li*. . . extended to the four limbs." Yet here again is the essential difference in their approaches: Tao-sheng's Sage, represented by Avalokiteśvara, is altruistically oriented, and *penetration* (or propagation) has to do with the salvation of other beings, whereas *penetration* in the *I Ching* remains impersonal and unrelated to others.

With regard to the idea of middle, Tao-sheng for the most part takes the Chinese frame of expression and instills therein a Buddhist content. Yet the concept does not necessarily agree with the metaphysical implication of middle path (*madhyamā-pratipad*) in the Buddhist Mādhyamika philosophy.[223] Rather, it uniquely reflects the Buddha's methodology as seen in the *Lotus*.

Tao

The term *tao*, after *li*, is the second most recurrent (101 times) abstract noun in the commentary. By the time of Tao-sheng, *Tao* had become a universal term inseparable from Chinese life and used by every system of thought, including Buddhism. It is present in the translated *sūtra*, though limited to some technical terms in compound forms. *Tao* occured profusely in the writings of the contemporary Buddho-Taoists, as a term more fully developed than *li*. By contrast, Tao-sheng's contribution to the further development of the concept of *Tao* is limited, and certainly less pronounced than his contribution to *li*, as far as the commentary is concerned.

The term *tao* as found in Tao-sheng's text embraces a wide spectrum of connotations, ranging from "path" (*mārga*), a usage already in the *sūtra* translation by Kumārajīva, to a self-subsistent abstruse entity. As in the case of *li*, two domains are considered, the relative and the absolute. Yet, upon deeper analysis, these two domains are interrelated, in that the higher, universal one subsumes the other. The frequent use of the word in the sense of the universal *Tao*, in fact, is overwhelmingly greater than in the sense of the particular *tao*. Again, as in the case of *li*, a particularized *tao*, especially the *tao* of "Śākyamuni," "the Tathāgata," "the Buddha," "the bodhisattva," or "the *Saddharmapuṇḍarīka*," does not conflict with the universal *Tao*. After all, "the *tao*(s) of various Buddhas is (are) the same"[224] and "one," and "the *Tao* is ubiquitous"[225] (397b17 et passim). Suggestive of a normative, ontological entity, the *Tao* denotes both the goal to be sought and the means or path by which one achieves the goal. Thus what can be said of the *Tao* also fits *li*. There is a shade of difference, of course, but what is attributed to one is generally applicable to the other. They are both "mysterious," "far reaching," "unobstructed,"[226] and so on. They are particularizable as *this* or *that*. In a few places they are juxtaposed within the same sentence or passage.[227]

The term *Tao* thus provided Tao-sheng with yet another functional tool for the exposition of his foreign Buddhist tradition. *Tao* by then was a fully developed concept, and with a wide scope of implications it could accommodate Buddhism. However, Tao-sheng prefers *li*, a concept not then as fully developed as *tao*.

Concluding Remarks

Tao-sheng was typical of Chinese Buddhist thinkers of the period in his dependence on words taken from the indigenous Chinese philosophical tradition. Yet, it can be said that his dependence on Chinese concepts is less marked than that of his contemporaries. For example, the *Pien-tsung lun*, an anthology of arguments on Tao-sheng's theory of enlightenment, as well as Seng-chao's writings, are both more densely filled with Confucian and Taoist terminology than Tao-sheng's writings. Everywhere, one encounters the universal, common use of the terms, *li* and *tao*. Another example is the *li*-related idiomatic expression *ch'iung-li chin-hsing* (the tracing of *li* to the consummate realization of one's nature), found in the text (398b4) and in the *I Ching* as its classical source.[228] Many Buddist writers of that time[229] cited this dictum as if it were a catchword describing the ultimate goal of religious practice.

Within the garb of borrowed language does Tao-sheng remain a Confucio-Taoist or does he emerge as a Buddhist convert? Tao-sheng normally did not lose sight of Buddhist doctrine. This does not mean, however, that his loan words were entirely free from their original, non-Buddhist meanings. Rather, the indigenous and Buddhist traditions are blended through Tao-sheng's vocabulary. In a given loan word, the original, indigenous Chinese meaning may interact with Tao-sheng's Buddhist use of the word in such a way that both are enriched or newly illumined and clarified. A good example is the concept of *li*. Because of its broadness, *li* lent itself well to Tao-sheng's uses. As he uses it, it is no more than a designation for something real or ultimate, that which underlies the Buddha's statements in the *sūtra*. Thus it is no different from the coinages of the later Mahāyānists in India—for example, *Tathatā* (suchness), *Tathāgata-garbha* (the womb of the Thus Come One), or *Ālayavijñāna* (the storehouse consciousness), let alone the concept of the "true self" represented in the *Nirvāṇa Sūtra*.

Tao-sheng did succeed, as Itano Chōhachi writes, "in surmounting Lao(-tzu)-Chuang(-tzu)'s thought."[230] His success was no less than that of his contemporaries, such as Hui-yüan and Sheng-chao, whose grasp of some of the Indian Buddhist doctrines, of Mādhyamika in particular, is deemed to have been unsurpassed among Tao-sheng's peers but whose language is heavily drawn from the Taoist lexicon.

Notes

1. See Translation of the Text, Notes to Preface, note 15.

2. Yet Ōchō finds the commentary structured in six parts. See Ōchō, "Jikudōshō sen . . .", p. 227; summed up in Hurvitz, *Chih-i*, p. 201.

3. See T'ang, *Fo-chiao shih*, II, p. 97. However, Ōchō, "Jikudōshō no hoke shisō," p. 155 treats Tao-sheng as though he had been the earliest commentator to do so. Cf. Sakamoto, *Hokekyō no Chūgokuteki tenkai*, p. 6 (summary in English).

4. Hurvitz, *Chih-i*, p. 81, n. 2.

5. See Fuse, *Hokekyō seiritsu shi*, pp. 244, 263, and 288; Kern, trans., *Saddharma-puṇḍarīka*, Introduction, p. xviii; Winternitz, *History of Indian Literature*, II, pp. 302ff.

6. I am referring to Liebenthal's article "The World Conception of Chu Tao-sheng," *MN*, 12(1956). I will juxtapose most of his translation in the notes to the Translation (Part III).

7. See T'ang, *Fo-chiao shih*, p. 96.

8. For example, *tao* from *mārga*, *fa* from *dharma*, *miao* from *sad*, as well as other nonsubstantives like *tzu-jan* in the sense of "of its own accord."

9. *Fang-p'ien* is a direct rendering of *upāya-kauśalya*, but *ch'üan* is a pure Chinese concept.

10. There are four commentaries that serve as the basic texts of neo-Taoism, by the two founders of the school, Wang Pi and Kuo Hsiang: on the *Lao-tzu*, *I Ching* (in part) and the *Analects*, by Wang, and on the *Chuang-tzu* by Kuo. The primary texts of this analysis are the commentaries on those scriptures, except one on the *Analects*, plus the three scriptures. For the *Chuang-tzu* and the commentary, I have used the *Chuang-tzu chi shih* (hereafter, *CTCS*) (Taiwan, 1972).

11. See T52.266a2.

12. Compare with another significant term *tao*, which occurs 101 times.

13. One who was closest to Tao-sheng in this regard may be Chih Tun (314–366). See Paul Dimiéville, "La pénétration du bouddhisme dan la tradition philosophique chinoise," *Cahiers d'histoire mondiale*, 1 (1956): 19–38, especially 28–31.

14. *CSPS*, 398b2–3. Cf. Kuo Hsiang, Commentary to the *Chuang-tzu* (hereafter, *CCT*), Chapters 3, 4, and 33.

15. *CSPS*, 398b4, and d5. Cf. *I Ching*, *shuo-kua*, Chapter 1.

16. *CSPS*, 406a17 and 407a13.

17. Ibid., 405d3.

18. Ibid., 410c11.

19. See *CSPS*, 402c5, 404c7, 406a12, 408a13, and 410c15. Cf. Kuo Hsiang, *CCT*, Chapters 1, 3, 6, 27, and 33.

20. Wing-tsit Chan, "The Evolution of the Neo-Confucian Concept *Li* as Principle," p. 57.

21. See Kuo Hsiang, *CCT*, Chapter 2 (*CTCS*, p. 40): "Every being has (its own) *li*, every affair has its own proper raison d'être." Also see Chapter 22 (*CTCS*, p. 325).

22. See ibid., Chapters 4, 5, 26, and 27. *Li* also is identified with *tzu-jan* (self-sonness) in Chapters 14 and 15, Wang Pi, commentary to the *Lao-tzu* (hereafter, *CLT*), Chapter 42. Tao-sheng follows the suit in his commentary to the *Nirvāṇa Sūtra* (hereafter, *CNS*), T37.377b10.

23. *T'ien-li* originally in the *Chuang-tzu*, Chapter 2 (*CTCS*, p. 56), found in Kuo Hsiang, *CCT*, Chapters 2 (*CTCS*, p. 28), 6(*CTCS*, p. 104), 15, and 23.

24. *Chih-li*, ibid., Chapters 2, 6, and 14.

25. Wing-tsit Chan, *A Source Book in Chinese Philosophy* (Princeton, N.J., 1963), p. 317.

26. Kuo Hsiang, *CCT*, Chapter 2.

27. See Wang Pi, *CLT*, Chapter 42.

28. Traceable to Kuo, *CCT*, Chapters 2 (*CTCS*, p. 38), 6, 14, and 33, it is originated in Wang Pi; see Wing-tsit Chan, "The Evolution of the Neo-Confucian Concept *Li* as Principle," pp. 58–59.

29. Chan believes that the idea was already established in the *Chuang-tzu*, see ibid., p. 49. Tamaki Kōshirō, *Chūgoku Bukkyōshisō no keisei* (Tokyo,

1971), vol. 1, p. 77ff., holds that an archetype of the theory is found in Tao-an (312–385).

30. *CSPS*, 402c10.

31. For example, the word *mi-lun* ("fills up and covers") is found in *I Ching*, *shuo-kua*, pt. 1, Chapter 4, and *wu-chih* occurs in the *Tao-te ching*, Chapter 28; *Chuang-tzu*, chs. 6 and 11; CCT, Chapters 3 and 6.

32. See *CSPS*, 402c9f., 403b14f., and 405d14.

33. Cf. Tao-sheng's Commentary to the *Nirvāṇa Sūtra*. T37.380c2: "The true *li* is self-so." See Kuo Hsiang, *CCT*, Chapter 5 (*CTCS*, pp. 91 and 99).

34. In seven places (402b17, 403d6, et passim), plus one presented as the word from the *sūtra* (T9.17b17), which is an adverb, rendered as "of themselves," or "of its own accord," in Hurvitz's translation, *Scripture of the Lotus Blossom of the Fine Dharma* (New York, 1976), pp. 89–90.

35. See, for example, *CCT*, Chapter 2 (*CTCS*, p. 121).

36. See *CSPS*, 403d6.

37. See *CNS*, T37.549a29f.; Liu Kuei-chieh, "Chu Tao-sheng ssu-hsiang chih li-lun chi-ch'u," p. 358.

38. See *CSPS*, 405d3, 407c12f.

39. The word *fan* occurs in ibid. *Pen* is used in 409d16 and 407c13. Cf. *Pien-tsung lun*, T52.226c7, where *fan-pen* is found. Also see *CNS*, T37.380c–81a in which Tao-sheng dwells on the two notions. A synonym, *kuei*, is used with *pen* in 407c13. A synonymous phrase *fu-kuei* is used similarly in the *Lao-tzu*, Chapter 28. Wang Pi identified *fu*, the twenty-fourth hexagram in the *I Ching*, with *fan-pen*. See T'ang Yung-t'ung, "Wang Pi's New Interpretation of the *I Ching* and *Lun-yü*," translated by Walter Liebenthal, *Harvard Journal of Asiatic Studies*, 10 (1947): 147; Fung, *History of Chinese Philosophy*, vol. 1, pp. 180–181; Hajime Nakamura, *Ways of Thinking of Eastern Peoples: India, China, Tibet, Japan* (Honolulu, 1964), p. 278. The idea of return to the original nature is touched on also in Kenneth Ch'en, "Neo-Taoism and the Prajñā School during the Wei and Chin Dynasties," p. 33.

40. *CSPS*, 401a12.

41. *CSPS*, 408b16 and 409c3.

42. See Kuo Hsiang, *CCT*, Chapter 2 (*CTCS*, p. 33): "The myriad beings in the heaven and earth are all existent in conformity with their proper allotments." For Wang Pi's idea of it, see T'ang, *Fo-chiao shih*, II, p. 144.

43. The term also occurs in *CSPS*, 412b15.

44. *CSPS*, 408d4 and 409c3.

45. *CSPS*, 398b9, 408d3, and 409c3.

46. *CSPS*, 412b4. For the rendering of the term *chi*, see Wing-tsit Chan, *Source Book*, p. 784.

47. See *CSPS*, 398c3, 406b5, and 412c15.

48. What appears implicit becomes explicit in the word "true-self" (*chen-o*) found in Tao-sheng's commentary to the *Nirvāṇa Sūtra*, T37.452a, 453b, and 463a. For the notion of self-nature, see the *Lao-tzu*, Chapter 17; Nakamura, *Ways of Thinking*, p. 278.

49. *CSPS*, 408c16.

50. Wing-tsit Chan, trans., *The Way of Lao Tzu* (Indianapolis, 1963), p. 184. Cf. *Chuang-tzu*, Chapter 22 (*CTCS*, p. 319).

51. *CCT*, Chapter 2(*CTCS*, pp. 38–39).

52. See *CSPS*, 406a14.

53. *CSPS*, 404a4.

54. *CSPS*, 400d10.

55. See *CSPS*, 410c11.

56. See *CSPS*, 410c14.

57. See *CNS*, T37.461a4f.; Liu Kuei-chieh, "Chu Tao-sheng," p. 359.

58. *CSPS*, 410c12. See also Tao-sheng's biographies in T55.111a2ff. and T50.366c14ff., which quote him as saying: "The purpose of words is to explain the Truth (*li*), but once Truth has been entered, words may be suspended, . . . few have been able to see the complete meaning. Let them forget the fish-trap and catch the fish. Then one may begin to talk with them about the Way (*Tao*)." (Derk Bodde, trans., in Fung, *History of Chinese Philosophy*, vol. 2, p. 270).

59. Section 4. Translation of the section is found in Hellmut Wilhelm, *Change: Eight Lectures on the I Ching* (New York, 1960), pp. 87–88.

60. See *CSPS*, 399b18.

61. See 399b14 and d17, 401a15 and b12.

62. The two facades of language, negative and positive also can be traced to the metaphysical schools of Wei and Ch in times prior to Tao-sheng's period to which Wang Pi and another neo-Taoist, Hsi K'ang (233–262), belong. See Fung, *History of Chinese Philosophy*, vol. 2, p. 184f.

63. See, for example, *CSPS*, 398d16, 411c18, 412b1ff.

64. Two terms are found in the same phrases in synonymous situations in *CSPS*, 398d13, 405d3, 407a3, c3, d12, 409d2, and 411c6.

65. See Arthur F. Wright, "Review of A. A. Petrov's Wang Pi (226–249): His Place in the History of Chinese Philosophy," *Harvard Journal of Asiatic Studies*, 10 (1947): 83.

66. T'ang Yung-t'ung, "Wang Pi's New Interpretation of the *I Ching* and *Lun-yü*," pp. 145–146.

67. Found in *CSPS*, 398d4 and 402c10. The compound *li-shu* "calendrical number" means "fate," but here, in this context, "course" or "consequence," is located in the *Chuang-tzu*, Chapter 27, and the *Confucian Analects*, Book 20, Chapter 1.

68. *CSPS*, 398d4. Cf. 402c10.

69. *CSPS*, 396d10.

70. Chapter 17.

71. See Chan, "The Evolution of the Neo-Confucian Concept *Li* as Principle," p. 64. For an overall survey of this point, see T'ang Chün-i, "Lun Chung-kuo che-hsüeh ssu-hsiang-shih chung li chih liu-i" (On the Six Meanings of *li* in the History of Chinese Philosophical Thought), *New Asia Journal* (*Hsin-ya Hsüeh pao*) 1, no. 1 (1955): 65–77.

72. To one of them he wrote a commentary, see T55.111b5. P. C. Bagchi, *India and China* (Westport, Conn., 1971), p. 102, says: "The real Buddha was the Dharmakāya Buddha, the Tathātā or the ultimate reality which could not be defined in words."

73. *CSPS*, 409c. T'ang Chün-i, "Lun Chung-kuo," 75ff., lists *k'ung-li* as one of the six meanings of *li*.

74. Found in the *Chuang-tzu*, Chapter 33 (*CTCS*, p. 463).

75. See Fung Yu-lan, *A Short History of Chinese Philosophy*, Derk Bodde, ed., (New York: 1966), p. 8.

76. *CSPS*, 407d5. Its variations are found in 397d1, 398a13, 399d2, 407d5, and 411c18.

77. *CCT*, Chapter 5 (*CTCS*, p. 85); Chapter 21 (*CTCS*, p. 316).

78. *CSPS*, 401b16.

79. The voice hearers (*śrāvakas*) of Hīnayāna are classified as belong to the category of the inside whereas the bodhisattvas of Mahāyāna belong to the outside, the inside having a limited area of application and the outside having an unlimited area. See *CSPS*, 397b15f. and 399d2.

80. Listed as one of the five features characterizing Kuo Hsiang's philosophy in Wing-tsit Chan, *An Outline and an Annotated Bibliography of Chinese Philosophy* (New Haven, Conn., 1969) p. 55.

81. *CSPS*, 401d10.

82. The monistic perspective can be traced as far as the *Chuang-tzu*, see Chapter 33. The monistic tendency of Tao-sheng viewed from a slightly different perspective, see Itano Chōhachi, "Dōshō no tongosetsu seiritsu no jijō," *Tōhō gakuhō*, Tokyo, 7 (1936): 164ff.

83. *CSPS*, 399d7.

84. *CSPS*, 412b4.

85. Tao-sheng is quoted in the eulogy for him by Hui-lin, T52.265c: "Teaching (*chiao*) is what causes conversion (*hua*) to happen. If one binds oneself to teaching, then one will be deceived into pseudo-conversion." So, there is a clear distinction between *chiao* and *hua*, which are sometimes coupled to make a compound found in *CSPS*, 411b8 and the *sūtra* (t. 927c), "teaching and converting," (Hurvitz, *SLFD*, p. 158).

86. See the *Chuang-tzu*, Chapter 13, the first few paragraphs; Kuo Hsiang, *CCT*, Chapter 6 (*CTCS*, p. 121); transl. found in Chan, *Source Book*, p. 333.

87. Found in the *Chuang-tzu*, Chapters 6, 12, and 14.

88. *CSPS*, 398b3f.

89. *CSPS*, 398d15f.

90. See, for example, the *Chuang-tzu*, Chapter 13 (*CTCS*, p. 216): "snare him in entanglement." (Watson, *Complete Works*, p. 151); *CCT*, Chapter 1 (*CTCS*, p. 7), Chapter 12 (*CTCS*, p. 182).

91. *Fan-nao*, see Yabuki, "Tongogi no shushōsa Jikudōshō to sono kyōgi," in Ōno Seiichiro, ed., *Bukkyōgaku no shomondai* (Tokyo, 1935), p. 792.

92. *CSPS*, 409d6.

93. *CSPS*, 404b7f.

94. *CSPS*, 405d14 and 404b7, cf. 410b18.

95. See Kuo Hsiang, *CCT*, Chapters 7(*CTCS*, p. 130), 9 (*CTCS*, p. 152), 12 (*CTCS*, p. 187), and 14 (*CTCS*, p. 234). The term also is found in Fukunaga Kōji, "Sōjo to Rōso shisō," in Tsukamoto Zenryū, ed., *Jōron Kenkyū* (Kyoto, 1955), pp. 259ff.

96. "Hataraki," Fukunaga, ibid.

97. Found in Tao-sheng's vocabulary too: *CSPS*, 412b15.

98. See *CSPS*, 402a4.

99. See *CSPS*, 403d18.

100. Legge, *The Texts of Taoism*, (New York, 1959), I, 70.

101. A. Rump, trans., *Commentary on the Lao Tzu by Wang Pi*, p. 82.

102. *CCT*, Chapter 1 (*CTCS*, p. 11).

103. *CCT*, Chapter 28 (*CTCS*, p. 426).

104. See *CSPS*, 401b1.

105. See *CSPS*, 403d18 and 407b2. Also see 401a11, 407b11, and 412d4.

106. See *CSPS*, 399c3 et passim.

107. *Ch'üan* occurs in at least nine places (399c4 et passim) whereas *fang-pien* is rarely found (400d11).

108. *CSPS*, 412a15. The word *wu-fang* "with no set pattern" is found in the Chinese texts associated with neo-Taoism in similar contexts. See Kuo Hsiang, *CCT*, Chapter 12 (*CTCS*, p. 184); *I Ching*, *Hsi-tz'u chuan*, I:4, "has no spatial restriction" (Chan, *Source Book*, p. 266).

109. CSPS, 403a9 and 17, 404b15, and 412b4; cf. 402b18.

110. *Hsi-tz'u chuan*, I:8 and 10; Chan, *Source Book*, p. 267 ("subtle activating force"), also see p. 784; appears also in the *Chuang-tzu*, Chapter 18, rendered as "mysterious workings" (Watson, *Complete Works*, pp. 195 and 196), and "great machinery (of evolution)" (Legge, *Texts of Taoism*, II, p. 10). Note that the world *chi* found in the *Chuang-tzu* is interchangeable with the word proper; see *T'su-hai* (Hong Kong, 1976), p. 486. Compare the phrase in *CSPS*, 404c5 with the similar one in *I Ching*, *Hsi-tz'u chuan*, I:5.

111. Chapter 7 (*CTCS*, p. 135f.), Chapter 18 (*CTCS*, p. 277), et passim.

112. *CTCS*, p. 135f.

113. *Chi-ken* or *ken-chi*. See *BGDJ*, I, 424c.

114. T9b and c et passim.

115. CSPS, 401a, and 406c.

116. In Chapter 6. Legge, *Texts of Taoism*, I, 238; Watson, *Complete Works*, p. 78: "Deep in their passions and desires, they are shallow in the workings of Heaven."

117. *CTCS*, p. 103; cf. p. 137.

118. *CTCS*, p. 208 (Chapter 13).

119. *CTCS*, p. 24 (Chapter 2). Cf. *CTCS*, p. 10 (Chapter 1).

120. *CSPS*, 398c3 and 403d1.

121. Note that Ch'eng Hsüan-ying (of T'ang), who annotates Kuo Hsiang's comments in the *CTCS* version, glosses *chi* in the *Chuang-tzu*, Chapter 7, with "spiritual *chi*," in *CTCS*, p. 136.

122. See the actual usage of the term in light of the contexts in *CSPS*, 397b8, 398c3, 400a5, 403d1, and 404b17; cf. 396d11f. Hajime Nakamura glosses it as *hazumi* (impetus, momentum, or chance) in *BGDJ*, I, 213b14ff.

123. Cf. *CTCS*, p. 208.

124. See *CSPS*, 296d11f., 398c3, 406b5, and 412c15f.

125. See *CSPS*, 397b8 and 412b2.

126. See Zürcher, *Buddhist Conquest*, vol. 1, p. 91.

127. *Chuang-tzu*, Chapter 22: See Kuo Hsiang, *CCT*, Chapter 12 (*CTCS*, p. 184): Chapter. 24 (*CTCS*, p. 378); *I Ching*, *Hsi-tz'u chuan*, I:10.

128. See *CSPS*, 406b1, 410c10, and 397b8.

129. See *I Ching,* Hexagram 31 (Hsien).

130. Fu (*-ying*): *CSPS*, 403a9, d1, and d17f, and 404d14; *Ch'ui* (412a18), if we take it to mean "stoop" as Chan, *Source Book*, p. 266, translates the word in *I Ching*, *Hsi-tz'u chuan*, I:4, but it sounds more accurate in the sense that Legge takes it (*I Ching*, p. 354): "by an ever-varying adaptation" (he completes [the nature of] all things without exception). The two phrases with the term, of Tao-sheng and the *I Ching*, are strikingly similar, which will be discussed later.

131. See *I Ching*, *Hsi-tz'u chuan*, II:2.

132. See *CSPS*, 398b2.

133. See *CSPS*, 409b11ff.

134. See *CSPS*, 398b2.

135. Ibid.

136. CSPS, 412b4f.

137. *I Ching*, *Hsi-tz'u chuan*, I:10.

138. T9.8a22, 9a22.

139. See *CSPS*, 399d6, 401c7, 402a2 and d8, 410b11, 411b4, and 412d5.

140. In Chapter 32, Watson, trans., *The Complete Works of Chuang-tzu*, p. 356. It should be noted that the expression *chien-chi*, "to combine saving (with the original mission or objective)" (CSPS 402a1) is found here in the same paragraph.

141. Chapter 37, Arthur Waley trans., *The Way and Its Power* (New York, 1958), p. 188.

142. *CLT*, Chapter 10; Rump, *Commentary*, p. 31: "If you do not inhibit the nature of things, things will succeed by themselves."

143. *CCT*, Chapter 18.

144. *CSPS*, 402a1f. Cf. *Mencius*, Book VI, part A, 7:3: "The sage and we are of the same kind," D. C. Lau, trans., *Mencius* (Harmondsworth, Eng., 1970), p. 164.

145. See, for example, the title of chapter 2, *Chuang-tzu*.

146. A. C. Graham, "Chuang-tzu's Essay on Seeing Things as Equal," *History of Religions*, 9, no. 1 (August 1969): 144. See also Kuo Hsiang, *CCT*, Chapter 2 (*CTCS*, p. 34). The Buddhists and Buddho-Taoists of the period were steeped in this line of Taoist thinking. For example, see expression by Hui-yüan (334–416) in T52.33a7f. See also *Pien-tsung lun*, compiled by Hsieh ling-yün (385–433), T52.226a1: Nonetheless, the notion is not unique to the original Chinese thought; see H. V. Guenther, *Philosophy and Psychology in the Abhidharma* (Berkeley, Cal., 1976), p. 241: "But before reality, which is one experience, is split up into subject and object, there is oneness with reality and sameness (*samatā*) of self and object. It is this oneness of reality in Buddhism which is the root of infinite compassion toward suffering mankind."

147. See Fung, *Chuang-tzu, A New Selected Translation with an Exposition of the Philosophy of Kuo Hsiang* (Shanghai, 1933), pp. 11, 45, and 61.

148. *P'ing-teng* (*samatā*), *CSPS*, 396d18.

149. *CSPS*, 397a2.

150. CSPS, 412a18. Cf. 401c7.

151. *I Ching*, *Hsi-tz'u chuan*, I:4. Translation adopted from Chan, *Source Book*, p. 256f., except "employs diverse approaches" instead of 'stoops' for the word *ch'ü*. See also Kuo Hsiang, *CCT*, Chapter 2 (*CTCS*, p. 37).

152. *Ta-tz'u*: 401c7, 402d18, and 403a13; *ta-pei*: 404a15, 407d18, 409b7f., cf. 404a18 and 408d18.

153. See the *Chuang-tzu*, Chapter 25 (*CTCH*, p. 381). "The love of the sage for others. . . . His love of others has no end, and their rest in him has also no end: all this takes place naturally" (Legge, *Texts of Taoism*, II, p. 116). Nonetheless, the sage remains free of desire, as is said in the *Chuang-tzu* (Chap-

ter 32) that to desire to save other belongs to the exercise of petty man's knowledge. And the neo-Taoists make it clear: "the Neo-Taoists defined the Sage as follows: 'Not even to have desire for this state of non-desire, this is the constant quality of the Sage. To have desire for this state of non-desire, this is the distinguishing quality of the worthy.'" (Kenneth Ch'en, "Neo-Taoism and the Prajñā School during the Wei and Chin Dynasties," p. 40). But ironically, Tao-sheng describes the Sage explicitly as having the desire to save beings (*CSPS*, 397d6; see 402a2 and a15).

154. Chapter 27. See Waley, *The Way and Its Power*, p. 117, note 4.

155. *BHSD*, p. 14.

156. The word in this sense (like *indriya*) is found in the technical terms "five or six feelings" (406d), which can be either Buddhist or Confucian-Taoist. But in wider, sectarian contexts, *indriya* may connote such virtues as confidence (*śraddhā*), strenuousness (*vīrya*), inspection (*smṛti*), absorption through concentration (*samādhi*), and discrimination (*prajñā*). See Guenther, *Philosophy and Psychology*, p. 240.

157. *CSPS*, 406c3.

158. *CSPS*, 408b14f.

159. *CSPS*, 404b15; cf. 404b9f.

160. *CSPS*, 404c11 and 405d4. Cf. *Pien-tsung lun*, T52. 225c8ff. Liebenthal renders the word with "vice" in *The Book of Chao* (Peking, 1948), p. 188. Chan uses "human desire" in "The Evolution of the Neo-Confucian Concept *Li* as Principle," p. 51. Also see Chang Chung-yüan, *Tao: A New Way of Thinking* (New York, 1977), p. 137: "passions".

161. *Pen*: *CSPS*, 403d17 and 404d3.

162. *Huo*: *CSPS*, 404b17.

163. *CSPS*, 407c5.

164. *CSPS*, 404b17.

165. *CSPS*, 401d15.

166. Cf. "innate tendency," T'ang, "Wang Pi's New Interpretation," p. 144.

167. See, for example, *CSPS*, 405d4.

168. *Shih-ch'ing*, *CSPS*, 398b7, c16; 401b12; *ch'ün-ch'ing*, 398c6, 407d13; 408c12. Cf. *shih-hsin* 398c8.

169. E. Conze, *Buddhist Thought in India* (Ann Arbor, Mich., 1969). p. 80.

170. For a comprehensive discussion on the question, see T'ang Yung-t'ung, "Wang Pi sheng-jen yu-ch'ing i shih" in his *Wei Chin Hsüan-hsüeh lun kao* (Peking, 1957) pp. 72–83, especially p. 72f. (The quotes of page 72 are translated by D. Bodde in Fung, *History of Chinese Philosophy*, vol. 2, p. 188).

171. See Fung, ibid., pp. 32, 161, 414, and 161.

172. See T'ang, "Wang Pi," p. 83. Cf. *The Doctrine of the Mean* (Chung Yung), Chapter 1.

173. See, for example, *I Ching*, *Hsi-tz'u chuan*, II:12.

174. See Kuo Hsiang, *CCT*, Chapter 18 (*CTCS*, p. 272).

175. *CSPS*, 400b4, 403c8, 406c4, and 411c18. Cf. *I Ching*, *Hsi-tz'u chuan*, I:1.

176. *CSPS*, 308d6, 399a6, 402a3, 14 et passim. See *Pien-tsung lun*, T52.225a11. *Yü* is listed in the neo-Confucian glossary as one of seven feelings.

177. See *Tao-te ching*, Chapter 3.

178. *CSPS*, 406c4; 405b1, 3.

179. *CSPS*, 398d16.

180. *CSPS*, 406a16f.

181. See note 91. Nevertheless, the word is found separately in *CSPS*, 405d and 406c. In 397d5, Tao-sheng identifies *lei* with *fan-nao (kleśa)* from the *sūtra*, T9.1c7.

182. *CSPS*, 406a17. Cf. 397d5f and *Pien-tsung lun*, 225c24.

183. *CSPS*, 400c7.

184. Quoted in T'ang, "Wang Pi sheng-jen," p. 72. A similar usage is found in the *Chuang-tzu*, ch. 33 (*CTCS*, p. 468).

185. *CCT*, Chapter 18. (*CTCS*, p. 292) Cf. *CSPS*, 406a17.

186. *CCT*, Chapter 33 (*CTCS*, p. 475).

187. *CCT*, Chapter 12 (*CTCS*, p. 182). Cf. *Pien-tsung lun*, T52.225c27.

188. Ibid., T52.225c and 227b.

189. Tao-sheng uses the word *chang* "veil" or "hindrance" in 400b10, 40218, 402b14, and *fan-nao*, "depravity" (*kleśa*) in 400c, 405d, and 406c. Cf. *huo*, "delusion" (*moha*) in 402a8 and 407c7.

190. In Chapter 32 (*CTCS*, p. 454). See Watson, *Complete Works*, p. 356; Legge, *Texts of Taoism*, II, 206. See also *CTCS*, p. 454; *Pien-tsung lun*, T52.225a12.

191. See *CSPS*, 401d8.

192. See *CSPS*, 396d13ff.

193. See *CSPS*, 399b10, 400c1, and 400d16.

194. See *CSPS*, 400b6, 402b12, 403b14, and (for the process) 398b13.

195. See *CSPS*, 396d16, 397a4f., 399b5f., 399d3, and 399d6.

196. T9.7b26f.; Hurvitz, *SLFD*, p. 31. Cf. Kern, *Saddharma-Puṇdarīka*, p. 42: "the Tathagatas, &c., use, skillfully, to designate that one and sole Buddha-vehicle by the appellation of the threefold vehicle."

197. *CSPS*, 400c13.

198. Wang Pi, *CLT*, Chapter 39, translation in Rump, *Commentary*, p. 119. Cf. Kuo Hsiang, *CCT*, Chapter 12 (*CTCS*, p. 190).

199. See *CLT*, Chapter 42.

200. *Tao-te ching*, Chapters 10 and 22; Kuo Hsiang, *CCT*, Chapter 33 (*CTCS*, 461).

201. *CSPS*, 405d3f. Cf. 411d9.

202. Rump, *Commentary*, p. 128.

203. See *CSPS*, 396d17, 397a1, 400a14f, 400c3, and 407a6. For one unity, see 400a14 and 403d2, and compare *Tao-te ching*, Chapter 47 and *I Ching*, Hsi-tz'u chuan, II:5.

204. Cf. *Tao-te ching*, Chapter 39: *te-i* (also see *Chuang-tzu*, Chapter 22).

205. See *CSPS*, 399d11: *Yüan-chi*, "source ultimate." For Wang Pi, Tamaki Koshiro, *Chūgoku Bukkyō*, p. 190, identifies Wang Pi's philosophical orientation with the search for "the (ontological) root-source."

206. See the *Chuang-tzu*, Chapter 12 (first and second paragraphs). A. Waley, *The Way and Its Power*, p. 171, translates *sheng-jen pao i* (*Lao Tzu*, Chapter 22): "The Sage clasps the Primal Unity." (See also p. 153). ibid., p. 191, speaks of the idea of unity discernible in Wang Pi's commentary to the *Confucian Analects*.

207. See C. S. Medhurst, *The Tao-teh-king* (Wheaton, I11., 1972), p. 10. The act of "union" is described in the term *kuei* (to return, belong to, or merge), used commonly by Tao-sheng (*CSPS*, 397a) and neo-Taoists.

208. *CSPS*, 396a, 399b8d, et passim.

209. See Chapters 34 and 42.

210. *CSPS*, 398b11.

211. *CSPS*, 402c17. *Cheng-tao* in 398b15, 403d6, and 401a10. For the first term, cf. the *Chuang-tzu*, Chapters 6, 12, and 26.

212. See the *Doctrine of the Mean* (Chung-yung), Chapter 6: "He took hold of their two extremes, determined the Mean," (Legge, *Confucius*, p. 388); the *Confucian Analects*, XIII:21 (Legge, ibid., p. 272).

213. See the *Doctrine of the Mean*, Chapter 1 (Legge, ibid., p. 384).

214. See the *Confucian Analects* XI:13: "hit the point" (Legge, ibid., p. 241). See also Fung Yu-lan, *The Spirit of Chinese Philosophy*, E. R. Hughes, trans., (London, 1962), p. 106: "Now this means reaching the point of being exactly good, by which is meant achieving the Mean."

215. On Hexagram *sung*, *Chou-i ching i t'ung-chieh* (Taipei, 1974), p. 62. Cf. *CSPS*, 403d18f. For the term "nondepravedness" (*pu-hsieh*) see the *Confucian Analects*, II:2 (Legge, ibid., p. 146).

216. Translated also in Fung, *The Spirit*, p. 107.

217. *Shih-chung*, the *Doctrine of the Mean*, Chapter 2; in the *I Ching*, Hexagram *meng* (Whilhelm, *Change*, p. 406; Legge, *Confucius*, p. 217).

218. *CSPS*, 402c17. This should be considered along with the fact that Tao-sheng is glossing the phrase *hsing-pu p'ing-cheng* ("whose tread is even", Hurvitz, p. 60) (T9:12c23), *p'ing* and *cheng* being recurrent terms in the *I Ching* and other texts.

219. Chapter 20, Chan, *Source Book*, p. 107; Legge, *Confucius*, p. 413.

220. *CSPS*, 411c12f.

221. See *I Ching*, Hexagram *k'un* (in *Wen-yen*:) . . . *ti-huang*, p. 395; Legge, *I Ching* p. 421. See also remark by Wilhelm: "Yellow is the color of the middle and moderation." Cf. Kuo Hsiang, *CCT*, Chapter 2 (*CTCS*, p. 52).

222. See *Choui-i ching i t'ung-chieh*. pp. 39 and 42.

223. Tao-sheng is said to have been exposed to the Mādhyamika doctrine in the earlier stage of his life and he wrote a commentary on one of the *Prajñāpāramitā Sūtras*, *Hsiao-pin* (*Aṣṭasāhasrikā*; see T55.111b). There are some traces of the doctrines in the commentary (see Ōchō Enichi's article on Tao-sheng in Sakamoto, ed., *Hokekyō no Chūgokuteki tenkai*, p. 158f.), but they are far from being significant.

224. *CSPS*, 412a13.

225. *CSPS*, 397b17 et passim.

226. Found in *CSPS*, 389b15 (for *tao*) and 403b14 (for *li*).

227. At least in nine places including 398d, 400a, 405d, 407a, c, and d, and 411c.

228. *Shuo-kua*, Chapter 1. See Wilhelm and Baynes, *I Ching*, p. 262: "By thinking through the order of the outer world to the end, and by exploring the law of their nature to the deepest core." Legge, *I Ching*, p. 423: "They (thus) made an exhaustive discrimination of what was right, and effected the complete development of (every) nature." Fung, *History of Chinese Philosophy*, vol. 2, p. 445, note (translated by Bodde): "They plumbed *li* to its depths and completely penetrated the nature." Cf. Kuo Hsiang, *CCT*, Chapter 31 (CTCS, p. 448): *ch'iung-li chih-ming* which can be regarded as an abbreviation of the sentence concerned in full, *ch'iung-li chin-hsing i-chih-yü-ming*.

229. For the quotes of the four-letter phrase by Tao-sheng's contemporary Buddhists including Seng-chao and Seng-jui, see Part III, ch. 1, note 42 (for the phrase in 398b4).

230. Itano Chōhachi, "Eon Sōjo no shinmeikan o ronjite Dōshō no shinsetzu ni oyobu," *Tōyō gakuhō*, 30, no. 4 (1943): 503–504.

Chapter 8

CENTRAL IDEAS

Main Themes

Let us first review the main theme of the *sūtra* itself: The three vehicles do not exist; in reality there is only One Vehicle, meaning that "there is only one form of Buddhism."[1] Hurvitz nonetheless draws out two component points.[2] One is that "there is only one Path to salvation, not three." The other is that "the Buddha is not to be delimited in time or space, or indeed in any finite terms." The first point portrays the three vehicles as a device to attract beings to Buddhist practice. In the *sūtra*, this first theme is dominant and has more significance, being illustrated by four parables (Chapters 3, 4, 7, 8). The second theme is confined to only two chapters (16 and 17; in the *CSPS*, 15 and 16) and is supported by one parable (Chapter 16).

In the *CSPS*, no theme is more pronounced than the three–One relationship. It is certainly the central leitmotif of the text. This is evident from the start. Every component of the title of the *sūtra* is explained by Tao-sheng in terms of the proposition that the three unreal vehicles eventually give way to the real One Vehicle. Three of his four *Dharma* wheels are based on this idea.

How this theme is immersed in the individual chapters can be seen in the first paragraph of each chapter, which serves as its synopsis. Even earlier, however, we find in the beginning of Tao-sheng's introductory chapter a tripartite breakdown of the *sūtra* according to this theme of three vehicles. In his analysis, the first thirteen chapters of the *sūtra* show that the cause of the three vehicles is really the cause of the One. The next eight chapters indicate that the effect of the three is to be identified with the effect of the One. The remaining six chapters are concerned with believers of the three in the process of becoming adherents of the One.

The theme of three in One appears as the topic of the initial paragraphs of eleven chapters (1, 2, 4, 5, 7, 10, 13, 14, 17, 18 and 22). They are the key chapters, in Tao-sheng's view. The balance of the *sūtra* contains parables to explain this main proposition, stories of some bodhisattvas in their past lives, and so on. The first seven chapters of the commentary-text are the longest. The first four chapters make up the first of two volumes of the commentary. Even the third chapter, not included in the eleven chapters cited earlier, on the parable of the burning house, deals in its seven segments with an allegorical story in which three carriages promised to some children are presented in the form of one big carriage or vehicle. In his mixed application of the terms *carriage* and *vehicle*, Tao-sheng does not draw a sharp line between the simile and the fact implied therein.

Although most of the chapters of the *CSPS* focus on the theme of three in One, many related matters also are treated, involving such problems as the underlying theoretical ground for the process of three transforming into One and its epistemological implications. This concentration on a single theme and related ideas suggests that the commentary is not a literary account but rather a thematic exegesis.

Why did the Buddha have to take the circuitous route of three vehicles in order to lead beings to the One Vehicle? Tao-sheng offers as answer the inequality of innate intellectual faculties in individuals. The idea is Tao-sheng's elaboration of what is loosely suggested in the *sūtra* (9b). It is further reinforced by his notion of an innate triggering-mechanism for the enlightenment process (396d, 398c, 401a, 406b–c, 412a). This in turn gives rise to the concept of "expediency in means" (*upāya*), which receives Tao-sheng's special attention and articulation with the help of the Chinese term "exigency" (*ch'üan*): The limited capacities of sentient beings forced the Buddha to invent a device that would tempt them on to the path to enlightenment; hence, the figurative nature of the multiple vehicles as opposed to the literality of the One Vehicle.

How the three vehicles are related to the One Vehicle, however, is a complicated matter. Although Tao-sheng relates essentially what is stated or suggested in the *sūtra*, he sounds somewhat ambivalent with respect to whether the vehicles have a negative or positive value. Three vehicles, being of exigent and temporary value, are identified as false, whereas the One is identified with what is real. Nonetheless, whereas the three (396d) or two (399d) are false, and thus antithetical to the One or Greater Vehicle (399c), they are ultimately subsumed by the One and cannot properly be thought of apart from this synthesis with the One (401b). One thus may call it a dialectical relationship. The process is best expressed in the word *miao* ("mysterious" or "wondrous").

This interpretation has the mark of Tao-sheng's own philosophical speculation. The *sūtra* has this to say: "the Buddha, by resort to the power of expedient devices, divide the One Buddha Vehicle and speak of three" (13c).[3] It thus seems to view the three vehicles positively. This is, however, a liberal rendering by Kumārajīva of the original text, which has no word for three.[4] The *sūtra* does not mention falsehood, as it only refers to the way the Buddha guides beings through the enlightenment process rather than to the device actually used. As the Buddha states in Chapter 3: "Śāriputra, just as that great man, first having enticed his children with three carriages and then having given them only one great carriage . . . is yet not guilty of falsehood, though he first preached the three vehicles in order to entice beings, then conveyed them to deliverance by resort to only the One Great Vehicle."[5]

In connection with the parable of the burning house (Chapter 3), Buddhists in the Sui and T'ang period were to raise the question as to whether there three or four carriages are involved in the story. The "great man" lures his children out of their burning house with the promise of three carriages, one ox drawn, one goat drawn, and one deer drawn. However, outside, the children find only a single great ox-drawn carriage. At issue here is whether the two ox-drawn carriages are identical or different. The problem gave rise to two theories: one involving three carriages, the other involved four. What is Tao-sheng's position? Really, the issue is whether or not the bodhisattva vehicle symbolized by the first ox-drawn carriage is identical with the Buddha vehicle, symbolized by the final, great ox-drawn carriage. Some modern scholars regard Tao-sheng as the progenitor of the three-carriage tradition, on the ground that the two other vehicles, voice hearers (śrāvakas) and pratyekabuddhas, are deemed by him to be false.[6] The following passage, which comments on the *sūtra* with respect to the phrase "[There are not other vehicles,] whether two (or second) or three (or third)" (7b3), is cited to support this view.[7] "'Two' means the second vehicle, and 'three' the third vehicle. Naturally it follows that there is no 'first,' either. The first does not contradict that which causes 'Great' [Vehicle], hence, it is not nonexistent. [Yet], since there is neither 'second' nor 'third,' 'first' is gone too" (400b18). Here the first vehicle refers to the bodhisattva vehicle. It is accorded a special status: This vehicle more than any other vehicle is to legitimately evolve into the One Buddha Vehicle.

One can also argue that Tao-sheng would not advocate the four-carriage theory, because this would contradict his view of the dialectical synthesis of three into One. Tao-sheng asserts that there are not three separate vehicles, but rather three anticipating the One.

Alongside this main thesis we find another recurrent notion in the commentary: gradual approach in the being's attainment of religious knowledge or enlightenment, which is apparently tantamount to a gradualist theory of enlightenment.[8] It poses an apparent contradiction to Tao-sheng's well-known doctrine of instantaneous enlightenment. Nonetheless, this gradualism is closely bound up with the three-into-One motif. It pictures two stages in the enlightenment process—that of the three vehicles and the One—and denotes a slow progress from the one to the other. A sentient being still at the first stage of the process thus is unable to apprehend the ultimate reality represented by the One Vehicle (400c). The *sūtra* itself clearly proposes a gradual learning process (18a, 19b, 20b, 21c, et passim), and in this regard Tao-sheng does not depart from it.

An Overview of the Internal Structure of the Commentary via the Term *Li*

By focussing on a single term and subjecting it to a comprehensive examination, we may gain an overview of the commentary. For this task there is no word better suited than *li*. It is ubiquitous, recurring 139 times, far more than any other significant term, including its closest synonym *tao* (101 times). *Li* may be seen as a key to the inner structure of Tao-sheng's thought as well as to his understanding of the *sūtra*.

In some cases it might seem appropriate to paraphrase or translate the term loosely, such as "in principle" or "it stands to reason that," but in the text *li* functions generally as an abstract noun. Translated variously in different contexts as "principle," "norm," "reason," "(cosmic) order," *li* perhaps was the most important philosophical concept in the Chinese tradition.[9] *Li* has no Sanskrit equivalent, at least as it was used by Tao-sheng.[10] Unlike the term *tao*, which is used for such technical terms as "path" (*mārga*), "(six) forms of existence" (*gati*), and sometimes "truth" (*satya*), *li* does not appear in the *sūtra*.

Syntactical and Contextual Position

The word *li* occurs fairly evenly throughout the text in all but five chapters (those five consisting mostly of a single passage), with its frequency of occurrence proportionate to the size of the chapter. The term rarely is absent from the synopses appearing at the beginning of each chapter. Syntactically, *li* is found in the position either of subject or object. In a complex sentence or equivalent structure, however, the word can be taken to represent an adverbial phrase or similar expression. When used as a corollary, *li* is a substantive and in some cases an adverbial expression. The term, most often stands by itself without a qualifier, though in many cases it is implicitly linked with something suggested earlier.

It remains an open question as to whether the word, when found independent, has the sense of an entity or universal reality. When accompanied by a modifier, qualification appears in three different ways. First, it occurs in the form of a compound. The qualifiers in this category center mostly around the Buddha and related terms including "Thus Come One" (Ju-lai/Tathāgata), "emptiness" (*k'ung/śūnyatā*), "Greater Vehicle" (Mahāyāna), "One Vehicle" (Ekayāna), "transformative teaching" (*hua*), "Saddharmapuṇḍarīka", and "the Buddha." When modified by other terms the particle *of* (*chih*) appears in between, as explicitly demonstrated in two places (403d18, cf. 403b14; 404c8). The adjectives *ultimate* (406b14) and *mysterious* (*miao*) also modify *li* in this way. Second, there are indicative adjectives such as *this* (408c3) and *that* (405a5) modifying *li*, as well as the negative adjective *wu* and other equivalent expressions (407d12, cf. 402b13). Third, the term often is modified by an adjectival phrase or sentence such as "the process of three turning into One" (402c5) and "of what the *sūtra* has elucidated" (410c15).

These patterns of qualification clearly suggest that *li* refers to or exists in a particular thing. There are different kinds of *li*, which are described in various ways. But if we assume an "ultimate" or universal *li*, as postulated in the neo-Taoist system of Wang Pi, then these various *li* simply represent diverse forms of the omnipresent noumenal reality. Particularization, on the other hand, stems from Kuo-hsiang's view of *li*. These two interpretations of *li* converge in Tao-sheng's use of the term.

Predicates, Properties, and Epistemic Implications

The adjectival words and phrases that predicate *li*, especially when it occurs alone without any direct qualification, are numerous and of a wide variety, as typified by expressions like *wide*, *distant*, *recondite*, *profound*, and *fathomless*. It is worth noting that these adjectives are taken from the Taoist and neo-Taoist lexicon, especially from the latter with respect to *li*. Therefore, *li* as envisaged by Tao-sheng may be tinted with the neo-Taoist metaphysics. It is "round", "immeasurable," "beyond empirical calculations" (402c10), and "mysterious." Yet, one can still "approach" (410a12) and "enter" it (409a5f), as if it were a place. Nonetheless, all these can be taken at the same time as the attributes of an abstract metaphysical concept; spatial references are transferred without modification to the mystical, extrasensory spiritual reality. Even the denotation *round* (*yüan*) can give way to the connotation *perfect*.

The object of *entering* can be not only a physical realm but also a spiritual domain. In that respect, *li* resembles *nirvāṇa*, which, as Tao-sheng puts it, one can, like the Buddha, "enter" (401d13). *Li*, like *nirvāṇa*, was thus understood as both a physical and metaphysical concept.[11]

Other verbs objectify *li*, besides the typical *to enter* and *to approach*: *li* is portrayed as something "to perceive," "to be traced to the end," "to know or become enlightened to," "to penetrate," and "to comprehend" (*chieh*). These words suggest an intellectual approach to comprehending *li*, which seems also to fall in line with the Buddhist view. *Li* is seen as requiring a "dark merging" (*ming*, 412d2), meaning an extrasensory intuition into a dark realm. It is so profound and lofty that it cannot be comprehended in a single "sudden step" (408c16) or "one encounter" (401a6), "one enlightenment" (406b13) or "speedily" (410d6); it remains inaccessible or unfathomable to those with superficial knowledge (412d2).

Another important phrase is *to go astray* (or *deviate*) *from* (*kuai*). *Kuai* occurs repeatedly in contexts suggesting the consequences effected by one's departure from *li*: "the preverted state leading to suffering" (403a12) and "delusion" (405d3). Hence, it follows that the process of learning *li* can be translated into the process of unlearning delusion; by turning against delusion one becomes enlightened to *li* (405d3).[12]

In Tao-sheng's use, *li* is not restricted in scope to a particular doctrine associated with the *Lotus* and is not entirely bound by the theme of the three vehicles merging into One Vehicle. In Tao-sheng's interpretation, *li* embraces the fundamental truths (*satya*) and path (*mārga*) the Buddha enunciated upon his own self-enlightenment. In more general terms, *li* has to do with what the Buddha himself "(empirically) merged with (or comprehended)" (406a17).

Li Viewed in Connection with Other Concepts

Purport (*i*)

Li is sometimes connected with *i* ("purport, tenor, or meaning"). *Li* implies a common, universal principle, whereas *i* is the intended purpose or implicit purport involved. An entire chapter (Chapter 3, Parable) is broken down into two major divisions, *i* and *li*. *I* refers to the part prior to the parable proper, and *li* refers to what the parable sets out to expound. *I* here is the overt meaning of the parable; *li* is the real import the story is designed to convey. *I* is explicit; *li* is implicit.

A similar pattern is identifiable in the apposition of *li* and *huai* ("to embrace, harbor") (412b4).[13] As he interprets the title *Avalokiteśvara* (Kuan-yin) ("One Who Observes the Sound of the World") (Chapter

2), Tao-sheng attempts to decipher it in terms of *li* and *huai*. He defined the *li* of the title as "all penetration" (or "universal propagation [of the *sūtra* or doctrine]," *t'ung*),[14] and the *huai*, the "embraced" implication, as "universal salvation." Here, Tao-sheng finds in the title, or rather reads into it, a personification of the Mahāyāna ideal of universal salvation with the accompanying mission of propagating the message of the *sūtra* (or with the "penetrating" [and sympathetic] "observation" [of all beings]). Like *li* and *i*, *li* and *huai* complement each other, describing a whole picture of the meaning of a given object. The difference between the two is too subtle to define; it lies somewhere between denotation and connotation.[15]

Li thus can be tentatively defined as something real or true lying behind symbols and expressions. The *li* of this kind is probably the most basic or typical *li* and can be traced to a distinct line of the indigenous tradition involving the philosophical issue represented by the terms *name* (*ming*) and *reality* (*shih*). These terms will be discussed later.

Linguistic Medium

In Tao-sheng's view, words cannot adequately draw out just what *li* is or what it symbolizes; *li* transcends words (404a4). Yet, rather than dwell on its ineffable nature, Tao-sheng focuses on the pragmatic need for words and symbols to serve as a kind of expedient, particularly for those who have not yet "seen" *li* (410c11). Words are to *li* what "traps and fishnets" are to animals and fish: once the job of delineating *li* is fulfilled, words are of no more use (410c12). The utility of words is epitomized in the Buddha's speeches, which fully express the nature of *li* (406a14, b11). In this and similar cases, *li* remains a final norm with which words are to comply. The *li* underlying different speeches and *sūtras* thus is all of identical "taste" (*rasa*) (399d1, 406a2) and "tenor" (397a1). In the temporal context, *li* represents actual facts mirrored in the recorded words of the *sūtra* (397b2); what is preached about *li* also can conveniently be codified in a charm (*dhāraṇī*) (412b10).

Facts Involved (*shih*)

Li is often found with *shih* or "wordly affairs or facts" in syntactical apposition or in compound or parallel construction. *Shih* later would become an important term in the Hua-yen philosophy, where *shih* and *li* are inseparably interrelated. *Li* and *shih*, when occurring in the same passages, similarly are predicated: "*li* is deep while *shih* is great" (411d6); "*shih* and *li* are both abstruse" (396d5). In this regard *shih* shares or reflects the multidimensionality of *li*. Yet in other passages *shih* is defined as "borrowed material" or "worldly imagery" serving to manifest the intangible *li* for the as yet unenlightened. Thus, *shih* is a teaching aid subservient to *li* and belongs to the category of expediency in means. Included in this definition of *shih* are the Buddha's supernatural wonders (408b15) and parables (401a6).

Suffering (*k'u*, *duḥkha*)

As observed earlier, *li* is seen as a remedy for suffering (397a3, 402b6). By turning one's back on *li*, one is led to delusion (405d3) and suffering (403a12) as one becomes immersed in desires (*tṛṣṇā*) (403a16) and attachment (399c13). As far as *li* in this context is concerned, Tao-sheng's interpretation remains firmly rooted in the basic framework of Buddhism. One can then easily identify *li* with the fundamental doctrines and truths espoused by the Buddha. *Li* thus extends beyond the principle of diversity in unity, the theme of the *sūtra*, to include the Buddhist teaching as a whole. In a more generalized sense, it can also be said that *li*, as the opposite of "evil" (408d16), encompasses the "good" (402c10), suggesting that *li* stands as the summun bonum or supreme good.

Tao

The word *tao* can be singled out as the term most closely related to *li*. They are similar in many ways, including grammatical function, usage and general import. It is unclear whether Tao-sheng sometimes uses them synonymously, but often finding the terms together, side by side, one can assume that they are not completely synonymous, because this would be redundant. By Tao-sheng's time, *tao*, unlike *li*, had already found its way into the Chinese Buddhist glossary. Some of the terms from the *sūtra* frequently quoted in the commentary that use *tao* include: "(five or six) states of existence" from the Sanskrit word *gati*;[16] "path" from *mārga*; "heretics" (literally, "eccentric or unorthodox path") from *tīrthikas*; "supreme (or unexcelled) path" adapted from *anuttarasamyaksaṃbodhi* ("unexcelled enlightenment"); and, probably, "middle path"[17] from *madhyamā-pratipad*. Of these, the term *path*, besides referring to the original source of the word (i.e., the fourth truth (*satya*) (406c13) of the Four Truths and Eightfold Path, which make up the contents of the Buddha's first sermon after enlightenment) also appears in compounds with words like *Buddha* and *bodhisattvas*, as well as independently, sometimes modified by particles and adjectives. It is hard to distinguish the *tao* derived from the Buddhist *mārga* from the *tao* derived from indigenous Chinese sources.[18] However, as far as actual substance is concerned, they may not be far apart: In Tao-sheng's system of thought, the *tao* of Buddhism can be seen as the embodiment of the universal *tao*. The same can be said of *li*.

Similarity also is visible in the predicates the two words share. *Tao*, like *li*, is "recondite," "mysterious," "profound and wide." Being "lofty," *tao*, too, covers three dimensions, as well as sharing *li*'s "mysterious" quality, though the expression *shen* ("deep"), frequently predicating *li*, is not found with it. The pattern "*li* is deep and *tao* is far-off" (407a3) abounds in various transpositions.[19]

In numerical terms, *tao* is "one and the same," and "unpolarizable" (cf. 400d15). It is also omnipresent (398b15), and free from obstacle and blockade (398b16). Concerning how it is "grasped," *tao* is the object of verbs such as *to know*, *to enter*, *to exhaustively trace*, and *to propagate* (or penetrate), which are all used for *li* as well.

The attributive adjectives or nouns for *tao* are the same as, or synonymous with, those for *li*. The indicative adjectives, including *this* and *such*, also are used for *tao*. Like *li*, (402c8) *tao* is modified by the phrase "of (the process of) three (vehicles) first One (Vehicle) later" (405c12). All these qualifiers indicate the diversity of the term *tao*. The range of qualification and spectrum of application of the term *tao* appears to be somewhat wider than those of *li*, probably due in part to the longer history of *tao*'s Buddhist usage. Yet the patterns of usage for *tao* are generally comparable to those for *li*.

The syntactical parallelism of the terms *li* and *tao* seems to indicate a larger scope for *li* than that circumscribed by the Buddhism of the *sūtra*; for, as it appears in Tao-sheng's commentary, the term *tao*, especially when unaccompanied by a qualifier, does not always remain a specific Buddhist technical term. Both *li* and *tao* often are used to represent the fundamental, essential reality. Sometimes, however, *tao* and *li* are defined more narrowly as specific technical terms from Chinese classical sources, as can be seen in the various expressions and idioms involving the two terms. (This will be discussed in Chapter 10.)

The two terms nevertheless often appear interchangeable, although *tao* is not applicable in the way *li* is, as the essential principle or truth underlying a given word or statement. Otherwise, however, the differences between *li* and *tao* are subtle. The two terms complement each other, together conveying a full picture of Tao-sheng's reality. It seems that *tao* tends to refer more to the external, whereas *li* refers to the internal. They also can be seen as form and content, respectively: If *tao* is the religious form, then *li* is the philosophical content. *Li* deals more with abstract substance, whereas *tao* deals more with the concrete aspect. From another point of view, *tao* is the path, way, or means leading to the goal that is *li*. Thus, as far as Buddhist practice is concerned, one can achieve enlightenment whether the focus is on *tao* or *li*. The two terms can be distinguished theoretically but may not differ practically.

In this respect, "perfecting the *tao*" (397c18) becomes identical with "enlightenment to *li*" (405d3), for, in the final analysis, "to consummate *tao*" (406c17) would not differ in substance from "to consummate *li*" (398b3).

Li and the Process of Enlightenment

As mentioned earlier, *li* is posited as the object of the noetic process of "understanding (or enlightenment)" (*wu*). It is also the object of such verbs as *to encounter* (401a6), *to grasp* (406b13), *to climb up* (or reach) (408c16). However, these often are found in expressions stressing the inaccessibility of *li*, in which *li* is depicted as impossible for beings to reach or grasp "speedily" or "at once." What makes enlightenment possible is the universal and all-pervasive, "profound," "deep," and "mysterious" nature of *li*, whereas the distance between beings and *li* is widened by the "murkiness" of beings (400c6). Typically, "*li*, being so recondite, is hard [to fathom] at one encounter" (401a6). What is thus in evidence throughout the text is nothing short of gradualism in the process of enlightenment. The position is fused with a much-cited Taoist dictum, as Tao-sheng declares: "*Li* cannot be arrived at instantaneously. . . . One should decreases [the existential crust covering up the real essence of being] and further decrease it until one reaches the point of no decrease" (408c16).

This gradualist view seemingly contradicts what Tao-sheng is well known for having advocated so fervently; namely, the doctrine of instantaneous enlightenment. At issue is Tao-sheng's understanding of *li*, which is a key word for determining the kind of process involved in the attainment of enlightenment. Faced with this apparent conflict between what one finds here at first glance in the commentary and what one can gather from other sources, one must strive to reconcile the sources themselves. For example, could it be that *li* as used in the commentary concerns a level of consciousness short of "enlightenment" in its fullest sense? In the commentary, *li* often seems to be less than ultimate comprehension, as the verbs connected with it often imply. But the range of nuance of both *li* and its verbs appears to embrace mystic apprehension.[26] Also, the various adjectives predicating *li*, such as *dark*, *wondrous*, *recondite*, and *profound*, invariably reinforce this interpretation. In terms of the schematized stages of enlightenment, *li* as expounded in the *Lotus* encompasses the tenth stage (*bhūmi*) (410c15), the acme of the process.

Li's position as the tenth *bhūmi* can effectively rule out the possibility that *li* is not the object of ultimate enlightenment. This leaves the possibility that Tao-sheng simply contradicts himself or that Tao-sheng may have shifted his initial position on the issue of enlightenment.

However, there is no record of such a momentous shift, one that would have been sure to create heated debate.

Another possibility is that the ideas in the commentary may not necessarily represent Tao-sheng's original thinking. As support for this view one may cite Tao-sheng's acknowledgement, in his Preface to the commentary, where he seems to declare that he only "edited" the materials, both old and new, including a lecture on the *Lotus* given by a certain master in his youth (396d4ff). Unless this statement is dismissable as mere modesty, the question then becomes: How much of his own thought is actually reflected in the commentary? To address this question we must peruse the commentary to see if the other doctrines appearing in it and attributable to Tao-sheng are in their original forms or have been altered in some way to allow the interpolation of foreign material, on the assumption that one doctrine cannot be readjusted without affecting others, especially in an integral system of thought like Tao-sheng's. Any major change in such an important doctrine as his theory of enlightenment would not occur without a ripple effect throughout Tao-sheng's thought as a whole. As stated earlier, however, there is no clear indication that any of these other ideas were modified. For example, Tao-sheng's doctrine of universal Buddha-nature appears unchanged in the text.[21] Furthermore, it is highly improbable that such a radical change in his theory of enlightenment would have gone unrecorded anywhere, unnoticed by any historian, and unmentioned by Tao-sheng himself.

This brings us to the last remaining possibility, that Tao-sheng actually proposes two conflicting theories of enlightenment. However, in reality these two apparently conflicting theories need not remain incompatible. As mentioned earlier, the enlightenment process is more complex than the polarity suggested by the terms *gradual* and *sudden*. The process really is two pronged,[22] so that the two different approaches associated with Tao-sheng may not necessarily be incompatible with each other, in that they represent two different phases of a single complex process. In this way, Tao-sheng's gradualist theory can be seen as referring only to the first phase of the total process, the culminating point of which should be an instantaneous breakthrough, which Tao-sheng somehow does not happen to mention in the commentary. This idea of a sudden breakthrough is intimated, however. The adjective *great* qualifying *enlightenment* (398b9, 407c7, cf. 404c5) is a case in point, as in the sentence "the great enlightenment is not far [from now]" (408b5). Likewise, this two-layer structure of the enlightenment process is in full view in this passage: "Internally he harbors wondrous understanding, and externally he has further practiced the six virtues to be perfected (*pāramitās*), which means that he is advanced in terms of both spirituality and things required to do. Thus, for him right awakening can come [any moment] in a short while ('in the morning or in the evening')" (410d10f.).

It may be debatable whether this "great" or "right" enlightenment is equivalent to "becoming a Buddha" as intended in the *sūtra*, which as seen in the prophecies of Buddhahood granted by the Buddha to a certain group of bodhisattvas (see Chapters 6, 8, and 9) is something that seems to require numerous eons to achieve. But Tao-sheng daringly rejects the terms of this prophecy by demythologizing it, calling it *untrue* (401b5). Tao-sheng thereby brings the process of realization closer to the human dimension.[23] He thus implies that "right" enlightenment does not differ in substance from *anuttarasamyaksaṃbodhi* or "supreme and right enlightenment." Viewed in this way, what *gradual* and *sudden* represent may not be two alternative processes, but two alternative approaches merely to the first half of a single process, the other half being equivalent to what was to be called later *cultivation* (*hsiu*) (though Tao-sheng still uses this term for the whole process referred to as *enlightenment*). The key term *wu* or enlightenment can refer to the whole process or any part of it, or either half, depending on the context; there is no precise division of application.

By stressing gradual cultivation in his commentary, Tao-sheng remains in line with the *sūtra*, which suggests nothing but a gradual approach to enlightenment, with reference either to teaching by the Buddha or to learning by beings (see 400a16), as symbolized in the gradual transition of three vehicles to One Vehicle. The need for a slow process of learning arises out of two causal factors: (1) limited individual potentiality, and (2) the "murky and evil age" of the "final period (or latter day)." The connection between *sūtra* and commentary is in evidence in this comment on the *sūtra* passage telling of the Buddha conjuring up and transforming numerous cosmic realms in gradual order: "Why is [the Buddha's] transformation [of the realms] gradual? The reason why [the Buddha] does so is that he wants to show that *li* cannot be attained to instantaneously. One should grind the coarse until one reaches the fine; one should decrease and further decrease until it reaches the point of no decrease" (408c16). This passage exemplified Tao-sheng's phraseology. Here, he rephrases a section of the story in the *sūtra* with words and phrases borrowed from a Chinese source, the *Tao-te ching* (Chapter 48) in this case, to make clear his own proposition that "*li* is not instantaneously reachable."

This description of *li* is diametrically opposed to that in the theory of sudden enlightenment, because the fundamental ground underlying that theory is that *li* is indivisible and consequently can be comprehended only in its entirety once and for all, not bit by bit.[24] However, as the sudden and gradualist theories turn out to be ultimately complementary, so it necessarily follows that *li* likewise must be taken as a double-faceted conception. The *li* addressed in the commentary may well be one aspect, different from the *li* subject to a momentary transformation. Yet "mysterious" (or "wondrous") *li* seems to account for something more comprehensive than these two aspects and thus requires an equally "mysterious" perception able to encompass both.

Concluding Remarks

Occurring in the text in a large number of cases, outnumbering any other substantive, the term *li* has been found to have a wide range of implications. Tao-sheng may not be credited with making the term a noticeably richer metaphysical medium, let alone coining it. It might be fair to say that *li* was already in the making as a philosophical concept. Nevertheless, Tao-sheng is still unique among his contemporaries in experimenting with such an extensive use of the term. Every possible meaning developed up to his time may have come into Tao-sheng's use of it in the commentary.

However, the primary aim of this section was not so much to study the concept per se as to investigate it as an intermediary and repository of Tao-sheng's understanding of the *sūtra*. Out of this analysis some facts have come to light. In some cases, especially when not modified, the term *li* still remains equivocal or ambivalent. Taken out of context, the term is open to identification with a sort of universal principle of cosmic order. In general, however, it seems that *li*, whether qualified or not, refers particularly to Buddhism, the Buddha, or the *sūtra*. Yet there must be some kind of interconnection between these two areas of meaning: How *li* the particular is related to *li* the universal hinges on the way Tao-sheng views the Buddhist system in respect to the idea of universal reality of truth. To Tao-sheng, Buddhism may appear by no means as claiming the "exclusive path" to salvation.

Also, the motif of the *sūtra*—that three vehicles, representing diverse approaches, merge into One Vehicle—is a subject Tao-sheng constantly focuses on and returns to again and again. This *One* is not restricted to a single thought system, and *three* does not apply only to the diversity of Buddhist thought, just as *li* as conceived by the neo-Taoists is not restricted to one single tradition. In his metaphysical view of *li*, Tao-sheng must have been influenced by the neo-Taoists or school of "Dark Learning"; but he went beyond the scope of meaning developed by the neo-Taoists. If we take *li* to be a basic internal structure penetrating external appearance, Tao-sheng obviously is in the line of tradition culminating in neo-Taoism. The pattern implied is *ming-li* or "names and principle," one of the six meanings associated with *li* throughout

Chinese history, according to T'ang Chün-i.[25] It is a variation developed from the pattern of *ming-shih*, "names and reality." In Wang Pi's system, the pattern is translated into "words" and "idea" (*i*). Tao-sheng breaks this down further into *li* and *i* ("connotation"), with *li* pointing to the more fundamental, deeper substructure as well as denotation.

Li thus remains open to various religious systems. Being simply a pattern or structure, *li* theoretically can accommodate any form of expression or idea. Naturally, in the case of the commentary, what is conveyed through *li* appears almost always to be connected to the words or doctrines of the Buddha as represented in the scripture. In short, Buddhism remains the primary frame of reference for Tao-sheng in his use of *li*. Far from being any transcendental object, self (*ātman*) or a positive entity (*bhāva*), *li* is a convenient interpretative tool or symbol, never conflicting with the fundamental principles set down by the Buddha and Buddhist interpreters. Hence, whatever is said of *li* in the commentary refers, first and foremost, to the *sūtra*.

Notes

1. Prebish, ed., *Buddhism*, p. 102.

2. *SLFD*, Preface, p. xviif.

3. *SLFD*, p. 64.

4. Cf. Kern, *Saddharma-Pundarīka*, p. 82: "in this way, Śāriputra, one has to understand how the Tathāgata by an able device and direction shows but one vehicle, the great vehicle."

5. *SLFD*, p. 64.

6. See Ōchō, "Jikudōshō sen," p. 263ff.

7. See Ōchō, ibid., p. 267.

8. See Hurvitz, *Chih-i*, p. 201: "But the commentary contains two central ideas, the gradualness of the Buddha's teaching method . . . and the idea that differentiations exist on the side of the Buddha's listeners."

9. "Arguable" only with respect to *tao*. Yet, it can be said that *li* is more broadly and commonly based when all three major religions—Confucianism, Taoism, and Buddhism—are considered together. Wing-tsit Chan qualifies it with "in the last 800 years," in "The Evolution of the Neo-Confucian Concept *li* as Principle," p. 123.

10. *DCBT*, p. 359, lists *li* with the Sanskrit words *siddhānta, hetu, pramāṇa*. But more often than not they are associated technically with the doctrines of

the Indian Buddhist Schools, especially in the Yogācara texts mostly translated by Hsüan-tsang (ca. 596–664).

11. Other eminent Buddhist thinkers like Chih Tun (314–366) and especially Seng-chao (384–414) already had identified *li* with *nirvāṇa*; see Chan, "Evolution of the Neo-Confucian Concept," p. 64. Cf. T. Stcherbatsky, *The Conception of Buddhist Nirvāṇa*, p. 25: "(*Nirvāṇa*) has to be realized within oneself. This is possible only when there is complete extinction of craving for sense-pleasure."

12. This resembles the Taoist approach of "reversion," see Chapter 6. The idea underlying the approach is the original purity of human nature. From this one can infer that Tao-sheng's theory of the Buddha-nature is connected to both traditions, Chinese and Buddhist.

13. This combination is unusual, occurring only once. I strongly suspect that the letter *huai* is a copying error, probably of *i* (meaning). Nevertheless, even if it is correct and is Tao-sheng's coinage, there is not much difference in meaning between them.

14. I take the word *t'ung* (occurring also in two more places in b4 and 5) to mean, as is the case in Chapter 17, *liu-t'ung* or "to propagate" rather than "to penetrate," which may sound too general and abstract, let alone out of context. See Chapter 17: 410d14ff., 411a5ff.; cf. Chapter 18: 411a13ff.; Chapter 26: 412d1ff.

15. The two words concerned, *i* and *li* in that order, with a similar implication under discussion, have found their way together into the current Chinese usage in the form of a compound, *i-li*, "the scope or sense of a passage" (*Mathews' Chinese-English Dictionary*, p. 499); "principle, reason" (Liang Shih-ch'iu, *A New Practical Chinese-English Dictionary*, p. 863). However, in the Japanese and Korean traditions the same compound means "sense of duty, sense of honour, obligation, justice" (A. N. Nelson, *The Modern Reader's Japanese-English Character Dictionary*, p. 725), which is akin and so traceable to the meaning "moral principle" taken by a line of tradition including *Book of Rites*, Mencius, and Hsün-tzu; see Wing-tsit Chan, "Evolution of Neo-Confucian Concept," pp. 48 and 51.

16. Cf. "three evil paths of transmigration (*gati*)" (401d1); also see 402a10.

17. *Chung-tao* (402c17) is traceable in the Taoist texts including the *Chuang-tzu*, Chapters 6, 12, and 26. For discussion see Chapter 6.

18. *Mārga* may be implied in "completing the *tao*" (397c18) and "achieving the *tao*" (398c2). Yet *tao* here can be related to the Taoist terminology.

19. See 405d3, 406a6, and 409d2.

20. See Ōchō, "Jikudōshō no tongosetzu," p. 107.

21. See 400b9, 401a13, 408b16, and 409c3.

22. Hypothetically the process as a whole is made up of two factors, "cultivation" (*hsiu*) and "enlightenment" (*wu*), subject to two temporary elements, "gradual" (*chien*) or "sudden" (*tun*). They are coupled in such a way that four alternative approaches are produced. Tsung-mi (780–841) of the Hua-yen school formulated the comprehensive schema of the process for the first time; see his introduction to the Ch'an source book: *Ch'an-yüan chu ch'üan chi tu-hsü*, in T48.399–413.

23. Tao-sheng's "existentialist" approach may be seen in his frequent use of the term *shih-ch'ing* (400a5 et passim), referring to a kind of collective sentiment of a given time or moment, and in his interpretation of the Buddha's prophecies of some bodhisattva's enlightenment in a remote future, which Tao-sheng treats in very rationalistic and realistic terms (see 401b5; cf. 408d8). Cf. *CVS*, T38.392a17: "Enlightenment in Mahāyāna basically does not consist in forsaking the birth-and-death realm in the near in order to seek it again in the far".

24. See *PTL*, pp. 224–228, especially 225a2, b15, and 26ff.

25. T'ang Chün-i, "Lun Chung-kuo che-hsüeh ssu-hsiang shih chung li chih liu-i" ("The Six Meanings of *li* in the History of Chinese Thought"), 65ff.

Chapter 9

TRACES OF TAO-SHENG'S DOCTRINES

As his only complete work available and possibly Tao-sheng's last major writing, the *CSPS* is a rich source for a study of Tao-sheng's thought. Although Tao-sheng's thought has been outlined earlier, a separate investigation of the *CSPS* to determine the extent of the influence of the *Lotus* on his thought also is in order. In our earlier attempt to reconstitute his individual doctrines, we turned to the work only when necessary for additional information. Now, the text will be scanned for any evidence of these doctrines. We may thus determine whether the commentary is an authentic vehicle of Tao-sheng's thought and, if so, how these ideas were integrated with the doctrinary frame of the *sūtra*.

Sudden Enlightenment

The problem involving Tao-sheng's theory of enlightenment viewed in the light of the *CSPS* has been partly dealt with in connection with the concept of *li* in the last section. This important question now deserves a review in the context of the whole text.

In brief, it has been suggested that a key to the question lies with the term *li* and that its indivisible nature presupposes or dictates the instantaneous pattern of illumination. Contrary to such a premise, however, *li*, remaining a key term in the commentary, is posited as something to be realized or awakened to in a progressive fashion. Most typically, as Tao-sheng puts it, "*Li* cannot be apprehended instantaneously; it requires one to grind and further grind the coarse [part of it] until one reaches its nucleus" (408c).

A graduated approach is the dominant position in the commentary. The orientation is abundantly clear either explicitly or implicitly in numerous expressions. A point of emphasis, for instance, is "a tiny bit of goodness" (396d, 297a, 400d). It is obvious that the term denotes a basic step of cultivation toward the goal of salvation. What is required is to accumulate one bit of goodness after another (400d). By the same token, the fundamental faculty one is born with, which enables one to achieve enlightenment, has to be cultivated gradually, finally reaching a point beyond learning or cultivation (409c).

In advocating this gradualist theory of enlightenment, Tao-sheng was constrained by the direction and scope of the *Lotus*, itself built on a gradualist theory clearly stated in Chapter 5: "By gradual practice all are to obtain the fruit of the Way,"[1] and again, "By the gradual cultivation of learning, you shall all achieve Buddhahood" (20b).[2] Yet, how can we account for the discrepancy in Tao-sheng's position? There is no ground to believe that Tao-sheng's had not been exposed to the *Lotus* before he thought of the idea of sudden enlightenment. Already there were four Chinese translations of the *Lotus* and these probably were available to Tao-sheng before Kumārajīva translated it in 406. To say that he realized the basic idea of the *sūtra* and its implications only later is to underestimate his acumen.

One may have to take enlightenment as a process in which two aspects, gradual and sudden, can be found compatible. From this comprehensive point of view, one can identify in the commentary some expressions suggestive of sudden enlightenment. The word for *sudden* does not occur in the text,[3] but we come across such words as *one single* and *great* modifying the word *enlightenment*. The implicit distinction is made even clearer in the expression *enlightenment proper* (410d) and in the context involved. As much as there is "ultimate knowledge (or wisdom)" (397a, 411b) to attain, there must be "ultimate illumination" (411b) to come by.

There also are some other terms by which the two aspects of enlightenment can be distinguished. Tao-sheng talks of ten stages (*bhūmi*) as if the tenth stage is still short of enabling a bodhisattva to realize a certain aspect of reality (409c). One term with significance in association with enlightenment is *fetters* (*lei*), which refers to the bondage of existence or birth and death (*saṃsāra*) and is identifiable with defilements (*kleśa*). Fetters can be subjected to gradual suppression, but their annihilation comes only with the complete realization of *li* (406a).[4]

Viewed from this perspective, the *CSPS* reveals the whole spectrum of enlightenment. Perhaps a more complete picture would involve a schema in which factors such as individual differences in ability are taken into account in considering the two alternative enlightenment processes. A complex schema with several variations was to unfold in the later tradition of Chinese Buddhism, but the germ of such a multidimensional structure already was in the making in Tao-sheng. One may conclude that the prevalence of one aspect of enlightenment over another in the commentary is the result of Tao-sheng's focus. The predominance of gradualism in this text coincides with the thrust of the *Lotus*.[5]

Buddha-Nature

The idea of Buddha-nature is conspicuous in many parts of the text. The Buddha-nature inherent in human beings is a basic presupposition that makes the interaction between the Buddha and beings possible, leading to the lattter's realization of the Buddha's teaching (412b4, cf. 403d1) and, by extension, to their enlightenment. The concept often is phrased in terms of the Chinese philosophical notion of natural provision (*fen*). As Tao-sheng puts it, "Beings are all possessive of the natural endowment of great enlightenment" (all, without exception, are potential bodhisattvas) (409c3, 398b, 400d, cf. 408d3). Parallel statements abound, as typically he declares: "All the beings are bound to become the buddhas" (401a12, cf. 408b16, 408d3).

The notion finds expression in still another Chinese term, *chi*, a subtle triggering mechanism (412b4 et passim). This spiritual spring force is connected with Buddha-nature in that the former represents the outer kinetic stratum of being that can be activated when the occasion arises, whereas the latter refers to the substratum. It is the outer part that gives individual variance from one being to another, whereas Buddha-nature remains universally equal.

Like *li*, the Buddha-nature also is presented as an object of understanding or enlightenment[6] and subject to cumulative learning. Yet although learning may aid one's discovery of one's potentiality for enlightenment, learning by itself is insufficient to bring about enlightenment (409c). Thus, two aspects of the enlightenment process, gradual learning and instantaneous awakening, are indicated here.

Miscellaneous

One can enumerate the subject matter Tao-sheng was associated with in terms of the expository writings attributed to him. The two major subjects just discussed are equivalent to two familiar expositions (*lun*): "One achieves Buddhahood through sudden enlightenment," and

"Buddha-nature is something one will come to possess in the future [when one gets enlightened]." Tao-sheng's other major subjects will be investigated in the following subsections.

A Good Deed Entails No Retribution

What the two key substantive terms, *good* and *retribution*, exactly represent is open to debate; yet. it seems obvious that the terms contain two different dimensions, religious and worldly or sacred and profane. For the sake of simplifying the problem, let us follow what Chi-tsang, the San-lun master, quotes Tao-sheng as saying in his exposition on the subject: "One minuscule part of a good deed counts toward achieving Buddhahood, not making one receive the retribution of birth-and-death (*saṃsāra*)."[7] Here, although *retribution* is defined clearly, *good deed* remains equivocal as to which dimension, sacred or profane, it points to. Nonetheless the "one minuscule part of good deed" made its way into the commentary as an emphatic expression, occurring several times (396d, 397a, 400d).

One bit of good conduct is presented as the initial step toward the goal of ultimate knowledge (396d). It also is the starting point in the diagram of four *Dharma* wheels embracing the Buddha's career as a teacher. Tao-sheng does not spell out the implications of the phrase, but we can infer from the preceding quotation that it may not be of an ethical nature and is likely to be noetic in its linkage with ultimate knowledge. In his interpretation of *good deed*, Chi-tsang speaks of "unattainable good" that results in "unattainable reward" and is linked with ultimate knowledge.

The idea of accumulation naturally denotes progressive advance toward the set objective of (supreme) enlightenment (400d15) and so mirrors the gradualist orientation of the commentary. Tao-sheng links means and goal as if the whole, after all, is the accumulation of its parts (397a2). However, this does not constitute the whole picture. There is something implicit in this process, suggested in the *sūtra*: "Gradually acquiring merit, / Then quickly achieving the Buddha Path" (50b23). Tao-sheng's metaphysical speculation partakes of a holistic tendency. This being the case, it presupposes something more than the accumulation of parts: one single, instantaneous illumination.

There Is [in Reality] No Pure Land in [the Realm of] the Buddha

Tao-sheng tackles the question of the Pure Land in Chapter 15: "The Life Span of the Thus Come One" (410b). He confronts, there, the *sūtra* phrase "My Pure Land is not destroyed" (43c12). Tao-sheng does not flatly reject the concept, but he attempts to prove that the purity symbolized by the Pure Land in fact is not connected to any actual location, because purity and land composed of "stone and sand" are in contradiction. He drives home the point that the Pure Land is as formless as the *Dharma-kāya*, whose life span is not limited to the present one. Thus the Buddha's description of the Pure Land as indestructible represents a ploy to deepen beings' aspirations for enlightenment. Likewise, in Chapter 6, in connection with the Sage, Tao-sheng says that the Sage, having penetrated *li*, is completely free of the fetters that give rise to images like land (406a).

The Dharma-kāya Is without Form

Tao-sheng equates the *Dharma-kāya* with the Pure Land. The predicate *pure*, descriptive of the Pure Land in its essence, can also be an attribute of the *Dharma-kāya* (410b). The notion of *Dharma-kāya*, which was originally a part of the Mahāyāna concept of triune body (*trikāya*), is interwoven with the notions of the Sage and *li*. The Sage, being in an unconditioned state (*wu-wei/asaṃskṛta*), is spatiotemporally omnipresent (409d). The *Dharma-kāya* is the manifestation of *li*, which pervades all *dharmas*, and so it is ubiquitous (404b), penetrating and filling up everything (402d). The substance (*t'i*) of the *Dharma-kāya* illuminates the ultimate (411b).

In Tao-sheng's view, even the Form-body (*Rūpa-kāya*), the corporeal component appearing to beings in response to their needs, is "without fixed, real shape" (409d). It holds more true of the *Dharma*-body. Situated beyond the scope of the form-body, it certainly transcends the representation of form. In suggesting that the *Dharma-kāya* is omnipresent by being formless, Tao-sheng borrows Taoist cosmology and terminology. Here the two perspectives, Buddhist and Taoist, find a synthesis.

On the Two Truths

The two truths (i.e., the absolute or real and the relative or conventional) do not occur by name in the text; nonetheless, the essence of Tao-sheng's conception of them (i.e., the necessity of conventional truth as a means and the eventual identification of the two levels, with the "real" as primary) is incorporated in the *Lotus*. The three vehicles belong to conventional truth, whereas the One Vehicle symbolizes the primary or real, and its convergence with the other level.

Li, also a symbol for the ultimate truth, remains immutably single and same natured despite variegated manifestations. The monistic pattern found in Tao-sheng's metaphysics, traceable to neo-Taoist philosophy, also applies to the concept and is not in conflict with the Buddhist (particularly the Mādhyamika) philosophy.

[The Buddha's] Response [to the Beings] Is Made in [Varying] Conditions (or Avenues of Approach)

Two key terms, *response* (*ying*) and *conditions* (*yüan*), are found separately in the commentary. *Response*, or reflex, which occurs more frequently, signifies what the Sage does after the incipient, subtle triggering mechanism (*chi*) in beings actively transmits (*k'ou*) to him their need. It represents a part of the process of awareness or edification involving an interaction between the Sage and beings. *Conditions* in the Buddhist terminology represents secondary conditions or causes (*pratyaya*) rather than primary causes (*hetu*). Tao-sheng is familiar with the distinction (399d), and in his curriculum of enlightenment, the Buddha-nature represents the primary cause.

The title of Tao-sheng's writing suggests that the Buddha's response requires concrete conditions to express itself; conditions that are bound to vary in accordance with the existential situations of beings. The Buddha's acts of response, according to Hui-ta's quotation of Tao-sheng's treatise, range from "being born in the state of suffering" to "opening up the *Tao* by way of the *Dharma* of goodness."[8] That scope generally applies to the Buddha as he appears in the *sūtra*, and in particular, the last act, opening up the *Tao*, seems to fit into the thrust of the commentary.

Explaining (the Proposition) that [a Bodhisattva], upon Entering the First Thought of the Eighth Stage, Is About (or Wishes) to Attain Nirvāṇa

The title remains somewhat vague. A key may lie in the word *yü*, which usually denotes wish or unfulfilled desire. Does this mean, then, that a bodhisattva in the eighth stage has not yet in reality achieved *nirvāṇa*, in spite of his hope? The word here rather denotes imminency, so the title can read "is on the point of attaining *nirvāṇa*."

Whatever the word may suggest, it is certain that the eighth stage is highlighted here. It is true that Tao-sheng constantly looks to the tenth stage and beyond in search of ultimacy in perception and knowledge (409c, 410c), but he also gives a special meaning to the eighth. A sharp line of demarcation is drawn between the seventh and the eighth stages: The former is compared to a small tree, whereas the latter is a great tree (406a). In the seventh stage a bodhisattva has suppressed the bondage of the three realms and disposed of passions (400b). In the eighth stage, the bodhisattva obtains a higher level of concentration (*samādhi*) (400b) and is even able to prognosticate the future development of the Buddha's preaching (399d).

The stress on the eighth stage conforms with the report that Tao-sheng was the sole advocate of the "Great sudden enlightenment," and other masters were the proponents of the "small sudden enlightenment," whose key stages were the eighth and seventh, respectively.[9]

Notes

1. *SLFD*, p. 108.

2. *SLFD*, p. 109.

3. The word occurs only in the *CNS*, p. 391c2. See Itano, "Eon Sōjo," p. 488.

4. Cf. *PTL*, p. 225cf.

5. Yet, the *Lotus*, too, at one point suggests two aspects: "Gradually acquiring merit, / Then quickly achieving the Buddha Path" (50b23: *SLFD*, p. 284).

6. See *CNS*, p. 547c16. Cf. *CNS*, p. 448c23.

7. T34.505a20.

8. *HTC*, vol. 150, p. 421b.

9. See *HTC*, vol. 150, p. 425b–c.

Chapter 10

CONCLUSIONS

The *CSPS* has extraordinary historical value. As the first commentary ever written on the *Lotus*, a work that itself was to become an increasingly important scripture in East Asia, it set many patterns for later commentators as well as founders of the Chinese Buddhist schools. Most likely, the *CSPS* is the first exegetical commentary in a full-fledged form in Chinese Buddhism. In that respect, it is probable that the work had a far-reaching impact beyond the area circumscribed by the *Lotus*, whether individual writers realized or acknowledged it.

The *CSPS* naturally had a considerable effect on the interpretation of the *Lotus*. The fact that Tao-sheng attached such importance to the scripture by writing a commentary foreshadows the rise of the *Lotus* as a basic text in the Chinese Buddhist tradition. The *Lotus* emerged as one of the most influential of the scriptures of Mahāyāna Buddhism.[1]

Tao-sheng's attempt at schematization and rationalization of the Buddha's diverse, if not contradictory, doctrines under a single teaching program in four units (396d) long prefigures the *p'an-chiao* systems of the T'ien-t'ai and Hua-yen doctrines. This rationalization is linked closely with the motif of diversity in unity, which was to be stressed especially by the T'ien-t'ai syncretists. As for the *p'an-chaio*, the T'ien-t'ai and the Hua-yen Buddhists owed Tao-sheng more than the general idea of it. In their *p'an-chiao* schemas are found the two components, sudden and gradual teachings, for whose conception, as fully seen in the *CSPS*, Tao-sheng was primarily responsible.[2] Thus one may say that the essence of Tao-sheng's understanding regarding the *Lotus* found its way into some of the more important theoretical works in Chinese Buddhism.

It would be presumptuous to claim that Tao-sheng originally conceived all the ideas found in the *CSPS*. Incorporated in the text, as Tao-sheng himself professed (396d), are many ideas and interpretations attributable to his masters. In the analysis of Fuse Kōgaku, the *CSPS* represents the line of tradition interpreting the *Lotus* in the earlier period of its introduction into China.[3] In this respect, Tao-sheng stood in the middle of the tradition and the commentary is a compendium of his own perceptions and the views he inherited.

Finally, the *CSPS*, which in many respects symbolized the culmination of Tao-sheng's scholarship, serves as an invaluable source of his philosophy, especially given the dearth of other extant works.

Situated at a historical juncture of two traditions, the assimilation of both indigenous and foreign philosophical currents was a matter of course for Tao-sheng and his contemporaries, whether they themselves were conscious of it or not. In fact, this syncretism may not be foreign to the *Lotus* itself. After all, the idea of One Vehicle denotes the unity of diverse means and paths. Tao-sheng merely expands this synthesis from one particular thought system to a different cultural tradition composed of multiple systems.

We also can view Tao-sheng, as revealed in the *CSPS*, in connection with many philosophically contrasting pairs, such as language and reality, mysticism and rationalism, theory and praxis. Ontologically, two realms of the absolute and the relative or the sacred and the proface had to be reconciled somehow. By the same token, epistemologically, subitism and gradualism had to find a common ground. For that matter one may say that Tao-sheng forged a compatible unity of "true emptiness" (*k'ung/śūnyatā*) and "mysterious existence" (*yu*). That description more properly refers to the two lines of Mahāyāna tradition, represented by the *Prajñāpāramita Sūtras* and the *Nirvāṇa Sūtra*, respectively. Tao-sheng found a formula for unifying them in the *Lotus*.[4] The *CSPS*, therefore, marks the culmination of Tao-sheng's scholarship.

The main tools of Tao-sheng's text for interpreting Buddhist concepts were Chinese philosophical terminologies, and it has been found that Tao-sheng's essential message remained Buddhist despite his indigenous philosophical vocabulary. There is no evidence that the original content of the *Lotus* was distorted. There might be some idiosyncratic renderings and interpretations, but the fundamental presuppositions of Buddhism remained intact. Rather, the Indian content found a new expression in the Chinese form.[5] At worst, Tao-sheng may be said to have constructed his own pavilion on top of the existing edifice. But it seems fair to say that he helped extend the expanse of the Indian system to a wider horizon. The Chinese terms and patterns in turn were tried out on a different system and proved applicable to another tradition, thus becoming universalized to some extent. Also, the epistemologically oriented Indian thought and the ontologically oriented Chinese thought[6] found a confluence in Tao-sheng. This marks a crucial point, the beginning of a long process of mutual challenge and response, culminating in the rise of Ch'an (Zen) Buddhism and neo-Confucianism.[7]

The cross fertilization resulting from Tao-sheng's ingenious grafting of symbols distinguishes Tao-sheng from other Buddhist writers who tried in various ways to translate foreign concepts using native terms. Most typical of these was the use of the *ko-i* method, a crude way of identifying parallel categories or concepts in Buddhist and Taoist literature, tried at one time or another by Chu Fa-ya, Tao-an, and Hui-yüan. But there is no such direct matching in Tao-sheng's phraseology. It is true that Tao-sheng often interprets Buddhist ideas in terms of the Chinese philosophical framework, but his style is more indirect and is not dominated by a word-for-word equation. By comparison, Seng-chao, also an advanced contemporary thinker, is less able to integrate the Buddhist message and the medium of the Chinese language.[8] Tao-sheng also does not belong to the naive syncretism found in the *PTL*, in which Hsieh Ling-yün, a contemporary neo-Taoist and dilettante Buddhist, interprets Tao-sheng's doctrine of sudden enlightenment as a sort of median theory composed of the Buddha's idea of the attainability of Truth and Confucius' view of the oneness and finality of Truth.[9]

A synthetic orientation pervades Tao-sheng's views of other issues as well. The balance he draws between the gradual process of learning, which is underscored in the text, and the monentary opening up of consciousness, implied there and reported elsewhere, symbolizes a pervading characteristic in Tao-sheng's pattern of thinking. This bifurcated approach stems from his view of the profound depth of reality[10] and human inadequacy. Tao-sheng shares the traditional view that language is not adequate to convey the meaning intended by the Buddha. It follows from the inadequate nature of language that reality has an ineffable aspect that requires transcendental apprehension or illumination.

Tao-sheng's thought, however, is fundamentally rationalistic. By *rational* I mean to contrast it not only with the mystical but also with the mythical and sentimental or emotional. Against the sometimes mythical and grandiose setting of the *Lotus*, Tao-sheng attempts to take a rational approach by interpreting mythological happenings symbolically. This approach is illustrated in his explanations of the glow emanating from the brow of the Buddha (398b), of the efficacy of reciting the name of Avalokiteśvara (Chapter 24), and of charms (*dhāraṇi*) (Chapter 25). Often Tao-sheng does not hesitate even to assert that the Buddha's statements are unreal; he frequently uses the phrase "false (or temporarily valid) saying," in the sense that these statements are devices designed to save beings (401b, 408d, et passim). It should also be noted that Tao-sheng, with respect to the Chinese tradition, inherited the traits of the rationalist line of neo-Taoist philosophy found in Wang Pi and Kuo Hsiang, rather than the sentimentalist line.[11] The term *li*, sometimes rendered as *reason* (or Reason),[12] may be regarded as a key to this kind of thought.

Exactly what methodology Tao-sheng advocates for attaining religious knowledge remains equivocal; yet it might be characterized basically as "noetic illumination,"[13] which involves different sources of knowledge including intuitive perception, reasoning, and testimony. There seems to be nothing in the description of Seng-chao by Robinson that is untenable in regard to Tao-sheng: "In short, he attempted to be rational, he aimed at a mystical goal, and he did not assert that there is any incompatibility between these two objectives." For Tao-sheng, intuition and learning remain essentially complementary to each other.

There is no question that Tao-sheng was equipped with the theoretical apparatus for acquiring religious knowledge. However, this does not mean that he was merely theory oriented rather than practice oriented. He was not just a philosophical theoretician but essentially a religious practitioner, and in the sense that theory is a reflection of practice for Tao-sheng, the two are inseparably interrelated. Thus, Tao-sheng's contribution to Chinese Buddhism is not limited to either theory or practice.[14] We can put Tao-sheng at the forefront of Chinese Buddhism more than any of his contemporaries. He was eclectic in developing many noteworthy areas of thought in accord with, not in deviation from, Buddhist doctrine.[15] Because of his originality and his relative independence from neo-Taoist patterns of thinking, the label *Buddho-Taoist* does not do full justice to Tao-sheng.[16]

Notes

1. *SLFD*, Preface, p. ix.

2. See Hurvitz, *Chih-i*, p. 197, note 1.

3. See Fuse Kōgaku, "Hokke korrū no kenkyū," p. 33.

4. One can also cite the *KSC*, p. 110.c29, stating that Tao-sheng penetrated and synthesized the essentials of both Mahāyāna of Nāgārjuna and Hīnayāna of Saṅghadeva, as one can consider that Hīnayāna and Mayāyāna become unified in the *Lotus*.

5. See Fang li-t'ien "Lun Chu Tao-sheng," p. 171. Cf. Robinson, *Early-*

Mādhyamika, p. 106: "Throughout his life, Hui-yüan strove to pour foreign wine into native bottles, to find "hidden meanings" in *Chuang-tzu* and the *I-ching*, to interpret the Chinese tradition as an upāya by which the Buddhas had prepared the way for the *Dharma*."

6. For this point see Mikiri Jikai, "Jikudōshō no hannyā shisō," p. 47.

7. See Fang Li-t'ien, "Lun Cho Tao-sheng," p. 237; Thomé H. Fang, "The World and the Individual in Chinese Metaphysics," in Charles A. Moore, ed., *The Chinese Mind*, p. 256: "His concept of the importance of Reason in gaining an insight into Ultimate Reality even anticipated the Neo-Confucianism of the Sung Dynasty (960–1279). In short, Tao-sheng was, in the one hand, the culmination of the line of thought in the linkage of Buddhism with Taoism, and , on the other, a bridge over which several schools of Buddhism were to make headway in alliance with some schools of Confucianism"; Itano, "Dōshō no busshōron," p. 23.

8. Cf. Dumoulin, *op. cit.*, p. 60: "In the work of Seng-chao the synthesis of Buddhism and the Chinese view of life was stated convincingly for the first time," and p. 61 on Tao-sheng: "He, too, belongs to the early generation of Chinese Buddhists who combined the Law of Buddha with Chinese thought and thus planted it in Chinese soil."

9. *PTL*, p. 225a, translated and discussed in Fung, *History of Chinese Philosophy*, vol. 2, p. 275ff.

10. See *CSPS*, 299b18f.

11. See Fung, *Short History of Chinese Philosophy*, p. 217.

12. For example, see Thomé Fang, "The World and the Individual," p. 256.

13. Robinson, *Early Mādhyamika*, p. 160. Cf. Hu Shih, "Ch'an (Zen) Buddhism in China," p. 15: "Tsung-mi was very fond of quoting Shen-hui's dictum: 'The one word "Knowledge" is the gateway to all mysteries.' That sentence best characterizes Shen-hui's intellectual approach."

14. See, for example, Thomé Fang, "The World and the Individual," p. 256: "His theory of sudden awakening by reverting to the inmost nature of the mind anticipated the later philosophy of Ch'an (Zen)."

15. See Dumoulin, *op. cit.*, p. 65: "Tao-sheng's doctrine encountered vigorous opposition. . . . In no sense did he feel himself to be innovator; rather, he was convinced that he was defending the true Buddhist teaching in accordance with Buddhist tradition. . . . There is no justification to assume a break with the past."

16. For a view on Tao-sheng's contribution to Chinese philosophy as a whole, see T'ang Yung-t'ung, *Wei Chin hsüan-hsüeh lun-kao*, pp. 112–119, especially p. 119.

PART III

A Translation of Tao-sheng's Commentary on the *Lotus Sūtra*

***Commentary on the Scripture of Lotus of Wondrous Dharma (Miao-fa lien-hua ching shu)*[1] written by Chu[2] Tao-sheng**

PREFACE

The subtle words[3] are so profound and abstruse, being mysteriously separated from hearing and seeing, that those who are led to [seriously] approach them and take an interest in them are very few, whereas those who just [superficially] touch and sneer at them are many. Is it not simply the case that the sacred order (or clergy) (*Tao*)[4] is in complete opposition to the secular order (or layman)?[5]

In my youth, I had the opportunity to attend some lectures[6] sitting humbly in the end row of the hall. I happened to find myself interested in the profound □,[7] which was rich[8] and broad in both[9] letter and meaning and recondite in both the fact involved [as explanatory medium] (*shih*) and [the underlying] principle (*li*).[10]

Because what is stored in one's memory does not [endure] like mustard-seed *kalpa* and rock *kalpa*,[11] one would find it impossible to keep it intact forever. Somehow on the days when there were lectures I just jotted down what I had heard during the day. To give an account of and record what I had heard earlier was like [re]producing a drum sound.[12]

Then, during the third month in the spring of the ninth year of the Yüan-chia era (432 A.D.),[13] while residing at the Tung-lin ("Eastern Grove") Monastery (*ching-she*)[14] on Lu-shan, again I put them in order and rearranged them. In addition, after collecting and consulting various versions, I edited them into one[15] roll.

It is hoped that 'men of virtue'[16] with discriminating enlightenment realize [my] follies [possibly committed here]. I hope they may be led to the outside □[17] (of?) the eternal bondage [of transmigration] by not abandoning the path (*Tao*) due to human insignificance.[18]

[Explaining the Title of the Sūtra]

0.1 **[396d10]** *"The Fine (or Wondrous)*[19] Dharma."

The ultimate image is without form; the ultimate music is without sound.[20] Being inaudible and subtle,[21] and in the sphere beyond the reach of trace[22] and speculation, how can [the *Dharma*] be expressed in terms of form?[23] This is why the *sūtras* are variegated and doctrines are different. Yet, how can *li* [underlying the *sūtras* and doctrines] be of such nature? It is only because the fundamental ability (or subtle triggering-mechanism) (*chi*)[24] and receptivity of ordinary people are not equal; there are a myriad of avenues of approach for prompting enlightenment. Hence, the Great Sage showed different styles of speech [for different groups of people] and manifested various teachings [for them].

0.2 From [the time of his enlightenment] under the bodhi tree till [the time of] his *nirvāṇa*, [the Buddha] preached (or turned) altogether four kinds of *Dharma* [wheels]"[25]

First, the good and pure *dharma* wheel, which begins with the discourse on one goodness,[26] and ends with that on the four immaterial heavens.[27] [Its aim] is to remove the impurities of the three [evil] paths.[28] Hence, we call it *pure*.

Second, the expedient *dharma* wheel. This means that one achieves the two kinds of *nirvāṇa*[29] by means of the constituents of enlightenment with outflows.[30] It [thus] is called *expedient device* (*fang-p'ien*).[31]

Third, the true and real *dharma* wheel. It is meant to destroy the falsehood of the three [vehicles] and thus establish the good ("beauty") of "the One" [Vehicle].[32] Hence it is called *true and real*.

Fourth, the residueless (*wu-yü*/*aśeṣa* or *anupādiśeṣa*) *dharma* wheel. This refers to the discourse on the [dialectical] merging and returning[33] [of the three Vehicles to the One] and thus to preach the mysterious and eternally abiding meaning. [Hence] it is called *without residue*.

0.3 The Sūtra Recognizes the *Greater Vehicle* (Mahāyāna) as Its Source of Origin (tsung).[34]

The Greater Vehicle refers to the universal[35] and great wisdom, and it begins with **[397al]** one goodness[36] and ends with the ultimate wisdom. By *universal* we mean that *li* has no different intentions but merges into the one ultimate.[37] *Great knowledge*[38] refers to just what one obtains at the end [of the process]. Speaking generally of what counts from beginning to end, all the tiny goods accumulated are included there.[39] What does *Vehicle* (*yāna*) mean? Its *li* lies in ferrying all beings to the other shore; the implied idea (*i*) underlying it is to relieve them of suffering (*duḥkha*).[40]

0.4 What is meant by *Wondrous?*[41]

If we talk of all sorts of speeches made by the Tathāgata and the teaching he promulgated, what *sūtra* would not be *wondrous*? The reason why this *sūtra* is specifically designated as *wondrous* is as follows: It is because the expedient three [vehicles] he (the Tathāgata) previously taught are not real, and now he declares that the three are nonexistent. As such, the words (of the *sūtra*) match *li* fully, and the falsity that appeared previously no longer remains. Hence. it is called *wondrous*.

0.5 What is *Dharma?*

In essence (*t'i*) there is nothing that is not *Dharma*; in truth there is no falsehood.

0.6 "Lotus Blossom (Puṇḍarīka)"

This is the term that praises the present *sūtra*. Indeed, of the worldly images none is more wondrous than that of the lotus blossom. The beauty of the lotus blossom is at its glory in the first opening of its bud. At the peak of the first budding, seeds fill inside and colors, fragrance, and taste become fully mature; then we call it *puṇḍarīka*. [The Buddha's] proclamation that the three are existent no more resembles this. When empty talk is gone, what remains is the true speech. As the authentic speech spreads, the fruit of [the three] returning to the One becomes manifested **[397a10]** in it.

0.7 What is *Scripture (Ching/Sūtra*[42]*)?*

The warp (*ching*)[43] and woof of the [conventional] world [etymologically] refers to uncolored silk. The warp and woof as referred to here would manifest their true illumination[44] on those who cultivate this scripture.

1. The text on which this translation is based is that of *Hsü Tsang Ching*, Vol. 150, 396–412.

2. Emend 笠 to 竺.

3. Cf. *logos* (λ'oγoς): "word, speech, discourse, reason" (*The Oxford English Dictionary*); "word, speech, argument, explanation, doctrine, esteem, numerical computation, measure, proportion, plea, principle, and reason" (*The*

Encyclopedia of Philosophy, P. Edwards, ed.,) This word is preceded by 夫, but being an initial particle, renderable sometimes as *now*, or *as regards the topic*, it is left out here in translation.

4. The word *Tao* otherwise will be either left untranslated, especially when it appears to retain some connotations as found in Chinese philosophical systems, Taoism and neo-Taoism in particular, or rendered by *path* or *Path*, also Leon Hurvitz's rendering of the term in the Chinese text of the *sūtra* translated by Kumārajīva, which is equivalent to the Sanskrit word *mārga*.

5. 道而俗反. *Tao* referring to the religious or absolute order, *su* to the relative. It represents a variant on the more standard phrase 道(之)與俗反, which is found *Pien-tsung lun*, T52.225a16 and 226c7; in Tao-sheng's senior contemporary Hui-yüan's writing *Sha-men pu-ching wang-che lun*, T.52.30b10; rendered as "the Way is opposed to common practice" in Leon Hurvitz, "'Render unto Caesar' in Early Chinese Buddhism," p. 100; *Ta-ch'eng ssu-lun hsüan-i*, Chun-cheng of T'ang, ed., *HTC*, 74.13a7. For other variants, see *Chao-lun shu* by Hui-ta, *HTC*, 150.443a10: 道俗相反; attributed to Bodhidharma, the legendary founder of the Ch'an school (sixth century): 理與俗反; in Hu Shih, "P'u-ti-ta-mo k'ao," *Hu Shih Ch'an-hsüeh An*, p. 57: 理與俗反. It is also important to note that a parallel opposition of the two orders occurs in the *Chuang-tzu*, Chapter 28. 此有道者之所以異乎俗("This shows how they who possess the Tao differ from common man"), Legge, *Texts of Taoism*, vol. 2, p. 149. Another typical rendering is "monks and laymen," as in Yampolsky, *The Platform Sutra of the Sixth Patriarch* (New York, 1967), p. 156 et passim.

6. Hurvitz, *Chih-i*, p. 197, presumes it to be Kumārajīva's as does Ōchō Enich, "Jikudōshō sen Hokekyōso no kenkyū," p. 228, and *Hokke shisō shih* (Kyoto, 1969), p. 229; Sakamoto Yukio in Sakamoto, ed., *Hokekyō no Chūgokuteki tenkai*, p. 2. But Liebenthal suspects it to be Fa-t'ai's in "A Biography of Chu Tao-sheng," p. 92.

7. 義 (meaning, doctrine), 談 (discussion), or 經 (*sūtra*)? Note that, as Ōchō points out, Tao-sheng in this commentary sets a pattern for the *hsüan-i* 玄義 and *hsüan-t'an* 玄談 of later Chinese Buddhism. See Ōchō, "Jikudōshō sen," p. 227; Hurvitz, *Chih-i*, p. 201. Anyway, it is obvious in the context that the lacuna refers to the *sūtra* concerned or something germane to it.

8. 愽 is emended to 博.

9. 俱. Ōchō, "Jikudōshō sen," p. 228, reads this as 但 ("yet, merely").

10. 事理 (the worldly affairs or facts and the principle), referring not exactly in this case to the apposition of two orders or realms, relative and absolute, which were to become the key terms in Hua-yen philosophy. Here rather they appear to denote the human affairs taken up as explanatory tools, such as parables and analogies, and the underlying messages or principles, respectively. For more discussion, see Chapter 7.

11. 芥石. Mustard-seed kalpa and rock kalpa: the first letter means "as long as the time it would take to empty a city 100 yojanas square, by extracting a seed once every century"; the second, "the time required to rub away a rock 40 *li* square by passing a soft cloth over it once every century" (*DCBT*, p. 280). Cf. also, the phrase 界石 ("firm as a rock") in the *I Ching*, hexagram Yu and Hsi-ts'u chuan (*Appended Remarks*, hereafter to be referred to as *AR*), Part II, Chapter 5.

12. 鼓生. Yün-hua Jan suggests 鼓 may be a corruption of 豉, so that the phrase means "preservation of food" (literally, "fermenting of beans"). Either way, we can discern the connotation that it is not easy for one to recount in written form in original detail what one heard before. Cf. the word 豉酒 in the biography of Hui-yüan, T50.361b, "bean-wine (a beverage made from the fermented juice of soy beans)." Cf. E. Zürcher, *Buddhist Conquest*, p. 253.

13. Of the Sung Dynasty (House of Liu) (420–479 A.D.).

14. 東林精舍 Liebenthal, "A Biography," pp. 67, 68, and 88, distinguishes this from the Tung-lin ssu 東林寺, the monastery proper. Then they must have been in the same compound on the mountain (Lu-shan). Yet, it is questionable if the two terms, *ching-she* and *ssu*, refer to two different residences or quarters, for *ching-she* is the word for *vihāra* commonly used in reference to the places or monasteries rendered as *ssu* where the Buddha stayed or resided; see 397b12. For the early history of Tung-lin ssu, see E. Zürcher, *Buddhist Conquest*, p. 209. See also T'ang Yung-t'ung, *Fo-chiao shih*, I, p. 251.

15. "One" is actually "two." See Hurvitz, *Chih-i*, p. 198, note 2: "The two-chüan arrangement must be the work of a later hand"; T'ang Yung-t'ung, *Fo-chiao shih*, II, 148; Ōchō Enichi, "Jikudōshō sen," p. 240.

16. *Chün-tzu* 君子: "superior man" (Wing-tsit Chan, *Source Book*; Fung, *History of Chinese Philosophy*); "gentleman" (de Bary, ed., *Sources of Chinese Tradition*). For the original idea of the term as defined by Confucius, see the *Lun-yü* (*Analects*) 1:2, 8, 14, et passim. In 407b11 (Chapter 8) the term refers to the arhants (28b).

17. 之 (of)? Cf. 398d4.

18. Out of this paragraph Hurvitz, *Chih-i*, p. 198, renders: "He hopes that gentlemen of learning, if they deign to read it, will not allow the shortcomings of the author to lead them to a condemnation of the subject."

19. 妙法 (*Saddharma*): "the True Law" (H. Kern), "the Wonderful Law" (Kato). Other than direct quotes from Hurvitz's translation, I will render 妙 as *wondrous* or less frequently *mysterious*. See note 40.

20. Cf. *Tao-te ching*, Chapter 41: 大音希聲大象無形 "Great music sounds faint. Great form has no shape." (Wing-tsit Chan, *The Way of Lao Tzu*, p. 174); *Chuang-tzu*, Chapter 17: 至精無形 "the ultimate essence has no shape."

21. Cf. *Tao-te ching*, Chapter 14, the words *inaudible* and *subtle* in particular.

22. The word 朕 ("sign") is used synonymously with trace in Kuo Hsiang's commentary to the *Chang-tzu* (hereafter, *CTC*), Chapters 2 (*CTI*, 1:21) 9 and 7 (*CTI*, 3:39). See 403b12.

23. Liebenthal translates the passage: "the absolute is free from individual features. Where things have got out of sight, where traces (of life) have vanished, what designation fits that realm?" "The World Conception," II, p. 74).

24. 機. See *I Ching*, *Hsi-ts'u chuan* or Appended Remarks, Part II, Chapter 5. I have borrowed the rendering from Wing-tsit Chan, *Source Book*, p. 267, see also p. 784. For a neo-Taoist use, see *CTC*, Chapter 13 (*CTI*, 5:6).

25. "The circuit (or wheel) of the *dharma*" was set in motion by the Buddha when he first preached after his enlightenment in the Deer park near Benareth (Sarnath). The "wheel" is able to crush all evil and all opposition, like Indra's wheel, and which rolls on from person to person, place to place, age to age. Hurvitz, *Chih-i*, p. 218, takes the four Dharma wheels to refer to the Hīnayāna canon, the *Prajñāpāramitā*, the *Lotus*, and the *Mahāparinirvāṇa*, respectively. But Tsukamoto Zenryū, *Collective Works*, vol. 3, p. 26, differs in the first (*dāna* or charity and *śīla* or morality) and the second (Hīnaỹana and Mahāyāna *sūtras*)

26. 一善. See 397a2, 400d15. Cf. *Chung-yung* (*The Doctrine of the Mean*) Chapter 8, Wing-tsit Chan, *Source Book*, p. 99, "one thing that was good". See also *I Ching*, *AR*, Part 1, Chapter 5: 一陰一陽之謂道繼之者善也"The successive movement of *yin* and *yang* constitutes the way (*Tao*). What issues from the way is good." Chan, *Source Book*, p. 266.

27. *Catur-ārūpya (brahmā) lokas*, the four immaterial or formless heavens, *arūpa-dhātu*, above the eighteen *brahmalokas*: *ākāśānantyāyatana*, the state of boundless space; *vijñānā-nantyāyatana*, of boundless knowledge; *ākiñcanyānāyatana*, or nonexistence; *naivasaṃjñānāsamjñāyatana*, the state of neither thinking nor not thinking. Ōchō, "Jikudōshō no Hokekyo shisō," p. 151, takes 四空 as 四空定 four stages of meditation (*dhyāna*) represented by four heavens.

28. 三塗, that is, 三惡道 three evil destinies (*apāya*): hells, hungry ghosts, and animals.

29. *Upadhiśeṣa-nirvāṇa* or *nirvāṇa* with remnants and *anupadhiśeṣa-nirvāṇa* or *nirvāṇa* without remnants.

30. *Anāsrava-bodhipākṣika-dharmas*. *Anāsrava* means evil influence, depravity, evil, sin, misery, "the influences which attach a man to the *saṃsāra*" (Edgerton, *BHSD*, p. 111). There are thirty-seven constituents conducive to enlightenment.

31. 方便, *upāya-kauśalya*, "skillful means."

32. 成一之美 Cf. the phrase 一爻之美 (the beauty of one line, a component of a trigram or hexagram) in Wang Pi, *Chou-i lüeh-li* (Simple Exemplifications of the Principles of the Book of Changes), 23b.

33. 會歸. Cf. *CTC*, Chapter 1 (*CTI*, 1:2). Cf. also the *Shu Ching*, V. iv. 14, Legge, *The Shoo King*, p. 332. The term can be paraphrased as 會三歸一 "The three together returns (or belongs) to the One", the idea set to be stressed later in the T'ien-t'ai tradition; see, for example, T34.363a27 et passim, T46.775b12.

34. *Tsung* 宗. See R. H. Robinson, *Early Mādhyamika in India and China*, p. 252, note 9.: (In reference to *Ideal* rendered for the term in Hui-yüan's writing, p. 112): "The term *tsung* 宗 means (a) Absolute Truth, (b) a proposition or thesis, (c) the goal of a quest, (d) an ideological school. Its connotations are those of the historically earlier meaning, 'clan shrine, clan'." But none of this is exactly equivalent to the present case. It refers to the line of tradition to which the *sūtra* belongs. Thus, it is closer to the renderings of the term in T48.360a27 et passim by Wing-tsit Chan, *The Platform Scripture*, p. 127: "fundamental" (cf. ibid., "school"); by Philip Yampolsky, *Sixth Patriarch*, p. 170, "the basic teachings".

35. 平等 (*sama*), literally, "level and equal."

36. 一善. See 400d15, note 24.

37. 同歸一極. See 399d17, 400b6. Cf. the *I Ching*, *AR*, Part 2, Chapter 5: 天下同歸而殊塗一致而百慮 "In the world there are many different roads but the destination is the same. There are hundred deliberations but the result is one" (Chan, trans., *Source Book*, p. 268). Also see Wang Pi, *CLT*, Chapter 42: 萬物萬形其歸一也: "The ten thousand things have ten thousand different forms, but in the final analysis they are one" (Rump, *Commentary*, p. 128); Chapter 47: "There may be many roads but their destination is the same, and there may be a hundred deliberations but the result is the same" (p. 137).

38. 大慧 (*mahāprajñā*).

39. Alternate translation: "All the accumulation of (many) a tiny part of good deed is what counts"; see 400d15. Liebenthal translates: "*Mahābodhi* is attained at the end, but during the progress each little bit of good counts" ("World Conception," II, p. 4). For punctuation and comment, see T'ang Yung t'ung, *Han Wei liang-Chin Nan-pei-ch'ao Fo-chiao shih*, (hereafter, *Fo-chiao shih*), II, p. 176.

40. See 402b6 and 404a7.

41. 妙 (sad), "Fine" (Hurvitz), "mysterious" (Zürcher). Cf. 妙道 in the *Chuang-tzu*, Chapter 2, rendered with "the Mysterious Way" (Legge, I, 193), "the Mysterious Way" (Watson, p. 46). See note 17. For an interpretation of the

rest of the paragraph from here on, see Ōchō, "Jikudōshō sen Hokekyōso no kenkyū," p. 249f.

42. *Sūtra* also means "thread."

43. On *ching*, E. R. Hughes, "Epistemological Methods in Chinese Philosophy," in C. A. Moore, ed., *Essays in East-West Philosophy*, p. 55, says: "The character *ching* meant in that age the warp set up on a loom. But after Confucius' time there came the practice of recording a teacher's noteworthy dicta, and these records came to be called *ching*, i.e., warp teaching on which disciples could weave the woof of their amplifications."

44. Ōchō takes this to mean enlightenment (*satori*). See "Jikudōshō no hokke shisō", in Sakamoto ed., *Hokekyō no Chūgokuteki tenkai*, p. 154.

Chapter 1

INTRODUCTION

(Synopsis of the *Sūtra*) [1]

(The *sūtra* opens with a description of the setting, typical of *sūtras*. The Buddha, surrounded by a huge number of followers consisting of various classes of beings, enters into *samādhi* (concentration). Subsequently, there appear some portents: the raining of the māndārava flowers, the trembling of the earth, and the emitting of a ray from between the Buddha's brows, which illuminates the universe and all the phenomena in it. These omens are designed to get the audience prepared to hear the Buddha promulgate doctrine that will negate the path of the three vehicles they have hitherto trodden. Nonetheless they cannot comprehend what these signs stand for. Maitreya turns to Mañjuśrī to resolve their doubts. Mañjuśrī, recalling the experiences he has had in the course of many eons, tells them that it must be the case that the Buddha is about to preach the *sūtra* named *Saddharmapuṇḍarīka*.)

1.1.1 "Introductory Chapter"

As regards the topic, initiating a speech and beginning a discourse must be done gradually. As [the Buddha] is about to issue (*ming*)[2] the subtle words, he thus manifests auspicious omens first. This [chapter] is organized as a general, organic introduction from which the rest of the chapters evolve;[3] it is [like] the sun and moon of the *Dharma Blossom* (or *Lotus*). Here [the Buddha] also intends to shock the vision and hearing of the beings so as to solemnize the mood of those who wish to hear [his words].

1.1.2

What this *sūtra* expounds can be divided into three sections in all. The [first] thirteen chapters from "Introduction" (1) to "Comfortable Conduct" (13) illustrate that the cause (*yin/hetu*) of the three [vehicles] becomes the cause of the One. The eight chapters from "Welling up out of Earth" (14) to "Entrustment" (21) distinguish the effect (*kuo/phala*) of the three [as identical with that of the one].[4] The six chapters from "Bhaiṣajyarāja" (22) to "Samantabhadra" (27) equate the men of the three [vehicles] with the men of the One [Vehicle]. These divisions are designed to brush off the feeling that [the vehicles] are blocking [each other] and are different, and to obliterate the impasses that helped divide the lines [of the Buddha's teaching].

1.2 "Thus"[5] (1c16, 1:1)[6]

This is the phrase of the transmitters[7] of the *sūtra*. How is it that the *sūtras* have been transmitted through generations and the voice of the Buddha has not been cut off? Because there are **[397b1]** certain factors that make it possible. It resembles the possession of a passport (literally, sealed tally)[8] by a person, with which he will not encounter any check point that he will not be able to pass through. The *sūtras* have five facts[9] established in the beginning [of the first passage] in order to make the path (*tao/mārga*) pass [down the generations] without difficulty. *Like* [of *like this* or *thus*] is the word suggesting that the words match *li*. When the words and *li* are in mutual accord, this is spoken of as *like*. *This* (or *right*) [of *like this* or *thus*] refers to the fact that everything the Thus Come One (Tathāgata) said is not wrong. This [word] points to all that the Buddha preaches.

1.3 "Have I heard"

He intended to transmit it to those who did not [directly] hear it. If there were just words [heard] but no information about transmission, it means that he merely followed the words he heard[10] [which could be subject to distortion]. The importance [of a document as an authentic scripture] lies not so much in preaching [as such] as in transmission. It can be said that the *Tao* values one who forgets himself.[11] [The reader is advised to] forget about (or cast off) "I" and to follow the word *heard*. *Heard* means that the words came from the Buddha himself; it clarifies that they did not come forth from "my" [the hearer's] mind. In this way, the *sūtras* have been handed down from generation to generation and the wondrous track [of the *Dharma* wheel] has not ceased.

1.4 "At one time"

Even though words be in accord with *li*, if they do not match the occasion (*shih*),[12] they will still be empty statements. Hence, next comes *at one time*. What *time* means is that the "subtle, triggering mechanism-force (*chi*)" within beings stimulates (*kan*) the Sage, and the latter responds [appropriately and helpfully] (*ying*)[13] to them; when religious interaction between ordinary people and the Sage does not miss a favorable opportunity (*chi*),[14] we call it *at one time*.

1.5 [397b10] "The Buddha was dwelling in the city of King's House (Rājagṛha)"

Although there is no place where the Dharma body is not present, if the place where the preaching took place were not recorded, it would look vague and diffuse.[15] Given that [the transmitter] had to introduce it in order to give evidence for the preaching, and there were five places in this mountain, [namely,] Rājagṛha, which is the one where the preaching took place? It was at the monastery on Gṛdhrakūta mountain ("Vulture Peak").

1.6 "Together with [twelve thousand] great bhikṣus"[16]

If it is said that [the transmitter] heard [the preaching] by himself, one would find it difficult to believe other factors, too. If he simply said *we* and *everybody* [vaguely, not specifically] he would not be any better than ("excepted from being")[17] a solitary [witness]. [So] he lists all the [specific] cohearers. These are all that I mentioned as [the five factors] witnessing the *sūtra*.[18] *Bhikṣu* is a general term referring to those who are in the process of destroying evils.[19] Why are the voice hearers (*śrāvakas*) listed first and then the bodhisattvas? This has to do with the difference of inner and outer; inner-directedness has a limited scope, whereas outer-directedness has no restrictions.[20] Hence, it should be in that order. It also suggests that the Buddha's transformative teaching covers all, starting from the near, extending to the distant; there is no place where [his] *Tao* is not existent.[21] *Great* (*Mahā*) refers to the assembly[22] of people that can [counter] ninety-six kinds [of heretical views or arguments].[23]

1.7.1 "Ājñātakauṇḍinya"

Ājñā(ta) means, in Chinese,[24] "attaining the unlearned knowledge." *Kauṇḍinya* is a surname **[397c1]**. He was the first one who attained the *Tao*; hence, the name.

1.7.2 "Mahākāśyapa"

Mahā means "great." *Kāśyapa* is a surname. Because he was an elder and virtuous, he was thus called by this name. *Kāśyapa* is a Brahman surname.

1.7.3. "Uruvilva [-kāśyapa]"

It is the name of a papaya grove. As he stayed always in this grove, the place became his name.

1.7.4 "Gayākāśyapa"

Gayā is the name of a town. He stayed by the town; thus, it became his name.

1.7.5 "Nadi [-kāśyapa]"

It is the name of a river.[25] He was born at the bank of this river. Because of this, he got the name.

1.7.6 "Śāriputra"

[*Śāri*] refers to his mother's name. His mother's eyes were like those of the śāri bird (stork); hence, this name. *Putra* means "son." This Śāriputra's mother was highly talented and skillful in debates. She was known all over the land. Therefore he came to have the name Śāri, after his mother.

1.7.7 "Mahāmaudgalyāyana"

His first name was Kolita. The surname came from a Brahman clan.

1.7.8 "Mahākātyāyana"

It was a surname of a Brahman (clan) of South India. So what originally used to be a surname became his name.

1.7.9 "Aniruddha"

In Chinese, it means non(*a*)extinction (*nirodha*) (i.e., "unextinguishable").

1.7.10 "Kapphiṇa"

It is a first name; it is untranslatable.

1.7.11 [397c10] "Gavāṁpati"

Gavām means cow (*go*); *pati* means foot (*pad*). When he was born, his feet were like cow's feet; hence, his name, "cow feet."

1.7.12 "Revata"

It is the name of a constellation. He was born when this constellation appeared in the sky; thus, he got the name.

1.7.13 "Piliṅgavatsa"

Piliṅga is the first name: *Vatsa* is a surname.

1.7.14 "Bakkula"

The name [translated into Chinese] is Fei-ch'eng ("fertile and prosperous").

1.7.15 "Mahākauṣṭhila"

The [Chinese] name is Ta-hsi ("great knee").

1.7.16 "(Mahā)nanda"

The [Chinese] name is Huan-hsi ("joy") (ānanda). He was the Buddha's younger brother.

1.7.17 "Suṇdarānanda"

The [Chinese] name is Jou-ju ("gentle and smooth"). It means "handsome" (*suṇdara*) and "joy" (*ānanda*).

1.7.18 "[Pūrṇa Maitrāyaṇiputra"

Pūrṇa is a surname; *Maitrāyaṇiputra* is a first name. He is also called [in Chinese] Man-yüan ("fulfilled wish"). *Maitrāyaṇi* was his mother's name. His mother's talent for debate[26] and great wisdom were known to many people. People[27] honored his mother. Hence, the son's name was taken from his mother's surname.

1.7.19 "Subhūti"

The [Chinese] name is Shan-chi ("good and lucky"). It also means "empty birth" (*su-bhū*).

1.7.20 "Ānanda"

He had a handsome appearance. People were delighted to see him. He was born on the day of the Buddha's enlightenment. Thus, he was called Huan-hsi ("joy") (*ānanda*).

1.7.21 "Rāhula"

In Chinese, it means "not letting go" (not released). He was **[387d1]** in the womb for six years. He thus came to be called *not letting go*.

1.7.22 "Known to the multitude"

All these voice hearers (śrāvakas) had "their virtues firmly established within and their fame reported without."[28] [People] far and near admired them [wholeheartedly]; who did not know them? This is why their names are listed and their virtues praised.

1.7.23

Great [of *great arhats*] tells that the *Dharma* of the Lesser Vehicle (Hīnayāna) is identical with the path of the bodhisattvas.

1.8.1 "Mahāprajāpatī" (1c26, 1:15)

Listed next are the group of mendicant nuns (*bhikṣuṇīs*). *Mahāprajāpatī* means, in Chinese, [the one who] loves the path (*tao*) greatly.[29]

1.8.2 "Rāhula's mother Yaśodharā"

[*Yaśodharā*] means, in Chinese, "keeps hearing from afar."

1.9 "Eighty thousand bodhisattva-[*mahāsattvas*]" (2a2, 1:17)

The voice hearers basically take the exhaustion of suffering as the aim [of life]; hence, it was said earlier (1b) that they had their bondages (*lei*)[30] destroyed. In the path of bodhisattvas, in which a person sets himself to embrace all [beings],[31] he does not stay [in the world] just to get rid of bonds of existence (*chieh*);[32] he wishes only to acquire such ways to help save beings.[33] [As such][34] they [i.e., the bodhisattvas] are the only people to be equipped with the magic charms (*dhāraṇi*) and the four kinds of [unhindered] powers.[35] Hence, their wondrous techniques for wheeling and uplifting[36] [beings to salvation] are introduced first, being followed at the end by a discussion of the innumerable people to be saved.

1.10 "Having made offerings to various (incalculable hundreds of thousands of) Buddhas"

This refers to the conduct that took place in the past [lives].

1.11.1 "Cultivating themselves through compassion"

[The passage] following this phrase illustrates the merits of the bodhisattvas through three kinds of deeds (*karman*).[37] Having sympathy for, and taking care of, the weak and the deprived is what is meant by "cultivating themselves through compassion." The word *body* [of *cultivating themselves* or, literally, *cultivating body*] **[397d10]** implies both mouth and mind as well.

1.11.2 "Having penetrated great wisdom"

This word (*great wisdom*) refers to what they have obtained for themselves. *Penetration* means "[reaching] to the substratum".

1.11.3 "Having reached the yonder shore"

This refers to what they have reached at the ultimate end.

1.11.4 "Their fame having been reported widely in countless worlds"

Whereas their virtues were established internally their fame spread outward. Their merit and fame having been established, the news spread outward.

1.12.1 "*Śakro Devānām Indraḥ*" (2a15, 2:13)

He is the second god-emperor, in charge of four regional god-kings.[38] He commands the dragons (*nāgas*) and demons (*pretas*), not letting them offend beings unrestrainedly but making them (beings) always cultivate meritorious virtues. He makes the sun and the moon shine clear and bright. He often acts as a main interlocutor who draws out remarks or sermons[39] [from the Buddha]. Hence, he is mentioned in the beginning [of the paragraph].

1.12.2 "Eight classes of ghosts (pretas) and spirits (devas)"

Spirits can have different forms and can change their appearances, sometimes into gods or men. Therefore, they belong to the category between the two, to be placed second.

1.13 "The four great god-kings"

In the east of Sumeru is [the king] called Dhṛtarāṣṭra, in the south Virūḍhaka, in the west Virūpākṣa, and in the north Vaiśravaṇa. They are controlled by Śakro Devānām Indraḥ.

1.14 "The eight dragon kings (nāgarāja)"

All these dragon kings are named *Joy*.[40] They were (once) reincarnated in human form and resided in **[398a1]** Rājagṛha. When suffering from drought, the king and ministers went to them to seek help. Immediately the sweet rain fell and the rain soaked the whole country. Seeing the rain fall, the people were very pleased; hence, the name *joy*.

1.15.1 "There were four kinnara kings" (2a:24, 2:29)

In Chinese [Kinnara] means "human cum inhuman"; they appear handsome, but their heads have one horn. They are the god-emperors' spirits in charge of music.

1.15.2 "There were four gandharva kings"

They also are the gods' music spirits. But they differ in that they have no horn.

1.16.1 "*Asura* kings"

A- means "no"; *sura* means "wine." In their past [life] they belonged to a Brahman clan, and led a clean life, abstaining from drinking; hence, the name.

1.16.2 "Garuḍa"

In Chinese, it means "flying in the sky." They are the spirits of the birds with golden wings.

1.16.3 "Vaidehī's son, King Ajātaśatru"

Vaidehī is the mother's name. King Ajātaśatru means, in Chinese, "hatred (*śātravaṃ*) [harbored] prior to birth." When he was in the womb, he kept harboring evil will against King Bimbisāra. Hence, the name *hatred before birth*. He was born of Vaidehī, thus he was called Vaidehī's son.

1.17.1 [398a10] "At that time, the World-Honored One, surrounded by the fourfold multitude" (2b7, 3:18)

The utmost virtue [of the Buddha] was so weighty that its majesty exceeded that of the sun and the moon. Hence, it brought men and gods to join together and intermingle with the same thoughts of respect; job imbued all beings, causing the false to go and the real to return.

1.17.2 "Showered with offerings, and paid respects" [41]

"Offering" is made by giving valuables, whereas "respect" is expressed by solemn manners.

1.17.3 "Revered and admired" [42]

Reverance means "to respect" and "to honor." Their affections in this case surpassed that for ruler or father. To paraphrase "admiration," it means that as they were pleased with the virtues [of the Buddha] within, [their pleasure] overflowed into chanting without.

1.17.4 "Preached a scripture of the Great Vehicle"

The three vehicles are [traces, which are used provisionally] in compliance with external [conditions]. [However], traces are diametrically opposed to *li*. Holding on to the words and deviating from the import,[43] how could they not be startled [by] the doctrine of the One Vehicle? [The Buddha] is about to preach the *Dharma Blossom*. Therefore, first he [attempts to] reach out to their psychological makeups by preaching "the Immeasurable Doctrine" (*Ananta-nirdeśa*). Because they have remained among traces (*chi*) so long, when they suddenly hear that there are [in reality] no three [vehicles], they will not suddenly deviate from what they have been found of so far. If they deviated from what they have been found of so far, then they would turn back while they gaze at [the other] shore. Turning back while gazing at the [other] shore means that the Great Path (*Tao*) is abandoned. Therefore, [the preaching of One] should be done gradually.[44] What is "the Immeasurable Doctrine"? It refers to something for which there is no external mark (*lakṣaṇa*) at all. There is nothing like "many or little" and "deep or shallow". It precisely speaks of the conduct of the Buddha. The import of his words contains **[398b1]** something [ultimately] real; we call it the *Doctrine Immeasurable*. *Li* is [so] broad that it liberates [one who gets in it] from the long passage of suffering; it is none other than the Greater Vehicle.[45] Only the bodhisattvas can learn it. [Thus] he preached it for them.

1.17.5 "A dharma to be taught to bodhisattvas"

The bodhisattvas are those who have not consummated *li* yet. [Hence], he must teach them about it.

1.17.6 "[A Dharma] that the buddha keeps ever in mind"

The Buddha has consummated *li*: he "keeps it ever." He has never forgotten or lost it: he [keeps it ever] "in mind".

1.17.7 "[He entered] the samādhi of [the Abode of] the Immeasurable Doctrine (ananta-nirdeśa-pratiṣṭhāna-samādhi)"

'Movement and quiscence'[46] apply only to beings, but certainly not to the Sage. 'The tracing of *li* to the end and the consummate realization of their nature (*hsing*)'[47] is referred to as the *samādhi* of the Immeasurable Doctrine. All that he will say after he rises from this *samādhi* should not allow any error. Thus, he has to verify it.

1.18 "Māndārava flowers" (2b10, 3:26)

As [the Buddha] entered and reached the *samādhi*,[48] his spirit moved heaven and earth. In heaven appear flowers of rain; on earth there is shaking (earthquake). As heaven and earth move, how can men remain silent?[49] Now that good omens have appeared there certainly will be an extraordinary preaching. The general mood at the time is full of speculation, and their doubts deepen. As deep doubts pile up, awakening, [if it happens] would necessarily be deep, too. The four kinds of māndārava flowers poured from heaven are designed to show the unreality of the four kinds of fruition.[50] The trembling of the earth is meant to demonstrate the nonabidingness (or transitoriness) of the four kinds of fruition. Also shown is the fact that the six kinds of living beings are all endowed with [the capacity for] great enlightenment.[51] It shows also [the truth of] impermanence (*anitya*).

1.19.1 [398b10] "Single-mindedly they beheld the Buddha" (2b16, 3:36)

Knowing for certain that there will be an extraordinary preaching, they wait to hear the unusual speech.

1.19.2 "Aglow from the tuft of white hair between his brows"

This is intended to illustrate the right middle-path[52] of the One Vehicle and the nonexistence of the two vehicles that are an illusion and hindrance. Its presence in the forehead signifies the mark of "impartiality."[53] When it shines, the [noble] knowledge will certainly become manifest.

1.19.3 "Illuminated . . . the East"

The East is the cardinal of all directions. This is to show [analogically] the mystery that the One Vehicle is [identical with] the three vehicles. Also expressed here is that one who becomes enlightened to [the meaning of] the Greater [Vehicle] is [no less than the one who has been] so darkly merged [with the ultimate foundation] that he cannot exhaust his illumination.

1.19.4 "Eighteen thousand worlds"

Although it illuminated in one direction, [the Buddha] intended to show that there was no place that such light could not illuminate. Thus by [the expression] *eighteen thousand* he meant to demonstrate that his illumination was not limited to one [direction].[54] That it illuminated throughout the regions above and below implies that 'there is no place where the *Tao* is not present.'[55]

1.20.1 "There could be fully seen . . . in those lands"

"Those" and "these" [lands] were [made] mutually visible, expressing the fact that the right path pentrates formlessly, without obstacle and without obstruction.[56]

1.20.2 "Six kinds of living beings"

The six "courses" illustrate that they were in such a state of existence because of their delusion (*moha*).

1.20.3 "There could also be seen . . . the Buddhas"

Because the deluded conditions of the six kinds of living beings[57] was shown, it seems necessary [to cite] also those who reversed the course of delusion. Those who reversed **[398c1]** the course of delusion were none other than the Buddhas.

1.20.4 "And the sūtradharmas preached by those Buddhas could be heard"

Those who wanted the know-how (or knowledge) for reversing the deluded state are required to hear the *Dharma* [preached]. What is said next (or as well) is that they heard the *sūtra* preached.

1.20.5 "Who through practice had attained the path"

All of them are those who turned around from the course of delusion.

1.20.6 "The various background causes and conditions"

It is illustrated here that the spiritual capacities of living beings are not equal. The ways for attaining enlightenment are myriad: [beings achieve it] sometimes by means of almsgiving (*dāna*) and morality (*śīla*), or sometimes through spiritual transformation; hence, the word *various*.

1.20.7 "There also could be seen those Buddhas who achieved [pari-] nirvāṇa"

These [Buddhas] are here shown to be contrasted with the present [Buddha]. They were supposed to realize that the Buddha's *nirvāṇa* was not long away, but were in such a state of mind that they were far from realizing it; they were urged to seek for the *Dharma* diligently.[58]

1.21 "Maitreya had this thought: . . . we have had these portents" (2b4, 4:18)

Now that the congregation had been mired so long, emotionally at a standstill, it held hard on to the idea.[59] When it saw all of a sudden the strange mark it had never seen before, it was at a loss, doubts arising within [each member]. Maitreya, who was in rank to become the next Buddha,[60] saw that his mind was becoming inquistive like those of the others. Sharing this [doubting] thought with the rest of the congregation, he availed himself of the opportunity (*chi*) (or the subtle triggering force in him) and became puzzled. As the doubts piled up inside to a great degree, enlightenment also could be incited quickly. Maitreya was the principal questioner because the one who sought to resolve these doubts would duly attain illumination.

1.22 "Then he questioned Mañjuśrī, . . . [398c10] a great ray emitted" (2c5, 4:34)

The reason why earlier, when [the Buddha] first entered the *samādhi*, [the phenomena of] the raining flowers and shaking earth appeared, was that he was going to expound the One Vehicle. This indicates that the transformative teaching[61] of the One Vehicle would follow later. However, [to preach] the One Vehicle was [the Buddha's] original purpose for convening the meeting. Therefore, Maitreya now first questions the emission of the ray. The order in which [the questioners] are arranged represents some meaning and intention in each case. It seems proper that the question about the rain flowers and the shaking of the earth follow next. [Yet], it is omitted and not mentioned [in the prose section]. That question then must be included in the *gāthās*.[62]

1.23.1 "Questioned in gāthās" (2c8, 5:4)

The composition of the *gāthās* is dictated generally by the following four aims: first, for the sake of those who will come later; second, for the sake of those who have not yet been enlightened [through the prose section]; third, to expand in the *gāthās* what has been briefly touched on (or left out) in the long lines (or prose); fourth, to chant and dance in tune with intense emotion. Maitreya has asked only the essentials. Now he speaks about them in full detail. The appearance of Mañjuśrī's name at the start is for the sake of drawing the congregation's attention; they regarded him highly and when they were to hear him speak later their affection for him would be very intense.[63]

1.23.2 "I will now tell them briefly" (3a6)

Because what he has seen and heard is so vast, it will be difficult for him to tell them in complete detail.

1.24 "I see in that land" (3a6, 7:4)

Many lines that follow this chant are [the recounting of] what has appeared earlier [in prose], **[398d1]** [including] "the various background causes and conditions [of the bodhisattva-mahāsattvas], and their various degrees of belief and understanding (*adhimukti*) (2b22, 4:10). [The word] *various* can refer to morality (*śīla*) or almsgiving (*dāna*). What it refers to is not limited to one kind. Listed next are various practices of the six perfections (*pāramitās*).[64] But there is no set order for them. [The sequential order] can be arranged high or low (or early or late) as [the Buddha] wishes. Why then are they put together here on this occasion and why are the good and the bad [practitioners] of them shown here? Because it is [the Buddha's] wish that [beings] are led to discard evil and cultivate good. Also illustrated there is the fact that there is no place the light of knowledge does not illuminate.

1.25.1 "Mañjuśrī said to . . . Maitreya . . . I surmise that" (3c11, 12:14)

The profound *li* is dark and deep beyond measurement. Not having realized for himself the deep *li*, how can [Maitreya] dare to explicate it? He has to rely on Mañjuśrī [as explicator, a role that requires expertise equal to that of] the famous artisan [Shih] of Ying (the capital of Ch'iu).[65] The phrase *I surmise that* indicates that comprehension must lie in the Buddha [himself], in whom all have their faith deepened.

1.25.2

The subsequent part consisting of four sections in all serves as an indication that the [Buddha's] preaching of the *Dharma Blossom* is imminent. [In] "the first segment," Mañjuśrī, knowing that *li* is subtle and sublime, dare not pinpoint, substantiate, or explain it. Therefore, he says: "I surmise that [the Buddha]. . . wishes to preach the great *Dharma*.

1.25.3 "You good man, once before, in the presence of past Buddhas, I saw this portent"

The second segment. [What happened in] the past is cited to explain [what happens in] the present **[398d10].** Even though the past and the present are distinguished, their *Tao* is not different. The past portents as such pointed to the fact that [the Buddha] would preach the great *Dharma*; [likewise] "it should be understood" that the present portents of Śākyamuni clearly signal that he is certain to preach the *Dharma Blossom*.

1.26.1

What will be plainly spoken of from now on is simply what happened in the remote past. [Mañjuśrī] is going to describe what really happened. It is the story of the Buddha Sun-and-Moon Glow.

1.26.2

The Thus Come One (Tathāgata) preached freely in accordance with his aims; thus it is referred to as *Immeasurable.* [66] But here just "ten" attributes[67] are mentioned. Why [*ten*]? *Ten* represents the full and ultimate number (or infinity), with the implication that the *li* of the Thus Come One is perfect and faultless and that the *Tao* is omnipresent;[68] hence, [the word] *ten* is employed.

1.26.3

What does [the title] "Thus Come One" (Tathāgata) (3c19) mean? Although the myriad *dharmas* are different from each other, they are one and in a [mysterious] way[69] the same. [Why did] the coming of the Sagely body [take place]? He has come [in incarnated form] to transform the myriad creatures; hence, the title *Thus Come One*.[70]

1.26.4 "Worthy of offerings (arhat)"[71]

The fertile fields of 'the utmost Tao'[72] can produce wonderful fruits. With both external marks (*lakṣaṇa*) and ties (*saṃyojana*?) dispelled, he can be called *[worthy of] offerings*.

1.26.5 "[The one who has] right and universal knowledge (samyaksaṃbuddha)"

There is no place that knowledge does not permeate: it is "universal." This knowledge is not depraved;[73] it is "right" (or correct).

1.26.6 "[The one who has] enlightenment and conduct perfect (vidyācaraṇasaṃpannaḥ)"[74]

When the actions (*karman*) of body, mouth, and mind are in conformity with knowledge, there is what can be called *enlightenment and conduct*. [The word] *perfect* means that as his wisdom is universal, his knowledge and conduct, too, must be complete and perfect.

1.26.7 "Well gone (Sugata)"

[The Buddha's][75] existence and disappearance provided beings with immeasurable benefits **[399a1]**. His trace was exhausted under 'the twin trees.'[76] He was then "gone" for [the good of] beings, and beings benefited from this. How can it not be "well"?

1.26.8

What does [the title] *[the one who] understands the world (lokavid)* mean? The five aggregates *pañcaskandhaḥ*)[77] are what make up the world. The Thus Come One came to the world and untied[78] the bonds and knots.

1.26.9 "The unexcelled worth (anuttara)"

The man is lofty; the path [to him] is cut off (or [his] *Tao* is absolute).[79] No one can stand equal with him.

1.26.10 "Regulator of men (puruṣadamyasārathiḥ)"

It is hard to regulate evils, and the immature and woeful [deeds caused by] body and mouth. The Buddha can suppress them and regulate beings. He thus can be called *regulator*.

1.26.11 "Teacher of gods and men (śāstādevānaṃ ca manusyāṇaṃ)"

Having completely mastered the wondrous technique of regulation, he can be the teacher of gods (*devas*) and men.

1.26.12 "Buddha, World-Honored One (Bhagavān)"

Buddha refers to awakening. He was awakened and enlightened to [the truth of] birth and death. Armed with the previous ten virtues, his general title [representing all his virtues] is *Buddha, World-Honored One*.

1.27

[The true Dharma] that is good at beginning refers to the voice hearers (*śrāvakas*); *good at middle* refers to the *pratyekabuddhas*; and *good at end* refers to the bodhisattvas. Listed next are those who belong to the three vehicles, and that is followed by a description of the events involved. The three kinds of transformative teaching (*hua*)[80] also were preached earlier; what was said there remains true in the present case, as well.

1.28.1 "In this way there were twenty thousand Buddhas" (3c27, 13:13)

The purpose underlying the description of twenty thousand buddhas as witnesses for Śākyamuni Buddha is to describe the transformative teaching of the two vehicles, and thus to expound[81] the beauty of the One Vehicle. Thus he must describe a wide variety of Buddhas. Although there are many [of these buddhas,] their **[399a10]** path (*tao*) is in the end one.

1.28.2 "He had eight [princely] sons"

The reason why the eight sons appear is twofold. First, to prove what Mañjuśrī says about what happened in the remote past, namely, that he was none other than the master of Torch Burner (*Dīpaṃkara*), [that is, Fine Luster (*Varaprabha*)], and that Torch Burner was in turn the master of Śākyamuni. As such, there can not be anything false in what Mañjuśrī has said. Second, speaking in reverse, [it suggests that] one's longevity [makes one] gradually open up one's eyes.

1.29.1 "At that time, the Buddha Sun-and-Moon Glow preached a scripture of the Great Vehicle" (4a8, 13:35)

The third[82] segment [begins here]. This is cited now in order to corroborate that the present portents are identical with [those in the past].

1.29.2 "Fine Luster (Varaprabha) and who had eight hundred disciples"

The eight hundred disciples are featured to indicate that it is not only now that Maitreya has sought advice from Mañjuśrī, but that in the past he also received instruction [from him] as his pupil. Now he has again become the one who inquires [about the portents]: he is bound to obtain enlightenment [this time].[83]

1.30.1 "At that time, the Buddha Sun-and-Moon-Glow, rising from *samādhi*"[84]

The fourth segment [begins here]. What he preached at this particular time he was going to continue preaching for sixty kalpas. How can this be true? This time span is used [merely] to express the utmost respect for the *Dharma*.

1.30.2 "At midnight, entered nirvāṇa [without residue]"

[Consequently] they sought for the *Dharma* earnestly with the utmost effort. The motive for [the Buddha's] gift to Womb of Excellence (*Śrīgarbha*) of the prophecy that he would later become a Buddha is to attract those with [excessive] self-esteem.[85] If they hear suddenly that the Buddha is about to [enter] *nirvāṇa*, which means that there will be no Sage [to guide them] from then on, they will then immediately stop their journey in the middle of the path they have trodden. Another reason **[399b1]** [the Buddha] confered the prophecy of his future Buddhahood on Womb of Excellence is because people of the world, seeking after fame and profit, tend to be very fond of holding on to what is near while rejecting that which is far off, and he wanted to admonish them from such proclivities.

1.31.1 "Proclaimed *gāthās*, saying" (4b:19, 16:4)

As for the way the *gāthās* are composed, what was [mentioned] before [in prose] may sometimes be omitted and not chanted [in the *gāthās*]; what was not previously [in prose] may sometimes be included in the *gāthās*]. It is also difficult to set a standard [on what is to be chanted]. It is possible only to determine provisionally at a specific point of time what should be [chanted].

1.31.2 "The doctrine of the reality marks of the dharmas" (5a10, 19:2)

There is no more falsehood of the two vehicles. He preaches only the reality of the Greater Vehicle.

Notes

1. Hurvitz, *Scripture of the Lotus Blossom of the Fine Dharma* (hereafter, *SLFD*), p. x, has a good summary of the contents chapter by chapter. I nevertheless have attempted a more extended summary for every chapter unless otherwise indicated. See also H. Kern, *Saddharma-Puṇḍarīka or The Lotus of the True Law*, p. xxixff.

2. 命 For the meanings of and theories about the term in traditional Chinese philosophy, see Wing-tsit Chan, *Source Book*, p. 78f.

3. Cf. 409b13. See B. Katō, *Myōhō-renge-kyō, The Sūtra of the Lotus Flower of the Wonderful Law* (Tokyo, 1971) (hereafter, MSLW), p. 1, note 1: "As an introductory chapter to the whole Sūtra it indicates (1) the order of the *Sūtra*; (2) the origin, or scene of the revelation; (3) the statement of the doctrine of the *Sūtra*."

4. See 409b13, 410d14, 411a13; Ōchō, "Jikudōshō no hoke shisō," p. 156.

5. *Evaṃ*. Tao-sheng dissects the word 如是 into "like (如) this (是)" for the exegetical purpose. Sanskrit words are based on U. Wogihara and C. Tsuchida, eds., *Saddharma-puṇḍarīka-sūtraṃ, Romanized and Revised Text of the Bibliotheca Buddhica Publication* (Tokyo, 1958).

6. The first reference is to the page, column and line of the text (*HTC*); the second to the page and line of Hurvitz's translation. For the original lines of the *sūtra*, I follow Hurvitz's translation unless otherwise indicated.

7. The transmitter is known to be Ānanda. See *MSLW*, p. 1, note 2.

8. Emend 苻 to 符.

9. 五事. They are, as listed in the following section, testimonial seal (*yin* 印), transmitter or witness, time, place, and other "cohearers," in that order.

10. 從設 Cf. 假設 "*Prajñapti*, ordinary teaching, doctrines derived from the phenomenal" (Soothhill, *DCBT*, p. 342), "*prajñapti*" being "manifestation in words, . . . verbal expression, . . . verbal convention, . . . arrangement, provision" (Edgerton, *BHSD*, p. 358).

11. 可謂道貴兼忘者也. See 407d18. For the expression 道,貴 see the *Chuang-tzu*, Chapter 17. (*CTI*, 6:12): 然則何貴於道邪 "What then is there so valuable in the Tao?" (Legge, *The Texts of Taoism*, Part I, p. 383); "If that is so, then what is there valuable about the way?" (Watson, *Complete Works*, p. 182). See also the *Analects*, VIII.4, 君子所貴於者三 "There are three principles of which the man of high rank should consider specially important" (Legge, *Confucius*, p. 209). For the expression 兼忘, see the *Chuang-tzu*, Chapter 17: 兼忘天下難, 兼忘天下易, 使天下兼忘我難. "[If it were easy to make my parents forget me,] it is difficult for me to forget all men in the world. If it were easy to forget all men in the world, it is diffcult to make them all forget me" (Legge, I, p. 347) Also cf. *CTC*, Chapter 12 (*CTI*, 4:12): 壽夭兼忘. E. Zürcher, *Buddhist Conquest*, p. 251, renders the two-letter phrase as "universal oblivion."

12. Apropos of the *I Ching*, Fung Yu-lan observes: "The development of a thing cannot go counter to its *shih* (time, i.e. circumstance, time plus environment). That is, for a development to succeed it must be at the proper time in the proper environment . . . on Feng Hexagram say, '. . . The heavens and the earth

cannot go counter to the *shih* factor'" (Fung, *The Spirit of Chinese Philosophy*, p. 98).

13. *Kan* and *ying* are also traceable to the *I Ching*, for instance, Hexagram *hsien*. Also see *CTC* Chapter 12 (*CTI*, 4:33). For a brief general observation on the terms in this regard, see Tsukamoto, ed., *Eon kenkyū*, p. 408.

14. Liebenthal translates: "When the spiritual state of a Being calls for the Sage, he is able to bend down and answer (the call). For the relation of the Sage to the Beings is reciprocal (like that of Heaven to Earth) and no true spiritual need is slighted" ("World Conception," II, p. 80).

15. Emend 猛 to 孟. The term *meng-lang* occurs in the *Chuang-tzu*, Chapter 2, 孟浪之言 "wild and flippant words" (Watson, *Complete Works*, p. 46); "a shoreless flow of mere words" (Legge, *Texts of Taoism*, Part I, p. 193); "nonsense" (A. C. Graham, "Chuang-tzu's Essay on Seeing Things as Equal," *History of Religions*, 9, no. 1 (August, 1969): 158).

16. More accurately, "a great congregation of bhikṣus." See Sanskrit manuscripts edited by U. Wogihara and C. Tsuchida, p. 1:7: "mahātā bhikṣu-saṃgheṇa", "a numerous assemblage of monks" (Kern, p. 1). But Katō, p. 1, note 6, has "Mahābhikshu, a 'great monk'".

17. Emend 勉 to 免. Cf. *sūtra*, T9.13b3&6.

18. See note 9; 397b1.

19. *Evil* may refer to "defilements" (*fan-nao*), as identified by Seng-chao and Kumārajīva, T.328b5 and 12. Cf, T'ang, *Fo-chiao shih*, II, p. 37. See 400c10.

20. That is, Hīnayāna followers are introvertive or self-centered whereas Mahāyāna followers are extraversive or altruistic.

21. 道無不在. See 398b15, 398d14. Cf. *CTC*, Chapter 33 (*CTI*, 10:35): 道無所不在; *Chuang-tzu*, Chapter 22: 道···無所不在. Hui-yüan also uses or cities this expression, see *Eon kenkyū*, p. 400.

22. Emend 㝡 to 冣.

23. What this number stands for is not immediately clear. According to Tao-sheng's commentary on the *Vimalakīrti-nirdeśa Sūtra*, refers to the kinds of the scriptures, possibly Mahāyāna ones (T38, 415c11f.). Seng-chao, however, speaks of it indicating as many heretics (*tirthikas*) (ibid., 329a and c). In a *sūtra* called *P'u-yao ching* (Chih-ch'ien and Dharmarakṣa, tran.) reference is made to *tao-shu*, see Tsukamoto Zenryū, *Shīna Bukkyō shi kenkyū*, p. 17. Hence, the number seems to suggest, as Kumārajīva, T.38.328b9ff says, the number of the heretical views that the Bhikṣus can counter and rebut or the very views they can hold against the heretical arguments.

24. Literally, "in the landuage of Sung," referring to the Sung Dynasty (House of Liu) (420–477) Tao-sheng belonged to at the time of writing.

25. Actually *nadī* is a common noun for *river*, not a proper noun as taken by Tao-sheng. So, Tao-sheng should say, "It means *river*."

26. 辨(c15) is taken here in the sense of 辯.

27. Here, as usual, the editor's note is respected: "母(c16) is suspected to be 人."

28. 德著於內名揚於外. Its variants occur in 397d11, 398a13, & 407d5; cf. *CTC*, Chapter 5, (*CTI*, 2:30): 德充於內應物於外 "Virtues are full within and [he] responds to the beings without."; see also Chapter 21, (*CTI*, 7:9; 7:13).

29. As in many other cases, Tao-sheng's literary rendering of the term does not exactly match with the Sanskrit equivalent. It rather means "Great Mistress of Procreator." This can support a generally held view that the Chinese Buddhists, except those who traveled to India, did not possess a direct knowledge of the Sanskrit language.

30. 累. It can be identifiable in the *sūtra* (1c17) with either *kleśa* ("anguish," Hurvitz; "depravity," Kern) or *saṃyojana* ("the bonds of existence," Hurvitz; "the ties which bound them to existence," Kern). Fung, *History of Chinese Philosophy*, vol. 2, p. 273, renders the Chinese term as used by Tao-sheng's contemporary Buddhists as "(mortal) ties." It is not certain in this particular context if *lei* is semantically synonymous and interchangeable with *chieh*, Kumārajīva's rendering of the term *saṃyojana* and the term Tao-sheng uses in the subsequent sentence (d6). It is basically a Taoist term, see the *Chuang-tzu*, Chapter 32, "fetters" (Legge, *Texts of Taoism*, Part II, p. 206), "entangled" (Watson, *Complete Works*, p. 356). For a discussion on the concept with reference to the neo-Taoist language, see Chapter 6.

31. 兼被. It occurs also in 406a11, 407d18; see also 398b12, 409b8.

32. See Hurvitz, *SLFD*, 1:6.

33. 濟物. Cf. the *Chuang-tzu*, Chapter 32: "But at the same time he wishes to aid in guiding to (the secret of) the Tao." (Legge, II, 206. Cf. also the *I Ching*, AR, Part I, Chapter 4.

34. In case the letter 然 (d6, "such") better be transposed to after 方 as the first letter in the next passage.

35. Inter. with 四無礙辯 (*catasrah-pratisaṃvidaḥ*): "unhindered speech" (Chinese) or "special knowledge" consisting of *dharma-pratisaṃvid (no obstacles in communicating the meanings) nirukti-p.* (no obstacles on communication in various dialects), and *pratibhāna-p.* (no obstacles in being ready to preach). In the *sūtra* only the word 樂說 (*pratibhāna*) (2a3) is represented, which Hurvitz renders as "preaching with joy and eloquence" (p. 1) (樂說辯才,

talented or excelled in being prepared to preach for any occasion) and H. Kern takes as "firmly standing in wisdom" (*Saddharma-Puṇḍarīka or The Lotus of the True Law*, p. 3) (*Mahāpratibhāna-pratisthair*, being conversant with the great way of being prepared to preach). What appear to be more appropriate English equivalents for *pratibhāna* are "readiness in speech," "quick-wittedness" as found in Edgerton, *BHSD*, p. 366r. Anyway, Tao-sheng interprets this term as representing the four powers.

36. Emend 秡 to 拔. See 412b2, *sūtra* 13a6, 27 and b9. Cf. also 404a15.

37. Action, word, and thought committed through body, mouth, and mind, the effects of which remain as agents for transmigration.

38. See 1.13 in text.

39. 對揚. See 399b17 and 407b11 (Chapter 8, note 1). Cf. the *Shu Ching*, IV. viii: "to respond to, and display abroad." (Legge, *The Shoo King*, p. 263).

40. This applies only to the first two kings, Nanda and Upananda, not to the eight as the word *all* would mean, referring to *nanda*.

41. Hurvitz puts what Tao-sheng takes as two phrases in the *sūtra* 供養恭敬 into one: "showered with offerings" (*SLFD*, 3:19).

42. "Deferentially treated and revered" (Hurvitz, *SLFD*, 3:13).

43. Ōchō, "Jikudōshō sen", p. 238, suspects the letter 旨 might be 昔.

44. Cf. Liebenthal's translation from "[The Buddha] is" up to this sentence: "With the aim of preaching the *Lotus of the Law* in mind (the Buddhas) lead (the believers) first to the goals of their own liking and give them all the Heavens they may wish (*amitārtha*). When then (the believers), having stuck to the word of the Scriptures so long, would suddenly hear that the three Vehicles (and their Heavens) do not exist, they might doubt the good (intention of the earlier revelation) and turn back in sight of the yonder shore. And the Great Path would be barred to them. Better proceed gradually" ("World Conception," II, p. 93).

45. See 397a3, 402b6.

46. 動靜. Cf. the *I Ching*, AR, Part I, Chapter 1; the *Chuang-tzu*, Chapter 33: 動靜不離於理.

47. 窮理盡性 *found verbatim in the I Ching*, *Shuo-kua*, Chapter 1. Wilhelm and Baynes, *The I Ching*, p. 262: "By thinking through the order of the outer world to the end, and by exploring the law of their nature to the deepest core." Legge, *I Ching*, p. 422: "They (thus) made an exhaustive discrimination of what was right, and effected the complete development of (every) nature." Liebenthal, "World Conception," II, p. 66: "(The sages), in perfect harmony with Cosmic Order, in realization of their own nature." Some contemporary Buddhists cited the phrase; for example, Seng-chao, T38.350c9; Seng-jui,

T18.536c15, 537a3; a certain Liu shao-fu, T52.224b17. Also see Hui-ta, *HTC*, 150.424c13.

48. Alternate translation: "entered the utmost *samādhi*".

49. Liebenthal translates: "When Heaven and Earth stir, how can men be silent?" ("World Conception," II, p. 81).

50. *Catvāriphalāni*, the four stages of the result of cultivation in Hīnayāna: stream-entrant (*srotāpatti*), once returner (*sakridāgāmi*), nonreturner (*anāgāmi*), and *arhat*.

51. It refers to the phrase in the *sūtra*: "trembled in six different ways" (2b12, 3:30).

52. 中正. This and its variant 正中 occur frequently in the *I Ching*, in Hexagram *Hsü* et passim.

53. 功平 (398b12) may be a misprint of 公平, which is found in Wang Pi's commentary on the *Lao-tzu* (hereafter, *LTC*), ch. 16, Rump, *Commentary*, p. 50.

54. The letter 無 (b15) seems to be unnecessary, as Ōchō questions it ("Jikudōshō sen," p. 258).

55. See 397b17, 398d14; see note 18.

56. *CTC*, Chapter 2 (*CTI*, 1:29): "故曰道通為一···唯達者無滯于一方" Thus it is said "the *Tao* makes them all into one. . . . Only those who have reached the (*Tao*) do not stagnate in one direction."

57. The six worlds 六道 or the six kinds of living beings 六趣, refer to the six forms of reincarnation: hell-dweller (*naraka-gati*), hungry ghost (*preta-g.*), animal (*tiryagyoni-g.*), malevolent nature spirit (*asura-g.*), human existence (*manuṣya-g.*), and heavenly existence (*deva-g.*).

58. Cf. the Buddha's last words: "all the constituents of being are transitory; work out your salvation with diligence" (H. C. Warren, *Buddhism in Translations*, p. 109). Cf. also the parting words of Hui-neng, the sixth patriarch of the Ch'an school: "After I have gone just practice acccording to the Dharma in the same way that you did on the days that I was with you" (Yampolsky, *The Platform Sutra*, p. 181f).

59. 意 (*i*), probably a copier's mistake of its homophonym 疑 (?).

60. Referring to (Hurvitz, *SLFD*, 4:24) "the Dharma-prince", (2b28), "prince royal" (Kern, *Saddharma-Poṇḍarīka*, p. 16).

61. I have emended 光 (c11) to 化. Cf. 399a8f.

62. 偈: Hymn or chant in form of metrical verse. This particular question is found in 2c10 (Hurvitz, 5:9f.).

63. 無間然. Cf. the *Confucian Analects*, 8:32. Legge takes the phrase to be 無閒然, *Confucius*, p. 215; *Tao-te ching*, Chapter 43: 無間 "with no space."

64. Besides the two mentioned already there are four more as the constituents of the six virtues to be perfected: patience (*kṣānti*), vigor (*vīrya*), meditation (*dhyāna*), and wisdom (*prajñā*).

65. See the *Chuang-tzu*, Chapter 24; Watson, *Complete Works*, p. 169; Legge, *Texts of Taoism*, Part II, p. 101.

66. See the *sūtra*, 2b8.

67. 十方 "ten directions," but here used as a synonym of 十號 (4a:1) ten "subsidiary designations" (Hurvitz, 13:17) or "titles."

68. The same phrase in 397b17, 398b15f. See note 21.

69. 如是. Cf. *sūtra*, 5c11f., "suchness" (Hurvitz, 22:29ff.); yet, it appears to be an adjective, *such*, and punctuation of the text may be correct. *MSLW*, p. 33f., has "such a."

70. Liebenthal translates; "Though the ten thousand *dharma* are manifold they are yet uniform (as integral parts of) the Self-same. The Sage, absorbed in the vision of their integral state 'comes'; 'coming' he transforms creation. He is therefore called tathăgata (same-coming or "nature developing")" ("World Conception," II, pp. 73–74).

71. Etymologically, the translation of the word *arhat* as 應供 is justified, for it is derived from the root *arh*: "to deserve, merit, be worthy of" (Monier Williams, *Sanskrit English Dictionary*, p. 93).

72. 至道. It is found in *CTC*, Chapter 1 (*CTI*, 1:7), Chapter 2 (*CTI*, 1:29), et passim.

73. 無邪. See the *Shih Ching*, IV, ii, I: 思無邪 "his thoughts are without depravity" (Legge, *The Shoo King*, p. 613), repeated in the *Analects*, II, ii: "having no depraved thoughts" (Legge, *Confucianism*, p. 146).

74. Hurvitz, *SLFD*, 12:29, has "clarity" from 明 instead of "enlightenment".

75. 無非, a misprint of 無比 (?). Cf. 397b3.

76. The śāla-trees under which the Buddha entered *nirvāṇa*.

77. The constituents of existence: forms or matter (*rūpa*), perception (*vedanā*), mental conceptions (*sañjñā*), volition (*saṃskāra*), and consciousness (*vijñāṇa*).

78. Tao-sheng obviously departs from what is supposed to be the original meaning of the Sanskrit word *vid* (knowing) by taking it in the sense phrased here, although the Chinese letter also has the connotation of *vid*.

79. See 400a6 and 412d2.

80. 化. It is a term of diverse meanings, traceable to Taoism and neo-Taoism. In the *sūtra*, it, rarely appearing by itself, means "to convert" (6c23) (Hurvitz, p. 28) and often makes a compound with "*chiao*" (to teach), "*chiao-hua*" (7a29 et passim). In the context of Hui-yüan's system of thought, which is believed to be close to Tao-sheng's, it can be taken as "transformation" (Robinson, *op. cit.*, pp. 198 and 281, note 36), or "transfiguration" (Hurvitz, "Render unto Caesar," p. 96, also see p. 98, note 42). For a further treatment of the term, see chapter 6.

81. Emend 筌 to 詮.

82. 二 should read 三.

83. 必明當? See 398c9. Cf. 399b15.

84. Hurvitz has omitted "at that time" (是時), in compliance with the Sanskrit text, where the words are not repeated; see *SPSR*, 18:24.

85. 自崖, 崖 interchangeable with 岸 (see 401b14). See also 403d14. Cf. *HTC*, 150.426a.

Chapter 2

EXPEDIENT DEVICES

(Rising from *samādhi* or concentration, the Buddha, addressing Śāriputra, speaks of the profound nature of the *Dharma* the Buddha has attained, especially unfathomable to the voice hearer and the pratyekabuddhas. He explains why, like past and future Buddhas, he has had to resort to various pedagogical devices to lead all beings to salvation. All ways and *dharmas* are directed toward the One Buddha Vehicle, replacing the other two or three vehicles, which are really no more than expedient devices.)

2.1

In the past [the Buddha] has hidden [his teaching proper] within the traces of the three vehicles, which his followers [mistakenly] regarded as the teaching proper. Now [the Buddha] wishes to reveal the One reality, showing what is true and right. Because he clarifies what is right by means of what is wrong, this chapter is titled "Expedient Devices." As the previous three vehicles are indicated as expedient devices, the One reality[1] **[399b10]** is clearly postulated here and, though how it is so is not mentioned, it is self-evident. If it is titled "One Vehicle," *li* will look like one. Hence, [the chapter] is referred to as *Expedient Devices*, and yet it is still expressive of 'the realm [of the One reality] which only superlative description (or praise) may befit' (or the 'ineffable realm').[2]

2.2 "[The World-Honored One] rose serenely from his samādhi" (5b25, 22:1)

As [the Buddha] has been to the profound realm [in his samādhi,] his recondite words are also [necessarily] deep. Because Mañjuśrī resolved Maitreya's doubts about the rain flowers and earth trembling, as mentioned earlier [in the first chapter], should this not have shaken off their confusion and cleansed their minds? Their minds being emptied, they would be ready to accept the One Vehicle. Thereupon 'the Sage set forth the track,'[3] acquiesced and 'moved,'[4] and then rising from his concentration, started speaking. What he said must be profound and proper. It being profound and proper, those who receive it must naturally become earnest.

2.3 "Proclaimed to Śāriputra"

The reason why [the Buddha] proclaimed to him [in particular] is because, although his trace seemed close in rank to the voice hearers, his actual illumination surpassed his peers, thus qualifying him to be 'respondent in the dialogue'[5] [with the Buddha].

2.4 "Wisdom is profound"

Although [the Buddha's] speeches are varied in myriad ways, yet the intent [of the words] lies in manifesting the One. When beings deviate from the import of the words, creating a "profound [chasm]" with respect to "wisdom," it is not because the "wisdom" [as such] is "profound," but merely because the beings themselves are far away (literally, "profound") from "wisdom."[6] [399c1] This expression laments the failure [of beings in reaching the Buddha's intent]. How can this be taken as a praise for "wisdom"?

2.5 "The gateways of their wisdom"

[The value of] wisdom consists in preaching. Preaching is what the *gateways* refer to. Not only is wisdom incomprehensible but the "gateways" also are hard to fathom. Fathoming the "gateways" means realizing that there are no three [vehicles]. Is not this something that is "hard to understand?"

2.6.1 "No voice hearer or pratyekabuddha can know them"

But then the three vehicles are all provisional exigencies (*ch'üan*).[7] And the Greater Vehicle does not contradict that by which it becomes great. Therefore, [the Buddha] does not mention it, [the Greater Vechicle]. The two vehicles are in diametrical opposition to the sphere of "great." This refers to [what they] "cannot know."[8]

2.6.2 "Why is this? . . . dharmas that had never been before"

If the reason why this is so is not explained, how can one believe it? [The Buddha] had to make repeated explanations. Accumulating [what he was supposed] to do in such a way, ["in former times the Buddha"] attained to the ultimate [achievement]; that is what is meant by "that had never been before."[9] [The phrase stating that the Buddha's wisdom is] incalculable (5b26) conjoins with the [next] phrase with the word *wisdom* (5b26). This thus explains effect by means of cause.

2.6.3 "What he preaches accords with what is appropriate"

Words and traces represent external compliance [with *li* or reality]. By following the traces one might overlook the meaning. Being ignorant of the meaning, one encounters difficulty in understanding [what is real]. This [phrase] joins with the phrase *the gateways of their wisdom*. Now that the reason has been explained, the subtle meaning will reveal its face (literally, "turn its head").

2.7 [399c10] "Since achieving Buddhahood . . . enabling them to abandom their encumbrances" (5c1, 22:11)

What has been stated so far is all about praising the Buddha's wisdom. The present statement is the direct recounting of what Śākyamuni says he did himself. Entitling the [present] chapter ("Expedient Devices") has yielded this phrase. The preceding words, *accords with what is appropriate*, may then be seen as bringing "encumbrances" (5c3); it is necessary thus to explain this again. [The Buddha] said "[what he preaches] accords with what is appropriate," in the sense that "in accordance with" the kind of disease there should be "what is appropriate." Diseases are myriad in kind. [By the same token] the teaching cannot be in a set pattern;[10] but its fundamental purpose is to lead [beings] to cast aside their "encumbrances." Otherwise [even] for a day, their "encumbrances" would not be loosened from (or "abandon") *li*. Hence, he said, "since achieving Buddhahood."

2.8 "Why is this? . . . He has perfected [all] the dharmas that have never been before"

Internally, [the Buddha] has consummated "expedient devices, knowledge and insight"; externally, he speaks with 'skillful measures applicable to all human situations.'[11] Explained again is the reason why he has consummated expedient devices; namely, because his illumination is perfect, without obstruction, and has reached the ultimate end.[12] [The statement] that his "*dhyāna* concentration" and his meritorious virtues "have deeply penetrated the limitless" explains the reason why his "knowledge and insight, and his *pāramitās* have [all] been acquired to the fullest measure."

2.9 "By making a variety of distinctions, [he] can skillfully preach the *dharmas*"

It has been stated already that [the Buddha's teaching methods are] without set patterns, although this statement appears contradictory to [the nature of] *li*, [which has to do with the One]. It is necessary to explain again the differences between the three vehicles, of which he says here, *a variety of*. By means of three, One is manifested and this is called **[399d1]** *skillful preaching*. His myriad statements are equally proper; there is no differing taste (*rasa*); [all] are in accord with it (the One), and there is nothing that goes against it, thus it is called *gladdening many hearts*. So far [the Buddha] has explicated internal comprehension; now here he talks about external conversion.[13]

2.10.1 "Cease, Śāriputra, we need speak no more"

Because it already has been declared that the three vehicles are not real, what should logically follow is an explication of the One Vehicle. Even though [the Buddha] has said that they are unreal, this is still short of what is proper, not yet sufficient to startle their minds from attachment to them. If he says it again, they are certain to be bewildered and puzzled. Hence, he shouts, saying, "cease." How could one argue that their puzzlement can be dispelled without speaking. Although the One has not yet been pinpointed, the idea has been roughly suggested. Hence, he says, "we need speak no more."

2.10.2 "Reality"

There is no counterfeit (facade) of the two vehicles any more. Only the One Vehicle is real.

2.11.1 "Such marks, [such] nature"

These eleven factors [qualified by *such*][14] represent myriad goodnesses. As smoke is the external mark (*hsiang*) of fire, burning is its nature. The external mark is based on the outside whereas nature is in charge of the inside.

2.11.2 "[Such] substance"

This is an integrated designation encompassing nature and mark.

2.11.3 "[Such] powers, [such] functions"

When one has an ability not yet harnessed it is called *power*. That which creates an actual use and makes application possible is referred to as *function*.

2.11.4 "[Such] causes, [such] conditions"

That which enables [something] to come into existence is its "cause" (*yin*/*hetu*); that which helps [something] grow exuberantly like the branches and leaves of a tree is its "condition" (*yüan*/*pratyaya*).

2.11.5 "[Such] effects, [such]retributions" **[399d10]**

When what one has willed and expected to happen duly come true, we call it *effect*. What is yielded from what one has seeded[15] is called *retribution*.

2.11.6 "[Such] beginning, [and such] end"

The start of myriad goddnesses is the "end"; the culmination of the Buddha's wisdom is the "beginning." Only the Buddhas comprehend those meanings,[16] and understand the ultimate source. Hence, in general conclusion, it is said, "the ultimate identity."

2.12.1 "Except for the multitude of bodhisattvas, whose power of faith is firm" (5c17, 23:32)

The Buddha earlier preached the three, but now he says that there are no [three], not yet, however, entering the track of the One. This idea is hard to fathom. Those who fathom it are few. Hence, those [whose faith is firm] are widely listed. Those [whose faith] is firm refer to those who are in the eighth stage (*bhūmi*) or beyond. Only they can fathom that the Buddha is about to preach the One Vehicle. Hence, it is said, "except for." Those of the two vehicles hold on but cannot fathom it.

2.12.2 Bodhisattvas who have recently launched their thoughts" (6a11, 24:24)

They are the ones who have understood their nature (*hsing*).

2.12.3 "Bodhisattvas who do not backslide"

They are in between the first and the seventh[17] stages. It cannot be said that they are not aware of it (the three as One); [the Buddha] wants to exalt and beautify the One Vehicle, causing people to worship and believe it. Hence, it is said thus.

2.12.4 "[The Buddha's] words are without discrepancy"

Li is the sole ultimate. The [Buddha's] words tally with *li*. Hence, it is said, "words are without discrepancy."

2.13.1 "At that time, in the midst of the great multitude. . . . twelve hundred persons" (6a28, 25:29)

The reason that [the Buddha] until now ceased to speak is to stop their [400a1] doubts. But more doubts arose in those ignorant [of the Buddha's true goal]. These voice hearers have heard the Buddha praising highly this path as being so profound, but they are far from realizing where his purport lies.

2.13.2 "The doctrine of unique deliverance, which means that, we, too, gaining this Dharma"

Even though there is distinction between superior and inferior in the merits and virtues of the three vehicles, there ultimately is no difference in that they all reach the abode of the eternal cessation of *nirvāṇa*. Hence, it is said, "unique deliverance" (*ekaiva vimuktir*), "unique" (or "one") meaning "the same." But they do not "know where the doctrine tends" (6b5) that the Buddha praised in such utmost earnest.

2.14.1 "Śāriputra, knowing of the doubts in the minds of the fourfold assembly" (6b7, 26:6)

Sharing the [collective] sentiment [prevalent in the congregation] at the time, [Śāriputra] has availed himself of the opportunity to raise a question. As the doubts intensify in his mind, his will to resolve them also becomes very strong.[18]

2.14.2 "On the dharmas attained on the platform of the path"

The path (*tao*) being lofty and *li* being recondite, who would dare to ask about them? If the Buddha did not preach, the traces would look like the *Dharma* they (the congregation) envisioned them to be. Therefore, the World-Honored One rose from *samādhi* and preached of his own accord, though unsolicited, praising the Buddha's wisdom as "extremely profound" and immeasurable. The *gāthās* that follow are designed to praise [the Buddha's wisdom] in a chant.

2.15 "The Buddha proclaimed to Śāriputra: 'Cease, cease! There is no need to speak further'" (6c7, 27:28)

By the first *cease* (5c9), the Buddha wanted them to cease harboring doubts. Body-son (Śāriputra) said [that the Buddha should] preach and then [they will] cease harboring **[400a10]** doubts. Hence, the repeated request. The two words show a vast difference [in what they refer to], and yet they are the same in that they are intended for dispelling men's doubts.

2.16 "At that time, the world-honored one declared to Śāriputra: 'Since you have not thrice earnestly besought me'" (7a5, 29:9)

As the Sage sets forth the teaching, his speech must be unfolded gradually; awakening, likewise, is achieved step by step.[19] As the request was made thrice, the doubts of the congregation were both prevalent and lingering; the doubts of the congregation being widely prevalent and lingering, their desire to hear was very intense.[20] The triple request was made not because the Buddha wished it, but because the circumstances of the time [with respect to his listeners] dictated it.[21]

2.17.1

In the next five segments [the Buddha] expounds the purport. The first segment is about distinguishing the difference between the true and the false. The second properly clarifies the process of becoming one at [the point of] the foundational-cum-ultimate.[22] The third illustrates that the tracks of the Buddhas in the three periods—past, present, and future—are identical. The fourth explains why preaching the three vehicles was not what the Sage [originally] wanted but that he could not help but appear [in the world to preach them]. The fifth is about the men who obtained [the Buddha's] original purport and those who did not.

2.17.2

The story of the five thousand men withdrawing [from the scene] (7a8). This belongs to the first segment, on distinguishing he difference between true and false. The speech proper is about to be revealed. Then true and false will be clear of themselves, which is, figuratively speaking, like when the sun and the moon shine brightly, the difference between black and white becomes distinct and clear. The purpose of showing this trace is to guide the collective sentiment of the time to a hushed readiness [for the doctrine] **[400b1]**. By showing it to those like the people with "overweening pride," who are not prepared to attend the auspicious assembly, [the Buddha wishes] to elate the mood of the time and lead to the point where all drive (literally, "flagellating") themselves toward faith and enlightenment.

2.18.1 "At that time, the Buddha declared to Śāriputra . . . No more branches and leaves" (7a12, 29:21)

This is the second segment. In the following part the Buddha attempts to explain the path of unification. The bothersome branches are gone; the firm trunk remains. "What he preaches accords with what is appropriate" (5b29); he preaches in the way that befits [the varying levels or existential conditions of] the various beings. Even though [the Buddha] speaks of the three, his emotional posture remains committed to manifesting the One. Hence it is said, "their purport is hard to understand" (7a18, 29:31).

2.18.2 ["The Buddhas, the World-Honored Ones] for one great cause alone appear in the world" (7a21, 30:1)

Earlier[23] a similar [statement] suggested this central theme[24] [of the preaching, namely, the One]. This [passage] represents the [Buddha's] further [attempt] to preach it. [The Buddha] already has stated that the three vehicles are expedient devices; now he explains that there is the One. The Buddha is for the One Ultimate. He has appeared [in the world] to manifest the One. If *li* consists in three, the Sage would appear for the sake of three. But there are no three in *li*, just the mysterious One alone.[25] Hence, it is said, "[the Buddhas] for one great cause alone appear in the world."

2.18.3 "They wish to cause the beings to open [their eyes][26] to the Buddha's knowledge and insight"

The idea of subtle speech and profound import becomes manifested here. These four phrases [making up the paragraph] from beginning to end are designed to express the doctrine of the One. Because all sentient beings **[400b10]** are originally endowed with the Buddha's knowledge and insight, although they are not manifested on account of defilement obstacles, when the Buddha opens [the original nature] and removes [defilement obstacles], they will be capable of achieving [what they are endowed with].[27] One theory [by a commentator][28] says that, from the first stage to the seventh, defilements (*kleśa*) are gradually removed, a process which is called *opening* (*k'ai*); nothing gets out of the luster of illumination, which is called *purity*.

2.18.4 "They wish to demonstrate the Buddha's knowledge and insight to beings"

It has been stated that [beings] have an original endowment of it. Instigated by the present teaching they can realize it. If realization is achieved through the teaching, this external "demonstration" (*shih*) is certain to bring about "understanding" (*wu*). By achieving "understanding" one is bound to "enter" (*ju*) the path (*tao*). One theory holds that [a bodhisattva] in the eighth stage attains *samādhi* by contemplating [the characteristic marks of] the Buddha. Eternity (*nitya*) and bliss[29] (*ānanda*) "demonstrate" the Buddha's wisdom.

2.18.5 "[Cause beings] to understand [the Buddha's] knowledge and insight"

One theory has it that a bodhisattva in the ninth stage gets good wisdom (*sādhumati*), and acquires a deep understanding of the Buddha's knowledge and insight.

2.18.6 "Enter into the Buddha's knowledge and insight"

According to one theory, a bodhisattva in the tenth stage, having the traces of defilements and the perfuming impression (*vāsanā*) discharged and destroyed by means of the diamond (*vajra*)-*samādhi*, turns to enter into [the realm of] the Buddha's wisdom. When we discuss the background and compare the contents [of the preceding passage], such a division and classification can be made. To sum it up, what a novice takes as a single enlightenment[30] consists practically of these four components.

2.18.7 "Whether two or three" (7b3, 30:18)

[The word] *two* means the second vehicle, and *three* the third vehicle. It is also natural that there is no first. The first **[400c1]** does not contradict what the *great* stands for. Therefore it is not nonexistent. [Yet,] now that there is neither "two" nor "three," "one" is gone as well.

2.19 "Śāriputra, the dharmas of the Buddhas [in all ten directions] are of this sort"

This is the third segment. [The Buddha] draws out the Buddhas of past, present, and future from the ten directions as witnesses. The Buddhas in the three periods all have preached and will preach the three vehicles first and manifest the One Ultimate later. In other words, although the periods are different and the men are varied, the paths (*tao*) are identical.

2.20.1 "Śāriputra, the Buddhas come into an evil world[31] stained with five defilements" (7b23, 31:16)

This is the fourth segment. The gist of this segment is as follows. The Sage did not intend to set up the doctrine of the three, but because beings mired in defilement were found to have difficulty in acquiring the one single enlightenment, [the Buddha] had no alternative but to come into the world to preach the three vehicles. How could he wish to do so [for his own sake]?

2.20.2 "The defilement of the kalpa (kalpakaṣāya)"

Beings in the earlier generations were of a natural disposition,[32] clean and void, and their bondages (*lei*) were minimal and thin. Compared with them, the contemporary generation can be characterized only as "defiled." *Kalpa* refers to time. Being in this evil state, beings sometimes encounter armed soldiers and sometimes face the scarcity of grains, diseases, or epidemics.

2.20.3 "The defilement of the agonies (kleśakaṣāya)"

Beings] being entangled with various delusions, how can the *Tao* be stimulated to arise [in them]?

2.20.4 "The defilement of beings (sattvakaṣāya)" **[400c10]**

This refers to the evil (or sufferings?) arising from the full-orbed activities of the aggregates (*skandhas*), five in total.[33]

2.20.5 "The defilement of views (dṛṣṭikaṣāya)"

The five false views[34] are in opposition to the true and are in conflict with *li*. Hence, they are listed separately.

2.20.6 "The defilement of life (ayuskaṣāya)"

The false [views] and life get intertwined, keeping [beings] from encountering the Path (*Tao*). How could this not be defilement?

2.20.7 "[The Buddhas. . .] make distinctions in the One Buddha Vehicle and speak of three"

As the Buddha thought that men in the defiled age had no lofty will, and because the *li* of the Buddhas was so profound and distant that they (men) were unable to believe in it, the Buddha designed the doctrine of the three vehicles in order to make it accessible to men. Although it is said that he preached the three, what he preached always [in reality] was the One. Men are now personally in contact with the Buddha. Isn't this a case of adaptation to make it accessible to men? Traces are closer to men. External demonstration is easier to apprehend. Even if it is possible to make it easy to learn, there is the distance inherent in its self-soness (*tzu-jan*). Moreover, it has been said that [followers of] the two vehicles had exhausted the bonds of existence; [and yet] they did not have [their] perfuming impressions (*vāsanā*) disposed of. By moving men close to [the One], [the Buddha] makes [it] easier to go beyond [the three]. If it is possible for them to go beyond [the three] and seek the self-soness [of the One at the same time], they will head for the total obliteration [of the three]. This is what "make distinctions in the One Buddha Vehicle and speak of three" means.

2.21.1 "Śāriputra, if a disciple of mine, thinking himself an *arhat*"

This is the fifth segment, on distinguishing men's attainment and loss [of arhatship]. Wishing **[400d1]** the *Tao* to prevail in the world, how can [the Buddha] not explain the distinction between attainment and loss, advising men to do away with [the cause of] loss and to follow [that of] attainment? If one calls oneself an *arhat* but does not know that the Buddha is [in the world] solely for converting [potential] bodhisattvas (9c27, 44:11), one is not an *arhat* [in the true sense of the word]. One is then a man of error and loss. When a man is able to keep this *sūtra*, he can be said to have attained [the arhatship].

2.21.2 "Except when, after a Buddha's passage into extinction, no Buddha is present"

[For the interim period] between two Sages, when there is no Sage-Lord,[35] unbelief may prevail. If one lives when a Buddha is present, one is certain to have faith and no doubts. Contemporary men have been taken unwittingly to where the Buddha is present, so there should be no [trace of] unbelief.

2.22.1

The *gāthās* that follow speak of [what is said in] the previous five divisions in the same order. The first four verses chant the first [theme] of "true and false." The next thirty-five verses chant "the one great cause" of the second [segment]. The following seventy-five verses chant of the Buddhas of the [three][36] periods as witnesses. The next two verses chant of the previous fourth segment, on the theme that [the Buddha] had no choice but to appear [in the world] to preach the three vehicles. The final five verses chant the fifth [theme] on the men of attainment and loss.

2.22.2 "That, receiving the frail form of a fetus" (8b14, 35:19)

Being within the delusion of the three realms,[37] they are referred to as *frail*. Only the *Dharma*-body (*-kāya*) **[400d10]** is great.

2.22.3 "By the resort to yet other devices, help to clarify the prime meaning" (8c10, 37:34)

Li is originally of the unspeakable [nature].[38] He has borrowed words to speak about it. They are called [*expedient*] *devices* (*upāya*). Again, the two vehicles are employed as [teaching] aids for transforming them (beings). They are called *other [expedient] devices*. The One Vehicle is so deep that it has to rely on them to be manifested. According to one theory, what was preached [by the Buddha] for forty-nine years belong to expedient devices. The subject of the present preaching, the *Dharma Blossom* (or *Lotus*), belongs to "other [expedient] devices".

2.23.1 "If there are varieties of living beings . . . there will be some who prostrate themselves ceremoniously" (8c11, 37:36)

What is shown in this and following paragraphs is that beings in the time of the past Buddhas planted the good seeds; one tiny part of[39] one kind of good deed after another, they were all accumulated to perfect the *Tao*.[40]

2.23.2 "Know that the dharmas are ever without a nature of their own" (9b8.41:16)

[This refers to] the doctrine of the [supreme or highest] emptiness (*śūnyatā*),[41] suggesting that *li* is the nondual ultimate.

2.23.3 "By virtue of conditions is the Buddha-seed realized"

The Buddha provides the conditions (*pratyaya*) for *li* to arise. Now that *li* is not dual, how can it afford to be threefold? "For this reason they preach the One Vehicle." (9b9, 41:19)

2.24 "The endurance of the *dharmas*, the secure position of the *dharmas*, in the world everabiding" (9b10, 41:20)

This articulates what was said earlier, [namely, the passage] "know that the *dharmas* are ever without a nature of their own (*svabhā-va*)." In this way, therefore, they came to "know that [the *dharmas*] are without a nature of their own."

2.25 "Throughout three weeks". (9c5, 43:1) [401a1]

The fact that for the first seven days [the Buddha] "beheld the Tree", means that he intended to express his desire to requite the favors [he had received]. That he "walked about" for the intermediate seven days means that as [the future Buddha], while walking around [in meditation], [he] perfected the *Tao* under the shady trees; these favors thereby must have been requited. For the final seven days, he meditated on how to ferry the multitudinous beings across [to the other shore]. [Then] the Brahmā king begged [the Buddha] to turn the Dharma [-wheel] (9c9 & 12). Perceiving (or stimulated by) (*kan*) [this request] [the Buddha] gave him transformative instruction.

Notes

1. Ōchō, "Jikudōshō sen," p. 251, suspects (一)顯 (399b10) to be 實.

2. See 399b17&c1, 400a1 and 8.

3. 聖人設軌. Cf. *I Ching*, *AR*, Part I, Chapter 2: 聖人設卦 "The Sage set forth the hexagrams"; 聖人···設教 (Hexagram *kuan*) "The Sage . . . set forth the teaching."

4. Cf. Wang Pi's commentary on the *I Ching*, on the latter passage in note 3: 以觀感化物者也 "by means of '*kuan*', he moves and transforms the beings." (Itō Togai, *Chou-i ching i t'ung-chieh*, p. 126)

5. 對揚: "One who drew out remarks or sermons from the Buddha" (*DCBT*, p. 423). The locus classicus of the term is the *Shu Ching*, Part 4. *Shuo-ming*, is translated to mean "to propagate [the will of the king] in response to

[the latter's decree]" or, in Legge's rendering, "to respond to, and display abroad, [your Majesty's excellent charge]" (Legge, *The Shoo King*, p. 262). See 397d14.

6. Hurvitz suggests in our discussion on the passage that this phrase seems to be out of place.

7. 權 See the *Chuang-tzu*, Chapter 17: 達理者必明於權 "Circumstances" (Watson, *Chuang Tzu: Basic Writings*, p. 104) or "all varying circumstances" (Legge, *Texts of Taoism*, Part II, p. 383). See Chapter 3, note 4.

8. Emend 致 (399d4) to 故. See Ōchō, "Jikudōshō sen," p. 265.

9. Liebenthal translates: "Consummation reached by accumulation of merit is 'marvellous'" ("World Conception," II, p. 94).

10. 無方 "without any set pattern." It is found in the *I Ching*, *AR*, Part I, Chapter 4: *CTC*, Chapter 12. (*CTI*, 4:33).

11. 無非 . Rather 無比 "Incomparable degree [of skillfulness]"(?)

12. Rephrasing the *sūtra*, 5c4f.; Hurvitz, SLFD, 22:17f.

13. Cf. the dictum that indicates the dual goal of a bodhisattva, 上求菩提下化衆生 "Above, he seeks *bodhi* or enlightenment; below, he converts all the beings." See Chih-i, *Mo-ho chih-kuan*, T46.6a18.

14. Hurvitz, pp. 22f., takes 如是 as a noun, "*suchness*," thus matching it with ten items, from "the suchness of the dharmas" to the "suchness of their retributions," which is discrepant from the generally accepted reading; that is, the way the passage is punctuated in Taishō edition (5c11ff.). Tao-sheng's reading is in agreement with the latter, taking the word as an adjective. He draws eleven factors from it by dissecting what others take as one the last factor, "beginning and end," into two. See J. Takakusu, *The Essentials of Buddhist Phi-*
ginning and end," into two. See J. Takakusu, *Essentials of Buddhist Philosophy*, p. 135.

15. 歷數所鍾. 歷數 means a calendrical, cosmic order, governing the divisions of times, that is, years, seasons, months, days. The term occurs in the *Shu Ching*, Chu-shu: Hung-fan; in the *Confucian Analects*, 20:1 (Legge, *Confucius*, p. 350, 天之歷數 "the Heaven-determined order of succession"); *Chuang-tzu*, Chapter 27. (*CTI*, p. 9:6), 天有歷數 "Heaven has its places and spaces which can be calculated" (Legge, *The Texts of Taoism*, II, p. 146) or "Heaven has its cycles and numbers" (Watson, *Complete Works*, p. 306). For 鍾 see *Chung-hua tai-tzu-tien*, p. 2753: 天所賦予 "What is endowed by the heaven."

16. Cf. Liebenthal's translation up to this point: "The (way of) good deeds begins at the end; it ends in the beginning with the attainment of the Buddha wisdom. Only the Buddha understands this" ("World Conception," II,

p. 74). Here Liebenthal fails to distinguish between the words from the *sūtra* and Tao-sheng's own words.

17. On the seventh stage, Takakusu, *Essentials of Buddhist Philosophy*, p. 125, says: "The seventh is the Stage of Far-Going (*dūraṇ-gamā*) which is the position farthest removed from the selfish state of two Vehicles. Here one completes the perfection of expediency (*upāya*)."

18. Cf. 398c8.

19. Emend 諧 to 階.

20. Cf. 398c17.

21. Liebenthal translates: "The Buddha is called three times, not because he is interested but because it is demanded by the state of the Beings" ("World Conception," II, p. 81).

22. See 409c11, 411d9. Cf. 397a1, 403d2, 407a7.

23. This may refer to 6b4, 26:2 "The Buddha has preached the doctrine of unique deliverance." See 400a2.

24. 宗: "the First Principle" (Hurvitz, "Render unto Caesar," p. 99).

25. Liebenthal translates: (from "The Buddha is") "'The Buddha is the one center (of the universe); to proclaim this oneness he has arisen'. . . . Cosmic Order (*li*) does not allow three (Vehicles); it is *unum mysticum* and nothing else" ("World Conception," II, p. 74).

26. Hurvitz renders 開 "open [their eyes]" as "hear of" (30:5), which can be drawn rather from 聞. Katō also takes it as "open" (44:7). The Sanskrit equivalent is "samadapana" (Wogihara, 37:7), which has the meaning of "instigation (of others) to assume, to take on themselves" (*BHSD*, p. 568).

27. Cf. Liebenthal's translation: "All the beings possess the innate ability to see what is known only to the Buddhas. But this knowledge is covered with rubbish. This the Buddha removes and thus makes (knowledge) possible" ("World Conception," II. p. 74).

28. Suspected to be one of Tao-sheng's contemporary scholars such as T'an-ying and Tao-jung, both Kumārajīva's disciples. See Ōchō, "Jikudōshō sen," p. 230.

29. 常樂: two of the four virtues of *nirvāṇa*, the other two being personality (我) and purity (淨).

30. 一悟, or "understanding the One" (?); see also 2.20.1.

31. "Ages" (Katō, *Myōho-Renge-Kyō*, p. 46).

32. 稟質. *Chih* (basic stuff) as used by Confucius and Tung Chung-shu (second century B.C.) refers to "man's inner, spontaneous nature," or "man's original nature in its totality"; see Fung, *History of Chinese Philosophy*, vol. 2, p. 33, notes 1 and 2.

33. 五盛陰惡 (苦?), the five being material form (*rūpa*). sensation (*vedanā*), conception (*saṃjñā*), predisposition (*saṃskāra*), and perception (*vijñāna*).

34. They are the heretical views that there is a real self (*satkāya-dṛṣṭi*); the heresy of extreme views (*antargrāha-d.*); false heretical views (*mithyā-d.*); attachment to perverted views (*dṛṣṭi-parāmarśa-d.*); and attachment to heretical practices and disciplines (*sīla-vrata-parāmarśa-d.*).

35. 聖主. See the *sūtra* (8c8): 大聖主 "the Chiefs of the Great Saints" (Hurvitz, *SLFD*, 37: 30).

36. The letter 三 (400d7) should be repeated.

37. 三界 (*triloka*): the realm of desire (*kāmadhātu*), the realm of form (*rūpadhātu*), and the formless realm (*arūpadhātu*).

38. 理本無言, cf. *CTC*, Chapter 2, (*CTI*, 1:34) 至理無言, and 理無所言, "The (ultimate) *li* cannot be expressed in words."

39. Emend 一 (400d15) to 之; see 397a2.

40. Liebenthal translates: "under past Buddhas the Beings have planted Roots-of-good. Little bits, single deeds, accumulating, secure salvation to the believers" ("World Conception," II. p.83).

41. 第一空義. It might rather be 第一義空 "the emptiness of the highest order" (*paramārtha-śūnyatā*). This phrase can be a strong candidate for the indicator that Tao-sheng was trained in the *Prajñāpāramitā Sūtras* and the Mādhyamika doctrine, the contention by Ōchō.

Chapter 3

PARABLE

(Śāriputra expresses joy at his understanding, without any more doubt and uncertainty about the Buddha's new doctrine of the One Vehicle. The Buddha confers upon him the prophecy of his complete enlightenment in the future, when he will become a Buddha named Flower Glow. Śāriputra, however, for the sake of other disciples with doubts and perplexities yet to be dissipated, beseeches the Buddha to give more explanations about the teaching. In response to the request, the Buddha takes up a parable of a burning house. The owner of the house, a rich elder, in an attempt to save his children from the burning house, who are immersed in playing, not knowing the disaster posed by the fire, devises an expedient. He promises them three kinds of carts drawn by goats, deer, and oxen. The children escape the fire and at their demands for the promised carts, the elder gives them one great carriage made of precious substances. As much as the elder cannot be guilty of falsehood, the Buddha, by the same token, is justified for having preached the three vehicles to entice beings, who will end up being saved by the Great Vehicle only.)

3.1

In faculties there is [the distinction between] keeness and dullness:[1] it follows that in enlightenment[2] there is [the differences between those who can be awakened] early and [those who can only be awakened] late. [The Buddha] hitherto has made a presentation of the

Dharma Blossom in a straightforward way, and those disciples with keen faculties have obtained an understanding of it, [as shown] in the preceding. Those who are dull have not been awakened yet. Thus [the Buddha] will explain it by resort to a parable. *Li* is so profound and unfathomable that it is difficult to grasp it in one encounter.[3] Therefore, [the Buddha] by evervarying adaptation,[4] resorts to worldly things (*shih*) and images to depict his recondite purport. The worldly things borrowed to be analogized with *li* are referred to as *parable*.

3.2.1 "Śāriputra danced for joy" (10b26, 49:1)

From this phrase to the beginning of [the parable of] "the burning house" (12b3) there are altogether three segments explaining the purport. The first [segment] explains that Śāriputra has achieved understanding within himself and issues outward what he has comprehended. Because his doubts, arisen earlier, were serious, his anxiety and worry were very deep. Now, **[400a10]** the first [among the congregation] enlightened to the One Vehicle, he expressed his pleasure, saying that he wanted to dance for joy. Unable to get over his pleasure, he could not help saying so. It is shown here that, by resort to the traces, [the Buddha] exigently[5] draws [the attention of] the congregation of the moment, making the collective sentiment at the time deeply earnest.

3.2.2 "What is the reason? . . . To miss the incalculable knowledge and insight of the Thus Come One"

[Śāriputra] has expressed his joy [for attaining] what he had wanted to understand formerly. His [long-held] intention to understand helped him to realize what he heard, namely, "such a *Dharma* as this." Hearing that all beings are bound to become Buddhas, and seeing the bodhisattvas receive the prophecy of their enlightenment, he was sorely grieved himself that he alone was not included in this. What he heard today tallies with [what he heard] in the past. Thus once the [doctrine] was passed to him, he was immediately awakened. He regretted in the past having missed the Greater [Vehicle];[6] now his enlightenment obviously made him delighted.

3.2.3 "I have dwelt alone in mountain forests and at the foot of trees . . . [our fault], not that of the World-Honored One"

The reason why he, upon hearing, was enlightened is because since earlier days he had had this thought every moment: "We will all equally enter into the Dharmahood; how could the Thus Come One limit it just to the Lesser [Vehicle] (Hīnayāna)? Yet it is our own [fault] that we have taken merely the Lesser. Why did the Buddha do [it] this way?[7] It is because [the Buddha] preached by means of a gradual process, namely, the Lesser first and the Greater later, certainly in that order [but not vice versa]. If I had waited for him to preach the Greater, I would have certainly obtained the Greater. But straight upon hearing [the Buddha] preach the Lesser, [I] immediately thought this to be the real **[401bl]** Lesser. Having befriended my own [self-] interest, and 'basing conclusions on it,'[8] [I] have always since been vexed at my own fault. Now hearing that they are one, and that we can enter into the Dharmahood without differentiating, [I] became awakened right away." The intention of [the Buddha] himself was not in the Lesser; the disciples were thus vexed at their own fault. Now [Śāriputra] being awakened in such a way, his joy must be boundless. *To wait* also means "[we] should have waited".

3.3.1 "At that time, the Buddha declared to Śāriputra: "I [now speak] in [the midst of the great multitude of] gods, men, *śramanas*" (11b9, 53:6)

This is the second segment. The gist of this part is that because there never has been the path of the Lesser Vehicle (*Hīnayāna*) it turns out that [the Lesser] merely has been pointing toward the Buddha [path]. The enlightenment Body-son [Śāriputra] has built up was so profoundly manifest that [the Buddha] granted him a prophecy of his enlightenment. The story of the prophecy should not be held to be true in a real sense. [It was designed] merely for leading forward those who aspired to the prophecy.

3.3.2 "Formerly I, in the presence of two myriads of millions of Buddhas . . . one that the Buddha keeps in mind"

Formerly [Śāriputra wrongly assumed] with delight that he was enlightened, but [the Buddha], contradicting him, admonished him to drive himself to achieve it. The fact that the Lesser Vehicle had no great hope in earlier times, but now [the Buddha] grants the group a prophecy, implies that there is no "lesser" in *li.* The [Buddha's] motive for reviewing the practices [of Śāriputra] in the remote past is to show that it was [Sariputra's own] merits that invited such prophecies, but he did not mention this, because he had his mind set on secretly directing the collective sentiment of the congregation at the time.

3.3.3 "By reason of his former vow he shall preach the Dharma of the three vehicles" (11b25, 54:2) **[401b10]**

The teaching of the three vehicles was designed originally for the impure ages. Now that the lands have been purified, there is no need for the three. But why does [the Buddha] speak of the three? He wants to show that the three are identical with the One; there is no separate "three" any more. What he formerly understood as three is the One; hence, *former vow*. He did not really mean to preach the three kinds of transformative teaching as such.

3.3.4 "Present a prophecy . . . to [the bodhisattva] Hard-Full (Dhṛtiparipūrṇa)". (11c6, 54:25)

The [Buddha's] intention in presenting further a prophecy to Hard-Full is to prove to Body-son that obtaining a prophecy is not an empty [word].

3.4.1 "At that time the fourfold multitude . . . endlessly for joy of heart" (12a7, 56:18)

This is the third segment. [Here, the Buddha] led those with [excessive] self-esteem to realize that they were [in fact] all endowed with [the capacity for enlightenment]; hence, *joy of heart.*

3.4.2 "Śāriputra addressed the Buddha, saying: 'I now have no more doubts or second thoughts'"

Insofar as one's virtue is great, one's concern [for others] is deep; when the *Tao* [one has achieved] is great, it extends to kingliness as well.[9] Body-son, having already been inducted into the path of enlightenment, wants others with the same intention [to receive a prophecy] to share his profound understanding. Therefore, on behalf of twelve thousand people, he raises the question and addresses the Buddha. These voice hearers had no doubts before, but they harbor some now. They should be opened up and put forward first, and then explanations [responding to their doubts] can follow.

3.4.3 "Having heard what they had never heard before"

Formerly they lived on **[401cl]** "three," now they have to take "One." Both are what the Sage has said, and so are contradictory to each other. Consequently they come to cast doubts on what they heard.

3.4.4 "For they who have intelligence gain understanding through parables" (12b12, 58:15)

What the Buddha has said up to now is aimed at cutting off the doubts they harbor. Now he mentions those who have intelligence in order to get them to the [main] idea. Intelligence counters stupidity. It was said earlier that men of intelligence, when hearing parables, can have their minds awakened.[10] By this statement, what was said before is further extended to encourage them to move toward a speedy enlightenment.

3.5 "Imagine that a country, or a city-state" (12b13, 58:17)

From this phrase on [the Buddha's] doctrine is explained analogically. There are seven segments, in total, illustrating *li*. The first segment relates the frequent occurrence of calamities and various misfortunes in the house. In the second is shown that only those who are awakened to these calamities and misfortunes are Buddhas. The third tells that the Buddha, having been awakened himself, has great compassion (*mahākaruṇā*) arising in him, [and that he means] to "rescue"[11] all children. In the fourth, as he will later offer the happiness of the three vehicles, he first talks about the dreadful happening in the house. Fifth, [the Buddha] offers them the happiness of the three vehicles. Sixth, [the Buddha] provides them with the utmost happiness of the One Vehicle, which is true and real. Seventh, it turns out that the three carts [the Buddha] promised earlier are not to be given at the end, [the promise] being empty and false.

3.6.1 [401c10]

A country refers to a place where cities are located. The multitudinous beings are situated in the cities of the three realms (*triloka*); we call them the *country*. The first segment [begins here]. *A city-state* refers to the supreme ultimate.[12] The ultimate is analogized as the *city-state*. [The Buddha's] limited approach to men is compared to "a municipality," which is synonymous with a city. The Buddha in accordance with doctrine follows [varying] existential situations (*shih*); thus all kinds of names have been created.

3.6.2 "Has a great elder"[13]

The Buddha is certainly in charge of them, and rules over them, being the one whom they pay respect to: he is "the elder".

3.6.3 "Advanced in years"

[The Buddha] reincarnated himself and advanced to the later stage of his life in order to set forth the doctrine of the three vehicles.

3.6.4 "Of incalculable wealth"

In preaching the *Dharma*, [the Buddha] uses wisdom-life as its source: it is "wealth." *Li* is inexhaustible and limitless: it is "incalculable."

3.6.5 "Owning many fields and houses, as well as servants"

Transformative teaching removes their defilements and produces shoots[14] of the *Tao* in them;[15] it is "fields." They come to reside in it [*Tao*]: it is "house." They comply with the teaching in their conduct: they are "servants." There is no place where it does not exist: it is "many."

3.6.6 "His house is broad and great"

They take delusions as their original source and are settled in them: this is what *house* represents. Delusions are everywhere: they are "broad and great."

3.6.7 "It has one doorway"

The Buddha teaches the passage to enlightenment: he is the "doorway." Only these people have passed through it, they are "one hundred or two hundred": **[401d1]** gods (*devas*) account for "one hundred"; men, "two hundred". The three evil paths (*gati*) of transmigration account for "five hundred." They rely on the [three] realms: they are "dwelling in it."

3.6.8 "The halls [and chambers] are rotting"[16]

The realm of sensuous desire (*kāmadhātu*) is the "hall." The two upper realms are "chambers." Gradual decay is "rotting."

3.6.9 "The walls crumbling"

Various delusions are prevalent in the four directions: they are referred to as *walls*. To do what is not good and what must be overcome is referred to as *crumbling*.

3.6.10 "The pillars decayed at their bases"

False views dwell in it: they are "pillars." Going astray from *li*, one is not stable: one has "decayed."

3.6.11 "The beams and ridgepoles precariously tipped"

[The beings] are brought to realize that they are in a state of ignorance and [self-] love; they [ignorance and self-love] are "beams and ridgepoles." *Li* can easily take them off: they are "precariously tipped."

3.6.12 "Throughout the house and all at the same time, quite suddenly a fire breaks out, burning down all the apartments"

Various sufferings are compared to burning. There is no place where there is no suffering: it is "throughout the house". It has come of [the path of] aberration;[17] thus "quite suddenly." The thing proper (or cause, *shih*) has arrived: it "breaks out." It burns "the apartments" of the five aggregates (*skandhas*),[18] [the constituents of 'self'].

3.6.13 "[The elder's] sons, ten, or twenty, or thirty of them"

Those who have already been converted are "sons". There is the differentiation of the three vehicles: it is "three" [of thirty or three tens]. There are so many [of those who have been transformed]: thus "ten" [of three tens].

3.7.1 [401d10] "The elder, seeing that great fire breaking out from four directions, is alarmed and terrified". (12b19, 58:27)

This is the second segment. The Buddha is awakened to the suffering [of the other beings]. [The fact] that [these living beings] are originally transformed does not correspond with the fact that suffering exists: he is "alarmed." Perceiving suffering makes his mind confused and he fears that the wisdom-life may be burned up in the fire; hence, he is "terrified."

3.7.2 "He then has this thought: 'Though I was able to get out safely through this burning doorway'"

The Buddha has his manifested form present in the house, also showing that he is in the state of suffering. The moment one enters *nirvāṇa*, the wisdom-life[19] is [mobilized] to produce the power of [*nirvāṇa*] with remnants (*upadhiseṣa-nirvāṇa*), which enables one to reach [*nirvāṇa*] without remnants. That is what [the word] *able* implies. To follow before everything else the Buddha's teaching is also what [the phrase] *able to get out [safely] through this burning doorway* means.

3.7.3 "Yet my sons [. . .] attached as they are to their games"

[The Beings'] minds roam in the five desires;[20] these are "games." Never discarding them at any moment, they are "attached" [to desires].

3.7.4 "Unaware, ignorant, unperturbed, unafraid"

They don't think that [desires] harm the [wisdom] life: they are "unaware and ignorant." Being "ignorant and unaware," how can they be made perturbed and afraid?

3.7.5 "The fire is coming to press in upon them . . . nor have they any wish to leave"

Injury pressing in upon the wisdom-life is not taken as a calamity. Without being told of what has happened, how can they have any wish to leave?

3.8.1 [402a1] "This great man has the following thought: 'I am a man of great physical strength, with [powerful] body and arms'"[21]

This is the third segment. The theme substantiated here is that the Buddha, in combination with [his own awakening, wishes to] save [other beings].[22] Having been awakened himself to [the truth of] suffering, he intends to cause other beings to become [awakened] like him.[23] Thus with great compassion [*mahākaruṇā*] arising in him, he has come to their aid. Originally the two kinds of transformation did not exist, but by going astray from the truth, they (beings) underwent suffering. [The Buddha] himself has to return to the use of the One Vehicle in order to teach them. Therefore he wants to set forth the doctrine of the One Vehicle. *Body* means the trace-body. The trace-body in essence (*li*) has the functional ability [of] holding and making contact [with beings]: it is [like] the "hands". Essential ability is "strength."

3.8.2 "In the folds of my robe"

A "robe" can be bent to wrap the sons. [The Buddha] appears [in the world] like a supernatural power, able to help beings out of the rugged mountains.

3.8.3 "On top of a table"

[A table with four legs symbolizes] the four virtues [which he manifests] equally to all.[24] [All the diverse] talk about *li* is universally similar and equal.[25]

3.9.1 "Again he thinks: "This house has only one doorway" (12b25 58:36)

This is the fourth segment. He wants to offer the happiness of the three carts later. He first[26] tells them about the frightening and dreadful happening in the house in order to terrify them. [The place] where various delusions are concealed[27] is the "house."

3.9.2 "Narrow and small"

The *doorway* to [the Buddha's] teaching is dark and deep. Those who have traveled to enlightenment are very few; few have advanced toward the *doorway*.

3.9.3 "[They] are in love with their playthings"

Though the Sage has introduced them **[402a10]** to the teaching [of the One], yet the children are too stupid to realize it, and they fall back again "to love of the playthings" of the five desires, and "they may fall victim to the fire" of the three evil paths.[28] Even though [the Buddha] wants to teach the One, they are not capable of making use of it. Therefore, it (the teaching of the One) is abolished temporarily.

3.9.4 "All they do is run back and forth playing, merely looking at their father"

Traveling through the five ways of existence[29] is what is meant by [the word] *run*. Revolving around and wandering in the six kinds of defilements[30] is referred to as *play*. Looking at [the Buddha] in his [transformation body (*nirmāṇa-kāya*)] sixteen feet tall, not advancing a single foot, that is what [the phrase] *merely looking at their father* means.

3.10.1 "At that time, the elder . . . aflame with a great fire" (12c4, 59:14)

This is the fifth segment. The Buddha wants to provide them with the happiness of the three vehicles. As he has told them about the frightening and dreadful happening in order to terrify them, they feel apprehensive, and when they hear the attractions of the three vehicles suddenly their hearts are filled with joy. This is not the real teaching; it is called an *expedient device*.

3.10.2 "The father knows what his sons are preoccupied with, what each of them is fond of"[31]

What living beings are fond of is replacing suffering with pleasure. Here he speaks of the joys of the three vehicles. These (joys) are what they are fond of; it looks as if they are [true joys], yet [in reality] they are not. What I mean by *replacing suffering with pleasure* is that in the absence of suffering there is pleasure, and in the absence of **[402b1]** pleasure[32] there is suffering. [However], [the statement] that there is no suffering eternally in the three vehicles must not be spoken of in this sense.[33] Traces follow the state of their minds, enabling them to pull themselves out of the stations of suffering, which is a consummate case of an expedient device. Because there are no three vehicles, how can there be pleasure? Yet it is suggested that there is pleasure. [Why?] This also is an expedient device. It has been stated that the joy of the three vehicles consists in bringing suffering to an end (*nirodha*) but, because suffering has not been destroyed and [the vehicles] have not been clearly revealed, again [it proves that] they are expedient devices. The Buddha's teaching is [for the sake of] others; those in the Lesser Vehicle follow their masters. These two teachings are compared to the ox and goat, which are the subjects of men. Because the pratyekabuddhas can neither teach [others] nor follow the masters, they are compared to the deer. Transmigration in the three worlds is represented in its walking and trotting the long passage of suffering. *Li* is capable of the unconditioned.[34] One may have joy by replacing walking [the long path of suffering] with it; it is symbolized by the carts. No sooner do they (beings) come out of the burning house through the *doorway* of the teaching, than they can get it (*li*). Hence, it is stated that "[they] are outside of the door."

3.10.3 "Then the sons . . . in a mad race, . . . leave the burning house"[35]

[The Buddha] tells them that because it is what they are fond of they will get it. Perceiving what they will get, they then practice the [required] deeds. That is what is meant by [the phrase] *in a mad race, . . . leave.* Following what [the Buddha] has said they run hard; they have to make every effort to obtain it first: They are "in a mad race to get ahead of the others."[36] If [the Buddha] tells them about it while offering nothing [as reward] **[402b10]** and they do not comprehend it, then they will return to the "fire" [of passion]; how can they be expected to leave [it, *saṃsāra]?*

3.11.1 "At this time, the elder, seeing that his children contrived to get out safely" (12c13, 59:30)

This is the sixth segment. Until now [the Buddha] has led them, exigently offering them the joy of the three vehicles. Here, he presents the joy of the great cart, the wondrous One. There are no more sufferings: they "have contrived to get out safely."

3.11.2 "At a crossroad"

Being present in [the realm] of the [ultimate] reality, there is no one that has not penetrated *li*: they are "[at] a crossroad." They have settled in it: they are "seated." There are no more "bondage and instigators of the passions,"[37] concealment (*mrakṣa*),[38] and obstructions (*āvaraṇa*):[39] they are in open space.

3.11.3 "All address their father, saying: 'Father, things you promised us a while ago'"

Even though they, having understood what they were told, know there are no three in reality, yet they have not yet come fully out of the doorway; this is tantamount to saying that they do not really know yet. As they have come out, they begin to realize that there are no three, though they still do not know the One. Hence there is the demand for the doctrine the [Buddha] promised [namely, of the three]. Yet as the Buddha himself has not previously promised them the One, they dare not demand the One. This is the reason why they demand the reward of the three. If *li* does not lie in three, it follows logically (*tzu-jan*) that [the Buddha] will give them the One. The meaning of their demand is such, with the implication that their subtle triggering-mechanism (*chi*) for grasping (*k'ou*)[40] the One has been so profoundly manifested[41] that [the Buddha], for their sakes, has devised this manner of speaking. *Carriage* **[402c1]** points to the consummate knowledge of the two vehicles; that is, the knowledge of nonorigination.[42] How could there be no "carriage" in the three spheres? [The Buddha] merely gives no names to them, because he wants to lead travelers[43] [to enlightenment] even in their ignorance. "Carriage" is [the means] that takes them to the ultimate destination. What does the Greater Vehicle refer to? Because the domain the Buddha is in is so subtle, profound, remote, and hard to connect with the coarse [world], [the Buddha] has brought himself close to men by means of the trace of [the Buddha,] [in the form of the transformation-body] sixteen feet tall. Hence, [the Greater Vehicle] points to the superficial level of knowledge of [the Buddha] sixteen feet tall; it is "carriage." The bodhisattvas in the seventh stage are the ones who have suppressed the bondage of the three spheres. The doctrine is outside of "the house" [of the three realms], and this is what men are demanding.

3.11.4 "[The elder] gives to each child one big carriage"

On account of their demand, they have obtained the discourse on *li*, that three are identical with the One. *Li* [in reality] does not consist in the three; now [the Buddha] gives them the One. The One has not been known as something to be given to them; it was not given in the beginning. What they previously understood turns out to be nothing; there is no point to resort again to metaphorical speeches. He has resorted to them only in order to awaken those who have not reached it. The reason why he has resorted to them is because men tend to believe in self (*ātman*) and are not willing to receive teaching. Because when they heard that [the One] appeared they did not comprehend it, [the Buddha] has to tell them about it. Now they have no alternative but to accept it, so that they may attain enlightenment.

3.11.5

The statement that the carriages are adorned with a "multitude of jewels" is designed to demonstrate the wondrous **[402c10]** *li* of the Greater Vehicle, which encompasses every kind of goodness that exists. With regard to "high and wide," *li* surpasses empirical calculation:[44] it is "high"; [it] fills up and covers[45] the illimitable [*wu-chi*]:[46] it is "wide". Concerning "a multitude of jewels", eighty-four thousand *pāramitās* in total are signified by *a multitude of jewels. A multitude of jewels* [surrounded by] *posts and handrails* analogize *dhāraṇis*.[47] *Little bells suspended on four sides* symbolize four kinds of [unhindered] eloquent speech.[48] *Parasols and canopies* symbolize compassion (*karuṇā*). *Miscellaneous jewels* refer to the jewels of the seven riches.[49] *Jeweled cords* are comparable to the great vows (*mahāpraṇidhāna*); they connect [being] with all the goodness and wondrous fruits. *Flowered tassels* refer to the flowers of the seven enlightenment [factors].[50] *Heaps of carpets decorated with strips of cloth* refer to various kinds of meditation. *Vermillion-colored cushions* symbolize various meritorious virtues, and *cushions* [symbolize] mutual support.

3.11.6 "A white ox . . . it can gallop like the wind"

The dustless purity of the Buddha's six supernatural powers (*abhijñā*)[51] is what *a white ox* symbolizes. [The Buddha] is utterly pure inside and outside: that is the implication of *skin is pure white. Li* is wondrous and all encompassing: it is what *his bodily form is lovely* implies. There is nothing that it can not break: [it has] "great muscular strength." Moving forward toward the middle path is what *its tread is even* means. There is nothing that it can not destroy or reach: it is "fleet like the wind." Applying and propagating the teaching of the Greater [Vehicle] and entrance into [the cycle of] the five ways of existence (*gatis*) is the intended meaning of the *yoke*. The phrase that [this ox] has many attendants illustrates that those who attend to [the Buddha] who teaches practitioners are gathered **[402d1]** [as many in number] as the trees in the woods. [The paragraph including] "What is the reason?" explains the reason why he intends to give [the doctrine] equally to them.

3.12.1 "Śāriputra, what do you think? . . . Is he guilty of falsehood or not?" (13a2, 60:22)

This is the seventh segment. He promised earlier to give them three carriages; now he gives them one [big carriage]. What has turned out is contradictory to the earlier promise, making it look like a false [promise]. Thus, conversely, [the Buddha] asks Body-son [Śāriputra] indicating that it is not false.

3.12.2 "But enabled his children . . . preserving their bodily lives"

The reason why it is not false is explained here. [Even] if [the Buddha] from the beginning really wanted to give them the three vehicles, but did not give them, he would still not [be guilty of] falsehood. "For what reason is that so?" [The Buddha] "has enabled them to preserve wholly" the wisdom-"life." Such munificence [shown by the Buddha] is very great, sufficient to make up for and neutralize what would otherwise be false. So, how can there be any falsehood?

3.12.3 "Had this great man given them not one tiny carriage, he would still be no liar"

And how much the more would it be true when [the elder] did not think of giving one big carriage in the beginning! The fact that now he has not given it is not contradictory to his earlier promise; how can it be false! How much the more would it be true when he gives them a great carriage! Thus what they have gained is great.

3.13.1 "The Thus Come One also is like this" (13a11, 61:4)

[The rest of the chapter up to the *gāthās*] following this sentence likewise can be divided into seven segments and it is conjoined by the preceding parable. The first four paragraphs deal directly **[402d10]** with the internal meaning, so that they are conjoined by the preceding parable. The latter three paragraphs first speak of the parable externally, later to be conjoined by the internal sense. Why? The latter three first discuss the three carriages; next, the giving of a great carriage; and finally, the fact that it is not false. [The Buddha] set up this discourse for the purpose of putting forth the One Vehicle, of course. This intent regarding the One Vehicle is manifested in the latter three [paragraphs]. That is the reason why I have said that [the latter three] first speak of [the external], then conjoin it with [the internal sense]. The first four paragraphs are designed to complete the latter three and, therefore, are directly connected with the preceding parable.

3.13.2 "The father of the worlds"

As he has become the Honored One of beings, his wondrous virtues are introduced first. [The paragraph] from this phrase to "*anuttara-* [*samyaksaṃbodhi*]," joins with the first [paragraph] of the parable regarding the conditions of the house.

3.13.3 "He sees that beings . . . by birth, old age . . . though they encounter great woes, they are not concerned"

This paragraph is connected with the second one of the parable, [which intimates] the Thus Come One's enlightenment to suffering.

3.13.4 "Śāriputra, having seen this, the Buddha then thinks: 'I am the father of beings . . . wisdom, thus causing them to frolic'"

This joins with the third [paragraph] of the parable [with the implication] that the Tathāgata harbors the intention of saving beings out of great compassion (*mahākaruṇā*).[52]

3.13.5 "Śāriputra, the Tathāgata also has this thought: **[403a1]** *'If I merely by resort to my spiritual power . . . the Buddha's wisdom?'"*

This joins with the fourth [paragraph] of the preceding parable, that although he plans to offer the happiness of the three carriages he describes the fearful happening [in the house] first.

3.13.6 "Śāriputra, just as that elder, [though] physically strong"

This joins with the fifth [paragraph] parabolizing [the] offering [of] the happiness of the three carriages. Listed here are the three carriages.

3.13.7 "Śāriputra, just as that elder, seeing his sons coming safely out of the burning house"

This joins with the sixth [paragraph] of the preceding parable, regarding the giving of the great carriage.

3.13.8 "Śāriputra, just as that elder, first having enticed his children with three carriages"

This joins with the seventh [paragraph] of the preceding parable, regarding nonfalsehood.

3.14.1 "Proclaimed *gāthās*, saying" (13c18, 64:17)

From this onward is a chant consisting of a double set of the preceding seven similes. The first thirty-seven *gāthās* chant the first paragraph of the parable, regarding calamities in the house. Omitted and not chanted in the *gāthās* is the second [paragraph], regarding "the doorway," [symbolizing] the Buddha's enlightenment to the various sufferings because its meaning is easy to perceive.

3.14.2 "Belonged to one man" (14a19, 67:4)

The subtle triggering-mechanism [of beings] in the previous transformative teaching has actively stimulated the Sage, who then condescends to respond to them.[53] [The process of] condescending to respond is represented in this [phrase], which means thus that **[403a10]** "the decayed house belonged to" the Buddha.

3.14.3 "The man had gone a short distance from the house . . . suddenly a fire broke out"

The purpose of the statement that "[the man] had gone a short distance" is to show, by pointing out that it was after he was gone that the fire broke out, that the outbreak [of calamity or suffering] comes from the multitudinous beings themselves and is not of the Buddha's making. The fact that the Sage's state of being, stimulated (*kan*) [in the previous encounter,] shortly disappeared is implied in the statement that "[the man] had gone a short distance." The effect of the transformative teaching in the past was that the superficial and a nascent beings chose themselves to go astray fro the transformative teaching.[54] By going astray from *li*, they were led into mistake and sufferings; that is what *suddenly a fire broke out* means.

3.14.4 "At that time the householder, standing outside the door"

The next three verses are the chant of the third paragraph, concerning the saving of beings by the Buddha out of [his] great compassion. The Thus Come One has transcended the three spheres: he is "standing outside the door."

3.14.5 "Heard someone say, 'Your sons, a while ago in play, entered this house"

[They] were born out of the transformative teaching they had received previously; they are "sons." The *li* of the transformative teaching is outside the three spheres; later they themselves chose to deviate from the transformative teaching to immerse themselves again in the five desires: they were "in play." Because of them (desires), they were reincarnated, they entered this house." "The householder" having come, the previous conditions also have been reactivated. The subtle triggering mechanism has temporarily become "human speech"; ("someone say") in order to actively stimulate the Sage. The Sage, able to respond [to the beings] and thoroughly propagage[55] [the transformative teaching], is obliged to listen to them.

3.14.6 "He uttered a warning to his children"

The next five verses chant of what is in **[403b1]** the fourth paragraph, speaking of the fearful happening in the house.

3.14.7 "At that time, the elder had this thought"

The next seven and a half verses chant of the fifth paragraph concerning the offering of the happiness of the three carriages.

3.14.8 "The elder, knowing his children able to get out of the burning house"

The next seventeen verse chant of the equal provision of the great carriages in the sixth paragraph. The seventh paragraph concerning nonfalsehood is not chanted.

3.14.9 "Had several carriages made"

The *li* of the Greater Vehicle is not "made.' But the sons did not know about it earlier; [the Buddha] made them know of it: therefore it was "made."

3.15.1 "I tell you, Śāriputra: I, too am like this" (14c19, 72:2)

The next four verses join with the first [part of] the preceding simile, regarding the conditions of the house.

3.15.2 "The Thus Come One, having already left the burning house of the three spheres"

This one verse joins with the second [part of] the parable.

3.15.3 "Now these three spheres are all my possession"

These two verses join with the third [part of] the parable.

3.15.4 "Even though I teach and command"

The next four verses join with the fifth [part of] the parable. The reason why they do not join with the fourth [part of the] parable is because telling them (beings) of the fearful [happening] is identical with offering the happiness [of the three]. Hence, they are not linked separately.

3.15.5 "You Śāriputra: For the beings' sake, I"

This one verse joins with **[403b10]** the sixth [part of] the parable. The seventh, concerning nonfalsehood, proves and completes the sixth, concerning the meaning of the One Vehicle. Hence, they are not linked separately.

3.16.1 "All of you, if you can believe and accept these words"

When a statement is lofty [in nature], as a rule, those who follow it are few.[56] *Li* is so deep that certainly very few believe in it. It has been said earlier of the path (*tao*) of the One Vehicle that its purport is very profound, far-reaching, dark, and signless.[57] It will be pretty difficult for those with a shallow consciousness to have faith in it. The next [verses] illustrate that [the Buddha] cannot commit falsehood by saying, for the sake of men, encouraging words, and by offering rewards.[58] Thus, how could those who are inclined to the [right] direction not drive themselves to believe in and understand them?

3.16.2 "The seal of Dharma*" (15b7)*

The wondrous *li* of the One Vehicle can have no obstruction.[59] Like the seals of the kings there is no place it cannot pass through.

3.16.3 "The sin and reward of this man" (15b25)

[The Buddha] wishes to transmit [the *Dharma*] to later generations; thereby, making the *Tao* prevail in the world. Thus, he has established the rule of gain and loss in order to admonish people. As for the *Scripture of Dharma Blossom*, there is no meaning (*i*) that it does not embrace; there is no goodness that it does not hold in its complete possession. If one follows it, there will be no fortune that one shall not collect.[60] If one goes against it, there will be no evil that one shall not encounter. Hence, a wide range of [the punishments and] rewards for sin and goodness are listed for the purpose of amplifying this idea.

Notes

1. Capacity 根 (*indriya*: "power," "faculty of sense," rather than *mūla*, "root") stands for the more frequently used terms 根機 or 機根, and a man's spiritual power of capacity is expressed in either way, "sharp" 利 or "dull" 鈍 as described here.

2. 悟 or "understanding" (Hurvitz), in the sense of awakening (*satori*) to the truth, accounting for the third (*pratibodhana*) of the four stages (開示悟入) as the purpose of the Buddha's appearance in the world.

3. See the *Analects* 7:8.

4. 曲. See the *I Ching, AR*, Part I, Chapter 4: 曲成萬物 "by ever-varying adaptation he completes (the nature of) all things" (Legge, *I Ching*, p. 354).

5. 權 denotes the temporal, provisional means of teaching, synonymous with expedient devices (方便), in contrast with the real facet (實). Cf. the

Chuang-tzu, Chapter 17 (*CTI*, 6:12): 達理者必明於權"he who has command of basic principles is certain to know how to deal with circumstances" (Watson, Complete Works, p. 182). See Chapter 2, note 7.

6. 失大. Cf. the *sūtra*, 10c18: "I have never lost the Greater Vehicles" (Hurvitz, *SLFD* 50:8).

7. Emend 示 to 爾 (?); see the editor's note in 401d6.

8. 取證(*sūtra* 10c10); Hurvitz, SLFD, 49:22.

9. 道大則兼王. Allusion to 內聖外王之道 "the *Tao* of sageliness within and kingliness without" (the Chuang-tzu, Chapter 33). Also cf. *Tao-te ching*, Chapter 25: 故道大天大地大王亦大 (Therefore *Tao* is great, Heaven is great, Earth is great, and the King is also great).

10. Referring to the *sūtra*, 7b4ff., or 12b9ff.

11. 拔濟. See *sūtra*, 13a6, "rescue" (Hurvitz). Cf. *Wu-liang-i ching* (*Amitārtha Sūtra*), T9.388c12.

12. 十無極. 十 is here not taken to mean numerically, but symbolically to mean "perfect," "ultimate," "final." See 410d3f.

13. "A man of great power" (Hurvitz, *SLFD*, 58:18); the Sanskrit equivalent, *gṛha-pati*: "the master of a house."

14. 牙 taken here in the sense of 芽; in fact, both are interchangeable.

15. Liebenthal translates: "Cultivating he removes the weeds that the sprouts of the *Tao* may rise" ("World Conception," II, p. 74).

16. 堂閣朽故. "And chambers" 閣 are added to Hurvitz's translation (58:22), to match with Tao-sheng's partition of the two letters into two separate words.

17. 橫造. One of the meanings listed in the Chinese dictionaries is 不順理 "non-conforming with *li*." It seems to be synonymous with the word 橫計 of the *Nirvāṇa Sūtra* as it is found in Tao-sheng's commentary to it (T37.454c20). So the word can be taken in the sense of false discrimination or imagining (*vikalpa*).

18. See 400c10; Chapter 2, note 32.

19. 惠命, interchangeable with 慧命.

20. 五欲, referring to either the set of desires for wealth, sexual love, eating and drinking, fame, and sleep, or the group of desires arising from the sense-objects; namely, form, sound, smell, taste, and touch.

21. For the purpose of following Tao-sheng's exegesis letter by letter, the phrase "with [powerful] body arms", which is obviously redundant, is added to Hurvitz's translation.

22. 兼濟. Cf. the *Chuang-tzu*, Chapter 32: 而欲兼濟道物 "But at the same time he wishes to aid in guiding to (the secret of) the Tao" (Legge, *Texts of Taoism*, Part II, p. 206).

23. Cf. the *Mencius*, Book VI ("Kao-tzu"), Part A: 聖人與我同類者 "The sage and I are of the same kind" (D. C. Law, *trans.*, *Mencius*, p. 164.)

24. 四等, which is the same as 四無量心 (*catvāri-apramānāni*): kindness (*maitrī*), compassion (*karuṇā*), joy (*muditā*), and indifference (*upekṣā*).

25. Alternate translation: "The *li* underlying the fact that a table has four equal [legs] is that [the Buddha's various] preachings are level, similar, and equal [in their validity]."

26. Emend 無 (402a8) to 先. See 401c7, 402a15.

27. 敞 (*ch'ang*, "open," "uncovered," 402a8) is taken as 蔽 (*pi*).

28. 三塗, 塗 (*t'u*) being used synonymously with 途 (*t'u*), which is in turn interchangeable with 道. Thus 三塗 appears to refer to nothing else than 三惡道, the three evil paths.

29. 五道. The five ways of existence (*gatis*) are five of the six *gatis* (六道), from which asura or evil spirit is excepted.

30. 六塵, or the six qualities (*guṇas*), which is the same as 六境 (*ṣadvi-sayaḥ*) or the six sense objects corresponding to the six sense organs (六根, 六入); namely, form (*rūpa*), sound (*śabda*), smell (*gandha*), taste (*rasa*), touch (*sprasṭavya*), and elements (*dharma*).

31. Hurvitz's translation, 59:17 is slightly modified here. (See 59:17).

32. The first 爲 of 於無爲爲苦 (402a18–402b1) is emended to 樂.

33. Emend 日 (402b1) to 曰.

34. It is possible that (無)爲 is the copying error of (無)苦. In that case, the sentence should be translated: "Speaking of *li*, it is capable of nullifying suffering, [providing] the pleasure replacing walking [a long way of suffering]", which is analogized by *carriage*. Cf. 402a18–b1, preceding note 32. Cf. also 397a3, 398b1. For the term *wu-wei*, see 404b8 (Chapter 4, note 23).

35. Emend 諍 (402b8) to 爭.

36. Again 諍 (of 諍前, 402b9) should read 爭·前 ("to go ahead of others") is Tao-sheng's coinage.

37. 結使. See *DCBT*, p. 386.

38. 覆, *mrakṣa*: "concealment of the good qualities of others, jealous disparagement, nasty disposition, ill-will" (*BHSD*, p. 441).

39. 障. There are two kinds of "obstruction" or "hindrance": *kleśāvaraṇa* 煩惱障 or moral fault and *jñeyāvaraṇa* 所知障 or intellectual fault, which build obstacles on the way to one's enlightenment.

40. 扣 literally, "to strike," "to fasten," or "to detain." When it occurs elsewhere (403a9 and 17, 404b16, 412b4), the object is always the "Sage" 聖; in those cases, I render it: "to stimulate actively."

41. Liebenthal translates: "That the children question in this way shows that the final day dawns which brings them in contact with the One" ("World Conception," II, p.81).

42. 無生智 (*anutpāda-jñāna* or *anutpāda-mati*), the knowledge an arhant attains by realizing the four noble truths, which is the tenth of the tenfold knowledge (十智). See *Abhidharmakośakārika* VI, 51 in "The Text of the *Abhidharmakośakārika of Vasubandhu*"; V. V. Gokhale, ed., *Journal of the Bombay Branch, Royal Asiatic Society*, n.s. vol. 22: 73–103.

43. 行者, which can also be taken as practitioner or novice (*acārin*). See also 397b:10.

44. 數表. See 398d4f. Cf. Hui-yüan's use of the term in T52.103a7.

45. 彌綸. Cf. the *I Ching*, *AR*, Part I, Chapter 4: "comprehend" (Wilhelm, *Change*, p. 293; Legge, *I Ching*, p. 353 "shows us . . . without rent or confusion"), "always handle and adjust" (Chan, *Source Book*, p. 265).

46. 無極. The *sūtra* has the word (12c15) later in the paragraph in the sense of "limitless," but it is more likely that the word denotes the absolute point of reality as taken by the Taoists. The term occurs in *CTC*, Chapter 2 (*CTI*, 1:45), which Chan renders, "the ultimate of nonbeing" ("The Evolution of the Neo-Confucian Concept Li as Principle," (rep.) in Chan, *Neo-Confucianism, Etc.*, p. 60.) Strikingly, the whole sentence of Kuo in which the term is found has another common word, *li*: 至理暢於無極 "the utmost *li* extends to the ultimate of nonbeing." The term *wu-chi* as such goes back to the *Chuang-tzu*, Chapter 11, (Legge, *Texts of Taoism*, Part I, 300: "the illimitable"), and Chapter 6, in which the term occurs adverbially, as "beyond the utmost limits of (things)" (Legge, ibid., 250). The term was later to be treated significantly in neo-Confucianism, especially by Chou Tun-yi (1017–1073) in his "*T'ai-chi T'u-shuo*" (Diagram of the Supreme Ultimate Explained), and D. Bodde renders the term "The Ultimateless" (Fung, *History of Chinese Philosophy*, vol. 2, p. 435). Kuo Hsiang employs the word in *CTC*, Chapter 1 (*CTI*, 1:1 & 5), Chapter 6, *CTI*, 3:21).

47. Magic formula or charm. One form of it is *mantra*, incantation or spell.

48. 四辨. This must be 四辯 or 四弁; that is, 四無礙辯. See 1.9, note 35 (397d7).

49. 七財, that is, 七法財, which are faith, zeal, morality, shame, obedient hearing, abnegation, and meditation-wisdom.

50. 七覺; that is, 七覺支 (*sapta bodhyaṇgāni*). The seven factors are mindfulness (*smṛti*), investigation of the *dharma* (*dharma-pravicaya*), vigor (*vīrya*), joy (*prīti*), repose (*praśrabdhi*), concentration (*samādhi*), and equanimity (*upekśā*).

51. 六通, the six miraculous powers the Buddha attained. They are associated with Mahāyāna whereas five are associated with Hīnayāna. The five are godly vision, godly hearing, insight into others' thinking, knowledge of former existences, and free activity, and the sixth is exhaustion of depravities (*āsrava*).

52. Cf. 407d18. Robinson, *Early Mādhyamika*, p. 282, note 52, renders 大慈 with "Great Kindness", and 大悲 with "Great Compassion."

53. Liebenthal translates: "The spiritual state created by a former contact (with the Sage) calls him. He then bends down and answers" ("World Conception," II, p. 80).

54. Cf. 403a16.

55. 感應遂通. The *I Ching*, *AR*, Part I, Chapter 10: 感應遂通天下之故 "when acted on, it immediately penetrates all things" (Chan, *Source Book*, p. 267). It should be noted that, besides the word *to penetrate*, *the Sage, moving* (*kan*), and *activating force* (*chi*) are the common terms shared by the present paragraph and the chapter concerned of the *I Ching*.

56. Cf. Idiom in current usage 曲高和寡 "(Literally) Highbrow music can be appreciated by only a few people: The profounder a theory is, the fewer its supporters are." (Liang Shih-chiu, ed., *A New Practical Chinese English Dictionary*, p. 487).

57. See 396d10; [Preface], note 22.

58. Emend 焉 (403b13) to 篤. See 408d9.

59. See 398b15.

60. For a discussion of preceding two passages, see Hurvitz, *Chih-i*, p. 201. See preceding 402c10.

Chapter 4

[403c1] BELIEF AND UNDERSTANDING

(Having witnessed the Buddha predicting the complete enlightenment of Śāriputra and the voice hearers, several other principal disciples including Mahākāśyapa tell a parable of a prodigal son to the Buddha as a means of giving voice to their amazement at their understanding of the Buddha's idea. The parable is as follows.

A father and son parted company while the son was still a very young man. In the course of time the father became very rich, whereas the son sank into the depths of poverty and beggary. Once, during the course of his wanderings, he happened to come to the palatial home of his father. The father, at once recognizing him, had him brought into his presence. This only frightened the poor man, and the father let him go. Then the father sent two men to ask the beggar whether he wished to do menial labor on the rich man's estate. The beggar consented, and worked in this way for many years. One day the rich man told the beggar that in view of his many years of honest and conscientious service he would reward him with the charge of all his posssessions. After several years more had passed, the rich man gathered his entire household and clan and told them that the beggar was his son, from whom he had been parted many years before, and that he was now reclaiming him and declaring him heir to all his possessions. When the beggar heard this, he was amazed, thinking that he had received something quite unexpected.[1]

In a similar manner, the disciples and the voice hearers, like the son, are being led secretly by the Buddha, as their father, to the Buddhahood of the Greater Vehicle through the Buddha's ingenius scheme.)

4.1.1

Although the four eminent voice hearers[2] have attained to enlightenment through the parable, it seems that their traces have not been thoroughly examined because they have become enlightened just lately. Therefore, they tell themselves [the parabel of] "the poor son" in order to [examine and] display their understanding. Their understanding must be thoroughly examined, which is then called *belief and understanding*.[3] Again, also illustrated here is the process (*tao*) of the three turned One.

4.1.2 "The unprecedented Dharma *they had heard from the Buddha" (16b9, 84:2)*

As a departure from what was mentioned as three, now they have heard that they are [in reality none other than] the One, and then [have witnessed] [the Buddha's] granting Body-son the prophecy [of his future enlightenment to] the unexcelled *Tao*. They heard these words directly pronounced by the Buddha, which they had never heard before. Thanks to this they realized it themselves. What they have attained is something beyond what they had expected; [naturally,] their happiness is double.

4.2.1 "Then they rose from their seats"

The next three [statements] describe why they are pleased. [In the paragraph] from [the clause] "[we], who were at the head of the *saṃgha*" to [the phrase] "made no effort to seek *annuttarasamyaksaṃbodhi* (unsurpassed, complete enlightenment)," they told [themselves] that they "had already attained" realization, and felt that they did not hope for anything further. [This is] the first [statement].

4.2.2 "The time is now long since [the World-Honored One], of old, began preaching the Dharma"

[This is] the second [statement]. In the past they heard the Buddha **[403c10]** preaching the *Prajñāpāramitā Sūtras*. Hearing them preached, they became "tired and idle," thinking solely of "emptiness" (*śūnyatā*) and "signlessness" (*animitta*), and giving up forever the will to transform the minds of living beings through the purity of the Buddha-land.

4.2.3 "Furthermore, we are now well advanced in years"

[This is] the third [statement]. They are already approaching the last stage of life, advanced in age. Being advanced in years, ["when the

Buddha instructed bodhisattvas"] in the unexcelled path,[4] [in their words], "this did not arouse in us the least thought of desire."

4.2.4 "Now, however, in the Buddha"s own presence we have heard a prophecy of the unexcelled path conferred on the voice hearers, our hearts are very glad"

The aforementioned three [statements] refer to the faults caused by self-esteem.[5] Now, as they suddenly hear the voice hearers receive the prophecy, their hearts are filled with joy but with no self-esteem. Thus, "the immeasurable amount of precious treasures, unsought by us, of themselves" have reached [them]. The meaning of their joyfulness is shown here.

4.2.5 "We now wish to tell a parable"

The men of the Lesser Vehicle from the beginning had no great hope; they had hope only in the two vehicles.[6] Again for the sake of them a parable is devised. This part, divided into three paragraphs, illustrates what "the immeasurable amount of precious treasures, unsought by us, of themselves have come into our possession" means. The first [paragraph] shows that formerly when they were in the place where twenty thousand Buddhas were, they were ignorant of the path of Śākyamuni. This formed the relationship of father and son. The second [paragraph] **[403d1]** explains that their spiritual triggering force grew so profound and manifest that Sākyamuni deigned[7] to respond to them, preaching the doctrine of the three vehicles.[8] The third [paragraph] discusses the purport of the One ultimate of the *Dharma Blossom*. This allows, as a secondary effect, the Buddha's idea to be manifested and helps them, as an immediate effect, to verify what they have heard.

4.3.1 "Suppose there was a young man who was young in years" (16b25, 85:2)

The first paragraph, which explains what father and son stand for. Formerly when they as bodhisattvas received the transformative teaching, the *li* of teaching was the One. The One came from the Buddha; it was the "son," and the Buddha is identical with the "father." The process of teaching began like that: it was "young in years."

4.3.2 "Forsaking his father and running off"

The process of the transformative teaching began very early, not yet bearing fruit. He returned to the depth of worldy delusion,[9] and delusion rode [over] the right path.[10] All [the achievements of] the transformative teaching also were gone. This is the implication of "forsaking his father and running off."

4.3.3 "Dwelt long in another country"

The self-soness (*tzu-jan*) of the transformation of sphere is "native land." The perversion of the [cycle of] birth and death (*saṃsāra*) is "another country."[11] It was a long period of departure from the transformative teaching and he stayed there as a human [*in saṃsāra*]": he "dwelt" [there].

4.3.4 "Whether ten, or twenty, or as much as fifty years"

[The word] *five* [of fifty or five tens] refers to the five forms of existence. [The word] *ten* means "dwelling long." It is not definite; hence, *or*.

4.3.5 "Not only did he grow old, but he also was reduced to destitution"

It is a long time since he abandoned the transformative teaching": he "grew old." He stumbled in [the cycle of] birth and death" **[403d10]**: he was "reduced to destitution."

4.3.6. "Running about in all four directions in quest of food and clothing"

He wandered through all the five forms of existence; no place was left unvisited: he "ran about in all four directions." Growing old, he sought after the joy of the Greater [Vehicle] and that of [the] parables; being in the state of destitution, he sought after the joy of the Lesser [Vehicle].

4.3.7 "In the course of wandering, he happened to head gradually toward his native land"

One does not suddenly receive the retribution of delusion: it is "gradual."[12] He was advancing gradually toward a nonoriginal place: he was [in the state of] "wandering." Responding to the force of the transformative teaching, he went back toward enlightenment; he "[happened" to head gradually toward his native land." He was led by unseen conditions to come [back],but it was not what he intended;[13] hence, *happened*.

4.4.1 "His father, who had preceded him, and who had sought his son without finding him, had stopped midway in a certain city" (16b28, 85:8)

The second paragraph demonstrates that he (the father) was incarnated as the Buddha in order to preach the doctrine of the three vehicles. The Buddha, having transformed himself and accumulated [meritorious] deeds, had always wanted to seek his sons who might have fallen into [the cycle of] birth and death. This ended badly, as [the Buddha was left] "without finding" them. His sons, having yielded to past conditions (*pratyaya*) [which were] bound to reach them [soon], had become attached to the pleasure of birth and death and had developed emotional inclinations of a direction different from those they had originally had. Their "father," in responding to them, condescended to become a Buddha.[14] The trace stopped short of reaching the real:[15] it "stopped midway." The *li* of the One Vehicle can **[404a1]** ward off what is wrong; it is the "city." [All beings from] the ten directions have converged on the transformative teaching: [in that sense] they are "one."

4.4.2 "The father's house was great and rich, with treasure and jewels immeasurable"

Even though he is the Buddha in human form, *li* encompasses all *dharmas*. This means that it is rich with the treasure of the *dharmas*, which is inexhaustible.

4.4.3 "Gold and silver, vaiḍūrya *. . . were all filled to overflowing"*

The seven sacred treasures[16] cannot be spied on [for stealing]: they are "[in] treasure houses." *Li* surpasses words:[17] it is "filled to overflowing."

4.4.4 "He had many attendants, servants, assistants, officers, and vassals . . . oxen and sheep without number"

The heretics (*tīrthikas*) are "attendants": the devils (*māras*) are "servants." They are destined to return and follow the transformative teaching: this is what *attendants and servants* imply. The bodhisattvas are "assistants," helping spread the right transformative teaching. The voice hearers are "officers," warding off and restricting the false and wrong. The multitudinous beings in the three spheres are "vassals"; the Buddha is the king who controls them. *Elephants and horses, oxen and sheep* refer to the meritorious virtues of the three vehicles and "five supernatural powers."[18] As for *carriage*, it means that *li* penetrates everywhere.[19]

4.4.5 "The profits that flowed in and out filled other countries"

The transformative teaching is what *out* refers to. Out of the transformative teaching they went: hence, "the profits that flowed." "The profits," belonging to the transformed throughout the five forms of existence, "filled other countries."

4.4.6 "Merchants and itinerant traders were **[404a10]** very numerous"

The bodhisattvas received the *Dharma* to transform [all beings in] the ten directions: they are "merchants and traders."

4.5.1 "At that time, the poor son, having visited various settlements . . . the city where [his father] was staying" (16c4, 85:17)

Past conditions led [him] toward the city where "his father" was staying: *li* is [what is to be] "reached."[20]

4.5.2 "The father and mother were thinking of their son . . . more than fifty years"

Compassion [arose in the Buddha], thinking they might go astray from *li*. Yet the "sons," after receiving the teaching, were lost and immersed in the five forms of existence: this is [the meaning of] "fifty years."

4.5.3 "Yet, without ever mentioning such matters to others"

This means that [the Buddha] never mentioned to others that the two vehicles would achieve Buddhahood. The Buddha's Great Benevolence[21] was originally aimed at uprooting the suffering [of others], but as they enjoyed birth and death, the true transformative teaching was then turned backward. Here arose the necessity for the exigency of the three. The three [were presented] in accord with the subtle state of their (beings') minds, and thereafter he would be able to produce the One for them.

4.5.4 "They merely thought to themselves, their hearts harboring regret and resentment"

[The Buddha] regretted that the earlier transformative teaching was not intensive, with the result that they (beings) returned to delusion and transmigration (*saṃsāra*). Entirely out of compassion he devised all-round, [provisionary] expressions.

4.5.5 "Thinking themselves: 'old and decrepit . . . constantly recalling our **[404b1]** *son'"*

[The words] *old and decrepit* refer to [the Buddha's] last stage of incarnation. [The statement] *we have no son* means that [the Buddha] has not yet said that the two vehicles will attain to the Buddhahood. [The Buddha] worries that there is nobody to whom to bequeath the treasure of the unexcelled *Dharma*.

4.6.1 "At that time, the poor son, hiring himself out as a laborer in his wanderings, by chance reached his father's house where, stopping by the side of the gate" (16c11, 85:30)

He practiced good [deeds] in his past stations of life in order to obtain worldly pleasures; he "hired himself out as a laborer." But in reality what he received was not good. Therefore he followed his past conditions: he "reached his father's house." The discourse of the Greater Vehicle is "the father's house." The place where he is made to appear is the "gate." His original conditions would have made him enter [the gate], but his emotion led him not to do so. Therefore he hesitated at the side of it.

4.6.2 "He saw in the distance his father seated on a lion throne, his feet resting on a jeweled footstool"

Their past conditions enabled them to see the intent of what was said of the Greater Vehicle: they "saw in the distance [their] father." *Li* as the *Dharma*-body (-*kāya*) [can] place itself [anywhere] fearlessly (or securely) [*abhaya*]:[22] [it is] "seated on a lion throne." He had his feet resting always in the unconditioned (*wu-wei*);[23] he had his "feet resting on a jeweled footstool."

4.6.3 "Brahmans . . . deferentially surrounding him"

All these gods (*devas*) hold in themselves pride and arrogance, but they all serve [the Buddha] as their master, because **[404b10]** [his] *li* has subjugated them.

4.6.4 "His body adorned with pearl necklaces"

There is not any form [of him] that is not *Dharma*;[24] hence, his bodies are adorned with the *Dharma*-treasures.

4.6.5 "Attended on his left and right by vassals and servants holding white feather dusters in their hands"

Like the "hands" of faith holding the teaching, they held the dusters of wisdom free from depravities,[25] which are meant to "attend on their left and right" and brush off dust and stupidity.

4.6.6 "With rows of precious objects that were given and received upon entering and leaving"

[The Buddha] had the external mark of the *Dharma* laid bare, making sure that they obtained it. They obtained it, and so the doctrine became their property: it was "given and received."

4.6.7 "As soon as the poor son had seen his father with great power, straightway, harboring great fear, he regretted having come to that place"

The *li* of the "father" is able to suppress the son's emotion: it has "great Power." What he was afraid of, the suppression of emotion, is what *fear* symbolizes. The subtle triggering-mechanism for embracing the Greater [Vehicle] actively contacted ("struck") the Sage: he "had seen his father." But his feelings deluded and blinded[26] his mind, being still unable to receive "the Greater":[27] he "regretted having come to that place."

4.6.8 "And privately thought: . . . not . . . the place for earning anything"

The subtle triggering-mechanism for the "Greater" [Vehicle] was not yet manifest. [Therefore the Buddha] set forth a wide variety of [provisionary] expressions.

4.6.9 "The best thing for me to do is to go to a poor village"

The three spheres are "poor villages." Practicing the five precepts[28] and the good virtues,[29] and seeking **[404c1]** the pleasure of men and gods (*devas*) are "easy to obtain" (16c20).[30]

4.6.10 "If I stay long [in this place], I may be coerced [to work]"

By "staying long," he certainly would be made to practice the path of the Greater. By being caused to practice the path of the Greater, he would certainly have to work for the sake of [other] beings. One who works for the sake of [other] beings does not [ascribe] the merit to himself ("me"). One who does not [ascribe] the merit to himself ("me") is made to see [the Greater] and is "coerced," [this is] what "others [are coerced to] work" means, which is [the antithesis] of "I [may be coerced to] work." He has thus quickly "run off" to the antithesis of worldly pleasure, where the calamities have quickly stopped.

4.6.11 "Seeing his son, he at heart instantly recognized him and greatly pleased at heart"

Past conditions became reactivated in a subtle way: it is like [the father] "seeing his son." Although he (the son) again felt like turning away, he was bound to realize afterwards the Greater [Vehicle];[31] for this reason, [the father was] "greatly pleased." The profoundly subtle triggering-mechanism arrived in a subtle way, although he did not realize this; thus, "quite suddenly, he came of his own accord."

4.6.12 "Immediately he dispatched an attendant"

The sixteen feet tall was not "that by which the Buddha was":[32] he was, as it were, "an attendant." The "attendant" wanted to set forth the teaching of the Greater [Vehicle]: he thus "dispatched" a messenger. "Going" to the Greater [Vehicle] was the first thing to do: it was [something] "to follow."

4.6.13 "[The messenger] running quickly, went and overtook him"

The wondrous *Dharma* of the Greater Vehicle is *li*, which grasps them firmly. *Li* does not allow any lapse; it is something that requires "running."

4.6.14 "The poor son was alarmed, . . . Why have I been seized?"

[The Buddha's] appearance was not what the son originally had anticipated: he was "alarmed." It greatly offended his feelings, and he "cried out resentfully," [because] it was like "committing no offense" and yet **[404c10]** ending up seized.

4.7.1 "The messenger, grasping him all the more firmly" (16c27, 86:26)

The Greater Vehicle "grasped" him, making his feelings meritorious; *li* could not be discarded; it [used] "force" [to hold him].

4.7.2 "At that time, the poor son thought to himself; 'I am guiltless . . . and helpless with agony, he fell to earth"

He felt extremely unhappy. He had faults but was innocent, and he came to grasp the transformative teaching of the Greater [Vehicle]. His mind was very much disturbed; he was "helpless with agony, and fell to earth."

4.7.3 "Seeing this from afar, the father . . . Do not force him to come with you!"

[Now, the Buddha provisionally] suspended and did not entertain the idea of [presenting] the transformative teaching of the Greater [Vehicle]. These are words [with] provisionary [value] (or metaphorical words) that he said merely to the messenger.

4.7.4. "Then, sprinkling him with cool water"

If [the Buddha] praises the transformative teaching of the Greater [Vehicle], the son would be "helpless with agony, falling [to earth]." So he simply suspended the transformative teaching of the Greater [Vehicle]. The son was then "brought to." [The phrase] *sprinkling him [with cool] water* expresses this. The statement that "the messenger said to the son, 'I am now letting you go'" also is a provisionary (or metaphorical) statement.

4.8.1 "He secretly dispatched two men, whose appearance was miserable and who had no dignity of bearing" (17a8, 87:6)

Two men symbolizes the *Dharma* of the two vehicles. [The Buddha] made up **[404d1]** his mind to bestow [it upon] them: thus he "dispatched." But he hid the real, thus the word *secretly*. *Li* did not illuminate itself completely: its "appearance was miserable". Also their inner understanding was not manifest: they had "no dignity of bearing." Such men were not "the [*Dharma*-] king's messengers."

4.8.2 "'You may go to that place . . .' where you will be given double wages"[33]

To follow his sentiment, but not his original [plan], is what is implied by *say gently*. He was made to work and practice and was provided with pleasure: they were in a "work place." What he was given surpasses [what he could enjoy] in the world: he was "given double wages."

4.8.3 "We two also shall work with you"

Dharma consists of men's practice: it is [what they] "shall work with."

4.8.4 "The poor son first took his pay"

He received what the messengers promised: he "first took his pay." He did not have any doubts: he "swept the dung with them."

4.9.1 "Then, on another day . . . soiled with dirt and dust" (17a14, 87:17)

Spiritual penetration is deposited in the six feelings; thus, "through a window he [they] saw." The body is not the outcome of meritorious virtues: it is "weak and emaciated." The bonds and the instigators of depravities (*kleśa* or *anuśaya*) [caused them to] receive it [i.e., the body]: it is "unclean with dirt and dust".

4.9.2 "Straightway he removed his necklaces . . . smearing dust over his body"

[The Buddha] hid the *Dharma*-body [in himself] in a mysterious way: he "removed (his) ornaments." This shows that **[404d10]** a bodhisattva becoming a Buddha is not merely interested in external pomp: he "puts on a dirty, tar-stained garment." Also he was reborn from the bonds and passion instigators: he was "smearing dust over his body."

4.9.3 "Took in his right hand a dung shovel. Now frightful in appearance"

He had not practiced [the path] free from depravities (*anāsrava*); this is what *took a dung shovel* means. It is convenient and easy; hence, "the right hand." It looked as if he had warded off depravities: he was "frightful in appearance."

4.9.4 "He addressed his workmen: 'You men, work! You may not slacken!'"

When [the Buddha] turned the *Dharma* wheel (*cakra*) at the Deer Park, he preached to that effect.[34]

4.9.5 "Thus by this expedient means he contrived to approach his son"

The *li* of the Buddha was cut off from men, [so that] [the Buddha], by condescending to demonstrate, "contrived" to establish contact [with men].

4.9.6 "Then he addressed him, saying, . . . I will increase your wages"

By entering into the path free from depravities, he was destined not to return to birth and death: he "worked here always, and did not go anywhere else." The pleasure he achieved surpassed that of the seven expedient positions [of the Lesser Vehicle];[35] hence, "increase your wages."

4.9.7 "Whatever you need . . . whose needs I supply"

Nowhere are the meritorious virtues free from depravities lacking or few: they are [like] "salt, vinegar, or that sort of thing." The spiritual penetration of the two vehicles originally is limited and weak: they are "other servants, aged and decrepit."

4.9.8 "You have never been deceitful, lazy . . . as like **[405a1]** *other laborers"*[36]

He felt at home in the *Dharma* of the Lesser Vehicle, which is meant in the statement, "I have never seen you guilty of these evils, as are the other workmen." *The other workmen* refer to the seven expedient positions [of the Lesser Vehicle]. It follows that the seven expedient positions are with "these evils."

4.9.9 "Called him his son"

Those who have obtained [the path] free from depravities have been "called" as if they were the Buddha's sons, but have not yet been spoken of as his real sons.

4.9.10 "The poor son, though delighted by this treatment. . . [for twenty years] he was kept constantly at work clearing away dung"

Seeing the truth and meditating on it have taken him ten [years] each: so it is said, "twenty years."

4.9.11 "Came and went at his ease"

[The Buddha] had him hear about the Greater Vehicle, and so he *came and went* to this *li at his ease* without harboring any doubt.

4.9.12 "Yet he was lodged in the same place as before"

He heard the teaching of the Greater Vehicle preached and was led to know that it was what he had already had, and yet he did not comprehend it: he was "lodged in the same place as before."

4.10.1 "At that time, the elder was taken ill, . . . to let nothing get lost" (17a29, 88:6)

They already knew that [the Buddha] had preached various *sūtras* of the Greater Vehicle, such as when, [for instance], he ordered Subhūti to preach the *Prajñā* (*-pāramitā Sūtras*) so that all might be taught that it was their own property.

4.10.2 "At that time, the poor son, upon **[405a10]** *receiving his instructions . . . still unable to discard [his lowly and inferior thoughts]"*

Although he received what he was entrusted with, he did not yet realize that it was his own property. He felt, therefore, [lowly and inferior].

4.11.1 "Then, when some time had passed, the father knew that his son had gradually become more at ease"

This is the third paragraph. His mind became open, and the incipient, subtle triggering-mechanism for embracing the Greater [Vehicle] was manifested. Following this [the father] gathered his kinsmen, announcing to them that he was his son: this refers to the preaching of the *Dharma Blossom Sūtra*.

4.11.2 "In such and such a city"

This refers to the place where formerly two trillion [future] Buddhas received transformative teaching. The merits of the transformative teaching had not yet matured, and he forsook "me" and ran off to hide himself in the three spheres.

4.11.3 "Suffered"

He drifted through the five forms of existence, ready to taste "loneliness" and "hardship."

4.11.4 "[These treasure houses] have come to me of themselves"

The preceding three paragraphs explain how the unsurpassed treasures reached him of themselves. Here this meaning is clearly shown.

4.12.1 "The great rich elder is the Thus Come One" (17b18, 89.2)

The next three [statements] are connected with the above three sections of the parable. This [sentence] conjoins with the first section of the parable, concerning the meaning of father and son.

4.12.2 "By reason of the three kinds of suffering (duḥkha)"

The Buddha spoke of the three states of sensation (*vedanā*)[37] as being the causes of the three kinds of suffering. When suffering becomes intensified, it is referred to as **[405b1]** "suffering as [ordinary] suffering (*duḥkha-duḥkha*)"; when [suffering] comes as the result of change, it is spoken of as "suffering produced by change (*vipariṇāma-duḥkha*)"; and when it is neither an unpleasant nor pleasant [sensation] and changes every moment as its life passes beyond [the present life], it is referred to as "suffering as conditioned states (*saṃskāra-duḥkha*)."[38] "By reason of the three kinds of suffering" is "by reason of the three kinds of sensation." Why? The sensation of suffering is bitter and cutting. Going against one's sentiment gives rise to anger (*dveṣa*). Following the way one is used to gives rise to desire (*rāga*). [In a state] neither unpleasant nor pleasant, and in an utterly disturbed state, arises stupidity (*moha*). Because of these three states of sensation, there arise the three evil faculties. As the three evil faculties are affected, the passion instigators become active. As the passion instigators spread out and thrive, *karma* is being committed by body and mouth. When *karma* and the passion instigators join forces, future retributions are induced.[39] Hence, it is said: "by reason of the three kinds of suffering, [in the midst of birth and death] we suffer various annoyances." Because birth and death are the outcome of "annoyances," it means that habits formed have not been overcome; hence, "erring and ignorant, we cling in desire to the lesser *dharmas*." [The rest of the paragraph] from this point on conjoins with their wandering from the transformative teaching.

4.12.3 "This day the World-Honored One commands us to take thought and to clear away"

This is connected with the second [part of the] parable, intended for preaching the doctrine of the three vehicles. [The words] *one day's wages* disparage the self-satisfied mind of the Lesser Vehicle. The merits they had accumulated when they were blind are equal to no more than those the bodhisattvas would accumulate in one day **[405b10]**. They are so little and are short of [reaching] the ultimate.

4.12.4 "Now, at last, we know. With regard to Buddha-knowledge the World-Honored One is unstinting"

This conjoins with the third [paragraph] on the *Dharma Blossom.*

4.13.1

Of the *gāthās* proclaimed, the first two verses chant of the three [statements] in the beginning of the chapter. The next two verses chant of the first [part of the] parable. The following thrity-two verses, [starting] from [the verse] "Then, when weary with the search," chant of the second [part of the] parable.

4.13.2

"Bookkeeping in ledgers," keeping count of the treasures, refers to the preaching of the *Dharma* of the three vehicles. Conferring the prophecy upon the bodhisattvas is referred to as *ledgers*.

4.13.3 "And your bedding is thick and warm" (18a.25, 93.27)

This symbolizes the joy of *nirvāṇa*, which does not lack any degree of sufficiency.

4.13.4 "Dwelling in a grass hut"

Making his way toward the gate of the Greater Vehicle, he was "dwelling in the hut" of the Lesser Vehicle.

4.13.5 "The father, knowing that his son's thoughts were at last broad and great" (18b1, 94:8)

The seven verses following this chant of the third [part of the] parable.

4.13.6 "The Buddha also in this way"

The verses following this summarily chant of the internal meaning. They do not do complete justice to the real [meaning], but they are temporarily proper for this stage of [the] process.

4.13.7 "[All dharmas*] without exception are empty and quiescent"*
(18b27, 96:15)

This explains why "[they should have taken absolutely] on pleasure therein". (18b26) Roughly speaking, it means that the nature of all *dharmas* is empty, making it difficult to investigate thoroughly, which leads one to **[405c1]** attain the Buddhahood. Thus it is that they "should have taken absolutely no pleasure therein."

Commentary on the Scripture of Lotus of Wondrous Dharma,
Roll the First

Notes

1. Hurvitz, *SLFD*, pp. xi–xii.

2. As listed in the *sūtra*, they are Subhūti, Mehākātyāyana, Mahākāśyapa, and Mahāmaudgalyayana. Mahākāśyapa is omitted in Hurvitz's translation.

3. 信解, faithful understanding, understanding resulting from faith, or understanding by faith. The Sanskrit equivalent *adhimukti* (*SPSR*, p. 95) means "confidence" (*SED*, p. 21) "earnest, zealous application" (*BHSD*, p. 14).

4. 無上道; *namely*, *anuttarasamyaksaṃbodhi.*

5. See 399b1 (Chapter 1, note 86), 401b14.

6. 二(乘) (403c16) seems to be an error of 大(乘).

7. Emend 府 (403d1) to 俯.

8. Liebenthal translates a part of this passage: "When an individual has mysteriously grown to a state of spiritual maturity which now shows, Śākyamuni bends down and responds" ("World Conception," II, p. 81).

9. Emend two 或 (403d5) to 惑.

10. Liebenthal translates: "He wavers in his faith, pursues mundane ends and also goes occasionally in the right direction" ("World Conception," II, p. 95).

11. Liebenthal translates: "Rise and decay, which are created by a mind, adverse to Nature, are the 'foreign country'" (ibid.).

12. Liebenthal here wrongly takes Tao-sheng's words and those from the *sūtra* as if they were one statement by Tao-sheng, as he translates: "A fruit does not ripe suddenly but very, very gradually" ("World Conception," II, p. 96).

13. Liebenthal translates: "Not knowing that such is demanded by his spiritual state, he feels an urge rising and contrary to his own intention finds himself longing (for the Buddha)" (ibid.).

14. Liebenthal translates: "Now the former impulse would bear fruit were he not attached to mundane pleasures. His will to live leads him away from Origin, and the father responding to his (unexpressed) demand, bows down and, though a Buddha, is incorporated into a human body" (ibid.).

15. Liebenthal translates: "His appearance on the phenomenal plane is not real" (ibid.).

16. 七聖財 (*sapta-dhanāni*) which is identical with 七法財, the seven *dharma-* riches: faith (*śraddhā*), morality (*śīla*), modesty (*hrī*), fear of evil (*apatrāpya*), learning (*śruta*), self-denial (*tyāga*), and wisdom (*prajñā*).

17. 理過於言. Cf. 理無所言 "*Li* cannot be spoken of," and 至理無言 in *CTC*, Chapter 2. (*CTI*, 1:34).

18. See 397a3, 402b6.

19. 五通 identical with 五神通, namely, heavenly vision (*divyacakṣus*), heavenly hearing (*divyaśrotra*), ability to know the thoughts of other minds (*paracittajñana*), knowledge of all former existences of self and others (*pūrvanivā sāmusmṛti-jñāna*), and power to be anywhere or do anything at will (*ṛddhisākṣātkriyā*).

20. 至 (404a12). But according to the *sūtra*, it should read 到, though there is no difference in meaning. Cf. Liebenthal's translation: "The former impulse leads him to the place where the Father lives. His time has come" ("World Conception," II, p. 96).

21. 大慈 (*mahāmaitra*). See R. H. Robinson, *Early Mādhyamika*, p. 282, n. 52: 大慈大悲 "Great Kindness and Great Compassion." But Tao-sheng does not seem to make a distinction between the two semantically, though the two are used separately, 大慈 occurring besides here in 407d18, 大悲 in 401c7, 402a2, 402d18, et passim. He interchangeably uses the two terms particularly in 408b6 and 409b8 with respect to the *sūtra*. Hurvitz, *SLFD*, 217:27, renders 大慈, "great good will."

22. Liebenthal translates in two ways: "*Li* is the *dharmakāya*; freedom from fear (vaiśāradya) is there enjoyed" ("World Conception," II, p. 77); and with the addition of the *sūtra* word *father*, the last word of the immediately preceding sentence, "The Father represents in the religious milieu (*li*) the *dharmakāya* where there is no fear (*vaiśāradya*)" (ibid., 96). On Dharma-kāya, D. T. Suzuki says: "The Dharmakāya, which literally means 'body or system of being,' is, according to the Mahāyānists, the ultimate reality that underlies all particular phenomena; it is that which makes the existence of individuals possible; it is the raison d'etre of the universe, it is the norm of being, which regulates the course of events and thoughts" (*Outlines of Mahayana Buddhism*, p. 46).

23. Probably not in the sense of the Taoist concept of nonbeing but in the sense of *asaṃskṛta*; that is, without (*a*-) *saṃskāra*: "*predisposition(s)*, the effect of past deeds and experience as conditioning a new state: . . . the second item in the *pratītya-samutpāda*, q.v. (arising from avidyā, and cause of vijñāna)" (*BHSD*, p. 542; see also p. 82, "*asaṃskṛta*").

24. Cf. 404a2.

25. 無漏 *anāsrava*; that is, without (*an*-) *āsrava*: "evil influence, depravity, evil, sin, misery" (*BHSD*, p. 111; see also 112).

26. Emend 或 to 惑.

27. Liebenthal translates: "He is afraid that the Order (*li*) of the Father may subdue his desire. He is entitled (mature) to be taught Mahāyāna: he calls the Sage. But his fancies dim his mind and make this impossible" ("World Conception," II, p. 96).

28. 五戒 (*pañca-śīla*). They are the first five of the ten commandments. The five involve prohibitions of killing, stealing, committing adultery, lying, and drinking intoxicants.

29. 十善 (*daśa-kuśalāni*). They, in addition to the first four of the five precepts, are the noncommittal of double-tongue, coarse language, filthy language, covetousness, anger, and perverted views.

30. Liebenthal translates: "'He decides to go to a poor hamlet', i.e., in the Three Worlds, to practice the five *śīlāni* and the ten *kuśalāni*, in order to be reincarnated as man or god. For this is the easy way" ("World Conception," II, p. 96).

31. Liebenthal translates: "Though he is still following his own will, he will awake to the Great Vehicle" (ibid., 97).

32. Cf. *CTC*, Chapter 9 (*CTI*, 3:53): 聖人者···非所以迹也 "The Sage is not that by which the trace is." For more on the term *so-i-chi*, see Fukunaga Kōji's "Sōjō to Rōsō shisō," in Tsukamoto Zenryū, ed., *Jōron kenkyū*, pp. 259ff. Wang Pi also uses a similar term 所以然之理 in his commentary on the *I Ching*, hexagrams numbers 16 and 1, rendered by Chan as "principle by which things are" ("The Evolution of the Neo-Confucian Concept *Li* as Principle," p. 56).

33. See the text of the *sūtra*, 17a:8–9. Hurvitz has translated: "'you may go to that place. . . . There is a work place here, to which we will accompany you'" (87:7). He obviously has taken 倍 (*pei*) as 陪 (*p'ei*). Katō is faithful to the *sūtra* as it is (p. 120). The Sanskrit version is in agreement with the Chinese version on this phrase: "*dvi-guṇāya*" (*SPSR*, p. 99:13). Tao-sheng, as will be seen, does not show any deviation from the text, as far as this point is concerned.

34. It refers to the last words of the Buddha: "All the constituents of being are transitory; work out your salvation with diligence" (H. C. Warren, *Buddhism in Translations*, p. 109).

35. 七方便(位). They are composed of the three sacred positions and the four good roots. The three are the five meditations (五停心觀), consisting of impurity, composition, causation, right discrimination, and breathing; reflection on the specific characteristics of all phenomena (別相念住); and reflection on the universal characteristics. The four are the *dharmas* of warmth (煗法), apex (頂法), patience (忍法) and the world first (世第一法).

36. Katō's translation has been adopted here (*MSLW*, p. 121). Cf. *SLFD*, 87:31.

37. The second of the five groups or aggregates (*pañcaskandha*). All sensations are divided into three: pleasant, unpleasant, and neutral.

38. For this and a more detailed sketch of the conception of *duḥkha*, see Walpola Rahula, *What the Buddha Taught*, pp. 16ff., particularly p. 19.

39. Liebenthal translates the preceding three passages: "When the *akuśala mūla* yearn (for external things) they stir up the *anuśaya*. These flare up and produce the three types of *karma*. *Karma* and the *anuśaya* in cooperation call forth retributions" ("World Conception," II, p. 80).

Commentary on the Scripture of Lotus of Wondrous Dharma,
Roll the Second
Written by the Dharma-Master Chu[1] Tao-sheng

Chapter 5

MEDICINAL HERBS

(The Buddha sanctions Kāśyapa's understanding of his doctrine, explained through the parable of the poor son, and extolls the Thus Come One's All-Knowledge, which encompasses all *dharmas* and applies to all beings. Taking up the examples of cloud and rain which reach equally everywhere without distinction as to grasses, trees, medicinal herbs, and so on, the Buddha stresses the nature of the *Dharma* preached by him, characterized as being of a single mark and a single flavor.)

5.1.1.

As four great voice hearers had achieved enlightenment by the first parable, subsequently they spoke of their faith and understanding, in order to express their enlightenment. Understanding had to be verified, [and it turned out that] they had comprehended in depth the Sage's idea of first the three and later the One. Because they comprehended the purport of what the Sage was driving at,[2] in this chapter the Buddha confirms the propriety of what they have said in order to perfect the meaning [of the doctrine]. Hence, he praised [them] saying, "well-done!" commending their rare achievement. [The Buddha] secretly guided them, undetected, making them equal with Kāśyapa [in understanding].

5.1.2

The title "Medicinal Herbs" conveys the fact that in the past they had received and maintained the Sage's teaching, and as the Sage's **[405c10]** teaching soaked their spirit, the disease of depravities (*kleśa*) was cured. Thus [the transmitter of the *sūtra*] used the [the words] *medicinal herbs* in titling the chapter.

5.2.1

[The part from the parable of] the burning house (Chapter 3) up to this [chapter] speaks of the *Dharma Blossom* through parables.

5.2.2 "Truly it is as he had said" (19a18, 101:3)

The Thus Come One's wisdom and meritorious virtues enabled him to preach the path of the three first and the One later, and Kāśyapa himself has spoken of it by taking up a parable. What he has said shows that he has attained to the Sage's meaning. Hence, in sanctioning it, [the Buddha says], "Truly it is as he has said."

5.2.3 "The Thus Come One also has incalculable. . . meritorious virtues"

What has been said [by Mahākāśyapa and others] is "true" and real because it relates to the region of the One. Now this passage deals with the boundlessness of the region of the One. The boundlessness of the region of the One, unexhausted for many *kalpas*, broadly verifies [the theme] that the transformative teaching of the three is [identical with] that of the One; how, then, can there be any mistake?

5.2.4 "The Thus Come One sees and knows [that to which] all dharmas [tend]. . . all manner of wisdom [to beings]"[3]

What is explicated here is how [the Buddha] has reached the state of All-Knowledge (*sarvajñā*): first, by investigating thoroughly **[405d1]** the profound intent of the *dharmas*; and second, by knowing where living beings' thoughts tend to go. Because he knew that medicines help regulate diseases, he took them, which led him to bring depravities and calamities to an end without fail, finally attaining to the All-Knowledge.

5.3.1 "Suppose, in the three-thousand-great-thousandfold world"[4] (19a25, 101:15)

Delusion arises when one deviates from *li*; delusions vary in a myriad of ways. By turning one's back [to delusion] one becomes enlightened to *li*. *Li* must be nondual; the *Tao* of the Thus Come One is one.[5] Beings go against [the One], calling it three. The three originated in beings' own disposition, but *li* has remained one always. It is like the fact that, though the clouds and rains fall equally [on all the medicinal trees], the medicinal trees themselves vary in a myriad of ways. It is the medicinal trees that are varied in a myriad of ways, not the clouds and rains.[6] What he said in parable of the difference and similarity was meant to show how [the three] turn out to be unified. Kāśyapa comprehended this purport, achieving the ultimate "rarely" (19c7) experienced by any. [The words] *three thousand* refer to the single domain of the Buddha's transformative teaching in its entirety.

5.3.2 "The mountains and rivers, the dales and vales"

This phrase illustrates that the benefit of the *Dharma* extends everywhere, leaving no corner unreached.

5.3.3 "Their different names and colors"

Conditions (*pratyaya*) and physical forms are not identical.

5.3.4 "A thick cloud spreads out, covering the whole three thousand"

Cloud symbolizes the *Dharma*-body; *rain* represents the preaching of the *Dharma*. The *Dharma*-body pervades everwhere, fully and thickly, and the *Dharma*-sound permeates all over equally.

5.3.5 **[405d10]** *"Raining down on every part of it equally at the same time"*

[The phrase] *at the same time* means that there is no [sequence of time], first or later. *Raining down. . . equally* means that [rain] falls without any distinction between much and little. The *Dharma* rains of the four virtues[7] with respect to *li* also are like that.

5.3.6 "Everthing rained on by the same cloud"

Rain "by the same cloud" implies that there is no water of a different taste. Although their genetic natures[8] are varied, all [beings of different] appellations seek to sustain life. The same "rain" of the previous conversion [causes] the shoots[9] of the *Tao* to issue forth: it is "the earth." The present preaching helps them to attain understanding: it is the "rain."

5.4.1 "The Thus Come One is also like this. . . as the great cloud rises" (19b7, 102:1)

The *Dharma*-body fills up [the ultimate of nonbeing];[10] the shade of compassion is like a cloud.

5.4.2 "With the sound of his great voice"

Li is broad and immeasurable: it is "great." There is no being that does not hear and know about it: it "pervades." It "pervades" and covers men and gods, so that they may be free of the heat (or passion) of depravities (*kleśa*).

5.4.3 "In the midst of a great multitude he proclaims these words: . . . in order to listen to the Dharma!"

Li becomes luminous: he "proclaims." They should pay attention to it: thus, he talks about it. The *Tao* spreads in the world. When conditions are met, they are certain to hear it. This is, "all should come here in order to listen to the *Dharma*!"

5.4.4 "At that time, numberless . . . hear the Dharma" **[406a1]**

Because the preaching of *li* has necessitated all kinds of [exigent] teachings, all join together in coming [to the preaching] "like that cloud." When its internal meaning is drawn, a connection can be made with the preceding parable.

5.4.5 "[The merit they gain] shall be unknown and unnoticed even by themselves" (19b26, 103:3)

The *Dharma* being of "a single mark", *li* has no different "flavors" (*rasa*). Even though living beings are all identically soaked in the marsh of the *Tao*, they do not realize that this is so.[11]

5.4.6 "What things [they] think back on"

What living beings "think back on" is not the same: it may be morality (*śīla*), or it may be almsgiving (*dāna*). Hence, it is said, "what things they think back on." "[What things] they think ahead to" and "[what things] they cultivate" also are like this.

5.4.7 "How they think back"

For the sake of attaining to the minds of the three vehicles, one is mindful of almsgiving. For the sake of attaining to the minds of men and gods, one is mindful of almsgiving. "[How they] think ahead" and "[how they] practice" also are like this.

5.4.8 "By resort to what Dharmas they think back"

In hopes of[12] gaining the fruits of the three vehicles, one is mindful of almsgiving. Expecting the retribution of men and gods, one is mindful of almsgiving.

5.4.9 "What Dharma they gain and by resort to what Dharma they gain it"

This sums up the three [statements] covered so far. *By resort to what* means "by means of what good deed as cause." *What dharma they gain* means "what retribution they receive as effect." Cause and effect all lead to the Buddha, but living beings do not realize it. All hold on to what they think is different; only the Buddha is aware that they all belong to the same [One].[13]

5.4.10 "The cloud is spread out, and hangs down" (19c18, 104:23)

This symbolizes that through the transformation body (*nirmāṇa-káya*) [the Buddha] makes contact with beings, so that he appears approachable [to them] step by step.

5.4.11 **[406a10]** *"These are called Small Trees" (20b14, 109:6)*

By this [the Buddha] intends to explain that the bodhisattva path is the superior one, comparing it again to trees. "Trees" are meant for shade and covering. The Greater Vehicle has the connotation of "covering":[14] [in this sense] it is similar to trees. [Those who are in] the seventh stage (*bhūmi*) and [those who are] below are referred to as *small trees* whereas [those who are in] the eighth or above are spoken of as *great trees*.[15]

Notes

1. Emend 笠 to 竺. See 396d2 (Preface, note 1).

2. Ōchō suspects 致 (405c7) as 教 "teaching" (see C9) in "Jikudōshō sen," p. 257. Then, it should read, "the purport of the Sage's teaching".

3. Emend 地 (405c16) to 慧. See T9.19a25.

4. *MSLW*, p. 140.

5. Cf. *Tao-te ching*, Chapter 42: 道生一 "*Tao* produced the One."

6. Liebenthal translates the preceding paragraph, beginning with a word from the *sūtra* as if it belonged to Tao-sheng's own words: "The three thousand chiliocosms constitute deviation from *li* and belong to illusion, the realm of manifoldness. Turn the back (to that manifoldness) and you face *li*. *Li* is never manifold; the *Tao* of the Tathāgata is one. The defectiveness of things is symbolized in the three vehicles; these originate in individual life (*ch'ing*). *Li* is only one, as the cloud which spends rain is one, while the grasses and trees (which it waters) are many. One cannot from the manifoldness of the grasses deduce that of the rain" ("World Conception," II, p. 76).

7. Kindness (*maitrī*), compassion (*karuṇā*), joy (*muditā*), and indifference (*upekṣā*).

8. See T9.19b5, "nature" (Hurvitz, *SLFD.*, 101:26), "nature and kind" (102:32).

9. 牙 "teeth" (405d13) should read 芽; see 401c15.

10. See 402c10.

11. Liebenthal translates: "All the Beings are watered in the marsh of the Tao yet they are unconscious of the source (from where the rain pours)" ("World Conception," II, p. 75).

12. Emend 斯 (406a5) to 期.

13. Liebenthal translates: (From "Such cause and effect") "All *Karma* is conducive to Buddhahood, but the Beings do not know and each of them aims at another goal. Only Buddha knows that (in fact) there exists only one goal for all of them" ("World Conception," II, p. 94).

14. See 397d6.

15. Cf. Liu Ch'iu, "Preface to the *Wu-liang-i ching*", T9.384a; Liebenthal, *The Book of Chao* (Peking, 1948), pp. 175f. and 169.

Chapter 6

BESTOWAL OF PROPHECY

(The Buddha confers the prophecy of future Buddhahood upon the four great disciples: Mahākāśyapa, Subhuti, Mahākātyāyana, and Maudgalyāyana.)

6.1

As regards this topic, as the task is achieved, then its effect is completed; this is the calendrical order (*li-shu*)[1] of self-soness (*tzu-jan*[2]).[3] That the four great voice hearers already had their roots planted in the distant past is shown in the present prophecy. What the Buddha has stated so far completes his preaching. What he has preached must be in compliance with *li*.[4] When *li* is complied with, the [natural] factors, as they converge, come to bear fruits. Therefore, the Buddha arranged for them (the disciples) to receive his prophecy. This bestowal of prophecy [is like] the blossom of the *Dharma*. Fetters cause the creation of all things and images [or phenomena], but when the Sage is united with *li*, these fetters are completely destroyed.[5] These fetters having been destroyed, it is illogical to claim the existence of a "land." Whereas it can be said that there is no "land," this does not [necessarily] imply the nonexistence of a "land." [For, although] there is neither body nor name, yet body and name both exist more really than ever (before). Therefore it should be understood that **[406b1]** what the "lands," the titles, and the bestowal of prophecy mean is that [the Buddha] merely devised such things as a way of responding to beings, in order to guide them to [feeling] unsatisfied [with themselves].[6]

6.2.1 "At that time, the great Maudgalyāyana, . . . all greatly agitated" (20c28, 122:16)

The way these men sought the prophecy [as it is described here] suggests that they entertained inwardly a wondrous understanding of *li*,[7] making them deserve to receive the prophecy, with the result that they came to the point of seeking it themselves. [The Buddha] secretly guided those unawakened, urging them [to drive themselves] toward awakening and understanding. Becuase their will to acquire understanding was so intense, [their will] to obtain the prophecy was also the same.[8]

6.2.2 "Twenty minor kalpas" (21a27, 124:2)

It is shown that there is [a distinction between] superior and inferior realms, and that there is [a difference] between long life and short life. Why is this? The Sage certainly has not made this so. [The difference in individuals of] the subtle triggering-mechanism accounts for it. Hence, [the Buddha] explains the difference.

Notes

1. 歷數. See the *Chuang-tzu*, Chapter 27: "places and spaces which can be calculated" (Legge, *Texts of Taoism*, Part II, p. 146), "cycles and numbers" (Watson, *Complete Works*, p. 306). It also occurs in *Confucian Analects*, 20:1, in the sense of "the represented and calculated numbers," or "order of succession" (Legge, *Confucius*, p. 350); the *Shu Ching*, V. iv. 8, "the calendaric calculations" (Legge, *The Shoo King*, p. 328), also II, ii, 14.

2. Unlike the case in, 405a15f., *tzu-jan*, used here as a noun, partakes of the Taoist metaphysics. *Tzu-jan* is synonymously identified with *t'ien* (heaven), *Tao*, and *li* in *CLT*, Chapter 13 (*CTI*, 5:10). Robinson renders the term, "autogenous, self-so," and "self-so-ness." (*Early Mādhyamika*, p. 278, n. 8).

3. Liebenthal translates (from the beginning): "It is prearranged in nature that good deeds must bear (good) fruits" ("World Conception," II, p. 94) Cf. *Tao-te ching*, Chapter 17: 功成事遂百姓皆謂我自然 "When his task is accomplished and his work done, the people all say, 'It happened to us naturally'" (D. C. Law, trans., *Lao Tzu, Tao Te Ching*, p. 73). Cf. 406d3.

4. 說必當理 See 397b2 and 7. Cf. *Han Fei-tzu, ju-hsiao*, 言必當理.

5. Cf. *Pien-tsung lun*, T52.225c24: 累不自除故求理以除累. Also see Chang Chung-yüan, *Creativity and Taoism* (New York, 1970), p. 126: "It is not until we have completely freed ourselves from all conditions and limitations that we can see 'the rising sun'."

6. The passage from "However, the coming into" is translated in Hurvitz, *Chih-i*, p. 199: "The coming into being of particulars and shapes is the work of the fetters [of existence]. Once the Sage has united with the Universal Principle, then subtly the fetters vanish. When the fetters have vanished, how can one admit the existence of 'lands'? But, though I say that there is no 'land', yet there is no 'not-land.' There is neither body nor name, but the more the body is not, the more does it exist. Hence one knows that Buddha-lands and Buddha-names and the meaning of the Buddha's prophecy vary with the beings [to whom these things are preached]."

Also cf. Liebenthal, "World Conception," II, p. 87: "All phenomena in the Buddha domains created by good *karman*, still feature inside World. As the Sage is in union with *li*, they disappear altogether, World has then disappeared. If so, what further purpose could Buddha domains serve? (But) though (in reality) there are no domains, yet all the domains there are; though there are no bodies and names (of Buddhas), yet none of them is lacking. It follows that the domains, the Buddha names, and the prophesies are responses answering the expectations of the Beings. They are expedients, not final." See also T'ang Yung-t'ung, *Fo-chiao shih*, II, p. 165, in which T'ang interprets the last phrase: "All [are devised to] lead men in such a way that they are made to turn to the good, [when they are not satisfied with themselves, they will turn to the good]."

7. *Chieh-li* 解理. Cf. *li-chieh*, "to comprehend; to understand" in current usage.

8. (406b2–4). Liebenthal translates this paragraph, changing, possibly by mistake, the letter 意 to 義: "Believers ask for an announcement of their impending liberation (*vyākarana*). For they feel that what they are pregnant with will be miraculously delivered. A natural law (*li*) demands that they be informed. So they ask. (The embryo) is secretly expected though not yet visible, it presses for delivery in an act of Illumination. When what is going to be delivered has become seed, the announcement is simultaneously due" ("World Conception," II, p. 81).

Chapter 7

PARABLE OF THE CONJURED CITY

(The Buddha tells about a Buddha in a remote past named Victorious through Great Penetrating Knowledge. After enduring for many *kalpas* that Buddha attained *anuttarasamyaksaṃbodhi*. Then his sixteen sons and their mothers that he had left, and later the Brahmā god-kings from all directions and lands, paid homage to him and made offerings, begging to turn the *Dharma* wheel. At their entreaties, that Thus Come One thrice turned the *Dharma* wheel of twelve spokes, which encompasses the four noble truths and the twelve chains of causation. The *Lotus Scripture* was also preached by that Buddha later. The sixteen *śrāmaneras*-turned-sons, having become Buddhas, were preaching the *Dharma* in the lands of all directions. The sixteenth of them is identified by the Buddha as himself. The Buddha then explained why there is the One Vehicle only, not two, the vehicles of the *śrāvakas* and the *pratyeka-buddhas*, which are expendient devices, by taking up an example of the conjured city.

A guide was leading a group of travelers to a spot where a treasure lay buried. On the way the travelers wearied, and some spoke of turning back. The guide accordingly conjured up an apparent city on the way, and successfully urged his companions to rest and refresh themselves there. When they had done so, they went on and reached the spot where the treasure was concealed. Then the guide told them that the city they had seen a while back had been an illusory city, and not a real one, which he had conjured up for the purpose of conquering their discouragement.[1])

7.1.1

Underlying the depiction of [the Buddha named] Victorious through Great Penetrating Knowledge (*Mahābhijñā-jñānābhibhū*) is a threefold meaning. First, because Victorious through Great Penetrating Knowledge also preached the three and the One, in that order, it lends support to and completes the present preaching. Second, the five hundred disciples and the great multitude were previously in the place of Victorious through Great Penetrating Knowledge and were converted by Śākyamuni. The story of what happened to Śākyamuni [in the past] is certain to lead beings to believe that [achievements made] in earlier times help one to accomplish **[406b10]** awakening now. Third, it means that the boundary of [the realm of] birth and death is so remote, and the Great Path (*Tao*) is so dark and distant, that [the Buddha] urgently devised the two vehicles, which are symbolized in the parable of the conjured city.

7.1.2 "Since that Buddha passed into extinction in a remote age, the time has been great and long indeed" (22a23, 130:9)

[What the Buddha] said here, that [that] Buddha passed into extinction a long time ago, is intended to express[2] that Śākyamuni reflects on the remote past as if he had thought of it today, in order to prove that the *li* he is now preaching is deep and proper.[3]

*7.1.3 "Just as he was about to gain [*anuttarasamyaksam*] bodhi, still the* Buddha Dharmas *did not appear before him" (22b20, 132:3)*

By stating that the *Buddha-dharmas* did not yet appear before him for ten minor *kalpas*, [the Buddha] means to show that the ultimate *li*[4] is dark and remote, and difficult to size up at once. Also expressed here is that the will of [the Buddha] Great Penetration was very strong and that his decisive mind could not be blocked, thus encouraging beings to cherish a longing for [complete enlightenment].

7.1.4 "The Brahmā [god] kings rained down [a multitude of divine] flowers"

The fact that men and gods congregate there, making offerings, [in multitudes] like forests, shows that the utmost virtue is so dignified and weighty that *li* has moved [even] the gods. The Brahmā kings are the lords of living beings, and yet they are among those who have come to pay reverence [to this Buddha]. Would it not be even more so for the rest [of the beings]?

7.1.5 "He had had sixteen sons"

Things caused in the past are depicted here.

7.2 [406cl] "At that time . . . to the East . . . aglow" (23a17, 135:5)

The fact that nothing was left not covered by the first illumination implies that there is nothing that the *Tao* does not mirror. That the Brahmā god [kings] from [all] the ten directions went far in search of this portent shows that, once [the Sage] is stimulated (*kan*), [beings] are certain to reach [the goal], regardless of the distance.[5] That they did not recognize the portent of the glow tells that *li* is outside the reach of the senses. Their gift of the palaces [to the Buddha] expresses again their infinitely [sincere, grateful] minds. They abandoned the joy of abstruse meditation and visited the Buddha, coming a long way, and because their sentiment had remained on the wondrous *Dharma*, they begged the Buddha to turn the *Dharma* wheel (23b2, 135:29).

7.3.1 "Thrice turned the *Dharma* wheel of twelve spokes" (25a2, 144:1)

[The Buddha] depicted [what happened in] the past to compare it with the present; this idea becomes evident here. [The Thus Come One] Victorious through Great Penetrating Knowledge preached the teaching of the three vehicles in the past for the Brahmā kings, and preached the scripture of the *Dharma Blossom* for the sixteen princes. That the youngest of the princes was Śākyamuni[6] means that for contemporary people he already had preached this *Dharma*. Now as he ascends a [*Dharma*] throne, he revives the past transformative teaching, preaching again the path of the One preceded by the three. "The three turns of the *Dharma* wheel" are as follows:

> The first [turn] was made for when the Buddha proclaimed to Kauṇḍinya [and four other mendicants, to the effect that] "[what constitutes the self or] body is suffering. You should know it, then you will attain the four 'spokes' of seeing, knowing, understanding, and awakening. This forms the root of what you have not yet known."
>
> The second was made for when the Buddha proclaimed **[406c10]** to the five men, [to the effect that] "you have known about suffering, and also obtained the four 'spokes' of seeing, knowing, understanding, and awakening. This forms the root of what you have already known."
>
> The third was made for when the Buddha proclaimed to the five men, [to the effect that] "you have known about suffering.

> You don't have to know again. You have also attained the four 'spokes' of seeing, knowing, understanding, and awakening. This forms the root of what you had no knowledge of."[7]

There are four courses and three turnings in one proclamation; hence, there are twelve (in total).[8] In this way, one who does not yet know should know: one who does not yet know the cause[9] [of suffering] should know it; one who does not yet know the extinction [of suffering] should know it; and one who does not yet know the path [to extinction] should know it. In this way in each truth [of the four noble truths] there are the four courses of seeing, knowing, understanding, and awakening. One proclamation encompasses the four truths. The three proclamations contain the *Dharma* wheel of forty-eight "spokes." "Twelve" is the outcome of [the four truths applied to] the three proclamations. The "forty-eight," when we speak of them in terms of the [four] truths, are "the twelve causes and conditions" (*pratītya-samutpāda*) [multiplied by] the four truths.[10] "The four truths" spell out the facts involved (*shih*) in detail, whereas the terms [of the process] are made brief. "The twelve causes and conditions" spell out the terms in detail, whereas the facts involved are made brief. As their faculties were sharp, when [the Buddha] preached merely the arising and destruction of the twelve [causes and conditions], they immediately comprehended for themselves, coming up with the *Dharma* medicine that would free them from suffering without fail, which means that they had reached the end of the path (*tao*).

7.3.2 "Ignorance[11] (avidyā)"

There are one hundred and eight kinds of depravities (*kleśa*),[12] **[406dl]** becoming numerous, [so to speak,] when they are applied to the various affairs. In reality, however, it can be said that there is no more than one kind of delusion. *Ignorance* represents all delusions. It is shown in desire (or "greed") and attachment (or "seizure"). Desire for and attachment to that which is useless and has been valued from the past, all this we call "ignorance."

7.3.3 "Karmic legacy (saṃskāras)"[13]

When *karma* committed through body, mouth, and mind appears in the present, it means that [a karmic legacy] exists, which causes a future effect to extist. When retribution is drawn to the background,[14] the process is then completed and phenomena come into existence.[15] When the creation of phenomena is passed, [what is left] we call *karmic legacy*. Karmic legacy has to do with transmigration in the realm of birth and death.

7.3.4 "Cognition (vijñāna)"

Cognition is the beginning of the present body, which means that the phenomenon of life comes into being.

7.3.5 "Name and visible form (nāmarūpa)"

As cognition becomes a seed, it can give rise to "name and visible form." The four aggregates (*skandhas*) are referred to as *name*; the fifth [aggregate, which is] consciousness (*vijñāna*), accounts for "visible form." They also are said to be in the womb, in an obscure and dark state. There is little consciousness of suffering and pleasure; there is no more than just "name."

7.3.6 "The six sense organs (saḍāyatana)"

The six sensations arise to appropriately match the six qualities (*guṇas*).[16]

7.3.7 "Contact (sparśa)"

Once sensations and qualities appear, the consciousness of body comes into existence. The body consciousness is delicate and subtle. The three things join together. "To join together" is what is meant by *contact*.

7.3.8 "Perception (vedanā)"

Once sensations and qualities join together, there is [the process of deciding] whether it is agreeable or not. Next the three states of perception[17] arise.

7.3.9 "Craving (tṛṣṇā)"

Pleasure conditions perception. To follow one's will is called *craving*. With craving one is attached to something. He who is attached to something **[406310]** is one whose root of birth and death (*saṃsāra*) is deep. Hence, stretching everywhere are the branches of [birth and death].

7.3.10 "Grasping (upādāna)"

Because of the obstruction caused by craving, the four categories of grasping[18] arise. By "grasping" one is able to grasp birth and death (*saṃsāra*).

7.3.11 "Becoming (bhava)"

Because of the four kinds of grasping, the three kinds of *karma*[19] are produced. They are referred to as *becoming*, in the sense that they can bring about "becoming."

7.3.12 "Birth (jāti)"

Because of the three kinds of *karma*, the shoots [of life] crave and grasp water and moisture, duly developing into birth.

7.3.13 "Aging and dying (jarāmaraṇa)"

As birth secures one in the state of undyingness, this is the residence of craving and compassion.

7.3.14

The twelve causes and conditions involve all the three periods of past, present, and future [lives]. However, the names [of the three] are invisibly revealed in accordance with the trace of transformation. How? Two are present in the past, eight in the present, and two in the future. Because of ignorance and karmic legacy, suffering in this life is induced; thus, if one intends to cut it off right now, then consequently [upon cutting it off] there will be no more birth and death. Birth and death are the locus of the various calamities. How can one not fear it? Thus these two beginnings are shown. Many made inquiries into the meaning of the words, but men drift in the three worlds because of the twelve [causes and] conditions; so if [causes and] conditions are destroyed, it means that stupidity and ignorance are cut dead by the knife of wisdom, and that the water of craving is scorched and dried off by the fire of knowledge. The lofty net [of knowledge] opens up over the four corners,[20] **[407al]** over the six forms of existence. Nonrebirth (*anutpatti* or *ajāti*) surpasses the eight apexes [of suffering?].[21]

7.4.1 "[At this time], the sixteen princes, [all] boys, left their household" (25a18, 144:34)

Until now he has preached the doctrine of the two vehicles. Now for the princes he preaches the *Dharma Blossom*.

7.4.2 "[At this time], this Buddha, entertaining the śrāmaneras' entreaty, when twenty thousand kalpas had passed"

This illustrates that *li* is so deep and the *Tao* is so recondite that they require meticulous scrutiny. This also makes beings admire and respect them.

7.4.3 "Straightway he entered a quiet room"

[By this the Buddha] wishes to manifest the virtues of the *śrāmaneras*.

7.5.1 "[All this] may be likened to . . . five hundred *yojanas*" (25c26, 148:16)

After [having given to them] the feeling of approximation and a low level of knowledge [about his meaning], [the Buddha now] intends to show that when he previously preached the doctrine of the three vehicles [it] was designed to manifest the One. [However], beings seek to hold on to the three. Because of this he again points them to their past conditions, improvising the parable of the conjured city. This parable suggests that the two vehicles are not real, eventually returning to the Path of the One. The Path of the One is very difficult to get to because of the workings of illusion. However, the three spheres are muddy and hilly, and the road of the two vehicles is dangerous. This [road], five hundred [*yojanas* long], is the path that bodhisattvas are required to take and [is] very hard to traverse.

7.5.2 "Empty and devoid of human beings—a frightful place"

Five hundred [*yojanas*] represent a very great distance: thus, "empty." They are determined to work out their solitary enlightenment[22] [just for their own sake]: [thus], "devoid of human beings" **[407a10]**. They have long endured hardships and suffering, subject to dangers that may come from anywhere, anytime: it is "a frightful place."

7.5.3 "There is a great multitude wishing to traverse this road to arrive at a cache of precious jewels"

The endowment of great enlightenment [innate in every being] issues forth: they "wish to traverse" the steep "road." [Those who] wish to traverse are not few; thus, "a great multitude." Traversing it, they will obtain all kinds of pleasure; thus, "a cache of precious jewels."

7.5.4 "There is a guide, . . . wishing to get through these hardships"

Meeting with *li* is what is meant by *passable*; going astray from it is what is meant by *impassable*. When it comes to "knowing well" the "features", there is just one person [who does]. By teaching the multitude to follow the "passable," [the Buddha] makes [himself] the master "who leads" them.

7.5.5 "The multitude being led get disgusted midway . . . We now wish to turn back"

They are confused about where they are heading, obviously far away from the Path of the Buddha. They have long endured hardships and suffering, suffering [the cycle of] birth and death. Those of the Lesser Vehicle tend to be content with substitutes [for suffering] and easily fall prey to being pleased with them: they "get disgusted." Despite this delusion, however, the original understanding is never lost: they "wish to turn back." They turn back to the *Dharma* of the "guide," which means that they proceed with the "guide," but they obtain no "comfort" from him. They then intend to make an "entreaty" to convey this [need].

7.6.1 "The guide, being a man of many skillful devices . . . conjures up . . . a city" (26a12, 148:25)

Proceeding with him but finding no comfort as they follow the "guide," they make their entreaty. The "guide" **[407bl]**, listening to their entreaty, sympathetically realizes that they are in a pitiful state. Thus, as a device, he invents the transformative teaching of the two vehicles, telling them that they will attain *nirvāṇa*. A city is originally designed to protect [its people] from evils; [likewise] only in *nirvāṇa* is there no calamity. This [nature of *nirvāṇa*] is analogized in the designation [i.e., "city"]. What [the Buddha] exigently shows is unreal: he "conjures up."

7.6.2 "He declares to the multitude, . . . You can quickly regain your composure"

The teaching of the two vehicles is the meaning implied here. [The Buddha] talks of it through a made-up story.

7.6.3 "If you then feel able to proceed to the jewel cache, you will also be free to 'do as you please'"[23]

The intent here is the teaching of the two vehicles, designed to enable them to obtain Buddhahood; but [the Buddha] does not reveal this, showing this also by way of a made-up story.[24]

7.6.4 "Thereupon the multitude . . . showing a sense of composure"

They have advanced to attain the result; that is, what they say to themselves [they have obtained],[25] *nirvāṇa*.

7.7 "At that time, the guide, knowing that the multitude . . . for the purpose of giving you a stop and rest, nothing more"

This again refers to *nirvāṇa*, which they say they have obtained: they "stop." They prepare themselves to advance further: they "rest." Because they have realized it, [the Buddha] preaches that the three are [in reality] the One: thus "dissovles the conjured city."[26] And he says that [the two vehicles] are made-up statements.

Notes

1. The synopsis of the parable cited from Hurvitz, *SLFD*, p. xii.

2. Transpose 者遠 (406b12) to 遠者.

3. Cf. 408b11, 398c9, 399a16 & b15.

4. 至理. Cf. Wang Pi, the commentary on the *I Ching*, hexagram l; *CTC*, Chapter 2 (*CTI*, 1:45), Chapter 13 (*CTI*, 5:8), and Chapter 33 (*CTI*, 10:39), et passim. See Wing-tsit Chan, "The Evolution of the Neo-Confucian Concept," p. 58.

5. Literally, "What calamities will leave them far off [from the goal]?"

6. It refers to 25c5: "The sixteenth is I myself, Śākyamunibuddha" (147:15).

7. Possibly referring to *Dhamma-cakka-ppavattana-sutta*, 9:20. See *Buddhist Suttas*, trans. T. W. Rhys Davids (New York; 1969; originally published in Oxford, 1881, as *The Sacred Books of the East*, vol. XI), pp. 150–152: for instance, "10. 'And Again, O Bhikkhus, that I should comprehend that this was the noble truth concerning sorrow, though it was not among the doctrines handed down, there arose within me the eye, there arose the knowledge, there arose the understanding, there arose the wisdom, there arose the light" (p. 150).

8. See ibid., p. 152: "21. 'So long, O Bhikkhus, as my knowledge and insight were not quite clear, regarding each of these four noble truths in this triple order, in this twelvefold manner."

9. Emend 習 (406c15) to 集.

10. Two letters 四諦 (406c16) should be repeated.

11. "Inclarity" (Hurvitz, *SLFD*, 144:6).

12. For what they are, see H. C. Warren, *Buddhism in Translations* (New York, 1972), pp. 188.

13. "Action" (Hurvitz, *SLFD*, 144:6).

14. Cf. Tao-sheng's statement found in Chi-tsang, *Erh-ti i*, T45.111b, cited by T'ang, *Fo-chiao shih*, II, p. 178.

15. See *Tao-te ching*, Chapter 17; Chapter 6, note 3 of this translation.

16. Sight, sound, smell, taste, touch, and idea.

17. Pleasant, unpleasant, and indeterminate.

18. *Catvāry-upādānāni*: clinging to desire, to enlightened views, non-Buddhist practices and observances, and ideas arising from the conception of self.

19. Deed, word, and thought committed by body, mouth, and mind.

20. The term 高羅四 (406d18) might be Tao-sheng's own coinage referring to *anuttarasamyaksaṃbodhi* (unexcelled, right enlightenment).

21. 八極, probably the copier's mistake of 八苦 (?), eight kinds of suffering put forward by the Buddha in his first sermon after his enlightenment.

22. 獨悟 seems to refer to the kind of enlightenment pursued by the practitioners of the Lesser Vehicle (Hīnayāna), which is self-centered in contradistinction to the altruistic type of enlightenment by the Greater Vehicle (Mahāyāna). This seems to be implicit in "great enlightenment" in the passage that follows.

23. (亦可) 隨意. This phrase (in 26a6) is put in place of (亦可)去 "to leave" (26a8).

24. Or "false words".

25. Cf. 27a17, 自謂己得度. "And saying to themselves that they have been saved" (Hurvitz, *SLFD*, 154:14).

26. See *DCBT*, p. 141, "化城 The magic, or illusion city in the *Lotus Sūtra*; it typifies temporary or incomplete *nirvāṇa*, i.e. the imperfect *nirvāṇa* of Hīnayāna."

Chapter 8

[407b10] RECEIPT OF PROPHECY BY FIVE HUNDRED DISCIPLES

(After Pūrṇa exhorts the Buddha's merits the Buddha prophesies that he, too, will attain *anuttarasamyaksaṃbodhi*. Also knowing the wishful thought of the twelve hundred *arhats*, the Buddha first confers the same prophecy on Kauṇḍinyabhikṣu and his five hundred *arhats*. The latter express their joy and repent for thinking themselves to have obtained what turned out to be pseudo-enlightenment, likening themselves to a man who is stricken by poverty not knowing that he had had a jewel sewn into his clothes by his close friend while he, having gotten drunk, visited the latter. Just like the friend who reminds the man of this, the Buddha points out to them again that they are open to the ultimate form of enlightenment.)

8.1

As regards the topic, [the disciples] can respond[1] to the teaching of the Sage, reflecting his trace like shadow and echo [that follow real form and sound].[2] This certainly is a case of exigency. Those superior men,[3] thrice[4] hearing it, were enlightened. The trace did not reach them earlier, and so they receive the prophecy later. Those who receive the prophecy later appear to be the truly dull receptacles. Now because [the Buddha] has disclosed that they are exigencies, the Path (*Tao*) is not available to dull enlightenment any more.

8.2.1 "Had heard about this wisdom" (27b14, 157:1)

This refers to [the part], from Chapter [2]: "Expedient Devices" to [Chapter 4:] "Belief and Understanding".

8.2.2 "Have powers of supernatural penetration"

They witnessed the story of what had occurred to [the Buddha] Victorious through Great Penetrating Knowledge as if it had happened today.

8.2.3 "[We] have not the words with which to express ourselves" (27b22, 157:17)

They have expressed that they have entertained inside their minds wondrous understanding. Their understanding has come from the Buddha; they have achieved[5] the task thanks to the Buddha.[6] Hence, [Pūrṇa said,] "In the face of the Buddha's merits, we have not the words with which to express ourselves." They wished in the depth of their hearts for the Buddha to show the trace of his path, proclaiming [the doctrine] that is not of the Lesser Vehicle. Therefore, it is said: "only the Buddha, [the World-Honored One], is able to know [the vows we once took] with deep thought."

8.3.1 "We are to be likened to the following case: There is a man" (29a6, 164: 29)

The five hundred *arhats*, after their subtle triggering-mechanism was awakened, were delighted and reproached themselves. Insofar as they reproached themselves, their pleasure **[407c1]** also was not a shallow one. Although the speeches the Thus Come One has made are so multifarious, with no set pattern, the *li* underlying them is by no means different. However, these five hundred people went astray from the [Buddha's] words, failing to grasp his import through their own extreme fault. Thus they themselves draw an analogy in order to express this idea.

8.3.2 "Who arrives at the house of a close friend"

Friend refers to the sixteen princes. *House* means the residence accommodating the teaching of the Greater [Vehicle]. Although these five hundred people in the beginning heard equally [the doctrine], their innate dispositions (*chih*)[7] varied [in absorbing the Buddha's speeches, like] white silk, which is dyed differently from one part to another. That is what *arrives at the house of a [close] friend* means.

8.3.3 "Where he gets drunk on wine, then lies down"

What the friend's words of advice mean is that beings' innate [nature], sufficiently [existent in them] has now become completely lacking (submerged). Although still unable to forget the [Buddha's] words, they have become deluded in thought. The deluded thought has turned passionate. They are intoxicated with the five desires and birth and death (*saṃsāra*), like the man "getting drunk and lying down."

8.3.4 "At that time, his friend, having official business, [is on the point of going away] . . . departs, leaving it with him"

Although it was said that they were in confusion and delusion, wouldn't they rather begin to have subtle understanding? Their understanding being truly subtle, the great enlightenment will arise from it; so, speaking of a cause in terms of its effect, one can say it is "priceless." It is covered with delusion like [the jewel] present in the interior of [the man's] garment. Because of "the friend," [the Buddha] has come; he "leaves" [it with them]. *Li* is never to be lost; it also is what that "friend" "sews." It was sewed secretly [into all] without discrimination; it cannot be overlooked. The import of the statement about the Greater **[407c10]** Vehicle is concealed, leaving them ignorant of this meaning; thus, they are "unaware of anything." After ["unawareness"] ends they can be transformed. The [Sage's] stimulus (*kan*) to teach is stopped temporarily, which is implicit in "having official business, [he] is on the point of going away."

8.4.1 "When he has recovered, he sets out on his travels . . . He is content with [however little he may get]" (29a8, 164:34)

Their previous understanding was activated, enabling them to oppose illusion: they "recovered" from lying down. "Recovering," they then listened to the teaching. But what they were following was not the original [path]; it is said: they "set out on their travels." The *nirvāṇa* of the two vehicles did not "belong to the original":[8] thus they "reached another country" to lead the pleasure-seeking life. Going astray from the path of the Greater [Vehicle], they suffered hardship in [reaching] *li*. The joy they found[9] there was less than that found in the Greater Vehicle, but it was something "to be content with" in comparison with that of the world.[10]

8.4.2 "Then his friend, encountering him by chance"

Following the teaching [of the three] is what they had grasped, still short of meeting their old friend. Now [the Buddha] has preached that the three are the One: Just now they have "encountered" it. It was not what they themselves had sought: they "encountered it by chance."

8.4.3 "Speaks these words to him: 'Alas, sir! . . . Suffering neither want nor shortage'"

"Once when I" was in the place of [the Buddha] Victorious through Great Penetrating Knowledge, "I sewed a priceless jewel" of *Dharma* "into the inside of your" hearts. **[407d1]** To show that they had obtained the One, [they] made up this story. As cause changes into effect, there is no pleasure that can not be obtained; there can not be any "want" in anything whatsoever.

8.4.4 "But later we forgot"

When formerly they received the transformative teaching, they had the subtle understanding "sewn" in. "Later" they were attached to the trappings (or disguised aspect) of the transformative teaching, or to the idea [itself] (or deluded thought): They "forgot."

Notes

1. 對揚. "Answering questions" (H. Nakamura, *BDJ*, p. 909); "One who drew out remarks or sermons from the Buddha" (*DCBT*, p. 423). See 397d14 (Chapter 1, note 34), 399b17.

2. 影響. See 410c6, 411c3, 412b10. Cf. the *Shu Ching*, "the shadow and the echo" (Legge, *The Shoo King*, p. 54).

3. 君子. Note that this term refers to "arhant". See 396d8 [Preface], note 16).

4. It refers to the three turns of the *Dharma* wheel. See 406c8ff (Chapter 7:3).

5. The first 成 (b16) is redundant and should be taken out. Cf. 408a2, 397b5f.

6. Liebenthal translates: (from "they entertain") "(The disciples) are longing for transcendental insight. This insight is given by the Buddha, and it is (only) through the Buddha that it can be achieved" ("World Conception," II, p. 95).

7. 質. "Basic stuff", Fung, *History of Chinese Philosophy*, vol. 2, p. 33; "The term 'basic stuff' (*chih*) had already been used by Confucius to designate man's inner, spontaneous nature" (note 2).

8. 歸本. Cf. Wang Pi's commentary on the *I Ching*, Hexagram "*fu*" 復: "復者反本之謂." "*Fu* means return to the origin" (T'ang Yung-t'ung, "Wang-Pi's New Interpretation," p. 147). See *CNS*, 531c, 532b.

9. 所所得之樂 (407c14) should read without one 所.

10. Liebenthal translates: (from "going astray") "The period of striving is opposed to the Great *Tao*; in comparison with *li* it is toil. Whatever happiness (the Lower Vehicles) may find there, it is always small when compared with the Great Vehicle, though it might look great enough when compared with worldly pleasures" ("World Conception," II, p. 79).

Chapter 9

PROPHECIES CONFERRED ON LEARNERS AND ADEPTS

(Prophecies of future enlightenment are bestowed this time upon Ānanda, Rāhula, and two thousand voice-hearing learners and adepts.)

The five hundred *arhats* are those who had "the virtues filled inside and their names flowing outside.'[1] Thus, they received their prophecies earlier. These learners and adepts are advanced very little in "name and actuality" (*ming-shih*);[2] hence, they receive their prophecies later. All that is dealt with throughout this one segment is [the Buddha's] bestowal of the prophecies upon them.

Notes

1. See 397d1 (Chapter 1, note 24).

2. 名實. See 412b15. For a discussion of the concept in the entire Chinese tradition, see Wing-tsit Chan, *Source Book*, pp. 40f., 232, and 787. Cf. a15; *CTC*, Chapter 13 (*CTI*, 5:11): 必由其名者名當其實故由名而實不濫也.

Chapter 10

DHARMA MASTERS

(Through the bodhisattva Medicine King, the Buddha tells the great worthies what merits and rewards, including complete enlightenment, will be accorded to those who pay the slightest respect to the *Lotus Sūtra*.)

10.1.1

What has been discussed so far, up to the preceding chapter, a total of three preachings and three prophecy bestowals, suggests the proposition that the cause of three turns out to be the cause of One, which can be arrived at either way [by way of preachings or bestowal]. The three preachings are, first, the chapter (2) on "expedient devices"; second, the chapter (3) on "parable"; and third, the chapter (7) on "[the parable of] the conjured city". The chapter (4) on "belief and understanding" deals with their self-examination **[407d10]** of their understanding. In the chapter (5) on "medicinal herbs" the Buddha tells that what he has preached is not of a separate category. The three kinds of conferment of prophecies are, first, the conferring on Śāriputra; second, the conferring on the four great voice hearers; third, the conferring on the five hundred disciples along with the learners and the adepts.

10.1.2

This chapter generally deals with [the Buddha's instruction] for propagating this *sūtra*. *Dharma Master* refers to one for whom there is no *li* that he cannot propagate. The one who is able to publicize and exhalt this path is referred to as *Dharma Master*. By praising it to [beings of] various sentiments, would they not be benefitted?

10.2.1 "Through [the bodhisattva] Medicine King (*Bhaiṣajya-rāja*)". (30b29, 174:1)

The reason why [the Buddha] addressed them through Medicine King is becasue he could burn his own body [as he did in his former incarnation in order to propagate the *Dharma*.][1] [The Buddha says that if] one rejoices over one single *gāthā* [of the *sūtra*, then one will be granted a prophecy]. If the is so with a few [*gāthās*], how much more so if one rejoices over many! So deep is the meaning here. If one harbors anger in the heart, one then separates oneself from other beings. When one [as a propagator] is separated from others, [one does] not then cause [others] to trod the path [also].[2] Therefore, [the Buddha] prasises one who "rejoices"; rejoicing means that the *Dharma Blossom* is propagated.

10.2.2 "Secretly for a single person preach" (30c27, 175:19)

What has been mentioned is the abundance of merits one obtains when one receives [the *sūtra*] for oneself. Now [the Buddha] talks about preaching it to another person, which represents an altruistic act, benefitting others. When one's Path (*Tao*) embraces [others] as well,[3] one's merits and rewards will be endless.

10.2.3 "An emissary of the Thus Come One"

The mind of Great Benevolence always **[408al]** cherishes the idea of propagating the *Dharma*. If a man is a practitioner of the *Dharma*, he is then "an emissary of the Thus Come One."

10.2.4 "Sent by the Thus Come One"

This explains that what they understand comes from the Buddha's understanding. I say "[their understanding] comes from the Buddha's," because certainly the Thus Come One is the source of understanding, and they act in compliance with him. The Thus Come One from the beginning takes propagating the *Dharma* to be his business. And he who can do so is said to be "doing the Thus Come One's business."

10.3.1 "If there is an evil man who with unwholesome thought . . . his guilt shall be very grave" (30c29, 175:25)

The Buddha is supreme among men and gods. To hate and "curse" him is but cursing the man, not cursing the *Dharma*. However, if a man who receives the *Dharma Blossom* "curses" it, this is tantamount to "cursing" the man and disgracing the *Dharma* as well. To "curse" men and disgrace the *Dharma* is identical with "slandering" the *Dharma*-body. The guilt of those who "slander" the *Dharma*-body is extremely "grave." [This injunction by the Buddha] is designed to strengthen the learner's drive, certainly with great effect.

10.3.2 "Borne about on the Thus Come One's shoulders"

The *Dharma* is [the same as] the Buddha Master. One should respect the *Dharma* in order to receive the*Dharma*, and what [the expression] *bearing about* means really is that one "bears about" the *Dharma* but not men. However, the descriptive trace of speech **[408a10]** as found here also is focused on man [as the agent of *Dharma*] in order to help strengthen learning.

10.4.1 "Whether already preached, now being preached" (31b7,) 178:6)

Whereas the preceding sections explicate the *Dharma* by way of man, the sections from here on explicate man by way of the *Dharma*. Because it is difficult to obtain the *Dharma*, it is difficult to find the men who receive and keep it also because it is difficult to believe and understand the *Dharma*.

10.4.2 "[The Thus Come One] shall cover them with garments" (31b23, 178:17)

Li is deep and covered completely. Through "garments," [the Buddha] manifests it.

10.4.3 "[These persons] shall have dwelt together with the Thus Come One"

When men feel intensely that they are entertaining doubtful thoughts, they are then on the way to wakening.[4] Wakened, one becomes identified with the man of the *Lotus Blossom*. As they comprehend and partake of the profound ultimate, their experience of understanding becomes an integral part of their thought; thus, a place is provided. Providing a place is the meaning intended by *dwelling together*.

10.4.4 "And shall have had their heads caressed by the head of the Thus Come One"

One who will keep the *Dharma Blossom* will be initiated as a son of the Buddha. A deep love is expressed by means of *caressing the heads*.

10.5.1 "Suppose, for example, there were a man hard pressed by thirst and in need of water" (31c9, 179:13)

Receiving and keeping the *Dharma Blossom*, while seeking enlightenment to the Path of the Buddha, at the apex of one's desire, is likened to [the state of a man] "[hard pressed by] thirst and in need of water." This analogy figuratively speaks of [the difference between] shallowness and depth, and gain and loss, in men keeping the *Dharma Blossom*. It was said earlier (31c4, 179:4) that there are those who "cannot **[408b1]** contrive to see and hear" the *Dharma Blossom*. It refers not so much to those who have not obtained the rolls [of the *sūtra*] as to those who have not comprehended the idea of the One Vehicle.

10.5.2 "[Though] on your high plain he digs in his search"

In contrast to the three vehicles, the One Vehicle is "the hardest to believe" (31b18, 178:8). Seeking understanding about the *Dharma Blossom* is like searching for water "on a high plain." Receiving, keeping, reading, and reciting it are symbolized in "to dig."

10.5.3 "Still he sees only dry earth . . . He knows that water must be near"

Not seeing the gate to the profound [realm] is like "seeing dry earth." Turning around to bring themselves to the deep [realm] is like seeing "mud." They already know that the great awakening is not remote: they "know that water must be near."

10.6.1 "The room of the Thus Come One is great compassion [toward all living beings]" (31c25, 180:4)

Compassion can fully cover [the whole realm] like a room providing shelter. *Room* should be read with the sense of "to enter."[5]

10.6.2 "The cloak of the Thus Come One is [tender forbearance and] the bearing of insult with equanimity"

"The bearing of insult" and the "forbearing" of pleasure are like a cloak protecting the body. *Cloak* should be read with the sense of "to put on."[6]

10.6.3 "The throne of the Thus Come One is the emptiness of all dharmas"

Being "empty", one is given "security." Attainment is likened to a "throne." *Throne* should be read with the sense of "to sit."[7] Isn't [the Buddha] thereby benefitting beings greatly?

Notes

1. See Chapter 23; Hurvitz, *SLFD*, 295:7.

2. See 410d15.

3. See 401b16. Cf. 397b5.

4. Emend 窹 (two cases in a14) to 寤.

5. Thus, it can be interpreted: "The Thus Come One enters [the room of] the thought of."

6. Thus, "The Thus Come One puts on the [cloak of] the thought of."

7. Thus, "The Thus Come One obtains and sits on [the throne of] the emptiness."

Chapter 11

[408b10] APPARITION OF THE JEWELED STŪPA

(An immense *stūpa* arises out of the earth, and the Buddha tells his listeners that it contains the body of a Buddha named Prabhūtaratna, who in a previous age preached the *Lotus*, vowing to produce his reliquary, after his *nirvāṇa*, wherever and whenever the *Lotus* should happen to be preached. Then the *stūpa* opens up, and Prabhūtaratna, seated within it, properly offers half his seat to the Buddha. A number of beings salute both Buddhas.[1])

11.1

The purpose of manifesting the *stūpa* is to verify that the *li* underlying the *Dharma Blossom* is certainly clear and proper, first, through the evidence of the *stūpa* and, second, through the evidence of the voice that issues forth therefrom.[2] Through the two events, beings come to bear faith to a full and deep extent. By extension it also shows that the ultimate fruit is subtly manifested, as it is ever existent.

11.2.1 "At that time, there appeared before the Buddha a seven-jeweled *stūpa*, . . . welling up out of the earth and resting in mid air" (32b17, 183:1)

Man's emotions [tend to make him] dark about *li*. [The Buddha] cannot help but cause him to nurture faith by resorting to supernatural wonders. In an attempt to manifest and prove [his preaching] through this method, [the Buddha] shows the jeweled *stūpa*. Throguh this event he reveals his meaning, making it manifest and visible.[3] It already was said that the three vehicles are the One. All living beings are [potentially] Buddhas and also are all in *nirvāṇa*. *Nirvāṇa*[4] and Buddhas are set apart by as little as [the difference] between beginning and end. Also why should there be any difference [between beings and Buddhas]? Only because of the instigators of depravities is [Buddha-nature] concealed, like a *stūpa* lying hidden, sometimes underground, covered by earth. The endowment of great enlightenment cannot be left **[408c1]** covered up. It is bound to be drawn out in due course, like the *stūpa* issuing forth. It cannot be stopped from coming out. It originally was existent in empty *li*,[5] like the *stūpa* resting in midair.[6] The sound of the voice issuing [from inside the *stūpa*], praising with the words, "How excellent! How excellent!" (32b38) expresses a final affirmation. The words *set about with sundry precious objects* implicitly show that the ultimate fruit encompasses all kinds of good. Thus, its *li* becomes manifest by way of the event [conjured up by the Buddha]. Though it is difficult and unbelievable, it can be obtained.[7]

11.2.2 "And also hearing the sound of the voice issuing forth from inside the stūpa, *. . . amazed at what had never been before" (32c3, 183:26)*

The fourfold assembly, seeing the *stūpa* issuing forth, did not know the reason. Then they "rose [from their seats]," and stood off ["to one side"]. They turned looking earnestly, wishing to hear about its meaning. This happening was beyond their comprehension, making them dare not to speak. [A bodhisattva-mahāsattva] named Great Joy in Preaching (Mahāpratibhāna) sharing doubts with the multitude, addressed the Buddha, asking him to reveal the motive behind the event he had conjured up.

11.3.1 "[He] took a great vow" (32c11, 184:13)

The fact that [a Buddha called] Many Jewels formerly had taken a vow and could fulfill it secretly drew the attention of the congregation at that time, and as a consequence all invariably wished to see this Buddha's body. By making them see [the Buddha] appear, [the Buddha] unequivocally showed them the evidence.

11.3.2 "Then may the Buddhas who are emanations of that Buddha's body . . . again gather in one place, for then and only then shall my body **[408c10]** *appear"*

No doubt [the Buddha] does not do this as an act of self-glorification. He wants to distinguish between the true and the false; therefore, he finds it necessary to summon the Buddhas to gather. It was said earlier (32c12 and 16) that in the ten directions there would be this teaching [of the *sūtra*]. It means that the present Buddha Śākyamuni is real. What the real Buddha has preached must be clear and proper.[8] Through this many gain faith and are enlightened, fully and deeply. Therefore [the Buddha] uses the vow of Many Jewels as a pretext for gathering them in one place.

11.4.1 "Then the Sahā world-sphere was starightway transformed into something pure" (33a9, 186:5)

The purpose of showing all the dirt and evils removed, gods and men cast away (33a13, 186:12), leading to the point when flowers and incense are offered (33b1, 187:2), is to suggest indirectly that evil[9] certainly can be destroyed and good cultivated.

11.4.2 "[The Buddha further] conjured up two hundred myriads of millions of nayutas *of realms" (33a21 and 33b3, 186:24)*

If he wanted to accommodate all the Buddhas, who were emanations of [that Buddha's] body, he would appropriately prepare and purify the realms [immediately], making it suffice for beings to accept [the Buddha's original thesis]. [But] why did he conjure[10] them up gradually? The reason for doing this is as follows: [The Buddha] wants to give expression to the thesis that *li* cannot be reached at once; the coarse should be ground until it is fine; it must be decreased further and further, until it comes to the point of no decrease.[11]

11.4.3 "Throughout, these realms was a single Buddha-land"

This is designed to express [the idea] that although there are causes, different in myriad ways, they result in one single effect.

11.4.4 "[The Buddha Many Jewels . . .] then half his seat [to Śākyamuni Buddha]" (33c5, 188:7)

The purpose of presenting the dividing **[408d1]** of the seat, in order to share [it with the Buddha], is to suggest that extinction [from the world] does not necessarily mean extinction and existence does not necessarily mean existence. The difference between existence and extinction originates in the various grades [of the capacities of beings]. How can the Sage be subject to them?[12] Also by showing that [the Buddha will enter] *nirvāṇa* not long hence, [the Buddha] makes them anxious to prepare for [receiving] the *Dharma*.

11.4.5 "With his power of supernatural penetration, touched the great multitudes, so that they were all in open space" (33.cll, 188:17)

Why did he touch them? Wanting to express [the idea] that living beings are endowed with the capacity for great enlightenment and that all [are geared to] achieve Buddhahood, [the Buddha] showed this scene.

Notes

1. Hurvitz, *SLFD*, p. xiii.

2. For what seems to be proper segmentation and punctuation and interpretation, see Ōchō, "Jikudōshō sen," pp. 259f.

3. Liebenthal translates: (from the beginning of the passage) "The passions becloud *li*; they must by miracles be induced to believe. The pagoda is raised in order to bear testimony for the truth (of the message). A visible demonstration is needed" ("World Conception," II, p. 99).

4. 泥 (408b17) should be complete with 洹 as Ōchō, "Jikudōshō sen," p. 259, suspects.

5. 本在於空理 (408c1). Yabuki Keiki takes 理 to be 地 in "Tongogi no shushosha Jiku Dōshō to sono kyōgi," p. 794. Ōchō, ibid., pp. 259 and 269, leaves it as it is. Cf. *CVS*, 335b:4 空地, 328a:4 理空, a:5 空理.

6. Liebenthal translates: (from "all the living beings") "We are all Buddhas, all in Nirvāṇa. In the eternal aspect what difference is there between Nirvāṇa and a Buddha? But (our Buddhahood) is covered by moral dirt (*kleśa-anuśaya*) as the pagodas when under the earth were covered by it. (Our true nature) is destined to appear in its glory, it cannot be covered forever. It must come to light all at once as the pagoda shoots forth from the earth. This cannot be hindered. For from the beginning we are in the heaven of *li* as the pagodas are in the sky" ("World Conception," II, p. 82).

7. Ōchō, "Jikudōshō sen," p. 259, suspects 難 (c4) to be 欲, in which case it would be rendered; "Even though they do not want to believe it, they can not help but obtain it."

8. The second 說 (c11) seems to be redundant or simply a misprint.

9. 樂. It may have to be emended to 惡 "evil" in line with the correlated term 善 that subsequently occurs.

10. 變 (c16), the same word for "conjured up" in the *sūtra* as rendered by Hurvitz.

11. Cf. Liebenthal's translation: (from "[But] Why") (408c16–17) "Why does (the Buddha) transform (the Buddha domains) by degrees (and not at

once)? This procedure shows that (the final state of) *li* cannot be reached in one instant. One must work through matter in order to reach the immaterial. 'Diminish and further dimihish in order to reach the undiminishable'" ("World Conception," II, p. 93) Cf. *Tao-te ching*, Chapter 48: "(The pursuit of learning is to increase day after day. The pursuit of *Tao* is to decrease day after day.) It is to decrease and further decrease until one reaches the point of taking no action" (Chan, *The Way of Lao Tzu*, p. 184). A variation occurs in the *Chuang-tzu*, Chapter 22.

12. Liebenthal translates: "Only of things we may say that they exist or do not exist. How to say that of the Sage?" ("World Conception," I, p. 85, note 54).

Chapter 12

FORTITUDE[1]

(The vow to keep and propagate the *Lotus* is taken by the bodhisattva-mahāsattva Medicine King and other bodhisattvas and arhats. More prophecies are conferred on the bhikṣunīs including the Buddha's aunt and Rāhula's mother.)

12.1

So far [the Buddha] has broadly drawn parables and explanations, speaking of those who kept this *sūtra*. What is said here is about the great beings (mahāsattvas), including Medicine King, who take vows to keep this *sūtra* and propagage it in the evil age.

12.2 "In other lands" (36a7, 202:16)

The people of this land are so evil-minded that arhats will not be able to transform them. Hence, they are "in other lands" (cf. 36a7, 36b8). [What appears to be a tacit] affirmation [by the Buddha, as he keeps silent about their vow to propagate the *sūtra* in "other lands"], of the impossibility of their mission should not be taken as real. [The Buddha's silence should be interpreted] merely as words of stern [warning] for serious application to their mission.

Note

1. Chapter 12 of Kumārajīva's translation as found in the Taishō edition is "Devadatta." Tao-sheng's commentary is no doubt based on Kumārajīva's

version. During the period of T'ien-t'ai Chih-i (538–597) the "Chapter on Devadatta" was added to Kumārajīva's version, and thus that version came to be made up of twenty-eight chapters, one more than the original twenty-seven.

Chapter 13

[408d10] COMFORTABLE CONDUCT

(At Mañjuśrī's request the Buddha teaches the congregation the four virtues with which a bodhisattva-mahāsattva is equipped to carry out the mission of propagating this scripture in the latter, evil age, which is the supreme, final and most profound preaching he has ever undertaken.)

13.1.1

The explication of the idea that the cause of three turns out to be the cause of One is to be completed here. In the chapter preceding the present one, it has been explained that the great beings (mahāsattvas) will propagate this *sūtra* and that the ranks of voice heareres also will propagate this *Dharma* "in other lands." Among these are those who wish to transmit this *sūtra* but do not know how to do it. [The Buddha] therefore sets up this chapter to teach them the practical modus operandi.

13.1.2

If one is able to "dwell securely in four *dharmas*" (37a12, 208:10), then the body becomes tranquil and the spirit is settled. When the spirit is settled and the body tranquil, then external suffering does not interfere with them (the four *dharmas*). When external suffering does not interfere with them, one can be said to be "comfortable" (cf. 38b16). Because they are then able to preach the *Dharma* tirelessly, beings receive its benefits. "The four *dharmas*" are as follows: The first *dharma* consists of the acts of dwelling and the acts of the two kinds of places "that [the bodhisattva-mahāsattva] approaches with familiarity."[1] "The place that he approaches with familiarity" enables them to keep a distance from evils and remain close to *li*. As the mind rests on *li*, body and mouth do not commit any faults. Body and mouth not committing any faults constitute the second *dharma*. The third one is the state of feeling no jealousy. The fourth one is the state of feeling Great Compassion. As the three kinds of acts are purified, compassionate thought also pervades their minds. Is not the propagation of the *Dharma* in this way also great?

13.2.1 [409a1] "How can [a bodhisattva-mahāsattva] preach this scripture in the latter, evil age?" (37a10, 208:6)

In the earlier ages it was not yet hard to keep the *sūtra*. [But] if it is very hard to keep it [in the latter age], the low level of knowledge[2] and self-confidence[3] [are the probable causes]. Hence, [Mañjuśrī] asked [the Buddha] about the way to guide learners in the evil age.

13.2.2 "If in the latter evil age [a bodhisattva-mahāsattva] wishes to preach this scripture, he must dwell securely in four dharmas*" (37a11, 208:9)*

Although keeping the *sūtra* in the latter age involves a lot of evils, if they dwell in four *dharmas*, the latter age does not mean suffering. Dwelling in them certainly leads to security; hence, it is said, "dwelling securely." As regards the *dharmas* for teaching the Path, the practical modus operandi are as follows.

13.2.3 "First, by dwelling securely in the place where the bodhisattva acts, in the place that he approaches with familiarity"

When, having entered *li*, [the bodhisattva] fulfills it, he is in "the place [where the bodhisattva] acts." Although he has not yet entered *li*, if he is familiar with it and close to it, he is in "the place he approaches with familiarity." Also they are, as beginning and end, conjoined as one thing [or *Dharma*].

13.2.4 "Dwells on the ground of forbearance: . . . Nor at heart becoming alarmed"

He who is in "the place [where the bodhisattva-mahāsattva] acts" regards from beginning to end forbearance as the primary [virture]. These five virtues (37a15f) belong to the beginning.

13.2.5 "If, further, he performs no act with respect to the dharmas"

So far the virtues of having *li* in mind have been explicated; now the abilities of "viewing" and "performing" are introduced. These four things (37a18) constitute the end of "the place [where the bodhisattva-*mahāsattva*] acts."

13.2.6 "[The bodhisattva-mahāsattva] does not **[409a10]** *approach with familiarity kings or princes of realms"*

Approaching with familiarity also has a beginning and an end. Not approaching the place where confusion arises means approaching *li* with familiarity. What follows next is concerned with the beginning of approaching the place.

13.2.7 "Lokāyatas *(materialists)"*

They refer to those who counter what people in the world argue for.[4]

13.2.8 "Those who oppose the Lokāyatas"

They refer to those who try hard to cling to what [people in the world] argue for.

13.2.9 "Natas *(dancers, actors)"*

They refer to those who make up their bodies in order to perform [various magical plays].[5]

13.2.10 "The five kinds of unmanly men" (37b5, 209:6)

The first kind are the men who are born impotent (*jātipaṇḍaka*), those whose original constitutions do not allow them to get an erection. The second are eunuchs whose organs are small and weak (*āpatpaṇḍaka*). The third refers to the men who are impotent for a half of [every] month (*pakṣapaṇḍaka*), which means that for half a month they change [feeling] for women. The fourth are men who are impotent because of jealousy (*īrṣyāaṇḍaka*): they cannot become potent by themselves, but seeing others perform sex, they immediately become jealous, and by way of jealousy they become potent. Fifth, the men who cannot ejaculate (*āsaktaprādurbhāvīpaṇḍakaḥ*). They can become potent only after others touch their bodies first.

13.2.11 "Views all dharmas *as empty, in accord with their true marks" (37b12, 210:3)*

The following ten-odd items, although the names are many, point in reality to no more than one **[409b1]** emptiness. This is the beginning of seeing, yet short of being able to enter, *li*: it is the end of "approaching the place with familiarity."

13.2.12 "Gāthās"

In the *gāthās* that follow, some [parts mentioned in the prose] are extened and some are summarized, and some also are not chanted. They can be regulated in accordance with the meaning.

13.3.1 "Whether preaching by word of mouth or reading the scripture itself, one must have no wish to mention the faults of men or the scriptural canon" (38a1, 213:26)

As for the second *dharma*, it is the committing of no fault through body or mouth. Although this does not refer to the *karma* committed through body, it is chanted in the *gāthās*. (38a10) [Although] this section may touch on the *karma* through mind, it is strictly meant to complete the theme that they (beings) should commit no fault through body or mouth; it does not deal with mind as such.

13.3.2 "Also, O Mañjuśsī, . . . shall harbor no thought of envy, flattery, or deceit" (38b2, 216:1)

The third *dharma* is the [harboring] of no envy or jealousy. Although this refers to *karma* committed through the mouth, it is designed to drive home the theme of [committing] no fault of *karma* through mind; it does not speak of mouth as such.

13.3.3 "[Again], O Mañjuśrī, . . . thinking with great good will of persons in the household and those gone forth from the household" (38c4, 217:25)

The fourth *dharma* is the state of feeling "great compassion" (*mahākaruṇā*). Because of its being "great," in altruistically embracing beings,[6] it is described later. If they can rest in these four dharmas, they will then not have fear or weakness. [If] they propagate the teaching by availing themselves of these [dharmas], the fruit will be a rich one.

13.3.4 "Suppose, for example, there is **[409b10]** *a wheel-turning Sage-king of great strength" (38c22, 218:16)*

This example symbolizes the *Scripture of Dharma Blossom*, which was not given earlier to men, but is given now.

Notes

1. 親近處 (37b11 and 17, 210:1 and 11). Katō renders it as "sphere of intimacy" (*MSLW*, pp. 271 and 272).

2. 淺識 (409a2), literally, "shallow or superficial knowledge," referring to

the information regarding the three vehicles in contradistinction to the knowledge of One. For a synonymous expression, see 403b13, 412b11 and d2.

3. See 399b1, 401b14.

4. *Lokāyatas* are classified as a heterodox school like the Buddhists in Indian tradition.

5. Hurvitz, *SLFD*, 209:1, breaks down what Tao-sheng takes as one group of people into two by translating the phrase concerned (37a:22) into "*naṭas* [dancers, actors], [practitioners of] any of a variety of magical games." Katō agrees with Tao-sheng: "to the various juggling performances of *Nartakas* and others" (*MSLW*, p. 270:9).

6. See 397d6 (Chapter 1, note 27).

Chapter 14

WELLING UP OUT OF THE EARTH

(Witnessing many bodhisattva-mahāsattvas follow the Buddha's suite, mahāsattvas from other lands also volunteer to hold the *sūtra*, only to be denied this role by the Buddha, as it was already sufficiently assigned to the mahāsattvas of his Sahā world-sphere. As witnesses, millions of bodhisattva spring up out of the earth with their innumerable retinues. Maitreya and others then wonder about the Buddha's great achievement in converting so many beings in such a short space of time.)

14.1

This chapter introduces an integral part[1] of the next [chapter], concerning the life-span [of the Thus Come One], and is designed to demonstrate that the effect of the three becomes that of the One. Earlier there was an introduction regarding the cause; in accord with that speech, flowers [rained down] and the earth trembled (Chapter 1). This chapter introudces the effect; in accord with this speech, a great number of bodhisattvas well up out of the earth. Here Maitreya harbors doubts, as he did before. It [the chapter] also manifests the everabiding meaning.

14.2.1 "Stop! [Good men], there is no need for you" (39c24, 225:10)

The reason for saying *stop* is to initiate the entrance of the bodhisattvas [equal in number to the sands of] sixty thousand [Ganges

Rivers]. Because the bodhisattbvas appear, [the Buddha] is able to show how his long life-span is brought about.

14.2.2 "My Sahā world-sphere itself has bodhistattva-mahāsattvas equal in number to the sands of sixty thousand Ganges Rivers"

The teaching of the Sage has its rise and fall; its deep purport is not fathomable. However, as it has widely prevailed throughout times earlier and later, **[409c1]** the meaning can be grasped. In the preceding [the Buddha] urged them to protect the *Dharma*, but now he says "[there is] no need." (32c24) [Why the discrepancy?] They are both [valid statements] each with its own purpose. The *Dharma* by which living beings emerge from delusion and are led to Buddhahood and *nirvāṇa* is designed to extinguish itself completely; they (beings) must volunteer to protect it. Hence, the words of exhortation, so that they may strengthen their will [to protect it]. However, living beings all are endowed with [the faculty of] great enlightenment; all are without exception potenial bodhisattvas. [In this respect] there is no time when it (the *sūtra*) is not protected. Then why does he have to rely on bodhisattvas from other regions [for protection]? Reliance on [bodhisattvas from] other regions makes it appear that the *li* of the transformative teaching is insufficient. Thus, [the Buddha] shows the rising-up [of the bodhisattva-mahāsattvas] in order to express this idea. *Six* [of *sixty thousand* or *six ten-thousands* (wan)] refers to the six states of existence (*gati*). *The sands of the Ganges Rivers* mean "a lot." *The earth* refers to the bonds and the instigators of depravites.[2] And the living being's endowment for enlightenment lies under these instigators of depravities. *(They all had been) under [this Sahā world-sphere], in an open space*[3] indicates that [beings] are in void-*li* [or *li* of emptiness (*śūnyatā*), the state of *li* devoid of instigators].

14.2.3

That the earth split and [the bodhisattvas] welled up suggests that living beings inherently possess[4] an endowment for enlightenment,[5] and it cannot remain concealed; they are bound to break the earth of defilements and emerge to safeguard the *Dharma*.[6]

14.2.4

It is said that [even] Maitreya did not recognize a single person (40c27, 230:26) because the [endowment] is such that [as an object of] enlightenment it cannot be empirically experienced [even by one who is] in the tenth stage.[7] That what welled up was not Buddhas but bodhisattvas means that this endowment for enlightenment has necessarily to be studied accumulatively **[409c10]** until there is nothing left to learn.[8]

14.2.5 "[At that time], [the bodhisattva-mahāsattva] Maitreya . . . at heart doubtful" (41b29, 233.29)

Riding on the thought of the multitude, [Maitreya] harbors doubts regarding [how] the Buddha since his attainment of Buddhahood could accomplish so many things [in such a short time]. [Maitreya] begs [the Buddha] to resolve these doubts for the multitude, showing them the ultimate within themselves. The everabiding, subtle meaning is gradually revealing itself in this way.

Notes

1. Cf. 397a13.

2. 結使 : *kleśa* or *anuśaya*.

3. The phrase is found in the *gāthās* (41b20), "under side, in open space, they dwell" (233:11).

4. 而 (c7). The letter still makes sense in the sense of 與 "to share in" (*Matthews' Chinese-English Dictionary*, p. 1142) but it seems safer if we emend it to 有 (see c3). Or it is rather unnecessary as in the immediately preceding line.

5. See 408b18ff.

6. The ten originally account for the stages, eleventh to twentieth, in the scheme of the fifty-two bodhisattva stages. But it often is interchangeable with the word 十地 (*daśa-bhūmi*). Cf. Liebenthal, *The Book of Chao*, pp. 169ff. In interpreting this passage, Ōchō, "Jikudōshō sen," pp. 269f., points to the passages of the two versions of the *Nirvāṇa Sūtra*, which states that the Buddha-nature innate in oneself cannot be perceived even by a bodhisattva in the tenth stage.

7. Another variation of the pattern similar to the passage in 408c:16, traceable to the Taoist texts, the *Tao-te ching*, Chapter 48, in particular. The word 積學 occurs in *CTC*, Chapter 32 (*CTI*, 10:11); see also Chapter 6 (*CTI*, 3:6) for the variations of the pattern and the term.

Chapter 15

THE LIFE-SPAN [OF THE THUS COME ONE]

The Buddha replies that the commonly accepted notions about the Buddha's life-span and teaching career have no ultimate truth, that the Buddha in fact is limitless in both time and space, assuming various forms in different ages and under different circumstances but all for one and the same purpose, the salvation of beings. He illustrates this with the following parable.

A physician who had been away from home a long time returned to find his sons suffering from an ailment. He prescribed for them an appropriate medicine, which certain of them took but which others, mad from the poison, refused. Those who took it were immediately cured, whereas the others continued to languish in their malady. The physician accordingly went away and circulated the rumor that he had died. This shocked the ailing sons back to their senses, after which they, too, took their father's medicine and were cured. When he heard of this, the father made his appearance again.

Just so, says the Buddha, are beings. When offered salvation some of them refuse it; so the Buddha stages a docetic *nirvāṇa*. This instills in them a sense of urgency, born of the fear that the Buddha will not always be among them. But for this, certain beings would continue forever to forego their own salvation.[1]

15.1

The profound mirror is void and clear,[2] it is outside the realm of phenomena. How can any being with a distinct form do away with life-span, long or short? However, the proposition that there is nothing that is with form and enjoys [a long] life-span stems from various delusions. There is no way that the Sage can be in that category. Only the deluded would count the actual life-span of the Buddha as a hundred years. Now such a [mental] impediment is driven out. [The Buddha] relies on [the theory of] longevity to dispel it. Thus this chapter is titled "Life-Span." *Life-span* is none other than that which prompted the Buddhas [to achieve] spiritual insight in the earlier chapters and is none other than the ultimate effect. Because the ultimate fruit has been shown, is it not true that they abide eternally? Furthermore, they tend to have an affinity for life and distaste for death. What is now **[409d1]** said about longevity must invigorate them greatly.

15.2.1 "The true speech [of the Thus Come One!]" (42b2, 237:2)

Maitreya has doubts and asks the Buddha to resolve them. The Buddha is about to answer them. Thus he addresses them three times, because *li* is so deep and the *Tao* is so wondrous that they cannot be spoken of in simple terms.

15.2.2 "We beg you to speak it!"

They beg for it three times, also expressing how intense is their aspiration.

15.2.3 "All say that the present Śākyamunibuddha *left the palace of the Śākya clan"*

Here is the point of which many are doubtful. Thus, he points it out to dispel the doubts. This day[3] [the Buddha] proves that his long life-span is real, thereby showing that [his enlightenment at] Gayā is unreal. If one perceives that Gayā is untrue, one also knows that [a] long or short [life-span] applies to beings, whereas the Sage is ever in the unconditioned state (*wu-wei*,[4] *asaṃskṛta*).[5]

15.3 "The time since my achievement of Buddhahood would exceed even this" (42b6, 238:16)

The Form-body (*Rūpa-kāya*) of the Buddha must be something visible and existent but without real form. If he is not real, how can he be spoken of in terms of life-span? However, the [different] modes and forms[6] [of manifestation] are directed to arrive at the same [goal]. He is one throughout the past and the present **[409d10]**; the past also is the present, and vice versa. There is no time when he is not existent. There is no place where he is not present. If there are times when something is not existent and there are places when something is not present,[7] it applies only to beings, but not to the Sage. For the reason, ultimately [the Sage] establishes the eternity [of the Buddha], suggesting that Gayā is [a part of] it. If Gayā is [a part of] it, there is no more Gayā. Because there is no more Gayā, how can eternity exist alone? [Therefore], eternity and shortness are not [separately] existent; this is the reason why both eternity and shortness remain existent.[8]

15.4.1 "[The Thus Come One] in full accord with Reality knows and sees the marks of the triple sphere" (42c13, 239:9)

He who has seen Reality never again sees what is not real. [The Buddha's] original intention was to ferry them over to Reality and awaken them to it. Thus, in accordance with the way they responded he devised expedients. Even though these are not identical their imports are not different. However, it is said here that [the Thus Come One] sees only "[the marks of] the triple sphere". He has already seen something more than that. Because [everything] he says contains his original [intention] he seeks to find the words and expressions in various forms [that would suit the existential situations of beings].

15.4.2 "The life-span I achieved in my former treading of the bodhisattva path even now is not exhausted" (42c22, 239:23)

When he was treading the bodhisattva path in the past, his life-span "was twice the preceding [number]." It should be known, therefore, that though [his life-span] was compared to the number of grains of sand, the tiniest part of it has not yet been exhausted. Now the Buddha is described by way of a bodhisattva; **[410a1]** the Buddha's life-span is long [in comparison with the bodhisattva's].

15.5.1 "For example, suppose there is a good physician . . . hundred or more" (43a8, 240:14)

This example symbolizes the Buddha who exists [for ever] in reality but who says he will soon be extinguished. Living beings formerly received [from him] transformative teaching; they are "sons" born of the bodhisattva. *Twenty* refers to the two vehicles. *Hundred or more* indicates "many." He who cures diseases on the basis of the [sufferer's] present [condition] is a "physician."

15.5.2 "On an affair of business, be goes far off to another realm"

Having transformed this [realm], he must also transform that [realm], without taking any rest.

15.5.3 "His sons, left behind, drink some other poisonous medicines and, as the medicines start becoming effective, they show agonized pain and confusion, rolling about on the earth"

Their understanding is small and they suffer from delusion; they are likened to those who "drink poisonous medicines." "Going astray from *li*," they belong to the "other." The condition (*pratyaya*) of delusion arises: "The medicines start becoming effective." Having received consciousness of death and birth,[9] they are likened to being in "agonized pain and confusion." [Being in the cycle of] birth and death, they are "rolling about on the earth."

15.5.4 "At this time their father returns home"

The *li* underlying the former transformative teaching is true; it is "home." The condition for receiving teaching overcomes them and they return to the city of Gayā and recognize it; they "return."

15.5.5 "The sons, having drunk poison, some of them have lost their sanity, though others have not"

Ever since they received the teaching, **[410a10]** [some of] them have practiced the right path all the time: they "have not lost their sanity". Going astray from it, [some of] them "have lost [their sanity]".

15.6.1 "All overjoyed at seeing their father from afar . . . welcome back to peace and security!" (43a11, 240:22)

Conditions develop in such a way that they overcome their ignorance, on a shallow level, and approach *li*, gradually, little by little: They "see from afar." But as they see that form [incarnated] in response[10] [to the different needs of individual beings] they are all "[over]joyed," and there is no one who does not offer alms to him and praise him.

15.6.2 "We in our folly have made the mistake of taking poisonous medicine"

The process of overcoming [ignorance] having been started, the true reveals the erroneous. What is said here is an unreal, tentative satatement.

15.6.3 "We beg you to heal us and restore our lives to us!"

They have appealed to him to heal them; he "heals" them, that is, he revives their wisdom-life. This also is an unreal, tentative statement.

15.6.4 "The father, seeing how acute were the agonies . . . ordering them to take them"

All that the Buddha has preached about the *Dharma*, in accordance with the way [beings] respond, has the same goal: it is "tasty." The words describe their external joy: they are "colorful." They have had their thought rectified inside and outside: it is "fragrant." The [Buddha's] teaching manifests the ultimate consequence, unity in the markless (*wu-hsiang/animitta*): he "pounded, sifted, and blended them."

15.6.5 "Speaking these words: . . . shall never again be subject to a host of torments"

He meant "to order them to take." This also is an unreal, tentative statement.

15.6.6 "Among the sons, those who had not lost their sanity **[410b1]** *. . . their sickness was completely removed and healed"*

They apprehended [the Buddha's] purport: they "took it." They had their delusions removed: they were "healed."

15.7.1 "The others, who had lost their sanity . . . said . . . was no good" (43a20, 241:1)

Although they knew that it was a medicine, they remained ignorant of its purpose; thus it was "no good."

15.7.2 "Straightway he spoke these words: '. . . I am now aged and infirm, and my time of death already is at hand'"

Likewise, the Buddha's age was eighty; his form was like a worn-out vehicle. He was just about to enter *parinirvāṇa*.

15.7.3 "This fine and good medicine I now leave here for you to take"

If the Great *Dharma* of the six *pāramitās* is not kept, it will disappear. *Li* is not subject to destruction; when practiced, it will remain.

15.7.4 "When he had given these instructions, he went again to another realm and then sent a messenger back to declare, 'Your father is dead!'"

[The Buddha] carried out again [his mission] to convert the rest; he "went again to another realm." He entered *nirvāna* under the twin trees; his words and traces were completely extinguished: he "sent a messenger back to declare, 'Your father is dead.'"

15.7.5 "At this time, the sons, hearing that their father had forsaken them . . . the poisons and the sickness were all healed"

Seeing the Buddha entering *nirvāṇa*, they were awakened to the fact that [the Buddha] did not exist eternally. They began to realize what the Buddha had said: it turned out to be "tasty." They apprehended the purport: they "took it."

15.7.6 "The father, hearing that his sons had all achieved a cure, then came back, enabling all to see **[410b10]** him"

They comprehended the profound meaning. They were beginning to see the Buddha, [yet] there were those who had not seen the Buddha in corporeal form. To them he also "came back."

15.7.7 "Is [he] guilty of the sin of willfully false speech, or is there not?" (43b7, 241:27)

The [Buddha's] intention was to make beings gain consciousness [of reality], and the result was that he saved beings. Even though the [Buddha's] words are lacking in consistency, [the underlying] *li* does not contradict the truth. Although [the Buddha] preached all day long, by preaching he did not commit "the sin of willfully false speech."[11]

15.8.1 "Emerge on the Mount of the Numinous Eagle (Gṛdhrakūṭa)" (43b24, 242:28)

The Buddha is at the stage of beginning to feel (*kan*) [the need of beings]: he "emerges."

15.8.2 "Ever am I on the Mount of the Numinous Eagle . . . yet the living beings,[12] seeing it consumed with flame" (43c5, 243:12)

The Buddha who was seen earlier is absent because of the multitudinous beings' impurity and evil. The Buddha is absent because of [beings'] impurity, which means that in the state of purity, [the Buddha] must be present. [Only] when there is no impurity is [the Buddha] positively present.[13] Hence, he clearly shows it by resort to the seven treasures,[14] which implies that there is no impurity of [the land of] stones and sands.[15] [The Buddha] himself did not [specifically] mention that its substance (*t'i*) is not impure. When it comes to talking about the formless (*wu-hsiang, arūpa*), how can it also be different from the basic substance (*chih*) of impurity? Hence, undefiled purity has the [real] meaning of *no land*. Through *land*, he refers to *no*; hence, he speaks of the Pure Land.[16] In that case, the purity of "no land" must be none other than that in which the *Dharma*-body finds representation. When impurity and **[410c1]** evil are burned [away] it is retribution for the sin of living beings. Also, how can [burning] harm the omnipresent and absolutely pure? Therefore, living beings see it being burned, and yet the "Pure Land" is not ruined, and it makes[17] them feel delighted in what is beautiful and esteem what they delight in. If they hear that the Pure Land is not ruined, they will then nurture longings in the depths of their thoughts. They are greatly benefitted by [the Buddha's attempt to make them] penetrate the darkly profound [realm] through [his own] example.

15.8.3 "I, everknowing living beings" (44a1, 244:28)

What is chanted here is concordant with [what is said in the prose section] that he preached the subtle, [wondrous *Dharma*]. (42c4)

15.8.4 "Each time having this thought"[18]

This is largely concordant with [what is said] likewise (43a23) [in the prose section].

Notes

1. Hurvitz, *SLFD*, p. xiv.

2. Cf. Seng-chao, *Chao-lun*, T45.153a2: 虛心玄鑒 "His empty mind mirrors the metaphysical." (Robinson, *Early Mādhyamika*, p. 213).

3. 今日 (c5), probably the copyist's mistake of 今曰 (?) "now he speaks" [to prove].

4. See 402b6 (Chapter 3, note 33); 404b8 (Chapter 4, note 23). Cf., Hurvitz, *SLFD*, p. 256, note; *sūtra*, 19a4.

5. Hurvitz, *Chi-i*, p. 200, translates (from "This day"): "This day, by holding to eternity as true, he shows Bodhgaya to be false. But if one can perceive that Bodhgaya is untrue, one must also understand that eternity is not true either. Hence one knows that long and short are on the side of the beings [who are the objects of the Buddha's salvation], and that the Sage is ever quiescent." Cf. *CTC*, Chapter 12 (*CTI*, 4:31) 壽夭兼忘所謂懸解 "Longevity and untimely death are both forgotten; it is what is said that someone has been released from hanging"; (4:37): 至人極壽命之長 "The superior man is the one who has brought the length of life to the extreme point."

6. 方形 (d9). Liebenthal reads it as (萬)形 "all the phenomena" ("World Conception," II, p. 85).

7. Another 有 is needed here to read: 若有時不有,(有)處不在者(d10f.), in agreement with Liebenthal (*loc. cit.*) and Sakamoto, in Sakamoto, ed., *Hokkekyō no Chūgokuteki tenkai*, p. 14.

8. According to Sakamoto, ibid., it should read: 長短斯非(亡)則所以長短(恒)存焉 (d13). The whole passage is translated by Liebenthal: "The mortal Buddhas appear as they are called. They have no definite shape and therefore also no definite age. It follows that (to the real Buddha) who integrates all the phenomena in all the ages the past is present and the present past. He is always and everywhere. If there existed any time or any place where he is not, he would be like other creatures. The Sage is different. If one agrees that the word *long-lived* is used as symbol for a *summum* and that this applies to Gayā also, (I maintain that) if Gayā is such, it is no more Gayā (the place on earth) and *long-lived* cannot refer to (mundane life which, though long, is limited). If (the life of the Buddha) is neither short nor long, it is potentially long as well as short" ("World Conception," II, p. 85).

9. 受死生識. Note that the four letters happen to account for four of the twelve links in the doctrine of conditioned origination or causation (*pratītya-samutpāda*) as discussed by Tao-sheng himself in 406d. Syntactically, they do not have any relevance with the chains. Yet, the implication of the life-and-death (*saṃsāra*) process is apparent here. Cf. 410b11.

10. Compare the meaning and terms of the phrase with the theory of multiple (triple, for example) body of the Buddha, by matching "form" (形) with the "corporeal body" (色身, *rūpakāya*) and "response" with "response body" (報身). See Suzuki, *Outlines of Mahāyāna Buddhism*, p. 250; *Studies in the Laṇkāvatāra Sūtra*, p. 308ff., especially pp. 310–311.

11. Liebenthal translates above two passages: "When penetrating to the meaning (of the Scriptures) we meet the Buddha in the medicine he offers though not in person. (The Buddha) came home to those children (who swallowed the medicine). . . . His intention was that they should accept (his message) and be saved in reality. Though words are not everlasting (truth), if they do not conflict with truth, then talk, though continued the whole day, does not involve the sin of untruth" ("World Conception," II, p. 98).

12. (43c12), which is taken by Tao-sheng as 衆生, by Hurvitz as "the multitude" (*SLFD*, 243:27).

13. 無必在穢. It may make sense in its own, but it is possible that it is a misprint of 無穢必在; that is, the phrase immediately preceding it, as it is quite usual that repetition of the same phrase occurs elsewhere in the text as Tao-sheng's style.

14. 七珍, identical with 七寶, which are gold (*suvarṇa*), silver (*rūpya*), lapis lazuli (*vaidūrya*), crystal (*sphaṭika*), agate (*musāragalva*), rubies (*rohita-mukta*), and cornelian (*aśmagarba*). They are the things that appear in the Western Paradise. It should be noted that the original title of Tao-sheng's essay,

"The Buddha is not found in the Pure Land," was "On the Seven Precious Things." See Chi-tsang, *Fa-hua hsüan-lun*, T34.442a; Liebenthal, "A Biography," p. 94.

15. Emend 名汝 (b16) to 石沙. See *CVS*, T38.337b, 338a; Fuse Kōgaku, *Nehanshū no kenkyū*, pp. 190, 196 (note 43).

16. Cf. a similar statement by Tao-sheng in *CVS*, 334c15ff.: "'Land' refers to the area to which the living beings belong. When it is undefiled we say it as pure; being undefiled, it is non-existent (*wu*) and, being what they belong to, it is existent (*yu*)."

17. 今 has been emended to 令. See T'ang Yung-t'ung, *Fo-chiao shih*, II, p. 165.

18. The phrase (410c4) slightly varies from the equivalent words in the *sūtra* (44a3).

Chapter 16

DISCRIMINATION OF MERITS

(The Buddha narrates the merit that shall accrue to those who venerate the foregoing chapter of the *Lotus* telling of the unlimited nature of the Buddha's life-span.[1])

16.1

Cause and effect entail each other. Faith is [related to the process] like shadow [is to the object] and echo [is to sound]. In the preceding they heard [the Buddha] preaching [his limited] life-span and so they have been doing their utmost in seeking advantages; by availing themselves of this [opportunity] to obtain the effect, they will reap the reward bountifully. Now [the Buddha] is going to distinguish its difference. Accordingly the chapter is entitled "Discrimination of Merits."

16.2.1 "*Ajita*"

In the Chinese language,[2] it means "[the one] not conquered". Maitreya is his style.

16.2.2 "Gained acceptance of [the doctrine of] the unborn dharmas *(*anutpattika-dharma-kṣānti*)"*

Why is there any need for talking about those who have been really enlightened **[410c10]**? The purpose of citing broadly those who obtained enlightenment is to glorify this *sūtra*, [helping] to generate and accumulate the various [stages of] understanding, so that by catering to the [need and situations of] beings in endlessly varied ways[3] [the Buddha] may secretly exhort those seekers [of enlightenment] to keep this *Dharma Blossom*. When one has not yet seen *li*, there is a need for the ferry of words; for one who has witnessed *li*, what is the use of words? They are like the fish trap and snare for catching fish and rabbits: when fish and rabbits have been already caught, what use do they have?[4] [It is said here that] once hearing the *sūtra* [preached], they immediately reach the one-birth-bound [stage][5] or [the state of] the forbearance of *dharmas*.[6] Yet, *li* certainly should not be so.[7] If originally there is no understanding, what can words add? The view that there are progress and regress [in the realization of *li*] is groundless. Yet, this is said in the writings to be so. [Why?] Because *li*, as enunciated by the *sūtra*, espouses the ten stages. Even though it is not something to resort to, it yet is put in the position of something to resort to; knowledge of the *sūtra* has no use, and yet it is said to possess the capacity for use. Through this demonstration [the Buddha] is able to make [past] facts of [attainment] manifest the meaning of the *sūtra*. If one follows and knows it, how can one be finished [as a practitioner]![8]

16.3

In [the phrase] *were destined after eight rebirths to gain the unexcelled bodhi (anuttarasamyaksaṃbodhi)* (44a17, 245:20), this [eight rebirths] refers to the eighth stage. Because for one who is beyond the eighth stage there is no more reincarnation, how can it be known whether his wisdom **[410d1]** is bright or dark? Therefore, by resorting to eight rebirths [instead of "stages"], [the Buddha makes beings] realize that the Buddha shall have been gone a long time before. "One rebirth" is the number through which Maitreya, for example, is destined to go. Likewise there may be two [rebirths] or three, up to eight. *Eight* refers to many births. Many births, hence, they know, or they may also be ignorant of it. [The Buddha] does not speak of ten rebirths, because *ten* is one ultimate of numbers, with the meaning of "a great many," and he intends to show that the bodhisattvas still have some delusions and instigators of depravities left, a little short [of annihilation]. Hence, *eight* is resorted to. [The Buddha] goes directly to "four births" without mentioning six [rebirths], wishing to demonstrate that the *sūtra* is so profound and deep, darkly drawing one to enlightenment and entrance into reality. [The bodhisattvas who are in the stages] from transcendence[9] to four rebirths reveal this intent. The fact that from four rebirths to one rebirth they proceed by degrees without skipping steps has the implication that *li* becomes [increasingly] wondrous [as they proceed]. That those who are enlightened also [gradually] become less [in number], and that it is hard to quickly attain [enlightenment], attests to this idea.

16.4.1 "Hearing of [the great length of] the Buddha's life-span" (44c20, 251:33)

[This refers to] the Buddha's wisdom-life. Now because hearing about [the Buddha's long] life-span is equivalent to practicing [the *pāramitā* of] *prajñā* or wisdom intensively, here it thus is said that the merit one can achieve by practicing the five *pāramitās* for [many] *nayutas* of *kalpas* may not equal [even the tiniest] part [of the merit one can achieve by hearing about the Buddha's long life-span].

16.4.2 "Who can keep this scripture and at the same time practice the spreading of gifts" (45c14, 253:27)

The meaning of what has been said in the preceding **[410d10]** is found here. When one holds the wondrous understanding within, and outwardly practices the six *pāramitās*, one has advanced [toward enlightenment], in both [inner] thought and its [outer] practical ramifications (*shih*); and so one's right enlightenment (*samyaksaṃbodhi*) is [so imminent that it can come at any moment] in the morning or evening.[11]

Notes

1. Hurvitz, *SLFD*, pp. xiv–xv.

2. Literally, "in the language of *Sung*", (Liu) Sung (420–479) being the state Tao-sheng belonged to at the time of compilation of the commentary.

3. 應物無窮. Cf. *CTC*, Chapter 25 (*CTI*, 8:33): 應感無窮 "He responds to and is moved by [the need of the beings] in endlessly varied ways"; Chapter 12 (*CTI*, 4:33): 應感無方.

4. The source of this analogy is the *Chuang-tzu*, Chapter 26: "The fish trap exists because of the fish; once you've gotten the fish, you can forget the trap. The rabbit snare exists because of the rabbit; once you've gotten the rabbit, you can forget the snare. Words exist because of meaning; once you've gotten the meaning, you can forget the words" (B. Watson, *Chuang Tzu, Basic Writings*, p. 140, and *Complete Works*, p. 302).

5. *Eka-jāti-pratibaddha*: "limited to one (more) birth" (*BHSD*, p. 152).

6. *Anutpattika-dharma-kṣāntiḥ*: "Intellectual receptivity to the truth that states of existence have no origination" (ibid., p. 27). It is a trait associated with the eighth stage (*bhūmi*).

7. Liebenthal translates: "Hearing the Sūtra once, one acquires the state of *ekajātipratibaddha* or that of *anutpatti dharmakṣānti*, but certainly that is not *li*" (*The Book of Chao*, p. 182). Compare another translation by him (see note

8). For the pattern of the last sentence (理固無然), see *CTC*, Chapter 1 (*CTI*, 1:2): 理固然.

8. Cf. translation by Liebenthal: (from "Why is there," 16.2.2) "Why (does the Buddha) tell that to one who has seen the Truth? It is done in order to praise this *Sūtra* that he enumerates all those who have reached Enlightenment. (For) it contains guidance for everybody, an inexhaustible (store) where each Being gets what he needs. Implicity he urges those who seek salvation to study this *Sūtra*. As long as *li* is not yet seen we must necessarily make use of speech; thereafter speech, as an effort of the mundane kind, is superfluous. Fishes and hares are caught in baskets and traps, but after the fishes and hares have been caught these devices are no longer needed. (We are told that) hearing the *Sūtra* once (the Saint) immediately attains the fruit of *ekāgamin* or *anutpattidharmakṣānti*. But in reality that is certainly not so. Would (the hearing of) the words (of the *Sūtra*) be of any use if (those Bodhisattvas addressed) were not already released? There is (for one released) no alternation possible, neither for the better nor for the worse. And the fact that the *Sūtra* (enumerates all these rewards) must be explained by its (above outlined) intention. *Li* occupies the tenth *bhūmi*. (It is the end.) Though (these rewards) are not lies they are yet, taken literally, lies. The story the *Sūtra* tells us is not (in itself) a means to salvation but the possibility exists that it becomes a means to salvation. The enumeration of rewards (given to those who hear the *Sūtra*) is therefore made, (not as an aim in itself, but) in order to draw our attention to the meaning (of the *Sūtra*). (Or, are we supposed) to be content with the knowledge gained (from listening to somebody else)? Is (what we are told in the *Sūtra*) our own experience?" ("World Conception," II, p. 92).

9. That is, transcendence to birth and death, which means no more rebirth.

10. "Five" because one, *prajñā*, is not included in the otherwise six "perfections" (see next passage).

11. Cf. the *Analects* 4:8: 朝聞道夕死可矣 "If a man in the morning hear the right way, he may die in the evening without regret." (Legge, trans., *Confucius*, p. 168). Cf. also I-tsing, *A Record of the Buddhist Religion*, J. Takakusu, trans. (Oxford, 1896), p. 185.

Chapter 17

THE MERITS OF APPROPRIATE JOY

(Again at Maitreya's question, the Buddha declares that the joy and merit of those who hear the *sūtra* surpasses that which can be had by practicing other virtues whatsoever.)

17.1

In the beginning when the Sage arranged the teaching, he did not expect that those who would be benefitted by it would be limited to contemporary beings; he desired strongly that the teaching be directed to the coming generations, admonishing and transforming numerous living beings. The thesis that the effect of the three makes that of the One, as has been explicated earlier, is roughly completed. This chapter is intended to deal with the topic of those who spread [the *sūtra*]. When a man wants to propagate the *Dharma*, it is essential that he hold joy and pleasure in his mind. If his mind is full of hatred and anger, he distances himself from [other] beings. How can the *Tao* be spread by one who distances oneself from [other] beings?[1] Hence, the chapter is entitled "Appropriate Joy."

17.2.1 "Maitreya addressed the Buddha" (46b19, 259:1)

Maitreya, who was formerly inclined to practice [the *Dharma*] with appropriate joy, now again asks the Buddha about its meaning.

17.2.2 "How much happiness shall he or she obtain?"

He demonstrates how much or little [happiness they shall obtain], in order to make stronger the beings' will to seek it.[2]

17.2.3 "Until it reaches the fiftieth person"

The purpose of taking up **[411a1]** the last person is [to say] that most of the people, in the beginning, hearing in person the wisdom-preaching, tend to accept it with deep pleasure, but if it is transmitted to other people, especially when it comes to the last person, their pleasure will be attenuated, and those with attenuated pleasure likewise will have their merits lessened. [Yet,] this time, it turns out that this is not the case; it is suggested that his happiness and recompense are limitless. How much the more would be [the happiness and recompense of] those who were present in the very first audience sitting and hearing firsthand [the Buddha preaching the *sūtra*]! It much also be deep!

17.2.4 "The living beings of the four kinds of birth"[3]

What they seek is [merit], [but their pleasure is] "not like the appropriate joy the fiftieth person would get in hearing the *Dharma Blossom*" (46c25). The merits of the four fruitions,[4] as mentioned earlier (26c17), are of limited measure [in comparison with this joy]. [In contrast,] the *Dharma Blossom*, on behalf of *li*, represents the complete penetration of the ultimate of nothingness.[5] Men have appropriate joys, which means that they have accomplished the path of Thus Come One. The path has been accomplished because of these men, so their merits cannot be easily kept down [from arising]. Hence, it is said, "[the merit] does not equal one-hundredth part, not one-thousandth . . . part." How can this be an empty [statement]?[6]

17.3.1 [He shall be] . . . never dumb"
(47a12, 260:23]

Why is the recompense ["for having rejoiced at hearing"] the *Dharma Blossom* administered this way? [The Buddha] merely takes up what men feel like [having]. Hence, [the Buddha] says: "[the body into which he is reborn] shall acquire . . . carriages, as well as palanquins fitted with precious gems" (47a4, 260:10).

17.3.2 "His breath never fetid"

There is nothing that can be disliked.

17.3.3 "And in the great multitude [explains] them to others" (47a22, 261:4) **[411a10]**

This refers to the forthcoming chapter. What has not been substantiated in the preceding, and what has so far been omitted, is how much merit there will be for those who rejoice appropriately, "explaining" by turns[7] and propagating [the *sūtra* to others].

Notes

1. Cf. 407d15f.

2. For a similar pattern, cf. *CTC, Chapter 32 (CTI*, 10:9).

3. *Catur-yoni*: "To wit, birth from eggs, birth from a womb,birth from moisture, and birth from transformation" (46c7, 259:1). Cf. the *Diamond sūtra* (*Vajracchedikā*), Chapter 3.

4. *Catvāri-phalāni*, the four stages of achievement in Hinayanic cultivation: as enumerated in the *Sūtra*, *srota-āpanna* (the first-stage *śrāvaka*), *sakṛdāgāmin* ("once returner"), *anāgāmin* ("nonreturner"), and *arhant*. (Hurvitz, *SLFD*, 259:18).

5. Or "complete penetration without bound".

6. Liebenthal translates: (from "they have accomplished") "The *Tao* of the Tathagata is adaptive complying with the status of each single Being. (The Buddha) is not deceitful. Promising a thousandfold reward (for the study of the SPS) he certainly does not tell a lie" ("World Conception," II, p. 98).

7. The term occurs in 46c28 (260:2, "albeit indirectly") and 47a26 (261:12).

Chapter 18

THE MERITS OF THE DHARMA PREACHER

(The merits to be accorded to those who take care of the *sūtra* are here enumerated in terms of the tangible rewards to be had by the six senses.)

18.1.1

The earlier chapter (10) concerning "preachers of *Dharma*" was aimed at preaching that the cause of three is that of the One. This chapter is aimed at making it widely known that the effect of the three is that of the One, and also at distinguishing the merit and reward of the *Dharma* as well.

18.1.2 "Whether reading it, reciting it, interpreting it, or copying it" (47c4, 264:3)

This refers to the *Dharma* preacher. It is said in the □ (previous?) chapter (17),[1] "and in the great multitude [he] explains them to others" (47a21). Here this statement is now substantiated.

18.2.1 "Eight hundred virtues of the nose . . . virtues of the mind"

As for the reward for those who practice the *Dharma Blossom* as they preach it, it is the great enlightenment wisdom. This wisdom is capable of clairvoyance and omniscience. If beings are to be given ultimate wisdom, it will be imparted to them imperceptibly. This is why it becomes present in men gradually, as if the joy could [only] be attained to step by step. The rewards are explained in terms of the six senses, in order to attract learners. □ (Hearing?)[2] it, learners **[411b1]** will be willing to practice the *sūtra* and accumulate the acts [as exhorted by the *sūtra*], working to achieve that by which they abide. As regards the statement that [the Buddha] resorts to the six senses [as teaching aids], [the faculty of] seeing the forms (*rūpa*) naturally is present in the eyes, and [the faculty of] perceiving the *Dharma* naturally is present in the mind. As already suggested, attainment through learning cannot make [one acquire] omniscience. Hence, the everpenetrating eyes stop at seeing "the three thousand" [chilocosms or great worlds]. On □ (this?)[3] basis it is possible to speak of the physical body.

The physical body exists close to [reality] in a coarse form and so we can say that it is still short of the *Dharma*-body. In the final analysis, [however,] the three thousand [chilocosms] being such, how can they be different from the ten quarters[4] [in their largeness]? They represent [the range of] the ultimate illumination by the substance (*t'i*) of the *Dharma*-body. The three faculties[5] are illustrated [with respect to] the [eight hundred] virtues in reading and preaching [the *sūtra*]. Thus, the numbers shown are not identical [with that of the other three]. What they represent in totality is the One; separately, they represent the immeasureable. They are all merely approximate numbers.[6] He who searches independently for the meaning of the chapter[7] must grasp it beyond the words.

18.3

"One thousand two hundred" meritorious virtues are based on the ten kinds of goodness. They are as follows. Self-practice, converting [others] through teaching, praise, and appropriate joy each have ten kinds of goodness, making a total of forty. One goodness in turn can be combined with the ten goodnesses. Forty goodnesses, all combined with the same, make the total of four hundred goodnesses. Four hundred goodnesses **[411b10]** have [three grades] each: superior, mediocre, and inferior, making twelve hundred. The three faculties, unlike [the other three], consist of two grades, mediocre and inferior, to produce eight hundred goodnesses. The rest of the faculties have a superior [grade], and so they consist of twelve hundred [virtues].

18.4 "[All] change for his lingual faculty into things of superior flavor" (49b18, 273:8)

Innate endowment[8] benefits and enriches us, enabling us to obtain the taste of the "sweet dew"[9] present in us. Yet the rewards we receive are originally not "bitter and astringent." How then can there be changes? But [the Buddha] says that there are, in order to draw them into a feeling of intimacy. The same is true when it comes to the rewards in connection with "sounds" and "scents." How can they be spoken of as "ugly"? Yet, worldly sounds and scents [can be distinguished as] good or bad. When the bodhisattvas hear it, what harm is there then?[10]

Notes

1. Probably 上 or 前 is the missing letter (a13).

2. As suggested by the editor, the missing letter is believed to be 听.

3. 此 (?)

4. 十方 *daśa diśah*: the four cardinal and the four intermediary directions plus up and down. See the *sūtra*, 48a25.

5. 三根 as deciphered by the editor is possibly 六根 (47c7) "six faculties".

6. Liebenthal translates: (from "the three thousand being of such nature") "As the Three Thousand (Buddha Worlds) are one, how can there be many spread out in the ten directions? Surely, in the light of the *dharma-kāya* (World) appears integrated, but the three types of human intelligences must be taught by means of scriptures and sermons. Thus the explanations vary. The general idea is one but expressed in innumerable ways. Explanations bring (the Buddha) near to us" ("World Conception," II, p. 75).

7. Two letters were unclear in the original and guessed by the editor. Hence, my translation must be tentative.

8. 資 (*tzu*) or natural property, possibly referring to Buddha-nature.

9. *Amṛta* (see 49c6, 274:8), nectar of immortality.

10. Cf. the *Analects*, 11: 25, "What harm is there in that?" Legge, *Confucius*, p. 248.

Chapter 19

[THE BODHISATTVA] NEVER DISPARAGING (SADĀPARIBHŪTA)

(More on the same, followed by the Buddha's narrtion of his own behavior in a previous era, in which, as the bodhisattva Sadāparibhūta, he was the object of much contmept and violence, but requited all actions with love and patience.[1])

19

As regards the respectful scripture of the *Dharma Blossom*, it is the source of many goodnesses and the luminous part of the ultimate wisdom. By going against it, one will see one's sins piled up like a mountain; by following it, one will reach the state of happiness [as great] as the ocean.[2] Although he has talked about it, [the Buddha] has not yet illustrated with concrete examples of men. Thus he draws from the past and proves the present **[411c1]**, so that [the number of] believers may increase. If one slanders and goes against it, the guilt will be like that of Bhadrapāla and the others. □ (If?)[3] one complies with it, one's fortune will be like that of the bodhisattva Never Disparaging (Sadāparibhūta). Having wanted to give testimonial to the *sūtra*, he thus set up this part,[4] pointing out those who committed guilt and those who received happiness, in order to help dispose of their doubts and slanders about it. [The Buddha] demonstrates that the fruit of the bodhisattva's attainment was the purification of his six faculties (51a6ff.) with a view to explaining that he had pure faith. Also expressed is the idea that guilt and fortune [entail each other like] shadow and echo; there cannot be any discrepancy as far as the underlying *li* is concerned.[5] This is what a disciple [of the antinomian school, which] adheres [just] to the learning of how to cleanse [oneself,] should be careful about.[6] The retributions for their guilt are like those mentioned in [the parable of] the burning house (Chapter 3).

Notes

1. Hurvitz, p. xv.

2. See 403b16ff.

3. The lacuna is probably 若 but the editor suspects it to be 信 "to believe in."

4. Emend 端 (c2) to 段, two being homophonym *tuan*.

5. Cf. *CNS*, 380c2f.; *CVS*, 415c6 (in Kumārajīva's words). Cf. also *CVS*, 414b28; Hui-jui, *Yü-i lun*, T53.41b4.

6. 可不慎哉 Cf. the *Chuang-tzu*, Chapter 4 (*CTI*, 2:20): 可不慎與 "Can you afford to be careless?" (Watson, p. 61); "ought he not to be careful?" (Legge, *Texts of Taoism*, Part I, p. 214). Also cf. *I Ching*, *AR*, Part I, Chapter 8: 可不慎乎 "may he be careless in regard to them?" (Legge, *I Ching*, p. 362). See 412a1 for a parallel statement of the idea expressed in the passage.

Chapter 20

THE SUPERNATURAL POWERS OF THE THUS COME ONE

(The bodhisattvas who have assembled from all over the universe promise to propagate the *Lotus*, whereupon both Buddhas stretch out their tongues, which extend very far, and emit a ray of light that illuminates the entire universe.)

20.1

It is described here that [both] cause and effect have come to an end, which means that *li* is perfected, and the related worldly facts (*shih*) [used as explanatory tools, analogies, and parables] have fulfilled [their assigned roles].[2] The words of the *Tao* and virtuous acts are completely propagated all over under □ (the heaven?)[3] However, lights illuminating the dark world [encounter] many opposing elements whereas profound voices [meet] adversities. [Likewise], when it comes to inspiring faith in the corrupt and final [age], [the Buddha] finds it hard to temporarily entrust them from then on with the *Dharma Blossom*. Thus he displays first supernatural powers that surpass any others of the kind, making the multitude overjoyed and awed. Envoys from afar in the ten quarters, saying *namaḥ*, vow to devote their lives to the Buddha. Thereupon [beings] become intensely faithful.[4]

20.2.1 [411c10] "Putting forth his long, broad tongue" (51c18, 286:17)

This implies that [the Buddha's] speeches are not empty.

20.2.2 "While his pores emitted rays"

This indicates that the □ (light?)[5] of the One ultimate □ (leaves?)[6] nothing not illuminated by it.

20.2.3 "Coughed and snapped their fingers"

Earlier it is shown that their tongues emitted rays of light, with the implication that their speeches were not false; wisdom illuminates [all] without leaving anything [in the dark]. [The Buddha's] Path (*Tao*) being such, it is clear therefrom that *li* spread down to the golden mean.[7] That *li* spread down to the golden mean finds expression in *cough*. Yet the voice reaching down to the golden mean must have a reason when it is mentioned, again finding expression in *snapping fingers*. *Li* has been propagated all over under □ (the heaven?);[8] hence, the statement, "These two sounds reached throughout [the world-spheres of the Buddhas] in all ten quarters" (51c23). Living beings in ten quarters began to sense their [innate] endowment of enlightenment:[9] thus "[the earth] trembles in six different ways."

20.2.4 "All together they scattered them from afar on the Sahā *world-sphere" (52a10, 287:26)*

Although these living beings are ignorant of the □ (One?)[10] yet they, thanks to favorable conditions, can have a glimpse of it "from afar." That they made offerings from afar with various kinds of treasures stands for giving □ the ultimate □. The purpose of showing this unreal appearance is to convey that the path [of the One] is not separate from [the path of the three].

20.2.5 "As if they had been one Buddha-land"

As their feelings become congealed within and reach their epitome, their sensing [of the endowment for enlightenment] appears without.[11]

20.2.6 "Turning into jeweled canopies, completely covered the Buddhas in this [region]"

What this and the subsequent segment stating that [the world-spheres] in all ten quarters become [411d1] one [Buddha-land] indicates is this: unless they have not sincerely exerted themselves and sensed the ultimate no one can do it.[12] What this implicitly signifies is that even though the causes are diverse in a myriad of ways, they finally return to the effect of the One.

Notes

1. Hurvitz, SLF̄D, p. xv.

2. Liebenthal translates: "When *Karma* draws to a stand, the consummation of existence is reached in *li*, then all affairs are settled" ("World Conception," II, p. 94).

3. (天?) (c6).

4. Or "without any interval"; that is, immediately.

5. (光?) (c10).

6. (遺?) (c11).

7. 理暢黃中 Cf. *I Ching*, *Wen Yen*, Chapter 2: 君子黃中通理···暢. "The superior man (emblemed here) by the 'yellow' and correct (color), is possessed of comprehension and discrimination . . . diffuses its complacency" (Legge, *I Ching*, p. 421), "The superior man is yellow and moderate; thus he makes influence felt in the outer world through reason . . . gives freedom" (Wilhelm and Baynes, *The I Ching or Book of Changes*, p. 395). As Wang Pi points out in his commentary on the same hexagram (*k'un*), yellow is regarded as the color of the center or middle (*CIC*, 1:23).

8. (天?) (c14).

9. Alternate translation: "sense their endowment of enlightenment coming to the fore."

10. (與?) (c16).

11. (411c18). Liebenthal translates: "When within longing is deepest it rouses the feeling (of the Cosmic Agent) which is expressed without (by a miracle)" ("World Conception," II, p. 81).

12. For the expression 孰能如此乎 (411d1), cf. the *I Ching*, *AR*, Part I, Chapter 10. (Legge, *I Ching*, p. 370; Chan, *Source Book*, p. 267).

Chapter 21

ENTRUSTMENT

(The Buddha now entrusts the *sūtra* to all bodhisattvas present, striking them on the crown of the head and asking them to go back to where they came from.)

21

Earlier when [the Buddha] preached about the cause, the entrustment [of the *sūtra*] was made as well.[1] Because the theme has not yet been wound up, there has been no separate chapter [for entrustment]. Here [the Buddha] now enunciates that both cause (Chapters 1–13) and effect (Chapters 14–21) have come to an end and that the preaching of *li* has been completed. As such, the great wisdom of the Thus Come One □ □. Here he entrusts them to keep this *sūtra*, while striking [incalculable bodhisattva-mahāsattvas] on the crown of the head, to show that *li* is so deep and the worldly facts (*shih*) [involved as descriptive tools] are so sublime, □ □. This chapter is established for this purpose.

Note

1. Probably referring either to Chapter 10 or Chapter 12.

Chapter 22

THE FORMER AFFAIRS OF THE BODHISATTVA MEDICINE KING

(The Buddha narrates an extraordinary act of devotion shown by the bodhisattva Medicine King in his past reincarnation, that of burning himself to death.)

22.1

In the preceding it has been explicated that the *li* of cause and that of effect are one, that there is no difference in purport. As the ultimate within became manifest, their understanding and discernment came to have [a distinct] presence. [The theme of] the section following this chapter, concerning **[411d10]** the men of three [vehicles] becoming the men of One [Vehicle], clarified that the children of two vehicles cannot help but become identical with □ (those?)[1] of the Greater [Vehicle]. Having finished preaching the *sūtra*, [the Buddha] now takes examples of those who propagated the *sūtra*. Earlier there were some examples of those who testimonially practiced [the teaching of] the *sūtra*. In the present chapter he marks out several people, showing the traces of their conduct in order to help verify [the effect of] the *Dharms Blossom*. These people were then in other realms, propagating this canon. Now again in this realm, they transmit and keep this *sūtra*, enabling the teaching of the Path (*Tao*) to benefit [beings] in the present time, and the fragrance of its virtues (*te*)[2] to spread and be known for a thousand years to come, so that those who advance to the destination proper, when they are in compliance with it, may reach it.

22.2

Now, as it appears here, the burning of [his own] body in the past is referred to as *the former affair*. What does burning [one's own] body signify? When it comes to what a man treasures and values, nothing exceeds bodily life, and when one burns it oneself, it is because there is something treasured as much as the body. If one is capable of grasping such meaning, even though one exists with the physical form, one is burning, as it were, all the time. [If] *li* is perverted in the attempt to understand it, even though one burns oneself all day long, [in reality] one is never burning. [The Buddha] hopes that they attain [*li*] free of its traces, and so be not stagnated in worldly facts (*shih*). The reason why the Sage thought of demanding □ □ is articulated here.

22.3 "[He was] born again [412a1] in the realm of the Buddha Pure and Bright Excellence of Sun and Moon" (53b19), (295:24)

This man had the cause planted not in vain; consequently the effect likewise is not empty. Those [antinomians] who diligently seek [just] to cleanse themselves may not be practicing acts deeply virtuous enough to induce the wondrous ultimate.[3] This example is cited, therefore, for the purpose of illustrating and proving [the need for practicing virtuous acts].

Notes

1. (于?) (d10). See Ōchō, "Jikudōshō sen," p. 254.

2. In using the two words, *Tao* and *Te* here in one statement, Tao-sheng seems to have had in mind *Tao* as principle and *Te* as its representation in individuals according to the *Tao-te ching*.

3. Cf. 411c3.

Chapter 23

[THE BODHISATTVA] FINE SOUND

(From another world-realm comes the bodhisattva Fine Sound, who attained various *samādhis* to pay homage to the Buddha, who tells the congregation about his achievement in a previous reincarnation.)

23.1

When the multitude heard of the former affairs of [the bodhisattva] Medicine King, they again praised the meritorious virtues of the *Dharma Blossom* with all the more faith and respect, all wanting to protect and keep [the *sūtra*]. The methods of propagating it must have a cause. [Of the possible] practices connected with this cause, in general there is nothing more penetrating than "the *samādhi* [of the manifestation] of the body of all forms" (56b18 and 28, 309:10 and 35). What is "the *samādhi* [of the manifestation] of the body of [all] forms?" It is none other than the wisdom of the *Dharma Blossom*. When men glorify and spread the *Dharma Blossom* they manifest this *samādhi*, easily changing appearances and preaching it in boundlessly varied ways. The [bodhisattva-mahāsattva] Fine Sound (Gadgadasvara) is himself the one [who has attained *samādhi*]. By resort to traces he goes back and forth [from one realm to another] in order to porpagate this *sūtra*. The benefit he gives is very great. [The Buddha] emits a ray of light [from] beween his brows to illuminate that realm because he wishes to let [the bodhisattva] Fine Sound come there.

23.2 "He magically created [eighty-four thousand] jewel-clustered lotus blossoms" (55b19, 305:3)

[The bodhisattva Fine Sound] wishes to come soon [to the *Sahā* world-sphere]. Hence, he first displays the wondrous omen of numerous flowers, so that living beings in this realm may begin to be fascinated and will long for it.

23.3 "[This] Thus Come One Many Jewels, [long extinct], for your sakes will display marks" (55c5, 305:32)

The purpose of making Many Jewels now [appear and] display marks is twofold: first, to show that Many Jewels will come for the sake of the *Dharma Blossom*; second, to show that the paths of various Buddhas are identical.[1]

Note

1. Cf. *CTC*, Chapter 12 (*CTI*, 4:52): 聖人道同.

Chapter 24

THE GATEWAY TO EVERYWHERE OF THE BODHISATTVA HE WHO OBSERVES THE SOUNDS OF THE WORLD

The Buddha tells the congregation about the efficacy of invoking Avalokiteśvara.

24.1

The Sage hangs the candle [of the *Dharma*], expediently leading [beings] in evervarying ways,[1] sometimes through supernatural wonders, sometimes by resort to the method of [invoking] a name. Because the subtle triggering-mechanism is uneven [from one individual to another], the way they take and refuse [what is given to them by the Buddha] is not identical. The name of Avalokiteśvara is singled out and glorified to cause living beings to find refuge in, rely on, and feel for one [person],[2] driving their feeling of respect to great intensities. If a man is capable of holding one [person] in high esteem, there is no one single [person] for whom he cannot do the same. [The Buddha's] exhorting beings to [do] this should not be interpreted as his favoring one over another.[3]

24.2

[The Buddha began] saving [beings] by resort to varied means, without leaving any out:[4] it is referred to as *everywhere* ("universal").

Following enlightenment he has penetrated **[412b1]** the supernatural: it is referred to as a *gateway*.

24.3

Those who, "suffering pain and torment, hear of the name of this bodhisattva He Who Observes the Sounds of the World (Avalokiteśvara)" "shall all gain deliverance" (56c6, 311:8). [One may argue in the following way.] The Sage pushes[5] [beings] in the beginning[6] [of the process].[7] The underlying *li* is that he cannot lift up those without faculty;[8] [in other words], if there is no religious mechanism (*tao-chi*)[9] within [a man], the Sage will not respond.[10] How [then] can one merely by invoking a name immediately gain deliverance (*chieh-t'o*/*mokṣa*)? Yet here [the Buddha] says so. Why? [I would answer in this way.] "Avalokiteśvara," in speaking of its *li*, is the one who is capable of propagating [the *sūtra* or its doctrine] to all; and, in speaking of its implicit [meaning], is the one who [sets out] to save all. Beings, possessing the subtle triggering-mechanism (*chi*) of enlightenment, actively stimulate the Sage. The Sage is equipped with the *Tao* of all-embracing propagation.[11] Now that the *Tao* of all-embracing propagation has been expounded, how can deliverance (*mokṣa*) be an empty [word]?[12] Isn't exhorting beings by glorifying a name also magnanimous?

24.4 "Who can be conveyed to deliverance by the body of a Buddha" (57a23, 314:7)

The bodhisattva Fine Sound appeared in various bodies, in order to attain the *samādhi* of the body of all forms. Here also Avalokiteśvara preaches the *Dharma*, appearing in various forms, all for the sake of propagating the *Dharma Blossom*. Men are different, [but] the path (*Tao*) remains the same, which shows that [various] cultivations are certain to lead to attainment [of the One].

Notes

1. (412a15). Cf. *I Ching*, *AR*, Part I, Chapter 4: 神無方 "spirit has no spatial restriction" (Chan, *Source Book*, p. 226); "spirit-like, unconditioned by place" (Legge, *I Ching*, p. 354).

2. See Hurvitz, *Chih-i*, p. 200: "The purpose, as here, is to fix the minds of the beings upon the One."

3. Cf. Liebenthal's translation: "When the sages hang up their lamps (in the darkness we are in) and guide (the Beings to salvation) making use of ex-

pedients, they may avail themselves of miracles or may argue. For Beings are in a varying state of maturity and (what they must be told to) acquire and to renounce cannot be the same (in all cases). Therefore, though (the *Sūtra* in this chapter) praises Kuan-yin alone, (this does not mean that the Buddha is a deity with definite characteristics, but that) it wishes to lead the Beings to the way home. (Thus it allows them to worship) any deity they like (if only they would do that) with their whole might and let their hearts be filled (with veneration). If they are able to worship one (deity) then (in that act) they have worshipped all others. (This *Sūtra* does not intend by its admonition (to worship Kuan-yin) to play off (one deity against another one)" ("World Conception," II, pp. 99–100).

4. 由濟無遺 (412c18). Cf. 曲成無遺 in *I Ching*, AR, Part 1, Chapter 4: "it stoops to bring things into completion without missing any" (Chan. *Source Book*, p. 266); "by an ever-varying adaptation he completes (the nature of) all things without exception" (Legge, *I Ching*, p. 354). Wang Pi recounts the theme in *Chou-i lüeh-li*, Part 2.

5. Or "sets in motion," "brandishes," or "ushers in."

6. 初. Leon Hurvitz in our private communication suspects the letter, in fact blurred in the original, as a corruption of 利 "sharply."

7. Cf. the meaning of the Buddha as the turner of the wheel of *Dharma* or the one who sets in motion the wheel (*Dharma-cakravartin*). Liebenthal reads 初 as (物) ("World Conception," II, p. 82).

8. Hurvitz seems to refer to this passage when he says, "As for being saved by virtue of a mere invocation of a name, it stands to reason that one cannot uproot that which has no roots" (*Chih-i*, p. 200). For the term 不拔 (b2), see the *Tao-te ching*, Chapter 54: 善建者不拔 "He who is well established (in *Tao*) cannot be pulled away." However, the nuance is different, to wit, it is positive in the case of Tao-sheng whereas the usage in the Taoist text has a negative connotation.

9. 道機 Or "subtle triggering-mechanism of the *Tao*."

10. Cf. *CTC*, Chapter 26 (*CTI*, 8:58).

11. For the phrase 遂通 cf. *I Ching*, *AR*, Part I, Chapter 10. See 403a17 (Chapter 3, note 53).

12. Liebenthal translates: (from "The Sage sets in motion") "The Sage can save a Being only when there is a root of which he can get hold. When he is not expected (literally, "when within there is not a spring of *tao*"; i.e., when the being is not impregnated before) he cannot respond. Can one attain salvation by the calling of the name (of Kuan-yin; i.e., by a magical act)? No. Then, what does (the *Sūtra*) mean expressing itself in this way: Kuan-yin is such that she reaches everywhere and releases every Being. If (a believer) desires earnestly to see (the Truth) (literally "has a spring of Illumination") and knocks (at the Gate of) the Sage, he possesses the means to guide him to the goal. He extends these

means to him and he will be released. (Thus understood it can be said that salvation is attained by calling the name of Kuan-yin and this calling) is not meaningless" ("World Conception," II. pp. 81f.). For an interpretation of the passage, see Ōchō, "Jikudōshō no hokke shisō," pp. 168–169.

Chapter 25

DHĀRANI

(Some *dhāraṇīs* or charms are pronounced by some listeners, which are designed to protect those who keep the *sūtra*.)

25.1

[412b10] The cause and conditions and calendrical numbers match with each other in the way a shadow [matches with a real object] and echo [matches with a real voice;] [this being the case], how can one escape luck or misfortune and calamities or happiness?[1] Yet, profound speeches and preaching on *li* are cut off from the general mass [by the dimension that can be expressed only as] wondrous or mysterious, with the result that those with shallow knowledge become [too] weak-willed to receive and keep [the *sūtra*]. [The Buddha] wants them to rely on incantation in order to make sincere the collective sentiment of contemporary beings. The people of the other realms believe in and respect incantation. The method (*fa*) of incantation can ward off misfortune and invite luck and is applicable to every situation. The latter age will see lots of fearful things happening; nobody will be able to cultivate the good without the risk of being harmed. Thus, the Sage, having sympathy for their stupidity and darkness, preaches these methods for them, [so that] those who are ignorant of *li* but hope to unite therewith may quickly come to have faith. Thus, he borrows the incantation of names to record[2] there the preaching of *li*. This way *li* can be preached anywhere, again achieving [the unity of] name and actuality.[3] Furthermore, the advent of fortune or misfortune has to do with demons and spirits. By using charms, one can order them not to do any harm. All those who are fearful of the bonds and are afraid of harm should cultivate [the casue of] the *sūtra*. Having reached [the stage of] cultivating [the cause of] the *sūtra*, naturally there is the need for secret words. As the comprehension of secret words become manifest, misfortune destroys itself.[4] Now, the *Dharma Blossom* being the ultimate inward level, the Buddha resorts to incantation in preaching it. People are pleased with the benefits of incantations and like to take advantage of it. They become inclined to and immersed in it; **[412c1]** they receive and keep it with great care.

25.2

Although the *li* of the incantation is one, the way the words are arranged is not identical. All have [the order of] right and left, which are solely entrusted to the Buddha. Therefore, again, because of this, the words are arranged in the order in which they were uttered by the Buddha. If any reversal [of the words] occurs later, □ (the sin?)[5] would be grave. If it is a charm for one who keeps [the *sūtra*], that is called *dhāraṇī*. Charms, being the words of demons and spirits, are not translatable.

25.3.1

Pūtaṇa (53c11, 321:15) is an inauspicious demon [haunting the people] of the world. One, when afflicted by the disease caused by it, is bound to die.

25.3.2

Kṛtya is a demon arising from a corpse.

25.3.3

Vaiśravaṇa is the heavenly king (*mahārāja*) of the North, primarily commanding the two demons, *yakṣa* and *rākṣasa*. The *mahārāja* controlling the East (Dhṛtarāṣṭra) has two demons under him: *gandharva* and *piśācāh*. The *mahārāja* of the South rules over two demons: *kumbhānda* and hungry ghost. The *mahārāja* of the West controls all [the remaining] dragons (*nāgas*) and *kinnaras*. Each of the four *mahārājas* thus is in charge of his own territory.

25.3.4

Daughters of *rākṣasas* (59a23, 322:15) and others, ten female demons, possess great powers in the world. They are the mothers of various demons. They respect and obey the Buddha's orders, as they also pronounce this charm. Even though the demons are wicked, they do not disobey **[412c10]** their mothers. As their mothers obey the Buddha, so their sons follow them.

25.3.5 "[The tenth named] Robber of the Vital Vapors of All Living Beings"

In the heart of a man there are seven [measures of] mucus sweet-water for nourishing human life. If a *rākṣasa* enters into a man's body, and drinks one mucus, then he (the man) suffers a head illness. If [the demon] drinks two, three, or four [measures of] mucus, then the man loses consciousness. This is curable, but if he is left there he is bound to die. Thus, he is "robbed of vital vapors."

25.3.6 "Apasmāraka" (59b7, 323:3)

This demon enters into a man's body, making the muscles of the hands and feet twisted, and making him expectorate from the mouth. It is a fever demon. If the demons assume these various forms, [it means that] they have penetrated the sick.

25.3.7

When "a branch of the arjaka tree" falls to the ground it makes seven pieces without fail. Hence, the analogy taken from this, [to express "Then may his head split into seven parts" (323:12)].

25.3.8 "The calamity visited on one for having pressed oil"

Many heretics (*tīrthikas*)[6] hold the view that all the grasses and plants bear life. The demons all believe this view. Therefore, they are afraid of committing a sin by pressing oil.

Notes

1. Cf. 411c3.

2. Rather a misprint of 銘 ("to inscribe")?

3. See 407d6 (Chapter 9, note2).

4. Liebenthal translates: (from the beginning of the chapter) "Whatever happens in this universe (is occasioned by *Karma* that) operates like a reflection and an echo; unavoidable are the changes of fortune (in consequence of this law). (Its function is wrapped in secret. For) the truth expressed in the Scriptures is beyond the understanding of common people. Their narrow minds harbor shallow desires; so to comply with the fashion of the time (the Sage) gave them the *mantras*. Foreigners favor *dhāraṇīs* because they give them power to call forth fortune and ward off disaster. There is nothing which they cannot control. In our period of decay people are afraid. They do the good for this

reason. Pitying their foolishness the merciful Sage taught them this means, so that those to whom final insight is denied, and who look with apprehension to their future may suddenly believe. He uses the syllables of the *dhāraṇīs* as symbols for truth which cannot be directly applied. (Apart from the real truth) he creates a symbolic truth. Further, good and bad luck comes from the demons whom the words of the *dhāraṇīs* order to desist from doing damage. Those people who fear for their future eagerly memorize sutras. At the end of that activity they must get behind the mere verbiage. Behind the verbiage is found the true meaning. When that appears, bad luck vanishes automatically" ("World Conception," II, pp. 98f.). This translation typifies the way Liebenthal tackles Tao-sheng's writings. It is a very liberal, or rather arbitrary translation, not faithful to either the letters or the meaning of the text, let alone Tao-sheng's thought as a whole.

5. (罪), following the editor's suggestion.

6. Reference, in particular, to Jainism. Hurvitz renders it with "the external paths" (336:2).

Chapter 26

[THE FORMER AFFAIRS OF] THE KING FINE ADORNMENT

(The achievements of some bodhisattvas in the past lives are traced here.)

26

[412d1] The wondrous path of the *Dharma Blossom* is so deep and recondite. Furthermore, the Medicine King and others have become its propagators. Thus, man is lofty whereas *li* is recondite,[1] separated from the mass [by the dimension of the] dark, [absolute realm]. Those of shallow intelligence have been slow in comprehending it and in fact have regressed.[2] Though they have wanted to propagate the *sūtra*, they have not dared to try to put it into practice. For this reason [the Buddha] takes up the example of the King Fine Adorment. The King Fine Adorment had earlier been [a man] with "crooked views" (60a2, 326:15). When his "crooked views" were rectified, he then became a propagator of the *Dharma Blossom*. Those with average intelligence thereupon resolved to propagate the *sūtra*. Expedient traces have been given [by the Buddha], with the result that those who are saved are many. Illustrated as well [in this chapter] is the significance of a good friend[3] (60c and 7, 329:26 and 33), implicitly revealing the beauty of learning lessons by way of observing another person.[4] Thus introducing the earlier, past conditions are "the former affairs."

Notes

1. Cf. 399b2, 412d2.

2. Cf. *CTC*, Chapter 2, (*CTI*, 1:42): 理有至極···則冥然自合.

3. Interchangeable with 善友 *kalyāṇa-mitra*: "*good friend*, regularly said of one (not as a rule a Buddha) who helps in conversion or religious progress" (*BHSD*, p. 174).

4. 切磋 (d5) denotes, first of all, persistent self-cultivation, as it is used in the *Shih Ching*, *Wei-feng*, Chapter 1.

Chapter 27

THE ENCOURAGEMENTS OF THE BODHISATTVA UNIVERSALLY WORTHY

Samantabhadra vows to be the protector of all who extol the *Lotus* and of all who appeal to him for help. The Buddha then entrusts the *Lotus* to him, once more dwelling on the merit that shall accrue to those who extol this scripture, as well as on the afflictions that shall attend all who harm such persons.[1]

27

Human sentiment is [the source of] blindness and ignorance; pure faith is something quite hard [to attain]. [As such], [the Buddha] has found it necessary to [devise] a universal measure[2] that is applicable to any circumstance; to resort to traces [instead of showing the reality itself]; and to corroborate [his theses] by means of worldly facts. [The process of] corroborating by means of the facts being shown, faith is then strengthened.

The bodhisattva Universally Worthy (Samantabhadra) made a vow in an earlier reincarnation, [saying] "if there is any place where people read and recite the *Scripture of Dharma Blossom*, [412d10] I will go there and encourage them, showing them what is false and wrong." [Hence], the chapter is entitled "Encouragements." Beings were pleased with the [Buddha's] response by way of the supernatural omen [in the previous chapter]. Thereupon [they have been made determined to] cultivate the *sūtra* with the utmost diligence and zeal.

***Commentary on the Scripture of Lotus of Dharma*,**
Roll the Second. The End.
Written by Chu Tao-sheng

Notes

1. Hurvitz, *SLFD*, p. xv.

2. In the current usage 曲尺 refers to "a (carpenter's) square", but Tao-sheng may have coined the word in the abstract sense that has bearing on the classical meaning as found in the *I Ching*; see 412a18 (Chapter 24, note 4).

Abbreviations

AR	*I Ching*, Hsi-ts'u chuan (*Appended Remarks*)
BGDJ	H. Nakamura, *Bukkyōgo daijiten*
BHSD	F. Edgerton, *Buddhist Hybrid Sanskrit Dictionary*
CCT	*Kuo Hsiang's* commentary on the *Chuang-tzu*
CLT	Wang Pi's commentary on the *Lao-tzu*
CNS	Tao-sheng's Commentary on the *Nirvāṇa Sūtra*, T37 (nr. 1763)
CSPS	Tao-sheng's Commentary on the *Saddharmapuṇḍarīka Sūtra*, HTC, vol. 150
CSTCC	Seng-yu, *Ch'u san-tsang chi-chi*, T55 (nr. 2145).
CTI	*Chuang-tzu i*
CTCS	*Chuang-tzu chi shih*
CVS	Tao-sheng's Commentary on the *Vimalakīrti-nirdeśa Sūtra*, T38 (nr. 1775)
DCBT	W. Soothill and L. Hodous, *A Dictionary of Chinese Buddhist Terms*
HTC	*Hsü Tsang Ching*
IBK	*Indogaku Bukkyōgaku kenkyū*
KHMC	Tao-hsüan, ed., *Kuang hung-ming chi*, T52 (nr. 2103)
KSC	Hui-chiao, *Kao-seng chuan*, T50 (nr. 2059)
LTI	*Lao-tzu i*
MN	*Monumenta Nipponica*

MSLW	B. Katō, trans. *Myōhō-Renge-Kyō, the Sūtra of the Lotus Flower of the Wonderful Law*
MSC	Pao-ch'ang, *Ming-seng chuan*
PTL	Hsieh Ling-yün, *Pien-tsung lun*, T52 (KHMC 18)
SLFD	Leon Hurvitz, trans., *Scripture of the Lotus Blossom of the Fine Dharma*
T	*Taishō Shinshū Daizōkyō*

Glossary of Chinese Characters

An-pan shou-i ching 安般守意經
An Shih-kao 安世高
Ch'an 禪
Ch'an-yüan chu-ch'üan chi tu-hsü 禪源諸詮集都序
Chang 障
ch'ang 常
Ch'ang-an 長安
ch'ao 超
Chao-lun 肇論
Chao-lun shu 肇論疏
chen 眞
chen-k'ung miao-yu 眞空妙有
chen-o 眞我
Chen Shun-yu
cheng 正
ch'eng 乘
Ch'eng-kuan 澄觀
cheng-tao 正道
cheng-yin 正因
chi (to reach, and) 及
chi (traces) 迹
chi (triggering-mechanism) 機
chi (ultimate) 極
chi-tu 濟度
chi-wu (making things equal) 齊物
chi-wu (saving beings) 濟物
chi-ken 機根
Chi-tsang 吉藏
chia-t'su 假辭
chiao 教
chiao-hua 教化
chieh (bonds) 結
chieh (release) 解
chieh-t'o 解脫

chien (gradual) 漸
chien (to see) 見
chien-chi 兼濟
chien-hsing ch'eng-fo 見性成佛
Chien-k'ang 建康
Chien-wu lun 漸悟論
chih (of) 之
chih (to reach, ultimate) 至
chih (substance) 質
Chih Ch'ien 支謙
Chih-i 智顗
chih-li 至理
Chih Lou-chia-ch'en 支婁迦讖
Chih Tao-lin 支道林
Chih Tun 支遁
Chih-yüan 智圓
chin 盡
ching (quiescence) 靜
ching (scriptire) 經
ch'ing 情
Ching-ming ching chi-chieh kuan-chung shu 淨名經集解關中疏
ching-she 精舍
Ch'ing-yüan ssu 淸園寺
ch'iung 窮
ch'iung-li chin-hsing (i-chih-yü-ming) 窮理盡性(以至於命)
Chou-i lüeh-li 周易略例
chu 注
ch'ü 曲
Chu Fa-t'ai 竺法汰
Chu Fa-ya 竺法雅
Ch'u san-tsang chih-chi 出三藏記集
Chu Tao-sheng 竺道生
Chu wei-mo-chieh ching 注維摩詰經
chüan 卷
ch'üan 權
Chuang-tzu 莊子
ch'ui 垂
ch'ui-ying 垂應
Chün-cheng 均正
ch'ün-ch'ing 群情
chün-tzu 君子
chung 中
chung-cheng 中正

chung-cheng-chih-tao 中正之道
chung-ho 中和
chung-sheng 衆生
chung-tao 中道
Chung-yung 中庸
Erh-ti i 二諦義
Erh-ti lun 二諦論
fa 法
Fa-hsien 法顯
Fa-hua chuan-chi 法華傳記
Fa-hua hsüan-lun 法華玄論
Fa-shen wu-se lun 法身無色論
Fa-tzu (Tao-tzu) 法慈(道慈)
Fa-yao 法瑤
Fa-yüan 法瑗
fan 返
fan-nao 煩惱
Fan Pao-lun (Fan-t'ai) 范伯倫(范泰)
fan-pen 返本
Fang-kuang ching 方廣經
fang-pien 方便
fen 分
Feng-fa yao 奉法要
fen-wu i 本無義
Fo-hsing tang-yu lun 佛性當有論
Fo-t'u-teng 佛圖澄(橙)
Fo wu ching-t'u lun 佛無淨土論
fu (to stoop) 俯
fu (to return) 復
fu-kuei 復歸
fu-ying 俯應
ho 和
Ho Yen 何晏
Hsi-ho 施護
Hsi K'ang 嵇康
Hsi-t'zu chuan 繫辭傳
hsiang 相
Hsiao-p'in ching i-shu 小品經義疏
Hsiao-wu 孝武
Hsiao Tzu-liang 蕭子良
Hsieh Ling-yün 謝靈運
hsien 咸
hsin (faith) 信

hsin (mind) 心
hsin-chieh 信解
hsing 性
hsing-ju 行入
hsing-pu p'ing-cheng 行步平正
hsiu 修
Hsü Tsang Ching 續藏經
Hsüan-hsüeh 玄學
hsüan-i 玄義
hsüan-t'an 玄談
hua 化
Hua-yen 華嚴
Hua-yen ching sui-shu yen-i ch'ao 華嚴經隨疏演義鈔
huai 懷
huang 黃
huang-chung 黃中
Hu-ch'iu-shan 虎丘山
Hui-kuan 慧觀
hui-kuei 會歸
Hui-neng 慧能
hui-san kuei-i 會三歸一
Hui-ta 慧達
Hui-yen 慧嚴
Hui-yüan 慧遠
Hung-ming chi 弘明集
huo 惑
huo-jan 豁然
i (thought) 意
i (meaning) 義
I-ch'eng fo-hsing hui-jih ch'ao 一乘佛性慧日鈔
I Ching 易經
i-li 義理
i-shu 義疏
ju 入
Ju-lai 如來
k'ai 開
k'ai-ch'üan hsien-shih 開權顯實
kan 感
kan-ying 感應
Kao-seng chuan 高僧傳
ken 根
ken-chi 根機
ko-i 格義

k'o-wen 科文
k'ou 扣
k'u 苦
kuai 乖
Kuang hung-ming chi 廣弘明集
kuei 歸
k'un 坤
k'ung 空
k'ung-li 空理
kuo 果
Kuo Hsiang 郭象
Lao-tzu 老子
Lao-tzu hua-hu ching 老子化胡經
Lao-tzu i 老子翼
le 樂
lei 累
li 理
lien-hua 蓮華
li-ju 理入
li-shih 理事
li-shu 歷數
Liu Ch'iu 劉虬
Liu I-min 劉遺民
liu-t'ung 流通
Lu Ch'eng 陸澄
Lu-shan 盧山
Lu-shan chi 盧山記
lun 論
Lun-yü 論語
Lung-kuang ssu 龍光寺
meng 蒙
mi-lun 彌綸
miao 妙
Miao-fa lien-hua ching shu 妙法蓮華經疏
ming 冥
ming-chiao 名教
Ming-chien lun 明漸論
Ming-fo lun 明佛論
ming-li 名理
Ming-pao-ying lun 明報應論
Ming-seng chuan 名僧傳
Ming-seng chuan ch'ao 名僧傳鈔
ming-shih 名實

Mo-ho chi-kuan 摩訶止觀
nei 內
Ni-heng ching i-shu 泥洹經義疏
Nieh-p'an ching 涅槃經
Nieh-p'an hsüan-i fa-yüan chi-yao 涅槃玄義發源機要
Pai-hei lun 白黑論
p'an-chiao 判教
Pan-chou san-mei ching 般舟三昧經
pan-jo 般若
Pan-jo wu-chih lun 般若無知論
Pao-ch'ang 寶唱
Pao-liang 寶亮
Pao-lin 寶林
pao-ying 報應
pen 本
pen-hsing 本性
pen-mo 本末
pen-wu i 本無義
P'eng-ch'eng 彭城
pien 便
p'ien-li t'i 駢儷體
p'ien-wen 駢文
p'ing 平
p'ing-teng 平等
Pien-tsung lun 辯宗論
P'u-chi ta-shih 普濟大師
pu hsieh 不邪
San-lun 三論
San-lun yu-i i 三論遊意義
San-pao lun 三報論
Seng-chao 僧肇
Seng-hsiang 僧詳
Seng-sung 僧嵩
Seng-jui 僧叡
Seng-lang 僧朗
Seng-liang 僧亮
Seng-yu 僧祐
shen (deep) 深
shen (spirit) 神
Shen-hsiu 神秀
Shen-hui 神會
sheng-jen 聖人
sheng-jen pao i 聖人抱一

shih (demonstration) 示
shih (phenomena) 事
shih (real) 實
shih (time) 時
shih-ch'ing 時情
shih-chung 時中
shih-hsiang 實相
shih-hsin 時心
shih-ju 事入
shih-shih 事事
Shih-shuo wen-hsüeh p'ien-chu 世說文學篇注
shu (commentary) 疏
shu (number) 數
Shuo-kua 說卦
so-i-chi 所以迹
su 俗
sung 訟
Ta-ch'eng ssu-lun hsüan-i 大乘四論玄義
Ta chih-tu lun 大智度論
ta-hui 大慧
Ta p'an-ni-heng ching 大般泥洹經
Ta p'an-nieh-p'an ching 大般涅槃經
Ta p'an-nieh-p'an ching chih-chieh 大般涅槃經集解
ta-pei 大悲
ta-t'zu 大慈
ta-wu 大悟
T'an-luan 曇鸞
T'an Wu-ch'eng 曇無成
tang 當
Tao 道
Tao-an 道安
tao-chi 道機
Tao-hsing 道行
Tao-i 道掖
Tao-jung 道融
Tao-sheng 道生
tao-shu 道數
Tao-te ching 道德經
Tao-yu 道猷
te 德
te-i 得一
t'i 體
ti-huang 地黃

Ti-kuan 諦觀
Ti-lun 地論
t'ien 天
t'ien-chi 天機
t'ien-hsia t'ung-kuei erh shu-t'u 天下同歸而殊塗
t'ien-li 天理
T'ien-t'ai 天台
T'ien-t'ai ssu-chiao i 天台四教儀
tso-wang 坐忘
T'su-hai 辭海
tsung 宗
tsung-chi 宗極
Tsung-mi 宗密
Tsung-pao 宗寶
Tsung Ping 宗炳
tun 頓
Tun-tsung 頓宗
tung 動
t'ung 通
Tung Chung-shu 董仲舒
Tung-lin ssu 東林寺
Tung-yü ch'uan-teng lu 東域傳燈錄
tzu-hsing 自性
tzu-hua 自化
tzu-jan 自然
wai 外
wan 萬
wang 王
Wang Fu 王浮
Wang Hung 王弘
Wang Pi 王弼
wei 僞
wen-chü 文句
Wen-yen 文言
wu (enlightenment) 悟
wu (nonbeing) 無
wu (objects) 物
wu-chi (triggering mechanism for enlightenment) 悟機
wu-chi (ultimate of nonbeing) 無極
wu-chih 無知
Wu-chih lun (般若)無知論
wu-fang 無方
wu-hsiang 無相

wu-hsin 無心
wu-hsing 無形
Wu-liang i ching 無量義經
wu-wei 無爲
wu-yü 無餘
yang 陽
yin (cause) 因
yin (negative principle) 陰
ying 應
ying-kan 應感
Ying yu yüan lun 應有緣論
yu (being) 有
yu (to worry about) 憂
yü 欲
yu-hsin 有心
yu-wei 有爲
yüan (condition) 緣
yüan (round) 圓
yüan-chi 源極
Yüan-chia 元嘉
yung 用

Bibliography

Sources

Works by Tao-sheng

Maio-fa lien-hua ching i-shu 妙法蓮華經義疏 (Commentary on the *Saddharmapuṇḍrīka-sūtra*, *CSPS*). *Hsü Tsang Ching*, (Taiwanese edition), vol. 150 (the text of the present study and translation). Also found in *Dainihon Zokuzōkyō* (New Edition) nr. 577 (vol. 27).

Ni-heng ching i-shu 泥洹經義疏 (Commentary on the *Nirvāṇa-sūtra*, *CNS*). Partly extant in the *Nieh-p'an ching chi-chieh* (大般)涅槃經集解, *Taishō*, nr. 1763 (vol. 37).

Wei-mo-chieh i-shu 維摩詰經義疏 (Commentary on the *Vimalakīrti-nirdeśa-sūtra*, *CVS*). Partly extant in the *Chu Wei-mo-chieh ching* 注維摩詰經, *Taishō*, nr. 1775 (vol. 38).

Works by the neo-Taoists

Kuo Hsiang 郭象. *Chuang-tzu chu* 莊子注 (Commentary on the *Chuang-tzu*, *CTC*). Editions used: *Chuang-tzu chi-shih* 莊子集釋 (CTCS) including the subcommentaries by Lu Te-ming and Kuo Ch'ing-p'an (Taipei, 1972); *Chuang-tzu i* 莊子翼 (*CTI*) or *Sōshi yoku* in Japanese) in *Kanbun taikei*, vol. 9. Tokyo, 1913.

Wang Pi 王弼. *Lao-tzu chu* 老子注 (Commentary on the Lao-tzu, *LTC*) in *Lao-tzu i* 老子翼 (*LTI*) (*Rōshi yoku* in Japanese) in *Kanbun taikei*, vol. 9. Tokyo, 1913.

———. *Chou-i chu* (Commentary on the *Chou-i*, CIC). Edition used: *Chou-i ching i t'ung-chieh* 周易經翼通解, *Kanbun taikei*, vol. 16. Tokyo, 1913; reprinted, Taipei, 1974.

———. *Chou-i lueh-li* 周易略例 (Simple Exemplifications of the Principle of the *Book of Changes*). Originally found in *Han-Wei ts'ung-shu*. Contained in *Chou-i*, Wang's edition of *I Ching*. *Ssu-pu Ts'ung-k'an*. Shanghai: Commercial Press, 1925–1936 edition, Chapter 10: pp. 180, 184, 186.

Other related works
Hsieh Ling-yün 謝靈運. *Pien-tsung lun* 辯宗論. *Taishō*, nr. 2103 (vol. 52), pp. 224–28.
Seng-chao 僧肇. *Chao-lun* 肇論. *Taishō*, nr. 1858 (vol. 45), pp. 151–61.

Secondary Works

Bagchi, Prabodh Chandra. "Indian Influence on Chinese Thought," *History of Philosophy Eastern and Western*, vol. 1 (London: George Allen & Unwin Ltd, 1957), pp. 573–589.

———. *India and China*, 2d ed. Westport, Conn.: Greenwood Press, 1971.

Capra, Fritjof. *The Tao of Physics*. Boulder: Shambhala Publications, 1975.

Chan, Wing-tsit. Comp. and Trans., *A Source Book in Chinese Philosophy*. Princeton, N.J.: Princeton University Press, 1963.

———. *An Outline and an Annotated Bibliography of Chinese Philosophy*. New Heaven, Conn.: Far Eastern Publications, 1969.

———. *Neo Confucianism, Etc. Essays by Wing-tsit Chan*, Charles K. H. Chen, ed. Hanover, N. H.: Oriental Society, probably 1968.

———. "Synthesis in Chinese Metaphysics." In C. A. Moore, ed., *Essays in East West Philosophy*, pp. 163–177. Honolulu: University of Hawaii Press, 1951.

———. "The Evolution of the Neo-Confucian Concept Li as Principle," *Tsing Hua Journal of Chinese Studies* n.s. 4, no. 2(1964): 123–149, reprinted in Chan, *Neo-Confucianism, Etc.*, pp. 45–87.

———, trans. *The Way of Lao Tzu (Tao-te Ching)*. Indianapolis: The Bobbs-Merrill Company, 1963.

Chang, Chung-yüan. *Tao: A New Way of Thinking*. New York: Harper and Row, 1975.

Ch'en, Kenneth K. S. "Anti-Buddhist Propaganda during the Nan-Ch'ao," *Harvard Journal of Asiatic Studies*, 15(1952): 166–192.

———. *Buddhism in China, A Historical Survey*. Princeton, N.J.: Princeton University Press, 1964.

———. "Neo-Taoism and the Prajñā School during the Wei and Chin Dynasties," *Chinese Culture*, 1, no. 2 (1957): 33–46.

Ch'ien Mu 錢穆. "Wang Pi Kuo Hsiang chu I Lao-Chuang yung Li-tzu t'iao-lu 王弼郭象注易老莊用理字條錄", *Hsin-ya Hsüeh Pao* ("New Asia Journal"), 1, no. 1 (1955): 135–156.

Conze, Edward. *Buddhist Thought in India*. Ann Arbor, Mich.: University of Michigan Press, 1967.

———, trans. *The Perfection of Wisdom in Eight Thousand Lines and Its Verse Summary*. Bolinas, Calif.: Four Seasons Foundation, 1975.

Creel, Herrlee G. *What is Taoism? and Other Studies in Chinese Cultural History*. Chicago: University of Chicago Press, 1970.

Dayal, Har. *The Bodhisattva Doctrine in Buddhist Sanskrit Literature*. Delhi: Motilal Banarsidass, 1970.

de Bary, William Theodore, ed. *The Buddhist Tradition in India, China and Japan*. New York: Modern Library, 1969.

Demiéville, Paul. "La pénétration du bouddhisme dans la tradition philosophique chinoise," *Cahiers d'histoire mondiale*, 3, no. 1 (1956): 1–38.

Dumoulin, Heinrich. *A History of Zen Buddhism*. New York: McGraw-Hill, 1965.

Dutt, Nalinksha. *Mahāyāna Buddhism*. Calcutta: Firma K. L. Mukhopadhyay, 1973.

Dutt, Sukumar. "The Ten Schools of Chinese Buddism," S. Radhakrishnan, ed., *History of Philosophy Eastern and Western*, vol. 1 (London: George Allen & Unwin Ltd., 1957), pp. 590–595.

Edgerton, Franklin. *Buddhist Hybrid Sanstrit Grammar and Dictionary*, vol. 2: Dictionary. New Haven, Conn.: Yale University Press, 1953.

Edwards, Paul. *The Encyclopedia of Philosophy*, vol. 5. New York: Macmillan, 1972.

Fang Li-t'ien 方立天. "Lun Chu Tao-sheng te Fo-hsüeh ssu-hsiang," 論竺道生的佛學思想, *Wei Chin Nan-pei-ch'ao Fo-chiao lun-ts'ung* 魏晉南北朝佛教論叢 (Peking: China Press, 1982), pp. 154–187.

Fang, Thomé H. "The World and the Individual in Chinese Metaphysics," Moore, Charles A. ed., *The Chinese Mind* (Honolulu: East-West Center Press), pp. 238–263.

Fukunaga Kōji 福永光司. "Sōjō to Rōsō shisō" 僧肇と老莊思想, Tsukamoto, ed., *Eon kenkyū*, pp. 252–271.

Fung Yu-lan. *A History of Chinese Philosophy*, Derk Bodde, trans., 2 vols. Princeton: Princeton University Press, 1952–1953.

———. *A Short History of Chinese Philosophy*, Derk Bodde, ed. New York: MacMillan, 1948; paperback, Free Press, 1966.

———. *Chuang Tzu, A New Selected Translation with an Exposition of Kuo Hsiang*. Shanghai: Commercial Press, 1933.

———. *The Spirit of Chinese Philosophy*, E. R. Hughes, trans. London: Kegan Paul, 1947; paperback, Boston: Beacon Press, 1962.

Furuta Kazuhiro 古田和弘. "Jikudōshō no hōsshin mushoku setsu" 竺道生の法身無色說, *IBK* 17, no. 2 (1969): 128–129.

———. "Jikudōshō no Butsu mu jōdo setsu" 竺道生の佛無淨土說, *IBK*, 19, no. 2 (1971): 313–317.

———. "Ryū-gyu no Muryōgikyō jo" 劉虬の無量義經序, *Ōtani Daigaku kenkyū nempō*, 27: 41–55.

Fuse Kōgaku 布施浩岳. "Hokke koryū no kenkyū," 法華古流の研究, *Shūkyō kenkyū*, 6, no. 6 (1929): 25–54.

———. *Hokekyō seiritsushi* 法華經成立史. Tokyo: Daitō Shuppansha, 1967.

———. *Nehanshū no kenkyū* 涅槃宗の研究, vol. 2. Tokyo: Kokusho kankokai, 1973.

Giles, Herbert A., trans. *Chuang Tzu, Mystic, Moralist, and Social Reformer*, 2d ed. London: Bernard Quaritch, Ltd., 1926.

Gregory, Peter N., ed. *Sudden and Gradual: Approaches to Enlightenment in Chinese Thought*. Kuroda Institute Studies in East Asian Buddhism 5. Honolulu: University of Hawaii Press, 1987.

Guenther, Herbert V. *Buddhist Philosophy in Theory and Practice*. Boulder: Shambhala, 1971.

———. *Philosophy and Psychology in the Abhidharma*. Berkeley, Cal.: Shambala, 1976.

Hamilton, Clarence, tr. *Vasubandhu: Wei Shi Er Shih Lun*. New Haven: American Oriental Society, 1937, 1967.

Hatani Ryōtai 羽溪了諦. "Saisho no Hokekyōso 最初の法華經疏", *Rokujō gakuhō*, 142 (1913): 33–44.

Hu Shih 胡適. "The Development of Zen Buddhism in China," *Chinese Social and Political Science Review*, 15, no. 2 (1932).

———. "Ch'an (Zen) Buddhism in China, Its History and Method", *Philosophy East and West*, 3, no. 1 (April 1953): 3–24.

———. "Ho-tse ta-shih Shen-hui chuan" 荷澤大師神會傳, *Hu Shih wen-ts'un* 胡適文存, vol. 4, pp. 245–288. Taipei: 1953.

———. *Hu Shih ch'an-hsüeh an* 胡適禪學案, Yanagida, Seizan 柳田聖山, ed. Taipei: Cheng-chung shu-chü, 1975.

———. *Hu Shih chiang-yen chi* 胡適講演集, vol. 1. Taipei: Hu Shih Chi-nien kuan, 1970.

———. *Shen-hui ho-shang i-chi* 神會和尚遺集. Taipei: Hu Shih chi-nien kuan, 1968.

———. "The Development of Zen Buddhism in China", *Chinese Social and Political Science Review* 15, no. 4 (January 1932): 475–505.

———. "The Indianization of China: A Case Study of Cultural Borrowing," *Independence, Converging and Borrowing in Institutions, Thought and Art*, pp. 239–246. Cambridge: Harvard University Press, 1937.

Hughes, E. R. "Epistemological Methods in Chinese Philosophy," Moore, ed., *Essays in East-West Philosophy*, pp. 49–72; reprinted in Moore, ed., *The Chinese Mind*, pp. 77–103.

Hurvitz, Leon. "*Chih-I* (538–597)". *Mélanges chinois et bouddhiques*, vol. 12. Bruxelles:. l'Institut Belge des Hautes Études Chinoises, 1962.

———. "'Render unto Caesar' in Early Chinese Buddhism," *Liebenthal Festschrift*, pp. 80–114. Santiniketan: 1957.

———. *Scripture of the Lotus Blossom of the Fine Dharma (The Lotus Sūtra)*, translated from the Chinese of Kumārajīva. New York: Columbia University Press, 1976.

Inari Nissen 稻荷日宣. *Hokekyō ichijō shisō no kenkyū* 法華經一乘思想の研究. Tokyo: Sankibo, 1975.

Itano Chōhachi 板野長八. "Dōshō no busshōron" 道生の佛性論, *Shīna Bukkyō shigaku*, vol. 2, nr. 2 (1938), pp. 1–26.

———. "Dōsho nō tongosetsu seiritsu no jijō" 道生の頓悟説成立の事情, *Tōhō gakuhō* 7 (1936): 125–186.

———. "Eon Sōjo no shimmeikan o rōn-jite Dōshō no shinsetsu ni oyobu", 慧遠僧肇の神明觀を論じて道生の新説に及ぶ *Tōyō gakuhō*, 30, no. 4 (1943): 447–505.

I-tsing. *A Record of the Buddhist Religion as practised in India and the Malay-Archipelago (*A.D. *671–695)*. Junjirō Takakusu, trans. Oxford: Clarendon Press, 1896.

Itō Takatoshi 伊藤隆壽. "Jōron o meguru shomondai 肇論をめぐる諸問題," *Komazawa Daigaku Bukkyō gakubū kenkyū* 40 (1982): 206–237.

Jan Yün-hua. "Tsung-mi. His Analysis of Ch'an Buddhism," *T'oung Pao*, 58 (1972): 1–54.

Kamata Shigeo 鎌田茂雄. *Chūgoku Bukkyōshi* 中國佛教史. Tokyo: Iwanami shoten, 1978.

———. *Chūgoku Kegon shisōshi no kenkyū*. 中國華嚴思想史の研究. Tokyo: Tokyo University Press, 1965.

———. *Chūgoku Bukkyō shisōshi kenkyū* 中國佛教思想研究. Tokyo: Shunjūsha 1968.

———. "Dōshō no tongoshisō to sōno tenkai" 道生の頓悟思想とその展開, *Komazawa Daigaku Bukkyō-gakubu kenkyū kiyō*, no. 20 (1962): 35–54.

Kanakura Enshō 金倉圓照, ed. *Hokekyō no seiritsu to tenkai* 法華經の成立と展開. Kyoto: Heirakuji shoten, 1970.

Katō Bunnō, trans. *Myōho-Renge-Kyō, The Sūtra of the Lotus Flower of the Wonderful Law*, revised by W. E. Soothill and Wilhelm Schiffer. Tokyo: Rissho Kosei-kai, 1971.

Katō, B., and Y. Tamura and K. Miyakawa, trans. *The Threefold Lotus Sūtra*. New York, Tokyo: Weatherhill/Kosei, 1975.

Kern, H., and B. Nanjio, ed. *Saddharmapuṇḍarīka*. Tokyo: Sankibo Buddhist Book Store, 1955.

Kern, H., trans., *Saddharma-Puṇḍarīka or The Lotus of the True Law. SBE*, vol. 21; reprinted, New York: Dover Publications, 1963.

Kino, D. *Hokekyō no tankyū* 法華經の探究. Kyoto: Heirakuji shoten, 1967.

Kobayashi Masami 小林正美. "Jikudōshō no jissō gi ni tsuite" 竺道生の實相義について, *IBK*, 28. no. 2 (1979): 759–764.

Kuno Hōryū 久野芳隆, "Hokushū Zen" 北宗禪 *Taishō Daigaku gakuhō*, no. 30–31 (March 1940): 131–176.

Lamotte, Étienne, trans. *L'Enseignement de Vimalakīrti* (*Vimalakīrtinirdeśa*). Louvain: Publications Universitaires, 1962.

Lau, D. C., trans. *Lao Tzu, Tao Te Ching*. Harmondsworth, Eng.: Penguin Books, 1963.

———, trans. *Mencius*. Harmondsworth, Eng.: Penguin Books, 1968.

Legge, James, trans. *Confucius. Confucian Analects, The Great Learning and The Doctrine of the Mean*. New York: Dover Publications, 1971.

———, trans. *I Ching, Book of Changes*, edited with introduction and study guide by Ch'u Chai with Winberg Chai. New York: University Books, 1964.

———, trans. *The Shoo King*, in *The Chinese Classics*, vol. IV. Hong Kong: Hong Kong University Press, 1960.

———, trans. *The Texts of Taoism*. New York: Julien Press, 1959.

Liang Shih-ch'iu 梁實秋. *A New Practical Chinese English Dictionary*. Hong Kong: Far East Book, 1974.

Liebenthal, Walter. "A Biography of Chu Tao-sheng," *Monumenta Nipponica*, 11, no. 3 (1955): 64–96.

———. *Chao Lun* (The Treatises of Seng-chao), 2d rev. ed. Hong Kong: Hong Kong University Press, 1968.

———. "Chinese Buddhism during the fourth and fifth Centuries," *Monumenta Nipponica*, 11, no. 1 (1955): 44–83.

———. *The Book of Chao*. Peking: Catholic University Press, 1948.

———. "The World Conception of Chu Tao-Sheng," *Monumenta Nipponica*, 12, nos. 1–2 (1956): 65–103 ("World Conception," I): nos. 3–4 (1956): 73–100 ("World Conception," II).

Link, Arthur E. "Shyh Daw-an's Preface to Sangharakṣa's *Yugacarabhūmi-sūtra* and the Problem of Buddho-Taoist Terminology in Early Chinese Buddhism," *Journal of the American Oriental Society*, 77 (1957): 1–14.

Luk, Charles, trans. *The Vimalakīrti Nirdeśa Sūtra*. Berkeley: Shambala Publications, 1972.

Liu Kuei-chieh 劉貴傑. "Chu Tao-sheng ssu-hsiang chih li-lun chi-ch'u" 竺道生思想之理論基礎, *Hua-kang Fo-hsüeh Hsüeh-pao*, no. 5 (December 1981): 357–375.

———. "Chu Tao-sheng ssu-hsiang chih li-lun t'e-se chi ch'i chia-chih i-i" 竺道生思想之理論特色及其價值意義, *Hua-kang Fo-hsüeh Hsüeh-pao*, no. 6 (July 31, 1983): 377–415.

Medhurst, C.S. *The Tao-teh-king*. Wheaton, Ill.: Theosophical Publishing House, 1972.

Mikiri Jikai 三桐慈海. "Jikudōshō no shisō" 竺道生の思想, *Ōtani gakuhō*, 46, no. 1 (1965): 150–176.

———. "Sōjo to tongogi" 僧肇と頓悟義, *Tōhō shūkyō*, no. 40: 12–23.

Mochizuki Ryōkō 望月良晃. "Itsusendai towa nanika" 一闡提とはなにか, *IBK*, 16, no. 1 (1968): 112–118.

Moore, Charles A., ed. *Essays in East-West Philosophy*. Honolulu: University of Hawaii Press, 1951.

———, ed. *The Chinese Mind*. Hononlulu: East-West Center Press, 1969.

Morie Shunkō 森江俊孝. "Jikudōshō no kannō shisō" 竺道生の感應思想, *IBK*, 21, no. 1 (1973): 140–141.

Murti, T. R. V. *The Central Philosophy of Buddhism*. London: Allen and Unwin, 1955.

Nakamura Hajime 中村元, *Bukkyōgo daijiten* 佛教語大辭典, 3 vols. Tokyo: Tōkyō shoseki, 1975.

———, ed., *Jiga to mūga* 自我と無我. Kyoto: Heirakuji shoten, 1974.

———. *Ways of Thinking of Eastern Peoples: India, China, Tibet, Japan*, Philip P. Wiener, ed. Honolulu: University Press of Hawaii, 1964.

Ōchō Enichi 横超慧日. *Chūgoku Bukkyō no kenkyū* 中國佛教の研究, vol. 2. Kyoto: Hozokan, 1971.

———. *Hokke shisō* 法華思想. Kyoto: Heirakuji shoten, 1969.

———. *Hokke shisō no kenkyū* 法華思想の研究. Kyoto: Hōzōkan, 1971.

———. *Hokekyō josetsu* 法華經序說. Kyoto: Hōzokan, 1962.

———. "Jikudōshō no hokke shisō" 竺道生の法華思想, Sakamoto Yukio, ed. *Hokekyō no Chūgokuteki tenkai*. Kyoto, 1972. pp. 145–173.

———. "Jikudōshō no tongosetsu" 竺道生の頓悟說, *Zen kenkyūsho kiyō* 3: 97–110.

———. "Jikudōshō sen Hokekyōso no kenkyū," 竺道生撰法華經疏の研究 *Ōtani Daigaku kenkyū nempō*, 5 (1952): 169–276.

———. "Muryōgikyō ni tsuite" 無量義經について. *IBK*, 2, (March 1954): 453–462

Park, Sung Bae. *Buddhist Faith and Sudden Enlightenment*. Albany, N.Y.: State University of New York Press, 1983.

Prebish, Charles S., ed., *Buddhism: A Modern Perspective*. University Park: Pennsylvania State University Press, 1975.

Radhakrishnan, S., ed., *History of Philosophy Eastern and Western*, vol. 1. London: Allen and Unwin, 1952.

Rahula, Walpola. *What the Buddha Taught*. New York: Grove Press, 1962.

Rhys Davids, Thomas W., trans. *Buddhist Sutras*. New York: Dover Publications, 1969.

Robinson, Richard H. *Early Mādhyamika in India and China*. Madison: University of Wisconsin Press, 1967.

———. *The Buddhist Religion*. Belmont: Dickenson, 1970.

Rump, Ariane, trans. *Commentary on the Lao-Tzu by Wang Pi*, in collaboration with Wing-tsit Chan. Honolulu: University Press of Hawaii, 1979.

Sakamoto Yukio. 板本幸男 ed. *Hokekyō no Chūgokuteki tenkai* 法華經の中國的展開 . Kyoto: Heirakuji shoten, 1972.

———. *Hokekyō no shisō to būnka* 法華經の思想と文化. Kyoto: Heirakuji shoten, 1965.

Sangharakshita, Bhikshu. *A Survey of Buddhism*, 4th ed. Bangalore, India: Indian Institute of World Culture, 1976.

Stcherbatsky, T. *Buddhist Logic*, vol. 2. New York: Dover Publications, 1962.

———. *The Central Conception of Buddhism and the Meaning of the Word "Dharma"*. Delhi: Motilal Banarsidass, 1970.

———. *The Conception of Buddhist Nirvana*, 2d ed. Delhi: Bharatiya Vidya Prahashan, 1975.

Streng, Frederick J. *Emptiness: A Study in Religious Meaning*. Nashville: Abingdon Press, 1967.

Suzuki, D. *Outlines of Mahayana Buddhism*. New York: Schocken Books, 1963.

———. *Studies in the Laṅkāvatāra Sutra*. London: Routledge & Kegan Paul, 1930.

Takakusu Junjirō. *The Essentials of Buddhist Philosophy*, Wing-tsit Chan and Charles A. Moore, eds. Honolulu: University of Hawaii, 1947.

Takachiro Tetsujō 高千穗徹乘. "Jikudōshō no kenkyū 竺道生の研究," *Rokujo gakuhō*, no. 234 (1921).

Tamaki Koshiro 玉城康四郎. *Chūgoku Bukkyō shisho no keisei* 中國佛教思想の形成, vol. 1. Tokyo: Chikuma shobō, 1971.

T'ang chün-i 唐君毅. *Chung-kuo Che-hsüeh yüan-lun* 中國哲學原論, 2 vols. Hong Kong, 1973.

———. "Lun Chung-kuo che-hsüeh ssu-hsiang shih chung li chih liu-i" 論中國哲學思想史中「理」之六義 (The Six Meanings of *Li* in the History of Chinese Philosophy), *Hsin-ya Hsüeh-pao* (New Asia Journal), 1, no. 1 (1955).

T'ang Yung-t'ung. *Han-Wei Liang-Chin Nan-pei-ch'ao Fo-chiao shih* (History of Buddhism in Han, Wei, the Two Chins, and Northern and Southern Dynasties), 2 vols. Shanghai: Commercial Press, 1938; reprinted Taipei, 1962.

———. "On 'Ko-yi,' the Earliest Method by Which Indian Buddhism and Chinese Thought Were Synthesized," in W. R. Inge et al., eds., *Radhakrishnan, Comparative Studies in Philosophy*, pp. 276–286. London: Allen and Unwin, 1951.

———. "Wang Pi's New Interpretation of the *I Ching* and *Lun-yü*," Walter Liebenthal, trans., *Harvard Journal of Asian Studies*, 10 (1947): 124–161.

———. *Wei Chin Hsüan-hsüeh lun kao* 魏晉玄學論稿. Peking: 1957.

Tokiwa Daijō 常盤大定. *Busshō no kenkyū* 佛性の研究. Tokyo: Kokusho kankokai, 1972.

Tsukamoto Zenryū 塚本善隆. *Tsukamoto Zenryū Chosakushū* 著作集 (Collected Works), vol. 3. Kyoto: Daitō Shuppansha 1974.

———. Jōron kenkyū 肇論研究. Kyoto: Hōzōkan, 1955.

———. *Shina Bukkyōshi kenkyū* 支那佛教史研究. Tokyo: Kobundo, 1969.

Ui Hakuju 宇井伯壽. *Zenshū shi kenkyū* 禪宗史研究, vol. 1. Tokyo: Shibundo, 1939.

Wach, Jochaim. *Types of Religious Experiences*, Chicago: University of Chicago Press, 1972.

Waley, Arthur. *The Way and Its Power*. New York: Grove Press, Inc., 1958.

Warder, A. K. *Indian Buddhism*. Delhi: Motilal Banarsidass, 1970.

Warren, Henry Clarke, tr. *Buddhism. in Translations*, New York: Atheneum, 1963.

Watson, Burton, trans. *Chuang Tzu: Basic Writings*. New York: Columbia University Press, 1964.

———, trans. *Complete Works of Chuang Tzu*. New York: Columbia University Press, 1968.

Welbon, Guy Richard. *The Buddhist Nirvana and Its Western Interpreters*. Chicago: University of Chicago Press, 1968.

Welch, Holmes. *Taoism, The Parting of the Way*. Boston: Beacon Press, 1966.

Wilhelm, Hellmut. *Change: Eight Lectures on the I Ching*, translated from the German by Cary F. Baynes. New York: Pantheon Books, 1960.

Whilhelm, Richard, and Cary F. Baynes, trans. *The I Ching or Book of Changes*, 3rd ed. Princeton, N.J.: Princeton University Press, 1967.

Winternitz, Moriz. *A History of Indian Literature*, vol. 2, translated from original German by S. Ketkar, 3rd ed. Calcutta: University of Calcutta, 1962.

Wogihara Unrai 荻原雲來. "Muryogikyō to wa nanika" 無量義經とはなにか. *Nippon Bukkyō gakkai nempō*, no. 7.

Wogihara, U., and C. Tsuchida, *Saddharmapuṇḍarīka-sūtraṃ*. Tokyo: The Sankibo Buddhist Book Store, 1958.

Wood, Ernest. *Zen Dictionary*. Middlesex: Penguin Books, 1977.

Wright, Arthur F. *Buddhism in Chinese History*. Stanford, Calif.: Stanford University Press, 1959.

———. "Fo-t'u-teng: A Biography," *Harvard Journal of Asiatic Studies*, 11 (1948): 321–371

———. "A. A. Petrov, *Wang Pi (226–249): His Place in the History of Chinese Philosophy*," *Harvard Journal of Asiatic Studies*, 10 (1947): 75–89.

Wu, John C. H. *The Golden Age of Zen*. Taipei: National War College, 1967

Yabuki Keiki 矢吹慶輝. "Tongogi no shushosha Jikudōshō to sōno kyōgi" 頓悟義の首唱者, 竺道生とその教義, Ōno Seiichiro 小野清一郎, ed. *Bukkyōgaku no shomondai*. Tokyo: 1936.

Yamamoto, K., trans. *The Mahāyāna Mahāparinirvāṇa Sūtra*, 3 vols. Ube City: Karinbunko, 1973.

Yampolsky, Philip B. *The Platform Sutra of the Sixth Patriarch*, the text of the Tun-huang Manuscript with translation, introduction, and notes. New York: Columbia University Press, 1967.

Zürcher, Erik. *The Buddhist Conquest of China*, 2 vols. Leiden: E. J. Brill, 1959.

Index

BQ 2055 .C553 K55 1990

Kim, Young-ho, 1941-

Tao-sheng´s commentary on
 the Lotus S¨utra

DATE		ISSUED TO

BQ 2055 .C553 K55 1990

Kim, Young-ho, 1941-

Tao-sheng´s commentary on
 the Lotus S¨utra

DEMCO